Montréal

Jeremy Gray

LONELY PLANET PUBLICATIONS
Melbourne • Oakland • London • Paris

Montréal
1st edition – May 2001

Published by
Lonely Planet Publications Pty Ltd ABN 36 005 607 983
90 Maribyrnong St, Footscray, Victoria 3011, Australia

Lonely Planet Offices
Australia Locked Bag 1, Footscray, Victoria 3011
USA 150 Linden St, Oakland, CA 94607
UK 10a Spring Place, London NW5 3BH
France 1 rue du Dahomey, 75011 Paris

Photographs
Many of the images in this guide are available for licensing from
Lonely Planet Images.
email: lpi@lonelyplanet.com.au
Web site: www.lonelyplanetimages.com

Front cover photograph
Olympic Stadium along Sherbrooke Street (Yves Marcoux/Stone)

Map section photograph
Street mural, St Denis district (Neil Setchfield)

ISBN 1 86450 254 1

text & maps © Lonely Planet Publications Pty Ltd 2001
photos © photographers as indicated 2001

Printed by The Bookmaker International Ltd
Printed in China

Contents

The Author

Jeremy Gray

A native of Shreveport, Louisiana, USA, Jeremy studied literature and business at the University of Texas at Austin before going to Germany on a one-year scholarship in 1984. Infatuated with Europe, he sensibly chucked his MBA plans in exchange for a glittering career as an English teacher and clerk for the US Air Force in Wiesbaden, Germany (specialty: plumbing translations).

Next came a master's degree in international relations at Canterbury, England, and a string of jobs in the rough-and-tumble of financial journalism – in Woking, England, and in equally lovely Frankfurt, Germany. While freelancing for the Financial Times in Holland, he tumbled into Lonely Planet, and has since contributed to a number of titles, including *Germany, France, The Netherlands, Georgia & the Carolinas* and *The USA*. He is also the author of LP's *Munich*. When he's not out gallivanting the globe for Lonely Planet, Jeremy resides in a canalside flat in Amsterdam, a city that is *almost* as fun as Montréal.

FROM THE AUTHOR

This book would have been sorely incomplete without the support of staff at the Centre Infotouriste and the Old Montréal tourist offices, who were friendly and efficient at every turn. I'd also like to thank Sam (Sara) Benson, the author of Lonely Planet's *Toronto,* for sharing information for the front-matter chapters. The kind travelers and Montréal residents who gave me a helping hand included Darren, Steve, Sharon, Mike, Adrian and Nora – you lot were effectively my roving reporters. *Merci* also to Mark Lightbody for allowing me to make liberal use of his Montréal research in LP's *Canada* guide. Back in Oakland, California, senior editor Robert Reid, editors Wendy Taylor and Suki Gear, assistant editor Paul Sheridan, senior cartographer Tracey Croom and cartographer Tessa Rottiers were a joy to work with. Last but not least, my deepest gratitude is due to my wife, Petra Riemer, for her boundless understanding and patience throughout this project.

This Book

FROM THE PUBLISHER

This first edition of *Montréal* was produced in the Oakland, California, office of Lonely Planet. The book was edited by Wendy Taylor, with the indispensable help of editor Suki Gear and assistant editor Paul Sheridan and with the unfailing guidance, support and good humor of senior editor Robert Reid and managing editor Kate Hoffman. The maps were created by cartographer Tessa Rottiers, under the supervision of senior cartographer Tracey Croom and with the assistance of Eric Thomsen, Andy Rebold, Kat Smith, Patrick Phelan and Molly Green. The expert technical assistance of Tim Lohnes was an important part of bringing the maps together.

The book was designed by Wendy Yanagihara, with the guidance of design manager Susan Rimerman; the colorwraps were put together by Jenn Steffey. Illustrations were coordinated by Beca Lafore, and illustrations were drawn by Justin Marler, Hugh D'Andrade, Hayden Foell, Beca Lafore and Jim Swanson. The cover was designed by Rini Keagy. Carole Nuttall, a native Montréaler in our own cartography department, helped by translating the boxed text 'Signs of Pride' into French, and the book was indexed by Margaret Livingston.

And last but not least, a warm thanks goes to our dear friend and comrade Gary, who so patiently posed for our chapter-end graphic. We love you Gary!

Foreword

ABOUT LONELY PLANET GUIDEBOOKS

The story begins with a classic travel adventure: Tony and Maureen Wheeler's 1972 journey across Europe and Asia to Australia. Useful information about the overland trail did not exist at that time, so Tony and Maureen published the first Lonely Planet guidebook to meet a growing need.

From a kitchen table, then from a tiny office in Melbourne (Australia), Lonely Planet has become the largest independent travel publisher in the world, an international company with offices in Melbourne, Oakland (USA), London (UK) and Paris (France).

Today Lonely Planet guidebooks cover the globe. There is an ever-growing list of books, and there's information in a variety of forms and media. Some things haven't changed. The main aim is still to help make it possible for adventurous travelers to get out there – to explore and better understand the world.

At Lonely Planet we believe travelers can make a positive contribution to the countries they visit – if they respect their host communities and spend their money wisely. Since 1986 a percentage of the income from each book has been donated to aid projects and human-rights campaigns.

Updates Lonely Planet thoroughly updates each guidebook as often as possible. This usually means there are around two years between editions, although for more unusual or more stable destinations the gap can be longer. Check the imprint page (following the color map at the beginning of the book) for publication dates.

Between editions, up-to-date information is available in two free newsletters – the paper *Planet Talk* and email *Comet* (to subscribe, contact any Lonely Planet office) – and on our website at www.lonelyplanet.com. The *Upgrades* section of the website covers a number of important and volatile destinations and is regularly updated by Lonely Planet authors. *Scoop* covers news and current affairs relevant to travelers. And, lastly, the *Thorn Tree* bulletin board and *Postcards* section of the site carry unverified, but fascinating, reports from travelers.

Correspondence The process of creating new editions begins with the letters, postcards and emails received from travelers. This correspondence often includes suggestions, criticisms and comments about the current editions. Interesting excerpts are immediately passed on via newsletters and the website, and everything goes to our authors to be verified when they're researching on the road. We're keen to get more feedback from organizations or individuals who represent communities visited by travelers.

Lonely Planet gathers information for everyone who's curious about the planet – and especially for those who explore it firsthand. Through guidebooks, phrasebooks, activity guides, maps, literature, newsletters, image library, TV series and website, we act as an information exchange for a worldwide community of travelers.

Research Authors aim to gather sufficient practical information to enable travelers to make informed choices and to make the mechanics of a journey run smoothly. They also research historical and cultural background to help enrich the travel experience and allow travelers to understand and respond appropriately to cultural and environmental issues.

Authors don't stay in every hotel because that would mean spending a couple of months in each medium-size city and, no, they don't eat at every restaurant because that would mean stretching belts beyond capacity. They do visit hotels and restaurants to check standards and prices, but feedback based on readers' direct experiences can be very helpful.

Many of our authors work undercover; others aren't so secretive. None of them accept freebies in exchange for positive write-ups. And none of our guidebooks contain any advertising.

Production Authors submit their raw manuscripts and maps to offices in Australia, the USA, the UK or France. Editors and cartographers – all experienced travelers themselves – then begin the process of assembling the pieces. When the book finally hits the shops, some things are already out of date, we start getting feedback from readers and the process begins again....

WARNING & REQUEST

Things change – prices go up, schedules change, good places go bad and bad places go bankrupt – nothing stays the same. So, if you find things better or worse, recently opened or long since closed, please tell us and help make the next edition even more accurate and useful. We genuinely value all the feedback we receive. Julie Young coordinates a well-traveled team that reads and acknowledges every letter, postcard and email and ensures that every morsel of information finds its way to the appropriate authors, editors and cartographers for verification.

Everyone who writes to us will find their name in the next edition of the appropriate guidebook. They will also receive the latest issue of *Planet Talk*, our quarterly printed newsletter, or *Comet*, our monthly email newsletter. Subscriptions to both newsletters are free. The very best contributions will be rewarded with a free guidebook.

Excerpts from your correspondence may appear in new editions of Lonely Planet guidebooks, the Lonely Planet website, *Planet Talk* or *Comet*, so please let us know if you *don't* want your letter published or your name acknowledged.

Send all correspondence to the Lonely Planet office closest to you:

Australia: Locked Bag 1, Footscray, Victoria 3011
USA: 150 Linden St, Oakland, CA 94607
UK: 10a Spring Place, London NW5 3BH
France: 1 rue du Dahomey, 75011 Paris

Or email us at: talk2us@lonelyplanet.com.au

For news, views and updates, see our website: www.lonelyplanet.com

HOW TO USE A LONELY PLANET GUIDEBOOK

The best way to use a Lonely Planet guidebook is any way you choose. At Lonely Planet, we believe the most memorable travel experiences are often those that are unexpected, and the finest discoveries are those you make yourself. Guidebooks are not intended to be used as if they provided a detailed set of infallible instructions!

Contents All Lonely Planet guidebooks follow the same format. The Facts about the Country chapters or sections give background information ranging from history to weather. Facts for the Visitor gives practical information on issues like visas and health. Getting There & Away gives a brief starting point for researching travel to and from the destination. Getting Around gives an overview of the transport options available when you arrive.

The peculiar demands of each destination determine how subsequent chapters are broken up, but some things remain constant. We always start with background, then proceed to sights, places to stay, places to eat, entertainment, getting there and away, and getting around information – in that order.

Heading Hierarchy Lonely Planet headings are used in a strict hierarchical structure that can be visualized as a set of Russian dolls. Each heading (and its following text) is encompassed by any preceding heading that is higher on the hierarchical ladder.

Entry Points We do not assume guidebooks will be read from beginning to end, but that people will dip into them. The traditional entry points are the list of contents and the index. In addition, however, some books have a complete list of maps and an index map illustrating map coverage.

There may also be a color map that shows highlights. These highlights are dealt with in greater detail later in the book, along with planning questions. Each chapter covering a geographical region usually begins with a locator map and another list of highlights. Once you find something of interest in a list of highlights, turn to the index.

Maps Maps play a crucial role in Lonely Planet guidebooks and include a huge amount of information. A legend is printed on the back page. We seek to have complete consistency between maps and text, and to have every important place in the text captured on a map. Map key numbers usually start in the top left corner.

Although inclusion in a guidebook usually implies a recommendation, we cannot list every good place. Exclusion does not necessarily imply criticism. In fact, there are a number of reasons why we might exclude a place – sometimes it is simply inappropriate to encourage an influx of travelers.

Introduction

No city blends the Old and New Worlds with more style and elegance than Montréal. Where else can you shop at London-style department stores, stroll among New York–sized skyscrapers and relax at a Parisian café, knowing that all these things somehow 'belong'? Its main influences may have been foreign, but ultimately, Québec's largest city succeeds in reminding you only of itself.

This uniqueness is most striking when it comes to language. Montréal is the largest French-speaking city outside France: Francophones account for more than two-thirds of the population, while Anglophones make up much of the rest. (Oddly enough, this also makes Montréal the largest English-speaking city in Québec.) While Francophones generally regard Anglo-Saxon culture with suspicion, there is a growing tendency – especially among the younger generation – to put the two languages on an equal footing. The city's atmosphere of tolerance has attracted many immigrants, and in some neighborhoods, you're just as likely to hear Chinese, Italian or Portuguese spoken on the streets as French or English.

In many respects, Montréal is a typically North American metropolis. It has a grid-pattern layout, and downtown, its wide, busy avenues are lined with modern corporate towers. The subway (Métro) is fast and efficient and joins an underground maze of shopping complexes that is the world's largest. Yet Montréal's romantic past is never far away: the attractive stone buildings of Vieux Montréal (Old Montréal) span four centuries of settlement, and residential areas such as Westmount and Plateau Mont Royal are showcases of Victorian architecture. Vestiges of the colonial era are sprinkled throughout downtown, and some modern public buildings, such as the Centre of Canadian Architecture, even straddle the epochs by incorporating parts of older structures.

By the 1960s, Montréal was overtaken by Toronto as the country's financial and economic hub, and an exodus of Anglophones during the following decades only accelerated this trend. Lingering uncertainty over Québec separatism, fueled by periodic referendums on the issue, tended to discourage foreigners from investing in the province. When recession struck in the 1990s, Montréal was already in the grip of economic decline, and the outlook was not better elsewhere in Québec.

In the past few years, the situation has improved dramatically. Montréal is reinventing itself as a high-tech center, and thousands of jobs are being created by new multimedia and telecommunication firms. Favorable exchange rates and an attractive setting continue to lure big-name US filmmakers, who spend over $1 billion in the city every year. Montréalers have more money to spend, and droves of new stores, some of them quite fashionable, are opening up in the shopping arcades along downtown's Rue Ste Catherine. Almost everywhere you look, there's construction under way. Enthusiasm for Québec sovereignty has died down as the economy has revived.

The upshot is that Montréal has more *joie de vivre* than ever but remains stunningly affordable, particularly for US residents. Hotels and restaurants charge up to half of what you'd pay in New York or Boston, even after adding in Québec's stiff taxes (which you can partly reclaim). The island city has an excellent location, too – it's close to beautiful recreational areas such as the Laurentian Mountains and Mont Tremblant. Québec City, the oldest walled city on the continent, and Ottawa, the nation's capital, are both less than a three-hour drive away.

Facts about Montréal

HISTORY

Montréal still mimics the Old Country with consummate skill. Stroll past the venerable residences along Rue Sherbrooke Ouest, and you're in a swanky London suburb; wander through Plateau Mont Royal, with its sidewalk cafés and wrought-iron balconies, to recall Napoleon's Second Empire. Discovering what makes Montréal tick, however, requires a look beyond the divisions of its colonial past, starting with the legacy of its indigenous residents.

Original Inhabitants

Despite the Viking expeditions around 1000 AD, the native societies of North America had developed for centuries in isolation from European influences. Long before the French arrived in Québec, the Algonquin, Huron and Iroquois shared the area – not always peacefully.

The Naming of Montréal

It is commonly assumed that Montréal derives its name from Mont Royal, its trademark mountain. However, there is some evidence that the city was named by French King François I after the Archbishop of Monreale in Sicily, who lobbied to have Spanish and Portuguese claims to lands in the New World annulled by the pope. Then there was Giovanni Battista Ramusi, who published a work in Italian on explorer Jacques Cartier's discoveries and translated 'Mont Royal' as 'Monte Real.' Last but perhaps not least, at the time of Cartier's voyage, there were a dozen-odd towns in France called Montréal – most with some kind of fortress on an elevated site. The Pontbriant family owned one such French castle, and son Claude just happened to be with Cartier when he climbed the mount. Hmmm....

By the 15th century, five groups of Iroquois speakers – the Mohawk, Oneida, Onandaga, Cayuga and Seneca tribes – had formed the Five Nations Confederacy of Iroquois, a league that kept its members at peace with one another and united them against their enemies. The Confederacy emerged as a force to be reckoned with – not only for neighboring tribes, but also for the Europeans.

The Mohawk of the Iroquois controlled the river stretch between Ontario and Québec City. North of and around Québec City, the Montagnais were the principal aboriginal group. Farther north was and is Cree homeland, and beyond that area, the Labrador Eskimo, Naskapi and Inuit peoples are dominant. The Montagnais and Naskapi are also known as Innu.

Founding of Montréal

With the ferocious Iroquois in mind, French explorer Jacques Cartier set off from his native St Malo for the New World in 1535. Not long after his arrival, he curried favor with the Iroquois chief of Stadacona, a settlement at present-day Québec City. The chief, Donacona, told Cartier of shiny stone at an Indian stronghold upriver, and the Frenchman, in search of gold and a passage to the Orient, set off to investigate.

On October 2, 1535, Cartier became the first European to set foot on the Island of Montréal, landing on the north side to be greeted by the local Iroquois. Cartier was led to the summit of the mountain – which he named Mont Royal – and planted the famous cross in tribute to his sponsor, King François I. Below him to the south lay a large, walled village called Hochelaga, on the site of present-day Montréal. The glinting stone turned out to be nothing more than quartz, but a lucrative venture soon emerged: fur trading.

More than seventy years later, another great explorer, Samuel de Champlain, shared Cartier's vision of riches and glory from the

New World. However, when he arrived in 1611, three years after founding Québec City, he found no trace of Hochelaga, nor of the Iroquois who had lived there. Undeterred, Champlain made plans to set up a fur-trading post at Place Royale on the Island of Montréal, but he had to postpone the project due to ferocious attacks by the Iroquois confederation on the French, who were allied with the Huron and Algonquin.

In 1639, a French tax collector named Jerome Le Royer, sieur de la Dauversière, formed a company in Paris to establish a settlement on the Island of Montréal. Two years later, the company sent a group of Catholic missionaries, led by Paul de Chomedey, sieur de Maisonneuve, to convert the Indians to Christianity. On May 17, 1642, Maisonneuve set up a religious mission named Ville Marie on what is now Place Royal. Retracing Cartier's footsteps more than a century later, Maisonneuve erected another cross on the mountain, which had been named Mont Royal (leading, perhaps, to the city's present name – see the boxed text 'The Naming of Montréal').

Ville Marie soon became a fur-trading center. The Iroquois renewed their attacks in an attempt to wrest control of the fur trade, just as they had nearly a century before. Despite this, the colony boomed as a religious center, an exploration base and a fur-trading post. A peace treaty was finally signed in 1701. Many of the buildings erected during this period can still be seen in Vieux Montréal today.

By the early 18th century, Ville Marie had become Montréal, the commercial hub of France's North American empire, Nouvelle France. By 1710, the town had 3500 inhabitants. Its location on the St Lawrence River made it an important trading center and linked it to the fur country, as well as to valuable forests along the Ottawa River.

The Conquest

The French and Indian War (1754–63) marked the turning point for French influence in North America. Québec City fell to the British in 1759 after a summerlong standoff (see the boxed text 'The Battle of Québec City,' in the Excursions chapter). The French moved their capital upstream to Montréal, but to little avail: British troops led by General Jeffrey Amherst captured the city the following year. The Treaty of Paris officially ended the war in 1763, making Canada a British colony. (French Québecers refer to this whole event, perhaps with a touch of bitterness, as 'The Conquest.') English-speaking settlers then came in droves to Montréal.

Soon, the rebelling American colonies were after the city. In 1775, General Richard Montgomery took Montréal without firing a shot. Benjamin Franklin and other American diplomats tried to win French-Canadian support against the British. Their efforts failed, however, because most French Canadians viewed the war as a quarrel between Britain and its colonies. Montréal was in the hands of the revolutionary forces only until the British beat back another group trying to take Québec City, at which time the revolutionaries fled.

Montréal began to expand to the north and along the southern part of the island in the late 18th century. English-speaking merchants gradually gained control of the town's economy; this was made easier by the departure of many French merchants to the Old Country after British troops captured the city in 1760. In the 1770s, a group of Montréal fur traders founded the North West Company as a rival to the powerful Hudson Bay Company, and a golden era of fur-trading dawned in the city.

19th-Century Growth

By the early 1800s, Montréal's population had risen to 9000. The St Lawrence River had been established as the main passenger route into Canada, and Canada's first steamboat, *Accommodation,* sailed from Montréal to Québec City in 1809. In 1821, the Hudson Bay Company bought the North West Company; the area around Hudson Bay became the chief marketplace for furs, and Montréal declined as a fur-trading center.

The Canal de Lachine was opened on the south side of Montréal in 1825. The route provided a detour for vessels around the treacherous Lachine Rapids, and this led to a sharp increase in travel and trade between Montréal and the Great Lakes area. Shipping replaced fur trading as the chief industry, and the city's port flourished.

In 1832, Montréal was incorporated as a city. From 1844 to 1849, it served as the capital of the United Provinces of Canada, triggering a further influx of settlers – including Loyalists, Irish, Scottish and English. In 1852, the majority of its burgeoning population (by now 58,000) were Anglophones, but it remained this way only until 1866. Nonetheless, the English-speakers retained control of the economy and gave the city its first university, McGill. English and Scottish merchants built plush homes at the southern foot of Mont Royal, a neighborhood known by some as 'the Golden Square Mile' (but it acquired this nickname much later, after WWII).

The mid-19th century saw Montréal develop as a transportation center. Rail lines were laid to New England, Toronto and areas farther west. Investment by wealthy English merchants helped make Montréal a major industrial center, and many factories were built along the Canal de Lachine. Thousands of immigrants from Italy, Russia and Eastern Europe, as well as French Canadians from other parts of Québec, came to Montréal to find work, and ethnic districts began to form. By 1870, more than 100,000 people lived in the city, about half of whom had French ancestors.

Founded in Montréal, the Pacific Railway Company completed the country's transcontinental railroad in 1885. This brought more prosperity to Montréal, and the population topped 260,000 by the end of the 19th century. The incorporation of several nearby communities boosted its size to 468,000 by 1911.

By 1900, Montréal was the commercial and cultural center of Canada. In the early part of the 20th century, there came a huge influx of Jewish Europeans – even today, Montréal has the largest Jewish population in Canada (about 100,000).

The World Wars & the Draft

During WWI, Canada backed the Allies, which included France, Britain and the United States. Both French- and English-speaking Montréalers supported the effort and volunteered for military service – that is, until Ottawa introduced a national draft in 1917, to which many Francophone Montréalers were opposed.

The period between the wars was difficult for Montréal. The early 1920s saw both inflation and unemployment soar, and the city developed a seamier side with the advent of Prohibition in the US (see the boxed text 'Sin City'). Montréal wasn't spared in the stock market crash of 1929, either. But there was progress, too: somehow, a middle class began to emerge, the city began to fashion itself as a manufacturing center, and New York–style skyscrapers began to spring up around downtown.

During WWII, a renewed conscription caused an outcry among French Québecers. In 1940, Montréal Mayor Camillian Houde urged citizens to ignore an Ottawa plan to

Sin City

From the 1920s onward, Montréal gained a reputation as Sin City, thanks in part to hordes of free-spending, pleasure-seeking Americans who visited during Prohibition. Brothels, gambling houses and gangsters thrived, and the nightlife was known far and wide; politicians and law-enforcers turned a blind eye. Long after alcohol was no longer taboo in the States, Montréal retained a flourishing red-light district. One leading personality of the period was Lili St Cyr, the flamboyant stripper whose affairs with high-ranking politicians, sports stars and thugs were as legendary as her stage performances.

This all came to an end with the arrival of squeaky-clean Jean Drapeau, who pledged to clean up the city when he was elected mayor in 1954. Some vestiges of the bygone era remain, such as the strip clubs and XXX bars along Rue Ste Catherine.

register data on all men and women in the country, fearing (quite rightly, as it turned out) that registration would pave the way for a draft for overseas military service. Most French Québecers opposed a draft, and Canadian government leaders had pledged not to introduce one. Houde was arrested, charged with treason and kept in a prison camp until 1944 – the same year that Ottawa finally launched conscription.

Grand Projects

By the early 1950s, Montréal's population had passed the one-million mark. Mayor Drapeau drew up plans for grand projects that would change the face of the city. He had plenty of time to do so: except for a five-year period in the early '60s, Drapeau remained mayor right into the mid-'80s. He was sometimes touched by scandal, and critics dubbed him 'Emperor,' claiming he was megalomaniacal. Whatever his faults, Drapeau remained popular and helped to develop Montréal's international reputation.

In 1958, the city embarked on a huge redevelopment program, which over the following decade included construction of a new subway system and the underground city (see the boxed text in the Shopping chapter). Montréal's harbor was enlarged, and the opening of the St Lawrence Seaway in 1959 was expected to lure hundreds of industries. (Ironically, the seaway eventually hurt Montréal, as trade bypassed the city for more attractive ports upstream.)

The skyline altered dramatically during the 1960s. Private developers razed old structures in the area and replaced them with banks, upmarket hotels and office buildings. The two tallest skyscrapers in Montréal, the 49-story Royal Bank of Canada Building and the 47-story Place Victoria, were built during this period. (They won't get much taller, either: city law forbade new buildings from being taller than Mont Royal, which is 232m high). Other landmark buildings that sprung up include Place Bonaventure, a mammoth shopping and hotel complex; and the Place des Arts, a rather boxy performing-arts center.

As Vieux Montréal lost its function as a business center, the focus of downtown moved slightly north to around the Ville Marie shopping complex and Squares Dorchester and Victoria. It was also in the 1960s that Montréal lost its place as Canada's economic capital to Toronto, which had been growing at a faster pace for decades.

New expressways were laid out and the Métro built in time to serve visitors to the 1967 World's Fair, which attracted over 50 million people. Many of the fair's facilities were built on two islands – Île Notre Dame and Île Ste Hélène. Île Notre Dame was created entirely from earth excavated when the Métro was built.

Montréal hosted the 1976 Summer Olympics, for which it built a grand new sports stadium (see Olympic Park, in the Things to See & Do chapter). The apartment complex for the athletes was rented out as public housing after the games. The city's professional baseball team, the Expos, began playing in the stadium in 1977.

Modern Montréal

In 1992, the city celebrated its 350th anniversary with yet more grand projects. The Musée d'art contemporain de Montréal (the Montréal museum of contemporary art) was moved to its new building on the Place des Arts, and two new museums (the Pointe à Callière Musée d'archéologie et d'histoire de Montréal and the Biodôme environmental science center) were also opened. Montréal's riverfront and the Vieux Port area were redeveloped, and parts of it are being reshaped for new projects.

The redevelopment of the downtown area has produced an alluring blend of European and North American forms, accompanied by plenty of debate on future projects. The Montréal you see today is a much cheerier, prosperous place than it was even five years ago as economic revival breathes new life into its streets. This, combined with its other assets – a terrific music and arts scene, thousands of affordable restaurants and an unparalleled nightlife, to name a few – makes Montréal a more attractive, intriguing place to visit than ever before.

GEOGRAPHY

At roughly the same latitude as Portland and Milan (but brrr! much colder in winter), the Island of Montréal occupies an island on the north bank of the St Lawrence River, which feeds into the Atlantic Ocean about 1600km to the east. It's the largest of 234 islands that make up the Hochelaga Archipelago, one of three island groups along the St Lawrence River.

The surrounding region is the Great Lakes–St Lawrence lowlands, a richly agricultural but also (relatively) highly populated area stretching from Lakes Huron, Erie and Ontario up to the Atlantic Ocean. The rolling countryside here was formed by glaciers: many lakes, plains and shorelines were carved by glacial streams. The plains are broken by the seven Moneteregian Hills of the Montréal region, of which Mont Royal (232m) is the highest.

The city itself is 57m above sea level and has an area of 158 sq km, but the greater Montréal area encompasses several towns on both sides of the St Lawrence that occupy almost 1100 sq km combined. For centuries, ships were unable to sail farther upstream due to the Lachine Rapids here, which forced them to dock and unload for land transport at Montréal. To the northeast rise the Laurentian Mountains (the Laurentides) – the southern edge of the Canadian Shield and the world's oldest mountain range, formed more than three billion years ago. Across the St Lawrence to the southeast, the alluvial plains begin to undulate in the Eastern Townships and become the foothills of the Appalachian Mountains near the US border.

CLIMATE

Even the earliest European explorers were surprised by seasonal extremes of Montréal. Not long ago Canada's finance minister blamed Montréal's high unemployment rate on the weather, although most residents seem to cope pretty well.

Although global warming has taken the edge off the winter, daily temperatures average between -20°C and -6°C, with spells of -25°C or colder. Snow can last from late

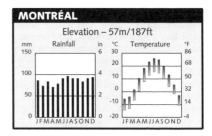

MONTRÉAL

Elevation – 57m/187ft

November to mid-March, sometimes piling a meter high in some unserviced areas (not sidewalks, which are cleared in town). The blasts of wind down the St Lawrence River are laden with bone-chilling humidity and make you very thankful for Montréal's climate-controlled underground city.

Summer arrives late – temperatures are very changeable with a break on the chilly side into early June. Summer doesn't get into full swing until July, but then it's brutal and steamy – air-conditioned hotel rooms become a major asset. Highs of 25°C or 30°C aren't uncommon between mid-July and late August. But temperatures cool sharply in the evenings, and you'll find yourself wearing warmer clothing by mid-September.

The seasons in between are short but delightful. The first spring buds don't appear until late April, and full blossom is only in mid-May, for a couple of weeks at most. Fall comes in a burst of color in late September, but it's all over by late October.

ECOLOGY & ENVIRONMENT

All in all, Montréal is a pretty healthy place to live. The city routinely ranks in the top 20 places on the planet, according to the United Nations' annual Human Development Index (HDI), which takes into account factors such as literacy, environmental pollution, life expectancy and earnings. Vancouver usually makes the top three cities. Canada as a whole has placed first in the national rankings since 1994.

The St Lawrence River has shaped the development of Québec more than any other single factor. Nearly 80% of the province's population lives along the St Lawrence, and 50% draws its drinking water from it. Shoreline urbanization, such as in the industrial zone of East Montréal, has an impact on the ecosystem in terms of water discharges and encroachment. Exhibits in the Biosphère explain these and other risks in detail (see Île Ste Hélène under Parc des Îles, in the Things to See & Do chapter).

Shipping, a major industry in Montréal, carries a serious pollution risk. The wave action caused by ships and deballasting puts stress on the river's ecosystem, and every year, several hundred thousand cubic meters of sediment have to be dredged from the St Lawrence Seaway.

Some of Québec's richest farmlands lie along the St Lawrence valley. The intense use of fertilizers and pesticides, as well the effects of erosion, have become major concerns. Moreover, one-third of the river's wetlands were lost to farming between 1945 and 1976.

On a more positive note, Montréal enjoys close proximity to a wealth of protected nature reserves and parks. In 1895, the Québec government created the first two such parks – at Mont Tremblant and in the Laurentian Mountains, to the north of Montréal. The decision was revolutionary because these areas had been controlled by Québec's powerful logging and paper-processing industries. Québec now has 20 nature parks, and about 10% of the province's forestland is property of the state.

Montréal was also the site of a historical environmental accord. Signed in 1987, the Montréal Protocol on Substances That Deplete the Ozone Layer stipulated that the production and consumption of chlorofluorocarbons (CFCs) and other ozone-depleting compounds were to be phased out by 2000. Some 29 countries representing 82% of world output initially signed the accord, and the list later increased to 173 countries. More recently, the city has hosted high-level international meetings on biosafety – the issues surrounding the trade and regulation of genetically modified foods. The Canadian government routinely faces protests from environmental and health organizations, as well as from farmers, for its support of these new foodstuffs, which critics argue haven't been adequately tested.

FLORA & FAUNA

This is Canada, a nature-lover's dream, so there's a cornucopia of plants and wildlife in the park-studded area surrounding Montréal. The nearby forests, notably in the Laurentian Mountains, feature a huge range of coniferous and deciduous treelife, including sugar maple, American beech, white spruce and firs. You'll also find the rarer yellow birch, Québec's official tree. This leafy habitat is shared by black bears, wolves, deer, porcupine and, of course, moose (watch out for them when driving). Keep an eye out, too, for beavers, Canada's national animal – they can be surprisingly tame, photogenic and aren't aggressive toward visitors.

Porcupine

You'll find a fantastic variety of birds, too – the golden eagle and snowy owls are prized sightings for bird-watchers. The shores of the St Lawrence River feature puffin, black ducks, great herons and marsh wrens. The eagle owl, a protected species, has been Québec's official bird since 1987 – it can be seen in the St Lawrence valley as it migrates south from the Arctic tundra in the fall.

The St Lawrence River teems with marine life. Local pike, perch and several species of trout turn up frequently on Montréal menus. Tens of thousands of Atlantic salmon return to Québec's rivers and streams

Golden eagle

to spawn every year, and some of them make it as far west as the Ottawa River.

In Montréal itself, the best place to view plant life is at Olympic Park's Jardin Botanique, which has 26,000 varieties. It's an orchestra of color and includes orchids, lilacs, roses and hyacinths. In town, the area around the Vieux Port contains a wealth of manicured flowerbeds and hedge sculptures in summer. See Olympic Park, in the Things to See & Do chapter, for more information on the botanical garden.

The catalogue of varmints in town is copious – squirrels, raccoons, skunks, chipmunks, rabbits and rats are common sights in or on the fringes of the city. (It's illegal to feed squirrels, pigeons or gulls – under threat of a $60 fine – in an effort to curb their populations.) Squirrels, mainly gray but also black varieties, number in the thousands in Montréal; as friendly as they are to passersby, these critters cause plenty of damage to trees in town. Mont Royal is a favorite dumping ground for homeowners who catch live squirrels.

Whales rarely make it this far up the St Lawrence. One celebrated visit to Montréal was in 1832, when an 18m-long specimen was harpooned, dragged to shore and put on display to a paying public.

Peregrine falcons, which neared extinction in Québec in the 1960s, can be found nesting downtown and in Vieux Montréal.

A good place to see them is on the 32nd floor of the Montréal Stock Exchange (see the boxed text 'The Precarious Peregrine,' in the Things to See & Do chapter). Great gray owls – which have a wingspan of over 1.5m – also make an occasional appearance.

Last but not least, you'll notice that Montréal has a large and active mosquito population in summer. Bring repellant if you're spending time in green areas, especially after dusk.

GOVERNMENT & POLITICS

Montréal has a mayor-council form of government. The 50 members of the city legislature are chosen by the broad electorate to four-year terms; the mayor has a seven-member executive committee, which prepares the budget and new laws.

Municipal politics in Montréal are made almost exclusively by the liberal-moderate Vision Montréal Party, led by Mayor Pierre Bourque. The opposition parties are small and badly fragmented (in the last election in 1998, their candidates got 55% of the vote but won only 12 of 52 seats).

Montréal gets some of its services from an agency called the Montréal Urban Community Council, which provides fire protection, law enforcement, health services and public transportation. This will probably change in 2001, however, with the creation of a so-called 'megacity' in Montréal, which will unite 105 on- and off-island municipalities. The controversial new entity hopes to save tax dollars by amalgamating public services such as public transit, social housing and waste disposal.

At the provincial level, Québec has more than a dozen parties represented in the Assemblée Nationale (National Assembly). However, the Parti Québécois – which advocates separation – has dominated completely in the past two federal elections. It now has 77 seats in the assembly, and is led by Québec Premier Lucien Bouchard.

The Parti Libéral du Québec (Liberal Party of Québec), led by Daniel Johnson, is the federalist party and has 47 seats. A single seat is held by the somewhat forlorn Parti de l'Action Démocratique du Québec

(Democratic Action Party of Québec), which is separatist but very conservative.

At the federal level, Prime Minister Jean Chretien is a Member of Parliament for the riding (district) of St Maurice in Québec. Despite this, he is not of the separatist mould. In the November 2000 general election, which he called almost two years early, voters elected his Liberal Party to a third consecutive term; unprecedented in post-WWII Canadian politics. Despite predictions that it would be a close race with the main opposition, Canadian Alliance Party, his government increased its absolute majority, taking 172 seats in the 301-seat parliament.

After what was often described as the country's most bitter campaign, the Canadian Alliance Party, led by Stockwell Day, failed to woo voters anywhere but in its western heartland, while the Liberals made requisite gains in the eastern provinces. But this, as well as the unique politics of Québec, means Canada remains a politically divided country, and Mr Chretien still has to represent a significant section of the population that didn't vote for his party.

Québec has an extra dimension due to separatist politics. The Bloc Québécois (BQ), founded by Lucien Bouchard in 1991, is the federal equivalent of the Parti Québécois (PQ). At the federal election in 2000, the BQ won 37 of the 75 seats allocated to the province in the national parliament in Ottawa, down seven seats from 1997. The prime minister's Liberals also won 37 seats, an increase of eight since 1997. The Liberals won more than 43% of the vote in the province; the BQ won 40.5%. (For more on separatism, see the boxed text 'The Separatist Movement,' later.)

ECONOMY

Montréal suffered a deep recession in the early 1990s, and poverty was a major problem: nearly one in four Montréalers lived below the poverty line. A slump occurred in many Western countries at the time, but the widespread relocation of companies to Toronto (due to uncertainties over Québec's separatist tendencies) made things even worse in Montréal.

Things look a lot rosier now. The Conference Board of Canada, the country's leading economic think tank, has predicted that Montréal's economy will grow by around 3% per year through 2004, after having topped 4% in 2000. Unemployment, which soared into double digits in the 1990s, is set to fall below 6% in the same period, and inflation isn't likely to exceed 2%.

The city's aerospace and telecommunication industries have emerged as locomotives of growth; companies such as Nortel Networks and Bombardier are creating thousands of jobs, and aircraft maker Bombardier alone accounts for about 8% of manufacturing jobs in the area. More than 130,000 jobs stand to be created by the end of 2004. Even economic standbys such as the textile industry – which was expected to reel after the North American Free Trade Agreement (NAFTA) was passed – are holding their own. New high-tech industries are also regarded with optimism (a huge multimedia complex, Cité du Multimedia, is expected to open in 2001). The pickup has fed through into new construction, and a boom in retail sales confirms that Montréalers have more money in their pockets.

On the downside, salaries in Montréal tend to lag behind those paid in Toronto or the US, and Québec's high taxes put the city at a disadvantage compared with, say, rival Toronto. The government is trying to run leaner at all levels, and cutbacks on university funding have begun to undermine the quality of higher education.

POPULATION & PEOPLE

With almost 3.4 million residents, Greater Montréal accounts for about 46% of Québec's total population. (The city proper numbers just over one million.) About 77% of Greater Montréal's residents were born in Canada. Since the end of WWII, hundreds of thousands of immigrants have settled in the city, creating a rich patchwork of languages and cultures.

About two-thirds of Montréalers have French ancestors; those of Anglo-Saxon descent now make up only 7% – less than half of what the figure was in the 1960s.

Italians account for another 7%. Other significant groups, in order of size, are Jews, Greeks, blacks, Chinese and Portuguese. More than one-quarter of Montréalers are descended from more than one group.

About half of the population speaks both French and English. Something like 400,000 people in the city speak only French, and 100,000 speak only English.

As the Anglo-Saxons controlled much of Montréal's large enterprises up through the 1950s, English used to dominate in the boardroom. Since 1977, however, all businesses that employ 50 or more people are required to use French as the language of business, which has discouraged more than a few enterprises from setting up in the city.

EDUCATION

Montréal has an unusual public (ie, tax-financed) school system, which is organized on the basis of language and religion. There are Roman Catholic schools, some of which teach entirely in English, and some in French; Protestant schools are set up the same way. Unfortunately, it's virtually impossible to pick and choose. In an effort to promote French among the younger population, Québec's 1977 language law allows pupils to attend these English-language schools only if their parents were also educated in English. This has been a source of friction not only with Montréal's Anglo-Saxon community, but also among many immigrant families.

School is obligatory from age 6 to age 16. Instruction is free through the end of secondary school, as well as at some community and professional colleges.

Four major universities are based in Montréal: at two, classes are taught mainly in English (McGill and Concordia), and the

The Separatist Movement

Québec separatism has its roots in the economic order established by the English in the mid-19th century, although more than a century passed before any organized resistance emerged. In 1960, the Rassemblement pour l'Independence National (Assembly for National Independence) was founded in Montréal with the chief aim of the separation of Québec from Canada. This was the beginning of the 'Quiet Revolution' that eventually gave French Québecers more sway in industry and politics, and which established the supremacy of the French language in the province.

Some not-so-quiet events followed. The Front de Libération du Québec (FLQ), a radical nationalist group committed to overthrowing 'medieval Catholicism and capitalist oppression' through revolution was founded in 1963. Initially, the FLQ attacked military targets and other symbols of federal power, but soon, it became involved in labor disputes. In the mid-1960s, it claimed responsibility for a spate of bombings.

In October 1970, members of the FLQ kidnapped Pierre Laporte (Québec's labor minister) and James Cross (a British trade official) in an attempt to force the independence issue. Pierre Trudeau, the flamboyant Montréal-born prime minister and a strong believer in federalism, declared a state of emergency and sent heavily armed federal troops to Montréal and other Québec cities to protect government officials. Hundreds of Québec intellectuals, political activists and labor leaders were imprisoned arbitrarily. Asked if he would use more force if necessary, Trudeau gave the famous answer: 'Just watch me.' But that didn't prevent Laporte from being murdered, which discredited the FLQ in many people's eyes (Cross was released unharmed). The troops were withdrawn in January 1971.

other two have classes in French (l'Université de Montréal and l'Université du Québec à Montréal). Founded in 1821, McGill remains one of Canada's most prestigious institutions of higher learning. L'Université de Montréal has about 60,000 students, making it the largest French-speaking university outside France.

ARTS
Dance

Every year, it seems as if there's another new miniseries, dance festival or performing-arts troupe to expand Québec's fertile contemporary dance scene. Increasing numbers of new choreographers pour out of schools or migrate to Montréal, Canada's dance capital – and competition is fierce. Newcomers and better-known experimentalists can be seen at Studio 303, which also mounts events such as IMF, a group of improvisers.

Montréal's most famous dance soloist is Margaret Gillis, who has been performing for over a quarter of a century. You can catch her exploring contemporary experiments or breathing new life into works by Leonard Cohen and George Gershwin. Choreographers on the cutting edge of things include Suzanne Miller, Allan Paivio, Lin Snelling, Hetty King, Lina Cruz and Lydia Wagerer.

Venezuela-born José Navas has built a formidable reputation as an intense and virtuoso solo performer and choreographer. His elegant abstract works have been presented at major European dance festivals and across Canada.

Montréal boasts several ballet troupes with international reputations. The Grand Ballets Canadiens attracts the biggest audiences to the Place des Arts with evergreens such as *Carmen* and *The Nutcracker.*

The Separatist Movement

The passage of the Québec French Language Charter in 1977 (see the boxed text 'Signs of Pride' under Language, later in this chapter) only fed the separatists' appetite for more rights. In a 1980 referendum, Québec's citizens voted to seek a 'sovereignty association' with the Canadian government, a compromise entity that would give Québec political independence but allow it to retain its economic ties to Canada. This proposal was given a lukewarm reception by the provincial governments, who failed to ratify it.

However, the separatists weren't about to let the matter rest. In 1987, Prime Minister Brian Mulroney and the 10 provincial leaders hammered out a set of constitutional reforms known as the Meech Lake Accord, which would recognize Québec as a separate, distinct society within Canada. However, this plan also faltered when two provinces, Manitoba and Newfoundland, declined to sign the agreement. Support for Québec independence surged, and the nationalist Parti Québécois gained control of the province in the 1993 elections. The next, and perhaps final, referendum took place in 1995 – with a whopping 98% turnout – in which Québec residents narrowly voted to stay within Canada by a mere 1% margin. (Montréal voted 70% in favor of the unionists.)

Now, after 40 years of acrimonious debate on the issue, the people of Québec may have decided to move on to something else. Polls over the past few years show that support for sovereignty is at its lowest point in a generation. The anger that sparked the 'Quiet Revolution' in the 1960s may have lost its edge – after all, French is now the dominant language, French-speakers have moved into key positions and the incomes of French- and English-speakers are almost equal. Economic recovery may have also dulled the separatist urge.

The point was driven home when Lucien Bouchard, Québec's separatist premier, opened a Youth Summit in Québec City in the spring of 2000. Student rioters used Molotov cocktails to disrupt the meeting, but constitutional politics was the last thing on their minds: the demonstrators were demanding lower tuition and more funding for social programs.

Music

Québecers love lyricism and poetry in music. Many established names have found it necessary to move to the USA, at least for a while.

Céline Dion, from the town of Charlemagne, about 30km east of Montréal, was a star in Canada long before *My Heart Will Go On* from the movie *Titanic* won her accolades for Record of the Year and Female Pop Vocal Performance. In 1983, she became the first Canadian to get a gold record in France. More recently, Dion turned entrepreneur and established Nickels, a chain of retro diners with outlets in Montréal.

A successful Montréal pop singer who has remained 'local' is Corey Hart, whose *Boy in the Box* album enjoyed modest success throughout North America in the 1980s. English-language folk singers are thin on the ground in Québec. The main exception is Leonard Cohen (see boxed text 'The Spirit of Leonard').

In the 1960s, Québec was more receptive to pop from France, with stars such as Johnny Halliday and Charles Aznavour topping the charts. But in the 1970s and '80s, a new generation of Québec singers emerged with its own brand, which mixed traditional Québec folksongs with rock, pop and chanson elements. Few artists from France generate strong sales in Québec nowadays.

Céline Dion hails from a town just east of Montréal.

Gilles Vigneault painted a portrait of the province in more than 100 recordings between 1960 and 1996. Along with Félix Leclerc, Raymond Lévesque and Laude Léveillé, Vigneault is the most prominent of a generation of songwriters who advocated independence for Québec. His chanson *Gens du pays* (People of the Country) is a favorite on nationalist occasions. Another veteran chansonnier is Jean-Pierre Ferland.

Meanwhile, Michel Rivard touched the conscience of the world with his song *La Complainte du phoque en Alaska* (The Plight of the Seal in Alaska). Other well-known names include Daniel Bélanger, Daniel Lavoie, Jean Leloup, Richard Seguin, Robert Charleboix and Diane Dufresne. Harmonium, Offenbach or Beau Dommage (with Michel Rivard) are popular groups. Montréal's Lhasa, singing in Spanish, surprises with her passionate global sound.

Legendary pianist Oscar Peterson is Montréal's most famous jazz musician, known for his dexterity and dazzling speed on scores of recordings. He plays one-handed for audiences after suffering a stroke several years ago. Screech trumpet star Maynard Ferguson has been leading his own brassy ensemble bands since the 1960s; his Big Bop Nouveau orchestra can be caught on tour in the US and Europe. Other high-profile jazz names include pianist and vocalist Diana Krall and pianist Oliver Jones.

Among personalities on the classical-music scene, the Orchestre Métropolitain's new director, Montréaler Yannick Nézet-Séguin, is among the youngest to lead a major orchestra in Canada.

Montréal's best-known classical composer was Jean Papineau-Couture, whose works are noted for their modern Stravinski-like style. Some of his experiments were too bizarre even for a liberal audience, eg, a 1986 concerto for double bass and contra-bassoon. Papineau-Couture died in 2000.

Literature

Montréal's contribution to English-language literature has been uneven but potent. Its leading light is Mordecai Richler, whose

The Spirit of Leonard

Best known as a pop icon of the 1960s, Leonard Norman Cohen remains one of the world's most eclectic folk artists. Born in Montréal in 1934, Cohen, the son of a Jewish engineer, studied English literature at McGill University and attended Columbia University in New York. While at McGill, he formed a country-and-western trio called the Buckskin Boys, but he began to write poetry after his early singing efforts failed to land a record contract. His first collection of verse, *Let Us Compare Mythologies*, appeared in 1956 when Cohen was just 21; this was followed by more volumes, including the controversial *Flowers for Hitler* (1964). His only novels, *The Favorite Game* (1963) and *Beautiful Losers* (1966), have sold nearly one million copies each.

Ever the restless, creative spirit, Cohen used his success as a writer to relaunch his singing career. His compositions carry an aura of romantic, semisuicidal despair and have been compared to that of Jacques Brel's chansons. He won the coveted Canadian Governor General's award for his debut album *Selected Poems* in 1968, but he declined it. Singers such as Judy Collins, REM and Nick Cave acknowledge his influence, and the group Sisters of Mercy even took their name from one of his early songs.

Extensive tours, poetry and movie soundtracks occupied Cohen through much of the 1970s. A second burst of major creativity occurred in the 1980s, when his dry, gravelly baritone could be heard on albums such as *Various Positions* (1984), a treatise on lovers' relationships, and the sleekly produced *I'm Your Man* (1988), which suddenly made him hip again to younger audiences.

Cohen's works reveal a deep interest in spiritual themes. In the 1960s, he settled with Marianne Jenson on the Greek island of Hydra, a center of the hippie-intellectual scene. He stayed there on and off for seven years. India was also his home for a while, and he studied Hindu mysticism there.

Now in his mid-60s, Cohen was recently sighted at a Buddhist monastery on California's Mt Baldy, preparing his inner self for a return to the recording studio. One of the best places to meet the bard – as well as hordes of tie-dyed devotees – is the annual Leonard Cohen Event, a conference held every spring in Montréal for a hefty participation fee (at last check, $100).

comic, biting prose in novels such as *The Acrobats* (1954) and *Son of a Smaller Hero* (1955) depicted life in the Jewish tenements and delis of 1950s Montréal. He has won numerous literary awards. He contributes to the *New Yorker*, and he writes a weekly column in the Montréal *Gazette*. His more recent efforts are often aimed at Québec politics and the topic of separatism in particular.

Other familiar names include poet Irving Layton, novelist and essayist Hugh MacLennan, and poet and novelist Mavis Gallant. Hugh Hood, who died in 2000, wrote a good collection of stories about Montréal called *Around the Mountain* (1967). In the realm of theater, David Fennario's *Balconville* scrutinizes the lives of middle-class Montréalers whose summer holidays are limited to their balconies.

The Montréal Group of poets caused a renaissance of Canadian poetry during the 1920s and '30s by advocating a break with traditional landscape poetry. Its members – who included AJM Smith, AM Klein, Leo Kennedy and Francis Reginald Scott – encouraged realism, metaphysical complexity and expressionist techniques already used by Ezra Pound, TS Eliot and others. Smith's *Book of Canadian Poetry* (1943) is regarded as a landmark work.

French Québec writers who are widely read in English include Anne Hébert, Marie-Claire Blais, Hubert Aquin and Christian Mistral. Roch Carrier's witty short story *The Hockey Sweater* can practically be taken as a microcosm of the country's French–English quarrels. Gabrielle Roy's *Bonheur d'Occasion* (The Tin Flute) is a colorful urban novel set in Montréal during the 1930s and WWII. Reclusive novelist Réjean Ducharme of Montréal is considered one of the major French-language writers.

Painting

Québec has produced mainly landscape artists, although other areas have gained in popularity over the past several decades. Clarence Gagnon (1881–1942) is known for his subtle snowscapes and dazzling autumn scenes; the work Jean-Paul Lemieux (1904–90) is more somber. In the early 20th century, Horatorio Walker (1858–1938) captured urban and country scenes of the Victorian era.

The city also inspired artists such as Adrien Hébert (1890–1967) and Robert Pilot (1897–1967), who became famous for their snowy portraits of Montréal and Québec City. Their lively street scenes were a departure from the romantic classicism that was popular among the previous generation of painters, which included William Brymmer (1855–1925) and Antoine Plamondon (1804–95).

Paul-Émile Borduas (1905–60) and Jean-Paul Riopelle (b. 1923) went a step further with their convictions. In a manifest entitled 'Refus Global' (Global Refusal), which they cosigned with writers in 1948, they rose against the traditional Canadian landscape painting of the era and dedicated themselves to abstract art.

Marc-Aurèle Fortin (1880–1972) became famous for his watercolors of the Québec countryside, particularly the treescapes of the Laurentian Mountains and Charlevoix. His portraits of majestic Dutch elms along Montréal avenues recall the era when they were not yet ravaged by disease.

Cinema

Québec's cinematic output is impressive, given the small size of its local audience. Filmmakers are subsidized by the National Film Board (NFB), which is based in Montréal. Although the bulk of Québec movies are in French, dubbing and subtitling have made them accessible to a wider audience.

Québec cinema has a long, albeit provincial, tradition going back to the 1930s, such as Maurice Proulx's documentaries about the colonization of the Abitibi, an immense, gold-rich region in northwestern Québec. But it was only in the 1960s that the directors began to explore freer, more experimental styles similar to those of Frederico Fellini and Jean-Luc Godard. Feminist films such as *Anne Trister* and *La Femme de l'Hôtel,* by Montréal director Léa Pool, showed uncanny parallels with the emerging nationalism of the period. *Sonatine,* by actress Micheline Lanctôt, deals with suicide and the problems of communicating with young people.

In the 1980s, local cinema burst onto the international scene with the highly acclaimed *Le Déclin de l'empire américain* (The Decline of the American Empire), by Denys Arcand, which casts a wry look at male/female relationships. Arcand also took a dig at the Catholic Church with *Jésus of Montréal,* which revolves around a modern production of the Passion Play. François Girard's stylish epic *The Red Violin* weaves together five stories about a single violin as it travels through three centuries and the hands of prominent owners. The film won an Oscar for best original score in 1998. Girard also directed *Thirty-Two Short Films about Glenn Gould,* which provides a fascinating insight into the mind of the eccentric pianist.

Feminism and female sexuality continue to be strong themes among Montréal's women directors. Léa Pool's *Emporte Moi* (Set Me Free), a drama about the emotional consequences of a young girl's emerging sexuality, won Best Canadian Film at the Toronto Film Festival in 1999. Margaret Wescott produced a powerful chronicle of lesbian history in *Stolen Moments.*

Other names to look out for include Attila Bertalou, Louis Archambault, Michel Brault and Charles Binamé. Bertalou's *Between the Moon and Montevideo* (2000), a futuristic tale with a film-noir atmosphere, recalls the sinister urban landscapes of US director John Carpenter's work.

Animation and multimedia technologies have become something of a Montréal specialty, thanks in large part to the success of Softimage, a company founded by Daniel Langlois, a special-effects guru and former director. Softimage created some of the first 3-D animation software and was behind the special effects used in *Jurassic Park*, *The Mask*, *Godzilla* and *Titanic*. Frédéric Back's Oscar-winning animated film *The Man Who Planted Trees* tells the story of a shepherd who transforms a desert into a lush oasis.

Montréal has also produced several high-profile actors, including William Shatner (better known as Captain Kirk from the original *Star Trek* television series) and Geneviève Bujold, who has starred in a variety of films in English and French, including *Anne of the Thousand Days*, for which she received an Academy Award nomination.

SOCIETY & CONDUCT
Traditional Culture

The Europeans did their best to crush the original cultures of Canada, and together with disease, loss of land and means of livelihood, they were largely successful. Traditions still remain in Québec's more remote communities, but today, the predominant religion is Christianity, and the languages of the indigenous inhabitants – the Amerindians and Inuit – are rarely heard outside of reservations or limited 'homelands.' For more information, see the Kahnawake Indian Reserve section in the Things to See & Do chapter, or the Oka section in the Excursions chapter.

Dos & Don'ts

Montréalers are generally a pretty relaxed bunch, but you'll make yourself more popular if you observe a few simple rules.

A few dos:

- If you don't speak French, it's polite to begin your queries in Francophone shops, restaurants and public places with *'Parlez-vous anglais?'* ('Do you speak English?') rather than launching straight into English.

Getting Creamed

The tradition of pushing someone's face into a pie, usually out of protest or the desire to ridicule, is alive and well in Montréal. Almost all Canadian pie-throwing incidents have occurred here, sponsored by the Québec anarchist group Les Entartistes (which is linked to Belgium's International Pie-Throwing Anarchists). Since 1998, there have been a dozen attacks on prominent public figures in Montréal, including mayor Pierre Bourque, Canadian Health Minister Allan Rock and actor Sylvester Stallone (a near miss, at the grand opening of the Planet Hollywood restaurant). The organization, whose grievances include state backing of genetically altered foods, celebrated its 'Cream Come True' in 2000, when Prime Minister Jean Chrétien was blitzed with a meringue *tarte* in Charlottetown, Prince Edward Island.

- When walking into a shop, say *'Bonjour, monsieur/madame/mademoiselle'* and *'Merci, monsieur…au revoir'* when you leave.

- As in France, it's customary among French Québecers who know each other to exchange *bises* (kisses) as a greeting (though two men rarely do this). The usual ritual is one glancing peck on each cheek.

• If invited to someone's home or party, it's a good idea to bring some sort of gift, such as good wine (not some $10 *vin de table*). Flowers are another good standby.

A few don'ts:

• Don't address waiters as '*garçon,*' which means 'boy' and is considered rude. Saying '*S'il vous plaît*' (please) is the way it's done nowadays.

• When buying fruit, vegetables or flowers anywhere except at supermarkets, don't touch the produce or blossoms unless invited to do so. Show the shopkeeper what you want and he or she will serve you.

• Don't address the topic of Québec separatism if you have less than half an hour to spare.

RELIGION

Roman Catholics, most of whom are of French descent, make up about 80% of the churchgoing population. The majority of religious English-speaking Montréalers are Protestant – Anglicans, Presbyterians and members of the United Church of Canada make up the largest denominations. About 3% of the population is Jewish.

Montréal has more than 300 churches – and their abundance led American humorist Mark Twain to quip that you couldn't throw a rock in town without breaking a church window. Many of the churches are of a weighty Gothic style, with monumental

Signes de Fierté   Signs of Pride

Je me souviens. (I remember.)
– Devise Québécoise inscrite sur les plaques d'immatriculations

Je me souviens. (I remember.)
– Québec motto featured on license plates

L'adoption en 1977 de la Charte de la langue française, la fameuse loi 101, bannie l'usage de l'anglais sur les enseignes publiques à travers la province de Québec. Les conséquences en ont été parfois ridicules. Les panneaux de signalisation indiquant 'STOP' ont tous été remplacés par des panneaux lisant 'ARRÊT' tandis que même en France les panneaux hexagonaux rouges lisent 'STOP.' Des détaillants renommés, tel que Ogilvy's et l'ancien Eaton's, ont été obligés de supprimer l'apostrophe de leurs enseignes afin de respecter l'orthographe de la langue française. L'ironie c'est que Eaton's, fondé par une famille canadienne anglaise, a éventuellement refusé d'afficher des enseignes en anglais pour se conformer aux exigences de la loi. Furieux, des anglophones se sont réunis au magasin en 1999 pour protester. Le plus insensé de tout c'est l'acronyme 'PFK' lequel remplace le fameux 'KFC' (Kentucky Fried Chicken) dont même la Chine, un pays communiste, en permet l'usage. La loi est mise en application par une sorte de police municipale de la langue française qui parcourt la ville cherchant des portes indiquant 'Push' au lieu de 'Pousser.'

The passage in 1977 of Québec's French Language Charter, the (in)famous Bill 101, banned the use of English on public signs across the province. Sometimes the consequences are just plain ridiculous. Stop signs in Québec read 'ARRÊT,' a word that actually means a stop for buses or trains (even in France, the red hexagonal signs read 'STOP.') Venerable retailers, such as Ogilvy's and the now-defunct Eaton's, were forced to remove the apostrophes from their storefronts in line with French usage.

(Ironically, Eaton's, which was founded by an English Canadian family, later refused to post signs in English to comply with the law, and irate Anglophones gathered at its store in 1999 to protest.) Perhaps most comical of all is the acronym 'PFK' for a leading fast-food chain – even communist China still allows signs for KFC (Kentucky Fried Chicken). The law is enforced by a sort of municipal language police, who roam the city looking for doors bearing 'Push' instead of 'Pousser.'

JEFF GREENBERG

entrance arches and a soaring steeple in the front. St Patrick's serves English-speaking Roman Catholics; the Notre Dame Basilica is attended mainly by French-speakers. The Cathedral of St Mary, Queen of the World serves as the seat of the Catholic archdiocese of Montréal.

St Joseph's Oratory, a pilgrimage church on the western slope of Mont Royal, attracts more than two million visitors a year – some of whom climb the steps of the tower on their knees.

LANGUAGE

The interaction of the English and the French languages lends charm to Québec, but it's also responsible for continuing conflict. You may feel it less in cosmopolitan Montréal, but many French Québecers believe that their language is the last line of defense against the encroachments of Anglo-Saxon culture.

The French may have long dominated the social spheres, but traditionally, it was the English who ran the businesses, made decisions, held positions of power and accumulated wealth. As the Québec separatist movement gathered pace, the Ottawa government sought to assuage Francophones by passing legislation in 1969 that required all services to be offered in French and English. Canada effectively became bilingual, and one result was that tourist brochures and public signs had to appear in both French and English. However, the separatists took things a step further and demanded the primacy of French in Québec, which was affirmed by the passage of Bill 101 in 1977 (see the boxed text 'Signs of Pride').

Some French Québecers believe that they speak an older and purer form of French than even the French themselves. There is some truth to this, as the relative isolation of Québec settlers from the 17th century onward meant that linguistic trends in France were not fully absorbed. This knowledge is small consolation for Québecers visiting Paris, who may discover that their lingo is not readily understood by the locals.

Young Montréalers today tend to be less concerned with the issue than their elders, and visitors to the city shouldn't let it deter them. A large proportion of residents grow up bilingual, and store owners, telephone operators, waiters and most public-service personnel switch effortlessly between French and English. As a tourist town, Québec City is used to accommodating English-speakers. Out in the countryside, however, you'll find that your French phrasebook will come in handy.

Facts for the Visitor

WHEN TO GO

Montréal is alluring any time of year, but late spring and early summer are arguably the most pleasant periods. From mid-May to early July, the sun is warm but not baking, and you'll catch world-famous events such as the Grand Prix and the Montréal Jazz Festival. By late July, the mercury soars to 30°C or higher and, depending on what you're used to, the humidity (and the mosquitoes) can cramp your style.

Still, in high summer, the days are wonderfully long, and a seamless procession of festivals will take your mind off the heat. You'll have plenty of company: Québec's schools go on summer break from late June until Labour Day, which is the period when most people go on vacation.

The colder seasons have their charms, too. Many attractions shut down, but the crowds are thinner, hotel prices drop and the pace slows considerably. Fall produces a blaze of colors that rival New England's. In winter, Montréal becomes a great base for winter sports, and despite Arctic temperatures, the city is remarkably livable (see the boxed text 'The Underground City,' in the Shopping chapter). The city's ballet, opera and symphony season also runs through the winter months, and Québec City's famous Winter Carnival takes place in February.

The French-English Divide

Blvd St Laurent is the traditional boundary between the French community (to the east) and the English (to the west), although this border has lost a lot of its significance.

Street names still reflect the distinction: East of St Laurent, they're given the Est (East) designation – eg, Rue Ste Catherine Est – and to the west, they're called Ouest (West). All streets are divided in this way.

ORIENTATION

Though it's not apparent at first, the city occupies the Island of Montréal, which is roughly 40km long and 15km wide at the confluence of the Ottawa and St Lawrence Rivers. The narrow Rivière des Prairies flows along the northern shore, separating Montréal from the Île de Jésus and the town of Laval. Bridges link all sides with the mainland.

The Island of Montréal's most striking landmark is Mont Royal, a 232m-high extinct volcano (known locally as 'the mountain'). The core of the city is actually quite small and lies below in the southern central section of the island.

Montréal is an easy place to navigate, thanks to its grid system of streets, which is roughly aligned east-west and north-south. (The grid is actually skewed left of true north, but the locals ignore this niggling detail.)

For descriptions of the individual neighborhoods and districts, see the boxed text 'Districts in a Nutshell,' in the Things to See & Do chapter.

MAPS

The free maps from the tourist offices are adequate for most visitors. Car rental agencies usually provide an atlas or road map with rented vehicles.

The best maps of Montréal are published by Mapart – indeed, some local bookstores don't stock anything else. The yellow-cover *Montréal Urban Community* covers the entire island in detail, while its larger-scale *Montréal Explorateur* focuses on downtown. Both versions highlight a wealth of tourist attractions in easy-to-read colors. Where available, Rand McNally's *Montréal & Québec City* gives a clear overview of both cities but without Mapart's depth of detail.

Mapart and Rand McNally also publish road maps for Québec province – both have six city insets and a distance chart. *Canada East,* by Hildebrand's Travel Map

Rue or Street?

Montréal is a bilingual city, even though approximately 70% of the population consider themselves more French than Anglo-Saxon in origin. The bulk of visitors are English-speaking, and English is widely used in the central districts. On top of that, many streets were named by the British, who dominated the city throughout its formative years.

However, in this book, Montréal's street names are labeled in French, the first language of Québec. Many squares, parks and other sites are known by their French names. It may seem odd to read 'Rue Peel' instead of 'Peel St,' but this matches the street signs and is the way most Montréalers refer to them.

⚜ ⚜ ⚜ ⚜ ⚜ ⚜ ⚜ ⚜ ⚜ ⚜ ⚜

(1:500,000), and the spiral-bound *Grand Atlas Routier du Québec*, by La Cartothèque, show more detail of smaller roads.

RESPONSIBLE TOURISM

Montréal's traffic and air pollution, not to mention your blood pressure, can be reduced by using public transportation. Do us all a favor and leave your vehicle at home.

Recycling containers for glass, metal and plastic are common in town. Supermarkets have automated machines that will pay you to return deposit bottles. There are also regular municipal pickups of recyclable items – just ask wherever you're staying.

If you'll be visiting Québec's nature reserves or parks, be sure to pack up your litter when you leave. Don't use detergents or toothpaste in or near watercourses, even if they're biodegradable. When camping in the wild, bury human waste in holes at least 15cm deep and 100m from any watercourse.

TOURIST OFFICES
Local Tourist Offices

Montréal and Québec province have one central phone number for tourist information offices (☎ 873-2015 or 1-877-266-5687). The airports also have information kiosks that are open year-round.

The city's chief tourist office, Centre Infotouriste, is at 1001 Rue Square Dorchester (Map 5), a short walk from the main train station, Gare Centrale. Staff are friendly and will supply you with information on all areas of Montréal and Québec. Hours are 9 am to 6 pm (until 8 pm from June to Labour Day). The center also has a bookstore, currency-exchange counter and Internet terminals, and the staff can arrange guided tours and car rentals. Hotel reservations are provided free of charge. Web site: www.bonjourquebec.com. ⓜ Peel.

The other main tourist office is in Vieux Montréal at 174 Rue Notre Dame Est (Map 4), not far from Place Jacques Cartier. It's busy, but the staff are extremely helpful. Hours are 9 am to 7 pm daily from late June to early October and 9 am to 5 pm the rest of the year. Web site: www.tourism-montreal .org. ⓜ Champ de Mars.

Both offices sell a museum pass ($20), which covers entry to 25 museums and galleries over a two-day period – it generally pays for itself after two museum visits. Note that many Montréal museums are closed Monday.

There's also a tourist information booth at the entrance to the IMAX/Centre iSci complex on Quai King Edward (Map 4). It's open 10 am to 7 pm daily in the summer.

Tourist Offices Abroad

Aside from Canadian embassies and consulates (see that section, later in this chapter), you may obtain general travel information and publications about Québec from the following offices:

Belgium
   Délégation du Québec (☎ 022 512 00 36, email qc.bruxelles@mri.gouv.qc.ca), Ave des Arts 46, 7e étage, 1000 Bruxelles

France
   Délégation du Québec (☎ 01 40 67 85 00, email qc.paris@mri.gouv.qc.ca), 66 rue Pergolèse, 75116 Paris

Germany
   Agence Culturelle du Québec (☎ 030 308 76571, email berlin@quebec-info@mri.gouv.qc.ca), Friedrichstrasse 108-109, 10117 Berlin

FACTS FOR THE VISITOR

Italy
Agence Culturelle du Québec (☎ 06-44-25-21-30, email daniela.renosto@mri.gouv.qc.ca), Via Nomentana 201, Interno 2, 00161 Roma

Japan
Délégation du Québec (☎ 03-3239-5137, email qc.tokyo@mri.gouv.qc.ca), Nissei Hanzomon Building, 5th Floor, 1-3 Kojimachi, Chiyoda-ku, Tokyo 102-0083

Mexico
Délégation du Québec (☎ 05-250-8222, email qc.mexico@mri.gouv.qc.ca), Avenida Taine 411, Colonia Bosques de Chapultepec, 11580 Mexico DF

UK
Délégation du Québec (☎ 20-7766-5900, email qc.londres@mri.gouv.qc.ca), 59 Pall Mall, London SW1Y 5JH

USA
Boston: Délégation du Québec (☎ 617-482-1193, email francois.lebrun@mri.gouv.qc.ca), 31 Milk St, 10th Floor, Boston, MA 02109-5104
New York City: Délégation du Québec (☎ 212-397-0200, email qc.newyork@mri.gouv.qc.ca), 1 Rockefeller Plaza, 26th Floor, New York, NY 10020-2201
Washington: Bureau du Tourisme du Québec (☎ 202-659-8990, email qc.washington@mri .gouv.qc.ca), 1101 17th St NW, Bureau 1006, Washington, DC 20036-4704

TRAVEL AGENCIES

Travel CUTS, known in Québec as Voyages Campus, has eight locations in Montréal, including the main office at 1613 Rue St Denis (Map 6; ☎ 843-8511). It sells the International Student Identity Card (ISIC) and cheap plane tickets, and it also sets up working holidays and language courses. Web site: www.travelcuts.com. Ⓜ Berri-UQAM.

Run by Hostelling International, the Boutique Tourisme Jeunesse (Map 8; ☎ 844-0287), 4008 Rue St Denis, sells books, maps, travel insurance, ID cards and plane tickets. It's open 10 am to 6 pm Monday to Wednesday and Saturday, 10 am to 9 pm Thursday and Friday, and 10 am to 5 pm Sunday. The travel service is closed Sunday. Ⓜ Sherbrooke.

The American Express Travel Agency (Map 5; ☎ 284-3300), 1141 Blvd de Maisonneuve, is open 9 am to 5 pm weekdays. Ⓜ Peel.

DOCUMENTS
Passports

Visitors from all countries but the USA need a passport, except for people from Greenland (Denmark) and St Pierre & Miquelon (France), who don't need passports if they're entering from their areas of residence. However, everyone needs to have valid identification.

For US and Canadian citizens, a driver's license is usually sufficient when entering via land border crossings. However, a certificate of birth, citizenship or naturalization, if not a passport, is recommended and may be required in some cases. Permanent residents of the US who aren't citizens should carry their green card, and US citizens arriving from somewhere other than the USA should have a passport.

Visas
For Canada Visas aren't required for visitors from nearly all Western countries. However, you'll need to apply for a visa if you're from Hong Kong, Korea, South Africa, Taiwan, developing countries or certain parts of Eastern Europe. Visa requirements change frequently, so it's a good idea to check with the Citizen and Immigration Canada call center in Montréal (☎ 496-1010) to see if you're exempt. Web site: www.cic.gc.ca. Checking with your Canadian consulate is another good way to find out if you need a visa.

Single-entry visitor visas ($75) are valid for six months, while multiple-entry visas ($150) can be used over a two-year period, provided that no single stay exceeds six months. Extensions, which cost the same price as the original visa, must be applied for at a Canadian Immigration Center one month before the current visa expires. A separate visa is required for visitors intending to work in Canada.

A passport and/or visa does not guarantee entry. The admission and duration of a permitted stay is based on a number of factors, including being of good health, being law abiding, having sufficient money and, possibly, having a return ticket out of the country.

If you are refused entry but have a visa, you have the right of appeal at the Immigration Appeal Board at the port of entry. People under 18 years old should have a letter from a parent or guardian.

For the USA Admission to the USA when you're arriving by land can work quite differently than by air or sea, and requirements can change frequently. The duration of the visit – whether for one afternoon or for three months – is inconsequential. Visitors to the USA from most developed countries don't need visas, but there are exceptions, one being South Africa.

You can apply for a US visa in Canada, but it's generally easier to apply for one at home, and your chances of being refused are reduced that way. Visas cannot be obtained upon arrival in the USA. Make sure that your Canadian visa is a multiple-entry visa; otherwise, you may find that Canadian officials won't let you back into Canada. Also, note that the period of any side trip to the USA will count as time spent on your Canadian visa.

Visitors to the USA who don't need a visa must pay a US$6 fee at the border. Air or sea travelers must also have a return or onward ticket in their possession. Travelers with young children should be aware that they may be required to document custody of their children.

For information in Canada on US visas, call the visa information line at ☎ 1-900-451-6330 (98¢ per minute), or contact a US embassy or consulate in your home country. Web site: www.usembassycanada.gov.

Travel Insurance

Travel insurance can cover you for medical expenses, luggage theft or loss, and cancellation or delays in your travel arrangements. The policies handled by Travel CUTS (Voyages Campus in Québec; see Travel Agencies, earlier) or other student travel organizations are usually a good value.

Coverage depends on your policy and type of airline ticket. Paying for your plane tickets with a credit card often provides limited travel accident insurance, and you may be able to reclaim the payment if the travel operator doesn't deliver.

The largest seller of medical insurance to visitors to Canada is John Ingle Insurance, which offers policies from seven days to one year. The 30-day basic plan costs $90 for an adult under the age of 55, $108 for people ages 55 to 64, $120 for people ages 65 to 69, and more (on a sliding scale) for age groups that are above that. Coverage includes hospital and doctors' fees, extended health care and other features. Payment can be made before or after arrival in Canada. Ingle's head office in Toronto (☎ 416-340-8115 or 1-800-216-3588) will send you a pamphlet. Web site: www.ingle-health.com.

Driver's License & Permits

Driver's licenses from your home country are also valid in Canada. An International Driver's Permit (IDP) comes in handy, however, when dealing with the police and car rental companies. An IDP can be obtained for a small fee from your local automobile association – bring along a passport photo and a valid license. In the US, IDPs are not necessary but also come in handy at times.

US citizens should get a Canadian Non-resident Interprovince Motor Vehicle Liability Insurance Card, which proves financial liability if you're involved in an accident. It's only available in the US – contact your insurance agent.

Hostel Cards

A Hostelling International (HI) card is necessary only at official *auberges de jeunesse* (youth hostels) – of which there are 17 in Québec. The card also entitles you to small discounts at non-HI hostels, museums, restaurants, attractions and shops. One- and two-year cards are available at HI hostels for $25 and $35, respectively ($12 for youth under 18). Contact the Canadian branch of HI for more details (☎ 613-237-7884 or 1-800-663-5777). Web site: www.hostellingintl.ca.

Discount Cards

An International Student Identity Card (ISIC) can pay for itself through half-price admissions, discounted air and ferry tickets and cheap meals in student cafeterias. In Montréal, ISIC cards are issued by Voyages Campus and other student travel agencies for $16 (see Travel Agencies, earlier). The International Student Travel Confederation is another good source for ISIC cards. Web site: www.istc.org.

If you're under 26 but not a student, you can apply for a GO25 card, issued by the Federation of International Youth Travel Organisations (FIYTO), which entitles you to much the same discounts as an ISIC and is also issued by student unions or student travel agencies. It costs $16.

Teachers, professional artists, museum curators and certain categories of students are admitted to some museums for free. An International Teacher Identity Card (ITIC) costs $16 and may be obtained through the International Student Travel Confederation.

Copies

Before you leave home, you should photocopy all important documents (passport and visa, credit cards, travel-insurance policy, air/bus/train tickets, driver's license etc). Leave one set of copies with someone at home and keep another with you, separate from the originals.

You can also store details of your vital travel documents in Lonely Planet's free online Travel Vault. Your personal password-protected Travel Vault is accessible online anywhere in the world. Web site: www.ekno.lonelyplanet.com.

EMBASSIES & CONSULATES
Canadian Embassies & Consulates

For embassies and consulates not on the following list, consult the Department of Foreign Affairs and International Trade. Web site: www.dfait-maeci.gc.ca/english/missions/menu.htm.

Australia
High Commission: (☎ toll free 09-309-8516), Commonwealth Ave, Canberra ACT 2600, www.canada.org.au
Consulate: (☎ 02-9364-3000, Visa Immigration Office 02-9364-3050), 111 Harrington St, Level 5, Quay West, Sydney, NSW 2000

Consulate: (☎ 03-9811-9999), 123 Camberwell Rd, Hawthorn East, Melbourne, Vic 3123
Consulate: (☎ 08-9322-7930), 267 St George's Terrace, Perth, WA 6000

Denmark
Embassy: (☎ 33-48-32-00), Kr Bernikowsgade 1, 1105 Copenhagen K, www.canada.dk

France
Embassy: (☎ 01 44 43 29 00), 35, ave Montaigne, 75008 Paris, www.amb-canada.fr
Consulate: (☎ 04 72 77 64 07), 21, rue Bourgelat, 69002 Lyon

Germany
Embassy: (☎ 30 20 31 20), Friedrichstrasse 95, 12th Floor, 10117 Berlin, www.dfait-maeci.gc.ca/~bonn/

Ireland
Embassy: (☎ 01-478-1988; after hours 01-478-1476), Canada House, 65/68 St Stephen's Green, Dublin 2

Israel
Embassy: (☎ 03-636-3300), 3/5 Nirim Street, Tel Aviv 67060

Italy
Embassy: (☎ 06-44-84-46), Via Zara 30, 00198 Rome, www.canada.it

Japan
Embassy: (☎ 03-5412-6200), 3-38 Akasaka 7-chome, Minato-ku, Tokyo 107-5803, www.dfait-maeci.gc.ca/ni-ka/contacts/tokyo/menu-e.asp

Netherlands
Embassy: (☎ 070-311-1600), Sophialaan 7, 2500 GV, The Hague, www.ocanada.nl

New Zealand
High Commission: (☎ 04-473-9577), 61 Molesworth St, 3rd Floor, Thorndon, Wellington, www.dfait-maeci.gc.ca/newzealand/welcome-e.asp

Spain
Embassy: (☎ 91-423-3250), Edificio Goya, Calle Nuñez de Balboa 35, 28001 Madrid, www.canada-es.org

Sweden
Embassy: (☎ 08-453-3000), Tegelbacken 4, 7th Floor, S-103 23 Stockholm, www.canadaemb.se

Switzerland
Embassy: (☎ 031-357-3200), Kirchenfeldstrasse 88, 3005 Bern, www.canada-ambassade.ch
Permanent Mission to the Office of the UN, Consular Section: (☎ 022-919-9200), 5, Avenue de l'Ariana, 1202 Geneva

UK
High Commission: (☎ 020-258-6600), Canada House, Consular Services, Trafalgar Square, London SW1Y 5BJ, www.canada.org.uk

Your Own Embassy

It's important to realize what your own embassy – the embassy of the country of which you are a citizen – can and can't do to help you if you get into trouble. Generally speaking, it won't be much help in emergencies if the trouble you're in is remotely your own fault. Remember that you are bound by the laws of the country you are in. Your embassy will not be sympathetic if you end up in jail after committing a crime locally, even if such actions are legal in your own country.

In genuine emergencies, you might get some assistance, but only if other channels have been exhausted. If you need to get home urgently, a free ticket home is exceedingly unlikely – the embassy would expect you to have insurance. If all your money and documents are stolen, it might assist you with getting a new passport, but a loan for onward travel is out of the question.

FACTS FOR THE VISITOR

Immigration Information: (☎ 09068-616644), 38 Grosvenor St, London W1X 0AA

Consulate: (☎ 0131-220-4333), Standard Life House, 30 Lothian Rd, Edinburgh, EH1 2DH Scotland

Consulate: (☎ 0131-220-4333), 378 Strandmillis Rd, Belfast, BT9 5BL Northern Ireland

USA
Embassy: (☎ 202-682-1740), 501 Pennsylvania Ave NW, Washington, DC 20001, www .canadianembassy.org

Consulate: (☎ 617-262-3760), 3 Copley Place, Suite 400, Boston, MA 02116

Consulate: (☎ 716-858-9500), 1 Marine Midland Center, Suite 3000, Buffalo, NY 14203-2884

Consulate: (☎ 312-616-1860), Two Prudential Plaza, 180 N Stetson Ave, Suite 2400, Chicago, IL 60601

Consulate: (☎ 313-567-2340), 600 Renaissance Center, Suite 1100, Detroit, MI 48243-1798

Consulate: (☎ 212-596-1600), 1251 Ave of the Americas, Concourse Level, New York, NY 10020-1175

Many other US cities have Canadian Consulate Generals; see www.dfait-maeci.gc.ca/english/missions/menu.htm.

Consulates in Montréal

Only the main consulates are listed here; check the yellow pages for a detailed list. Australian citizens should call the Australian High Commission in Ottawa (☎ 613-236-0841).

Cuba (☎ 843-8897) 1415 Ave des Pins Ouest
Denmark (☎ 877-3060) 1 Place Ville Marie
France (☎ 866-6511) 1 Place Ville Marie
Germany (☎ 931-2277) 1250 Blvd René Lévesque Ouest

Italy (☎ 849-8351) 3489 Rue Drummond
Japan (☎ 866-3429) 600 Rue de la Gauchetière Ouest
Netherlands (☎ 849-4247) 1002 Rue Sherbrooke Ouest
Spain (☎ 935-5235) 1 Square Westmount
Sweden (☎ 345-2727) 8400 Blvd Décarie
Switzerland (☎ 932-7181) 1572 Ave Docteur Penfield
UK (Map 5; ☎ 866-5863) 1000 Rue de la Gauchetière Ouest
US (Map 5; ☎ 398-9695) 1155 Rue St Alexandre

CUSTOMS

If you're entering Canada by car, you should know that vehicles that look suspiciously full are likely to be searched. Keep the car's weight to a minimum, and stow your belongings in the trunk.

Adults age 18 and older can bring in 1.14L of wine or liquor (or a case of beer), 200 cigarettes, 50 cigars and 200g of tobacco – all are cheaper in the USA, incidentally. You can also bring in gifts valued up to $60 plus a 'reasonable amount' (up to the agent's discretion) of personal effects. Most fruit, vegetables and plants can be confiscated. Boats powered by motors under 10hp can be brought in without special licenses.

Don't get caught bringing in drugs – including marijuana and hashish – as sentences can be harsh. Mace, pepper spray, pistols and firearms (except hunting rifles) are also prohibited.

For the latest customs information, contact the Canadian embassy or consulate in your home country.

MONEY

All prices quoted in this book are in Canadian dollars ($) unless stated otherwise. The strong US dollar gives American visitors a favorable exchange rate, although Canadian federal and provincial taxes cut into that buying power.

For a range of financial travel services, visit American Express (Map 5; ☎ 284-3300), at 1141 Blvd de Maisonneuve, open 9 am to 5 pm weekdays. Ⓜ Peel.

Thomas Cook (☎ 284-7388) has an office in the Centre Eaton (Map 5), 705 Rue Ste Catherine Ouest; it's also open Saturday. Ⓜ McGill.

Currency

Canadian coins come in one-cent (penny), five-cent (nickel), 10-cent (dime), 25-cent (quarter), $1 (loonie) and $2 (toonie) pieces. Amounts less than $1 are represented in cents with a ¢ following the amount (eg, 25 cents is 25¢). The gold-colored loonie features the loon, a common Canadian waterbird. When the toonie was introduced in 1996, Canadians made a sport out of separating the aluminum-bronze core from the nickel outer ring.

Paper currency comes in $5 (blue), $10 (purple), $20 (green) and $50 (red) denominations. The $100 (brown) and larger bills are uncommon and could prove difficult to change. Some denominations have two styles, as older versions continue to circulate.

Exchange Rates

country	unit		Canadian dollar
Australia	A$1	=	C$0.84
European Union	€1	=	C$1.36
France	10FF	=	C$0.21
Germany	DM1	=	C$0.69
Hong Kong	HK$1	=	C$0.20
Japan	¥100	=	C$1.39
New Zealand	NZ$1	=	C$0.65
UK	UK£1	=	C$2.21
USA	US$1	=	C$1.53

> Unless otherwise noted, all prices in this book are in Canadian dollars.

Exchanging Money

It's best to change your money at a recognized bank or financial institution. Currency booths, as well as hotels, tourist shops and some restaurants, will exchange money for you, but their rates aren't very good. Always convert some money before leaving home.

ATMs tend to offer superior rates, and most also give you a cash advance through your Visa or MasterCard (see the Credit Cards section, later). Montréal has plenty of ATMs – not only in banks, but also in pubs, convenience stores and hotels – that are linked to the international Cirrus, Plus and Maestro networks. Many charge a $1.50 fee per use, and your own bank may levy an extra fee – check before leaving home.

Rue Ste Catherine has oodles of bank branches. Among them, there's a Banque de Montréal at 1205 Rue Ste Catherine Ouest (Map 5; Ⓜ Peel) and in the Village at 1700 Rue Ste Catherine Est (Map 6; Ⓜ Papineau). In the Plateau, there's a Banque Laurentienne at 3730 Blvd St Laurent (Map 8; Ⓜ Sherbrooke).

Currencies International (☎ 392-9100), 1230 Rue Peel, offers good rates. It's open daily to 9 pm weekdays, to 8:30 pm Saturday and to 6 pm Sunday (Map 5; Ⓜ Peel).

At Dorval Airport, there are foreign-exchange desks in the departures and arrivals sections. To find an ATM after you arrive, take the escalator to the departures level – you can't miss it.

Cash & Personal Checks Most Canadians don't carry large amounts of cash for everyday use, relying instead on credit and debit cards. Unlike in the US, shops and businesses rarely accept personal checks.

Traveler's Checks American Express, Thomas Cook, Visa and MasterCard are the best traveler's checks to use, either in US or Canadian dollars. They offer good exchange rates but not necessarily better than those offered at ATMs. Traveler's checks in Canadian dollars will be accepted as cash at most hotels, restaurants and stores.

American Express and Thomas Cook offices don't charge fees for cashing their

Aerial view of the Vieux Port at dusk

Street performer on Place Jacques Cartier

Characteristic mural in the Plateau

Fireworks over Pont Jacques Cartier

Entrance to Montréal's Chinatown

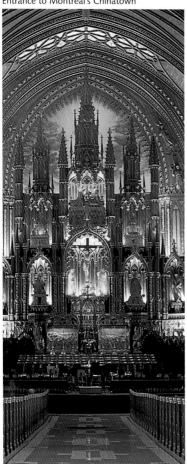

Interior of Basilique Notre Dame

Striking mural on St Denis

Pretty buildings all in a row

own traveler's checks. Otherwise, Banque de Montréal and Scotiabank charge the lowest fees.

If your traveler's checks are lost or stolen, call the appropriate toll-free numbers: American Express (☎ 1-800-221-7282), Thomas Cook (☎ 1-888-823-4732), Visa (☎ 1-800-227-6811). Keeping a record of the check numbers will help you get a swift refund.

Credit Cards Credit cards are widely used in Canada. They're also a good form of identification and may be required for security deposits on rented cars or bicycles. Credit cards enable you to get cash advances at banks and ATMs, generally for a 3% transaction fee or a minimum of $5. The following are some toll-free numbers for locating an ATM near you: American Express (☎ 1-800-227-4669), MasterCard (☎ 1-800-307-7309), Visa (☎ 1-800-847-2911).

Visa, MasterCard, and to a lesser extent American Express and JTB credit cards, are widely accepted in Canada. Beware that many US-based credit cards now use unfavorable exchange rates when billing foreign charges. Call your credit-card company before leaving home to inquire about rates. If your card is lost or stolen, call the appropriate number listed above.

International Transfers Telegraphic transfers are not very expensive, but despite their name, they can take several days to reach their destination. Be sure to specify the bank and the branch address where you'd like to pick it up.

It's quicker and easier to have money wired via American Express (☎ 1-800-668-8680), which charges a fee of US$50 for US$1000. Western Union's Money Transfer system (☎ 1-800-325-000) and Thomas Cook's MoneyGram service (☎ 1-800-926-9400) are also popular. A transfer should go through within 15 minutes.

Costs

By North American standards, Montréal is a cheap place to visit. If you're on a tight budget, you could scrape by on a mere $30 to $40 a day by staying in hostels, self-catering and limiting your entertainment. Staying in a cheap motel or B&B, eating in budget restaurants and allowing yourself a few drinks in bars could easily run you up to $90 a day. Eating your main meal at lunch rather than dinner can save a lot of money. Car rentals start at around $40 per day. Remember that most posted prices don't include taxes.

Tipping & Bargaining

A tip of 15% of the pretax bill is customary in restaurants. A few restaurants may include a service charge on the bill for large parties. No tip should be added in these cases, unless you feel the service was extraordinary and deserving of even more. It's acceptable to hand the tip directly to staff or to discreetly leave it behind on the table. Tipping is expected for bar service too, and it especially helps to give a fat tip on the first order – after that, you won't go thirsty all night.

Tips of 10% to 15% are also given to taxi drivers, hairdressers and barbers. Hotel bellhops and redcaps (porters) at airports and train stations should get a dollar or two per item minimum.

Taxes & Refunds

The federal goods and services tax (called TPS in Québec and GST in the rest of Canada) adds 7% to just about every transaction. Québec also charges a provincial sales tax (TVQ) of 7.5%, which – to the ire of the general populace – is also levied on the TPS (ie, taxing a tax).

Visitors are eligible for refunds on TPS paid for accommodations and nonconsumable goods (ie, not food or drink), provided you spend at least a total of $200 and apply for the refund within one year of purchase. However, the catch is that each eligible receipt must be for $50 or more. Tax paid on services or transportation is not refundable. You must keep the original receipts and have them stamped by customs before leaving the country. Instant cash refunds of up to $500 can be obtained at land border crossings with participating duty-free shops. Otherwise, you'll need to mail a tax-rebate form (widely available at shops and hotels) with your stamped receipts.

Many tax-refund services are run by private companies, which take a fee of up to 20% of your refund. The Maple Leaf refund office (☎ 847-0982) in the Centre Eaton (Map 5), 705 Rue Ste Catherine Ouest, is one such service. ⑩ McGill.

POST & COMMUNICATIONS
Post

The national mail service, Canada Post/ Postes Canada (☎ 1-800-267-1177) is neither quick nor cheap, but it's reliable. Standard 1st-class airmail letters or postcards cost 46¢ to Canadian destinations and 55¢ to the US (both are limited to 30g). Those to other destinations cost 95¢ (limit 20g). Web site: www.canadapost.ca.

The main post office (Map 5; ☎ 846-5401) is at 1250 Rue University. ⑩ McGill. There are also many smaller branches around Montréal. Stamps are often available at newspaper shops, variety stores and hotels.

Poste restante (general delivery) is available at Station Place d'Armes, 435 Rue St Antoine, Montréal H2Z 1H0 (Map 4). It's open 8:30 am to 5:30 pm weekdays. Mail will be kept for two weeks and then returned to the sender. American Express and Thomas Cook (see the Money section, earlier) will also hold mail for their customers – showing one of their traveler's checks may be enough to qualify.

Telephone

The city's area code, which applies to the entire Island of Montréal, is ☎ 514. Other area codes are indicated with telephone numbers throughout this book.

Almost anywhere in Québec, dial ☎ 911 for police, fire, accident and medical emergencies. When in doubt, dial ☎ 0 and ask the operator for assistance. For nonemergency police matters, consult the local telephone book for the phone number of the station. See Emergencies, later in this chapter, for more information on what to do in tricky situations.

Bell Canada, one of Canada's regional phone services, serves all of Québec. Rates are low for local use but tend to be costly for long distances, and they are certainly more expensive than in the US.

Local calls from a payphone cost 25¢ for three minutes. All Canadian business and residential phones are billed a flat monthly rate for local calls, so don't feel guilty about the cost of using a friend's telephone if you're making local calls.

Dialing the operator (☎ 0), directory assistance (☎ 411) or the emergency number (☎ 911) is free of charge from both public and private phones. For long-distance directory assistance, dial 1 + area code + 555-1212, which is also free. Some older telephones may not be equipped to make long-distance calls (in an effort to prevent phone-card fraud), but the newer ones with an LCD display are.

The peak and off-peak periods for long-distance calls depend on the country being called. The cheapest rates apply between 6 and 10 pm on weekdays and all weekend, while peak rates are charged weekdays during business hours. The evening rates listed next also apply on weekends.

Charges for calls to the USA vary. A weekday call to New York City costs 54¢ per minute 8 am to 6 pm and 22¢ per minute 6 pm to 8 am (plus a $3.54 connection fee if you call from a public payphone). Connections to farther-flung destinations (such as Los Angeles or Miami) cost more.

To the UK, you'll pay 67¢ per minute 10 am to 6 pm and 50¢ per minute 6 pm to 10 am; calling Australia costs $1.05 per minute 8 am to 8 pm and 79¢ per minute 8 pm to 8 am. From payphones, there's a $6.50 connection fee for both countries.

Dialing direct is cheapest. With operator assistance, calls in increasing order of cost are station-to-station, collect (reversed charge) and person-to-person.

Remember that hotels charge dearly for telephone use – often 50¢ or more for a local call.

Toll-Free Numbers Many businesses and tourist organizations have toll-free numbers, which begin with 800, 888, 877 or 777 and must be preceded with 1. Some numbers are good throughout North America, others only within Canada and still others in just one province. You won't know until you dial.

Dial-Around Services Dial-around services allow you to bypass the local long-distance carrier and bill your credit card or home phone account. Toll-free access numbers in Canada include AT&T (☎ 1-800-225-5288), MCI (☎ 1-800-888-8000) and Sprint (☎ 1-800-366-2255) – all are US-based. Prepaid phone cards, however, are a better proposition.

Phone Cards There's a wide range of local and international phone cards. Lonely Planet's eKno Communication Card is aimed specifically at travelers and provides cheap international calls, a range of messaging services and free email – but for local calls, you're usually better off with a local card. You can join eKno online at www .ekno.lonelyplanet.com, or by phone from Canada by dialing ☎ 1-800-294-3676. To use eKno from Canada, dial ☎ 1-800-808-5773.

International Dialing

To call someone outside Canada, dial the international access code (☎ 011), the country code, the area code (without the initial zero if there is one) and the local number. The country code for Canada and the USA is 1; you needn't dial 011 before the country code if you're calling the US. Other country codes include the following:

Australia	☎ 61
Hong Kong	☎ 852
Germany	☎ 49
Japan	☎ 81
India	☎ 91
Ireland	☎ 353
New Zealand	☎ 64
Singapore	☎ 65
South Africa	☎ 27
UK	☎ 44

Many local phone cards offer rates better than Bell's. The cards, sold at many convenience and magazine stores, have catchy names such as Chit-Chat, Nuvo and WOW, and they come in denominations of $10, $20, $30 and $50. For instance, Nuvo charges a flat 5.6¢ per minute for calls between Montréal, Toronto, Ottawa and Vancouver; 7.5¢ for calls to the US and UK; and 9.3¢ for calls to Australia and New Zealand. There's no connection charge.

Bell Canada's prepaid Puce card, sold in denominations of $10, $20 and $50, works only in public telephone booths, while its Allô! card can be used from both public and private phones. Both cards are sold at vending machines around town. You'll pay connection charges for long-distance calls (generally $1.54 to $1.75), and the per-minute rates aren't as good those offered by other phone cards.

Fax & Telegram

Fax machines are available to the public at major hotels and post offices and at a range of small businesses.

Bureau en Gros (Map 5; ☎ 875-0977), 770 Rue Notre Dame Ouest, charges 89¢ for sending a fax within Canada or to the US, $2 to Europe and Australia and $3 elsewhere. It's open 24 hours, seven days a week. Ⓜ Square Victoria.

Tip Tours (Map 5; ☎ 878-9594), in the basement of the Centre Infotouriste on Square Dorchester, is slightly more expensive and closes at 7 pm. Ⓜ Peel.

Even in the cyber age, you can still send telegrams. To do so, contact AT&T Canada (☎ 1-800-387-1926).

Email & Internet Access

If you're taking a computer to Canada to access the Internet, you may need a universal AC converter, a plug adapter or global PC-card modem – often it's easiest to buy these before you leave home.

Major Internet providers have local dial-up numbers in Montréal. It's a good idea to open a free Web-based email account, which will allow you to email from cybercafés and other access points. Lonely Planet's eKno offers just such a service. Web site: www .ekno.lonelyplanet.com.

The central public library (Map 6; ☎ 872-5923), 1210 Rue Sherbrooke Est, offers Internet access on its 12 terminals for free (two-hour limit). ⓜ Beaudry. Other public libraries around town are also equipped for free Web surfing. You'll need to show your passport or driver's license.

Chapters bookstore (Map 5; ☎ 849-8825), 1171 Rue Ste Catherine Ouest, has eight terminals on the 2nd floor and charges $2 for 20 minutes. It's open until 11 pm daily. ⓜ Peel.

Most hostels and some B&Bs offer Internet access to guests for around $6 per hour. Internet cafés in Montréal include the following:

Cyberground Netcafé (Map 7; ☎ 842-1726), 3672 Blvd St Laurent, has 16 computers and charges $4 per half-hour. It's open 10 am to 11 pm daily. ⓜ Sherbrooke.

Cybermac (Map 5; ☎ 287-9100), 1425 Rue Mackay, is a pleasant café with 11 terminals in modern cubicles. It charges $4/5.75 per half-hour/hour. Hours are 9:30 am to 10 pm weekdays and noon to 8 pm Saturday. ⓜ Guy-Concordia.

Le Café Electronique (Map 5; ☎ 871-0307), 1425 Blvd René Lévesque, has a dozen online terminals and charges $5.50/8.80 per half-hour/hour. Hours are 9 am to 8 pm weekdays. ⓜ Lucien L'Allier.

Centre Infotouriste (Map 5; ☎ 878-3847), 1001 Square Dorchester, has 13 Macs and PCs in the basement with printers and scanners. The rate is 10¢ per minute and hours are 10 am to 6 pm daily. ⓜ Peel.

INTERNET RESOURCES

The World Wide Web is a rich resource for travelers. You can research your trip, hunt down bargain airfares, book hotels, check on weather conditions and chat with locals and other travelers about the best places to visit (or avoid!).

There's no better place to start your Internet explorations than the Lonely Planet Web site (www.lonelyplanet.com). There you'll find succinct summaries on traveling to most places on earth, postcards from other travelers and the Thorn Tree bulletin board, where you can ask questions before you go or dispense advice when you get back. You can also find travel news and updates for many of Lonely Planet's most popular guidebooks, and the subWWWay section links you to the most useful travel resources elsewhere on the Web.

Web sites are listed throughout this book. The following is a list of English-language sites with many useful links:

Tourism Montréal
   www.tourisme-montreal.org
Canada Tourism Commission
   www.canadatourism.com
Tourism Québec
   www.bonjourquebec.com
Montreal Gazette
   www.montrealgazette.com
Mirror Magazine
   www.montrealmirror.com
Montréal Bars & Restaurants
   www.bar-resto.com
Montréal Online
   www.montrealonline.com
Montréal Jazz Festival
   www.montrealjazzfest.com
Just for Laughs
   www.hahaha.com
Montréal Radio Stations
   www.canehdian.com/radio/bycity/montreal.html

BOOKS

If you want to delve deeper into Montréal in print, the bookstores listed in the Shopping chapter are excellent sources of information.

Note: Most books are published in different editions by different publishers in different countries. As a result, a book might be a hardcover rarity in one country but readily available in paperback in another. Fortunately, bookstores and libraries can search by title or author, so your local bookstore or library is the best place to advise you on the availability of the following recommendations.

Lonely Planet

Lonely Planet's *Canada* is the essential companion if you're touring the country;

LP's *Toronto* and *Vancouver* are the definitive guides to those cities, and its *French phrasebook* is a handy primer for *la langue française*. Readers of French should pick up a copy of *Québec,* which has blanket coverage of the province from the Eastern Townships all the way up to Hudson Bay.

Other Guidebooks & Travel

There are a few good specialist guidebooks to Montréal. A good, easy-to-digest guide with insights into history, society and architecture is *Montréal Up Close: A Pedestrian's Guide to the City* (1998), by Kirk Johnson and David Widgington. Exhaustively researched, the book features numbered walking tours on color foldout maps based on aerial photographs.

Although it has nothing to do with crustaceans, the best-selling *Lobster Kid's Guide to Exploring Montréal* (2000) has 150-odd activities perfect for families in Montréal and its environs. The author, John Symon, has also written a similar book for Ottawa-Hull.

Foodies whose tastes routinely exceed their budget will enjoy *Cheap Thrills: Great Montréal Meals for Under $10* (2000), by Simon Dardick and Nancy Marrelli.

Jan Morris, a Welsh travel writer who has written about many cities around the world, published *City to City* in 1990. Written after traveling Canada coast to coast, it's a highly readable collection of essays of fact and opinion about 10 Canadian cities, including Montréal. This book also appeared under the title *O Canada: Travels in an Unknown Country.*

History & Politics

Of the few history books devoted to the city, the 400-page *Montréal in Evolution* (1981), by Jean-Claude Marsan, gives a pretty balanced account of the past four centuries. The emphasis is on architecture and urban development. (It's more interesting than it sounds.)

A Short History of Québec (1993, revised 2000), by John A Dickenson and Brian Young, is good for anyone looking for a general introduction to the province. Focused on the social and economic development of Québec (but far from dry), it stretches from the pre-European period all the way to the constitutional struggles of the present.

If you enjoy photojournalism, *Montréal's Century* (1999) provides a gripping account of the news and people who shaped the city in the 20th century. The collection was assembled and published jointly by the *Montréal Gazette* and *Journal de Montréal.* It's hard to put down once you start leafing through.

For all of Canada, *The Illustrated History of Canada* (2000), edited by Craig Brown, is a well-crafted work with fascinating prints, maps and sketches. Another good basic primer on the country's history is *The Penguin History of Canada* (1988), by Kenneth McNaught.

Peter C Newman, who is primarily a business writer, has produced an intriguing history of the Hudson's Bay Company, *Caesars of the Wilderness* (1987), beginning with the early fur-trading days.

For insights into the lives of Canada's indigenous inhabitants, *Native Peoples and Cultures of Canada* (1995), by Allan Macmillan, includes both history and current issues.

The seminal work on the topic, however, is *The Indians of Canada* (1932), by Diamond Jenness. It has been reprinted many times. Originally from New Zealand, the author spent years living with various indigenous peoples across the country.

General

No survey of Montréal literature would be complete without the critical articles, essays and novels by Mordecai Richler (who also writes a column for the *Montréal Gazette*). Richler, a Jewish Anglophone who grew up in the Plateau, rose to fame in the 1950s with novels such as *The Acrobats* (1954) and *Son of a Smaller Hero* (1955), which vividly depicted life in Montréal's Jewish ghetto. More recently, the author directed his biting wit and social commentary at the issue of Québec separatism in *Oh Canada! Oh Québec!* (1992). *Home Sweet Home: My Canadian Album* (1984) is a collection of tongue-in-cheek essays on the country.

FACTS FOR THE VISITOR

Montréal in the Literary Imagination: Storied Streets (2000), by Bryan Demchinsky and Elaine Kalman Naves, looks at the city through the eyes of writers and poets, including Charles Dickens, Harriet Beecher Stowe and Mark Twain, as well as contemporary scribes.

William Weintraub's *City Unique: Montréal Days & Nights in the 1940s and '50s* (1996) is full of engaging tales of Montréal's twilight period as Sin City. Its colorful characters include gangsters, the acid-tongued mayor Henri Bourassa and legendary stripper Lili St Cyr.

For an Anglo-Saxon take on living in Québec, *Feeling Comfortable* (2000), by Martha Radice, examines the decline of Anglo-Saxon influence in Montréal and its effect on the English-speaking residents over the past few decades. This readable university study includes dozens of interviews with Anglo Montréalers.

The Hockey Sweater (1979), a short story by Roch Carrier, strikes a chord with most Canadians. A Toronto Maple Leafs sweater is given to a Montréal Canadiens fan and becomes a symbol of friction between the country's Anglo and French populations.

FILMS

Montréal is an ideal city for shooting movies. It has an abundance of atmospheric locations that are ready-made for Hollywood productions, especially in Vieux Montréal. The strong US dollar, excellent technical facilities and proximity to New York also make Montréal a convenient bargain for American filmmakers, who dominate the scene.

The 500-plus cinema and TV films shot partly or entirely in Montréal include Sergio Leone's epic *Once Upon a Time in America* (1983), with Robert De Niro and Elizabeth McGovern; *12 Monkeys* (1995), Terry Gilliam's twisted sci-fi flick starring Bruce Willis and Brad Pitt; *Batman & Robin* (1997), with George Clooney and Chris O'Donnell as the caped crusaders; and the spine-tingling thriller *Wait Until Dark* (1967), with Audrey Hepburn and Richard Crenna. And let's not forget *Jesus of Montréal* (1989), directed by Québec's own Denys Arcand, in which an unorthodox production of the Passion Play sparks a bitter conflict with the Catholic Church.

NEWSPAPERS & MAGAZINES

The daily *Montréal Gazette* is the major English-language newspaper, with good coverage of national affairs, politics and the arts. The Friday and Saturday editions are packed with entertainment listings.

You'll also often see the Toronto *Globe & Mail,* which is sometimes termed 'Canada's newspaper' and is sold across the country. Regional dailies that turn up include the *Ottawa Citizen, Toronto Star* and *Vancouver Sun.* The *National Post* is a quality national paper with an emphasis on business. As for foreign papers, the *Financial Times, New York Times, Wall Street Journal, USA Today* and the *International Herald Tribune* are available at larger newspaper stores.

Readers of French should have a look at both the federalist *La Presse,* the largest-circulation French daily, as well as the separatist-leaning *Le Devoir. Le Journal de Montréal* is a popular French-language broadsheet.

Maclean's is Canada's weekly news magazine; it's quite thin but high quality. Not unlike its US cousin, the monthly *Canadian Geographic* carries excellent articles and photography on a range of Canadian topics from wildlife to weather.

RADIO & TV

The Canadian Broadcasting Corporation (CBC) airs national and regional broadcasts on both radio and TV. It carries more Canadian content in music and information than any of the private broadcast companies – much like the BBC in Britain.

CBC Montréal (88.5 FM) is the local flagship for news, educational and cultural programs in English. Tune in between 9 am and noon on weekdays for *This Morning,* a show offering a well-rounded view of the nation's opinions.

FM stations tend to specialize in a single style of music. English-language stations to try include CHOM (97.7 FM), for rock and alternative; Mix 96 (96.5 FM), for pop; Q92 (92.5 FM), for soft rock and oldies; and CBC 2 (93.5 FM), for classical and jazz (in the evenings).

Many private AM broadcasters favor the talk-radio format, with a baiting host and opinionated callers – CJAD (800 AM) is a prime example. CIQC (600 AM) runs talk and pop; CKGM (990 AM) plays oldies.

The CBC also operates a French radio and television network under the name Radio-Canada (95.3 FM and TV channel 4). The other major national TV network is the Canadian Television Network (CTV, channel 11). It's the main commercial channel, and it broadcasts a mix of Canadian and US programs, as well as a popular national news program every night.

Canadians can readily tune into TV and radio stations from the US, and often do.

VIDEO SYSTEMS

Four types of video systems are in common use across Canada: VHS, VHS C, Beta and 8mm. These tapes are readily available at electronics retailers such as Future Shop (Map 5; ☎ 393-2600), 460 Rue Ste Catherine Ouest. VHS tapes are incredibly cheap: A regular Sony 120-minute tape should cost less than $3. VHS C tapes will cost around $6 for 120 minutes. ⓞ McGill or Place des Arts.

Note that the PAL (Phase Alternative Line) system predominant in most of Europe and Australia isn't compatible with the American and Japanese NTSC or French SECAM standards. This means prerecorded videotapes bought in countries using PAL won't play in North America and vice versa, unless you happen to have a dual-system VCR.

PHOTOGRAPHY

Transparency film (slides), digital and video camera equipment and supplies are generally available only at camera shops. Pharmacies, department stores and corner convenience shops carry basic Kodak and Fuji print film. For a roll of 24-exposure Kodak Gold, expect to pay about $5 for 100 ASA (ISO) and $7 for 400 ASA.

Most film bought in Canada doesn't include processing. You can have your film developed onsite at camera shops in as little as one hour, which costs about $12 for 24 color prints, depending on the size. A second set of identical prints doesn't cost much more. Cheaper rates apply for one-day or three-day processing.

Some retailers offer cheaper development services. The Jean Coutu pharmacy, at 974 Rue Ste Catherine Ouest (Map 5), charges $10 for one-hour development of a 24-exposure roll of print film; the 24-hour service costs just $5. ⓞ Peel.

The X-ray scanning machines at Canadian airports should pose no problems to most films. But for specialized film, such as film with an ASA (ISO) speed of 400 or higher, X-ray damage is a real threat. When in doubt, pack your film in a transparent plastic bag (a resealable one is good) and show it separately to airport security officials.

TIME

Montréal is on Eastern Time (EST/EDT), the same time zone as New York City and Toronto. When it's noon in Montréal, it's 9 am in Vancouver and Los Angeles, 1 pm in Halifax, 5 pm in London, 6 pm in Paris, 2 am (the following day) in Tokyo and 3 am (the following day) in Sydney.

Canada switches to Daylight Saving Time (which is one hour later than Standard Time) on the last Sunday in April, making the daylight hours lusciously long. Standard Time returns on the last Sunday in October.

Official times (train schedules, film screenings etc) are often indicated using the 24-hour clock, also known as military time (eg, 6:30 pm is represented as 18:30).

ELECTRICITY

Canada, like the US, operates on 110V, 60-cycle electric power. Non-North American visitors should bring a plug adapter for their own small appliances. Note that gadgets built for higher voltage and cycles (such as 220/240V, 50-cycle appliances from Europe) will probably run more slowly, and tape recorders not equipped with built-in adapters may function poorly.

Canadian electrical goods have a plug with two flat, vertical prongs (the same as the US and Mexico) or sometimes a three-pronger with the added ground. Most sockets can accommodate both types.

WEIGHTS & MEASURES

Canada officially changed from imperial measurement to the metric system in the 1970s. Most citizens accepted this change only begrudgingly and even today, both systems remain for many day-to-day uses.

All speed-limit signs are in kilometers per hour, and gasoline is sold in liters. However, supermarket items such as hamburger meat and potatoes are still often sold by the pound. Radio stations will often give temperatures in both degrees Celsius and Fahrenheit.

Measurements in this book are given in metric. For help converting, see the chart on the inside back cover of this book.

A Note on Numbers

For numbers with four or more digits, Québecers commonly use periods or spaces where the Americans or British would use commas: One million, therefore, appears as 1.000.000 or 1 000 000. For decimals, on the other hand, the French use commas, so 2.75 becomes 2,75.

LAUNDRY

Montréal has plenty of self-service laundries ('laundrettes' in this book) with rows of coin-operated washing machines and dryers. Called *buanderies* or *laveries* in French, these places have machines for dispensing change and soap, but it's more reliable and cheaper to bring both. A wash and a dry costs a couple of dollars. You usually need $1 or 25¢ coins.

The Buanderie du Village (Map 6), 1499 Rue Amherst, is a big, comfortable laundry with potted plants and rows of machines. It's open 9 am to 9 pm weekdays and to 7 pm weekends. **Ⓜ** Beaudry. There's also a laundry opposite Fairmount Bagel in Mile End (Map 9). **Ⓜ** Laurier.

TOILETS

That dirty word is rarely used by English-speakers in Canada, who prefer 'washroom,' 'bathroom' or 'restroom' (although French-speakers have no qualms about saying *les toilettes*). Public washrooms are virtually nonexistent, but Montréal's many department stores and shopping complexes have facilities. You can also duck into a café, restaurant or museum and ask politely (with a hint of urgency) to use the washroom.

LUGGAGE STORAGE

The Gare Central (Map 5) has a left-luggage service in its main concourse (to the left of the VIA Rail information counter) that charges $2 per piece of luggage for 24 hours. It's open 7 am to 7 pm. A similar service is available at the central bus station (Map 6).

There are lockers in the basement of the Centre Infotouriste (Map 5) at Square Dorchester ($5 per day). The HI Auberge de Montréal (Map 5) also has luggage lockers for its guests; the cost is $2 per day.

HEALTH
Medical Treatment

There are no reciprocal healthcare arrangements between Canada and other countries, so non-Canadians have to pay up front for treatment and get reimbursed by the insurer later. Consider taking out travel insurance to cover any eventual expense (see Travel Insurance, earlier).

Medical treatment in Canada is expensive: The standard rate for a hospital bed in a city hospital is around $600 a day and can go up to $2500 a day in the major centers for nonresidents. Cutbacks in healthcare budgets have led to long lines and a shortage of beds in many Montréal hospitals, so you may have to wait several hours in the emergency room if your condition isn't diagnosed as 'urgent.' That said, the quality of treatment (when it comes) is generally excellent.

Hospitals & Clinics

The best hospital option for English-speaking patients is the Royal Victoria Hospital (Map 7; ☎ 842-1231), 687 Ave des Pins Ouest. ⓂMcGill. Admittance to the emergency ward at this hospital costs $310; the walk-in service at one of the city's many CLSCs (community healthcare centers) costs $110. Expect to pay the charge in cash and up front, as checks and credit cards are usually not accepted. French-speaking patients should go to Hôpital Notre Dame (Map 6; ☎ 281-6000), 1560 Rue Sherbrooke Est. ⓂPapineau or Beaudry.

For minor ailments, you can also visit a CLSC in your neighborhood – call ☎ 527-2361 for the address of the closest one. You can (and in some cases must) contact your travel-insurance agency first for referrals if you intend to make a claim later. Consulates often carry a list of recommended physicians and dentists (see Embassies & Consulates, earlier in this chapter).

For dental care, contact the Côtes des Neiges Dental Clinic (Map 5; ☎ 935-5145), 3550 Ch de la Côtes des Neiges. It's open during the day and evening and offers emergency treatment. ⓂGuy-Concordia.

Pharmacies

The Pharmaprix chain of pharmacies has branches around town, including one at 1500 Rue Ste Catherine Ouest (Map 5; ☎ 933-4744). It's open 8 am to midnight daily. ⓂGuy-Concordia. There's a 24-hour location at 5122 Ch de la Côtes des Neiges (Map 2; ☎ 738-8464), west of Mont Royal. ⓂCôte des Neiges.

Predeparture Planning

Canada is a typical First World destination when it comes to health. No vaccinations are required from visitors unless you're coming from an area with a history of certain diseases – immunizations against yellow fever or cholera are the most likely requirements. However, some routine vaccinations are recommended for all travelers. They include hepatitis B, polio, tetanus and diphtheria, and sometimes measles, mumps and rubella. These vaccinations are usually administered during childhood, but some require booster shots. Check with a doctor before you go.

It's a good idea to pack a basic medical kit (an antiseptic, aspirin or paracetamol, bandages etc). If you're packing medication, bring copies of your prescriptions to avoid problems at customs.

Water

Montréal tap water is perfectly safe to drink. If you intend to be out in the wild on outdoor excursions, the simplest way to purify water is to boil it thoroughly – a vigorous five-minute boiling should be satisfactory, even at high altitudes (where water boils less quickly).

Sexually Transmitted Diseases

These diseases include gonorrhea, herpes and syphilis. Sores, blisters or rashes around the genitals and discharge or pain when urinating are common symptoms. In some STDs, symptoms may be less marked or not observed at all, especially in women. While abstinence from sexual contact is the only 100% effective prevention, using condoms is also effective. Gonorrhea and syphilis are treated with antibiotics.

HIV/AIDS

Infection with the human immunodeficiency virus (HIV) may lead to acquired immune deficiency syndrome (AIDS), which is a fatal disease. Any exposure to blood, blood products or body fluids may put an individual at risk. The disease is often transmitted through sexual contact or dirty needles – vaccinations, acupuncture, tattooing and body piercing can be potentially as dangerous as intravenous drug use. The government estimates the number of AIDS cases in Canada at around 20,000, and nearly 46,000 people are registered as HIV-positive.

Catie (☎ 1-800-263-1638) runs a Canada-wide HIV/AIDS helpline that is open 10 am to 6 pm weekdays and until 7 pm Tuesday, Wednesday and Thursday. Staff provide information and advice on relevant topics, such as transmission risks, the side effects of certain drugs and alternative therapy.

Info-Sida (Map 6; ☎ 521-7432), 1000 Rue Sherbrooke Est, gives out information on prevention and treatment, as well as referrals to relevant social and medical organizations. Its bilingual staff are available weekdays 9 am to 5 pm. Ⓜ Beaudry.

WOMEN TRAVELERS

Montréal holds high standards for women's safety, especially when compared to major US cities. Still, the usual advice still applies – avoid walking alone late at night, especially in North Montréal.

It's illegal in Canada to carry pepper spray or mace. Instead, some women recommend carrying a whistle to deal with potential dangers. If you are sexually assaulted, call ☎ 911 or the Sexual Assault Center (☎ 934-4504) for referrals to hospitals with sexual-assault care centers.

GAY & LESBIAN TRAVELERS

Canada's national attitude of social tolerance makes Montréal a popular getaway for lesbian, gay, bisexual and transgendered travelers. The main center of Montréal's gay community is the Village (see the boxed text 'Districts in a Nutshell,' in the Things to See & Do chapter). Gay Pride Week takes place in early August.

Gai Écoute (☎ 866-0103) and Gay Line (☎ 866-5090 or 1-888-505-1010) provide information, counseling and referrals to organizations within the gay community. Gai Écoute is staffed 11 am to 11 pm daily; Gay Line is staffed 7 to 11 pm daily. For a complete list of local gay events, call the 24-hour Gay Event Line (☎ 252-4429). The Gay and Lesbian Association of UQAM is at ☎ 987-3039.

There are several gay-operated and gay-friendly B&Bs in the Village area – see the boxed text 'Gay-Friendly Accommodations,' in the Places to Stay chapter.

DISABLED TRAVELERS

Most public buildings in Montréal are wheelchair accessible, including tourist offices, major museums and principal attractions. Many restaurants and hotels also have ramps and other facilities suitable for the mobility-impaired. Unfortunately, access to the Métro is more difficult, as most stations don't have elevators to the platforms.

VIA Rail will accommodate people in wheelchairs with 48 hours' notice. Long-distance bus lines will assist passengers and take wheelchairs or any other aids, providing that they collapse and fit into the luggage compartments. Airlines are accustomed to dealing with disabled passengers and provide early boarding and disembarking as a standard practice – Air Canada is extremely well equipped.

Kéroul (Map 2; ☎ 252-3104) is a well-known specialist in mobility-impaired travel, offering attractive packages to destinations in Québec and Ontario. It also publishes the bilingual *Accésible Québec* for $13 ($14 from the US, $20 from Europe, including postage), which is a guide to 300 disabled-accessible hotels, attractions and restaurants in the province. Write to 4545 Ave Pierre de Coubertin, PO Box 1000, Station 'M', Montréal, Québec H1V 3R2 (provide a credit card number). Web site: www.keroul.qc.ca. Ⓜ Pie IX.

SENIOR TRAVELERS

Visitors over the age of 65 (sometimes 60) can qualify for discounts on transportation and many attractions, parks, museums, historic sites and cinemas. Some hotels and motels may also offer reductions. Carry your passport, driver's license or other photo ID to prove your age.

Elderhostel specializes in inexpensive, educational packages for people 55 years or older. Regular programs include field trips to Québec City, the art and architecture of the Eastern Townships and French language courses. Accommodations are in university dorms or the like. Contact Elderhostel (☎ 978-323-4141 or 1-877-426-8056), 75 Federal St, Boston, MA 02110-1941 USA. Web site: www.elderhostel.org.

For people over 50, the Canadian Association of Retired Persons (CARP; ☎ 1-800-363-9736) offers information on RV, mobility-impaired and discount senior travel, as well as savings on car and travel insurance. An annual membership costs $16.

Members of the US-based American Association of Retired Persons (AARP) can take advantage of many CARP services. Web site: www.fifty-plus.net.

MONTRÉAL FOR CHILDREN

Traveling successfully with children of any age requires preparation and effort. Lonely Planet's *Travel with Children,* by Maureen Wheeler, can give you some valuable tips.

In Montréal, kids are given discounted admission at major attractions, sometimes up to half off. Family passes (meaning two adults and two children) are usually a better deal.

Front desks at hotels can also recommend babysitting services if none are available in-house. To get the little ones off your hands for a day, the YMCA on Rue Stanley offers educational day programs for youngsters from 18 months to five years. Half- and full-day (from 9 am to 5 pm) fees are $13 and $22.50, respectively. There are also activity days (swimming, gymnastics, tennis, movies, museums and more) for children ages five to 12; the cost is $26 per day. Call ☎ 849-8393, ext 767, or check the Web site at www.ymca.ca.

It's easy (if expensive) to keep kids entertained in the summer at the La Ronde amusement park on Île Ste Hélène (Map 10). At any time of year, kids will enjoy the Dow Planetarium (Map 5) or the creepy-crawlies at the Insectarium in the Jardin Botanique (see the Olympic Park section of the Things to See & Do chapter). The Vieux Port area offers a number of popular options, such as the interactive Centre iSci and the IMAX cinema (Map 4).

For more ideas and details on these and other sights, see the Things to See & Do and Excursions chapters.

USEFUL ORGANIZATIONS

The Canadian Automobile Association (CAA) provides assistance to member motorists. It has reciprocal arrangements with the American Automobile Association (AAA) and other national auto clubs – check in your country of origin before you leave.

The CAA's services include 24-hour emergency roadside assistance, trip planning and advice, free maps and traveler's checks. For information, contact the Québec information line (☎ 1-800-686-9243) or the Montréal office (Map 5; ☎ 861-5111), 1180 Rue Drummond. An annual membership costs $75. Web site: www.caa.ca. ⓜ Lucien L'Allier.

Hostelling International (HI) Canada (☎ 613-237-7884 or 1-800-663-5777) has its head office at 205 Catherine St, Ottawa, ON K2P 1C3.

LIBRARIES

The central public library (Map 6; ☎ 872-5923), 1210 Rue Sherbrooke Est, is open 10 am to 6 pm Monday and Thursday, 10 am to 10 pm Tuesday and Wednesday, noon to 6 pm Friday, 10 am to 5 pm Saturday and 1 to 5 pm Sunday. You can use the Internet terminals there for free. ⓜ Beaudry.

The Bibliothèque Nationale du Québec (Map 6; ☎ 873-1100), in a beautiful Beaux Arts building at 1700 Rue St Denis, has the most complete library of works on the subject of the province, with impressive special collections of rare books and prints. Check out the pretty stained-glass windows by Henri Perdriau. Hours are 9 am to 5 pm weekdays in the summer; it is closed Monday in winter. ⓜ Berri-UQAM.

The university libraries are also open to visitors (see below).

UNIVERSITIES

Founded in 1821 – thanks to a donation by James McGill, a wealthy Scottish fur trader – McGill University (Map 7; ☎ 398-4455) is the oldest and most prestigious of Montréal's four universities. It's perhaps the finest English-language university in Canada, with some 15,000 students. The biggest faculties are in medicine, law and engineering, but the music and drama schools are also prominent. Singer and author Leonard Cohen is among its leading lights (see the boxed text 'The Spirit of Leonard,' in the Facts about Montréal chapter). The campus is a showcase of Victorian architecture and an oasis of calm at the foot of Mont Royal.

The much larger, French-language Université du Québec à Montréal (UQAM; Map 8; ☎ 987-3132) is at the heart of the Quartier Latin and has more than 40,000 students. The only relief in the university's expanse of brick and concrete is the Gothic steeple of the Église St Jacques, which was rebuilt after a fire in 1852.

The Université de Montréal (Map 2; ☎ 343-6111), north of the mountain at 2900 Blvd Édouard Montpetit, has about 60,000 students, making it the second-largest French-language university in the world. The main building is an Art Deco structure with a striking tower, but it's a bit out of the way for a visit. ⓜ Université de Montréal.

The second English-language institution, Concordia University (Map 5; ☎ 848-2424), is the youngest of Montréal's universities, founded in 1974. Its campus is split between a modern downtown (ⓜ Guy-Concordia) and more venerable Victorian premises in West Montréal (Map 2; ⓜ Vendôme); see the boxed text 'University Lodging,' in the Places to Stay chapter.

CULTURAL CENTERS

Montréal has a dense network of active cultural organizations. Among them, the Forum Action Québec (Map 4; ☎ 398-3960), 901 Rue de Bleury, is a nonpartisan organization that holds events to promote a dialog between the French- and English-speaking communities. Things arguably get most interesting when the dialog breaks down. ⓜ Square Victoria.

The National Friendship Centre Montréal (Map 5; ☎ 499-1854), 2001 Blvd St Laurent, is a conduit for Inuit and indigenous Indian activities. It holds a large powwow at the Vieux Port every August. There's a library and information service, too. It's open 9 am to 4:30 pm weekdays. ⓜ St Laurent.

The Union Française (Map 4; ☎ 845-5195) is Montréal's French cultural association. It holds (mostly French-language) lectures and exhibitions on France in its lovely late-19th-century villa at 429 Ave Viger Est. Bastille Day (July 14) is celebrated every year in Square Viger, opposite.

The library is open weekdays 10 am to 4 pm. ⓜ Champ de Mars.

The British Council (Map 5; ☎ 866-5863, ext 200), in the skyscraper at 1000 Rue de la Gauchetière Ouest, is open weekdays 9 am to 5 pm. It has a visitor's library and organizes talks, films and other events.

DANGERS & ANNOYANCES

Some people seem to think Canada is a perpetually icebound wasteland, but health problems due to extreme cold are unlikely. On winter days when frostbite is a possibility, the radio will broadcast warnings about how many minutes of exposed skin is acceptable. It's best to dress in layers (including a waterproof outer garment) and wear a hat.

Montréal is generally a pretty safe place, but some of the outlying districts should be avoided – North Montréal in particular, where gangs sometimes take their conflicts to the streets. Otherwise, exercise big-city common sense: Don't flash cash, watch your valuables, and remember that pickpockets flourish in crowded tourist areas.

Pedestrians should take special care at crosswalks in Montréal. Technically, drivers are required to stop, but don't bet your life on it.

EMERGENCIES

Almost anywhere in Québec, dial ☎ 911 for all police, fire, accident and medical emergencies. When in doubt, call ☎ 0 and ask the operator for assistance.

Should your passport get lost or stolen, contact your nearest consulate, which will issue a temporary replacement and inform you when and how to go about getting another. You may not need another, depending on your travel plans. See Embassies & Consulates, earlier.

For lost or stolen traveler's checks or credit cards, contact the issuer or its representative (see Money, earlier). For other types of theft, if you plan to make an insurance claim, be sure to contact the police as soon as possible for an incident report. Ask for the report reference number and/or a photocopy to send to the insurance company.

LEGAL MATTERS

Driving motorized vehicles, including boats and snowmobiles, while under the influence of alcohol is a serious offense in Canada. Offenders could land in jail overnight, followed by a court date, a heavy fine and a suspended license. The blood-alcohol limit is 0.08%.

In Québec, the legal drinking age is 18. It's an offence to consume alcohol anywhere other than a residence or licensed premises, which puts parks, beaches and the rest of the great outdoors technically off-limits.

Parking regulations are strictly enforced, and fines are stiff ($30 minimum) – even for an expired parking meter. Be sure to check the signs: Some are incredibly specific and forbid *stationnement* (parking) a couple of days (or even hours) a week.

If you're charged with an offense, you have the right to public counsel if you can't afford a lawyer. For less serious matters, the McGill Legal Information Service (☎ 398-6792), 3480 McTavish, Bldg 320, Room 21G, is staffed by law students who dispense free information and suggestions for whatever bind you're in.

BUSINESS HOURS

Standard business hours are 9:30 am or 10 am until 6 pm Monday to Wednesday; on Thursday and Friday, many shops stay open until 9 pm. Many larger retailers, especially department stores, stay open until 9 pm every night on weekdays. Most stores commonly open on Saturday, and some on Sunday, from 10 am to 5 pm.

Convenience stores tend to remain open 24 hours, as do some gas stations, supermarkets and drugstores (chemists). Post offices are generally open 9 am to 5 pm weekdays, but outlets in retail stores stay open later and on weekends. Banking hours are usually shorter, from 10 am to 4:30 pm Monday to Thursday, to 5 or 6 pm Friday. Only some branches are open Saturday morning.

PUBLIC HOLIDAYS & SPECIAL EVENTS

On national public holidays, banks, schools and government offices close, while museums and other services go on a Sunday schedule. Holidays falling on a weekend are usually observed the following Monday.

The summer season opens with Victoria Day, in late May, and closes with Labour Day weekend, in early September. These two dates also mark the opening and closing of many businesses, attractions and services, and more limited hours of operation for others.

Gay Pride Week takes place in early August, mostly in the Village.

Jean-Baptiste Day is Québec's national holiday and is named for St John the Baptist.

Canadian Thanksgiving (the same as the US holiday but held earlier, on the second Monday in October) is really a harvest festival. The traditional meal includes roasted turkey.

Halloween (originally a Celtic pagan tradition) is a time for costume parties. Nightclubs in particular are often the scene of wild masquerades.

The following public holidays are celebrated in Québec:

New Year's Day January 1

Good Friday & Easter Monday late March to mid-April

Victoria Day May 24 or nearest Monday

Jean-Baptiste Day June 24

Canada Day July 1

Labour Day first Monday in September

Canadian Thanksgiving second Monday in October

Remembrance Day November 11

Christmas Day December 25

Boxing Day December 26

While not a statutory holiday, National Aboriginal Day falls on June 21, the first day of the summer solstice, when Canada's heritage of First Nations, Inuit and Métis cultures is celebrated at public and private institutions.

DOING BUSINESS

Compared to Toronto and other major Canadian cities, Montréal offers significant cost advantages in terms of office rents, skilled labor and other business facilities.

Many of the large hotels offer basic office services, rent out meeting spaces and host conferences.

Montréal International (☎ 987-8191), 380 Rue St Antoine Ouest, is a joint government and business organization with services that include access to private offices, project counseling and relocation services. Web site: www.montreal-intl.com.

HQ Global Workplaces (☎ 934-5518), 1200 Blvd René Lévesque Ouest, provides turnkey office facilities, conference rooms, and secretarial and administrative support for short- and long-term purposes. Office packages begin at about $120 per day; terms are negotiable for longer use.

For cheap photocopies and a variety of documentation services, including scanning, binding and computer-aided design, Bureau en Gros (Map 5) is open 24 hours a day. For contact information, see Fax & Telegram, under Post & Communications, earlier.

WORK

It's difficult to get a work permit in Canada, as employment opportunities go to Canadians first. To get a permit, you'll need to show a valid job offer from a specific employer to your local Canadian consulate or embassy.

Employers hiring casual workers often don't ask for a permit, but visitors working legally in the country have Social Insurance numbers. If you don't have one and get caught, you will be told to leave the country.

One-year working-holiday visas are made available to 4000 Australians and 400 New Zealanders between the ages of 18 and 30 every year. Apply as early as possible, and allow 12 weeks for processing. Application forms are available through the consulate in Sydney (see Embassies & Consulates, earlier).

The Student Work Abroad Program (SWAP) offers 3500 working holidays every year for people 18 to 25 years of age in nearly 20 countries, including Australia, Britain, France, Japan, South Africa, the US and New Zealand. Participants are issued with a one-year, nonextendable visa to work anywhere in Canada. Most 'Swappers' find jobs in the service industry as waiters, hotel porters, bar attendants or farmhands. SWAP Canada (email swapinfo@travelcuts.com) and student travel agencies can provide details.

Getting There & Away

AIR

Some simple nuts-and-bolts knowledge about the airline business can save you a bundle of money when buying tickets. The summer months and Christmas holidays are the most expensive seasons; buy early, as advance booking of 14 to 21 days (also known as Apex) reliably produces the best fares. One-way tickets are rarely a bargain, except from Asia. Avoid flying on Fridays and Sundays, and take 'red-eye flights' (in the early morning or late evening). Keep an eye out for standby fares, as well as for specials posted by airlines and travel services on the Web.

Montréal has two airports. Dorval, 14 miles west of downtown, serves most domestic, US and overseas flights. Mirabel, 34 miles northeast of downtown, serves mostly charter flights. (Mirabel was originally built to replace Dorval as the main international passenger terminal, but it never quite took off.)

Departure Tax

Montréal's Dorval Airport (Map 2) levies an 'improvement tax' of $10 on all international flights before you leave. The special payment counter takes cash or, if you've spent all your Canadian dollars, major credit cards. Mirabel Airport doesn't charge extra to leave.

Other Parts of Canada

The home market is dominated by Air Canada and its affiliates, such as Canadian Airlines. For the best deals, check with Travel CUTS (see Travel Agencies in the Facts for the Visitor chapter), the travel section of the *Montréal Gazette* and the Web sites of competitors (such as Royal Airlines, Air Transat and Canada 3000). Regional operators, such as CanJet Airlines and Roots Air, are also worth a look.

From Vancouver, low-season return fares can be remarkably cheap (eg, $206 on Royal Airlines, tax included), but prices balloon to between $400 and $500 in summer. Along the heavily traveled Toronto-Montréal route, return fares start as low as $120, including tax – cheaper than the train or bus. From St John's, Calgary and Edmonton, roundtrips range between $300 and $350 in the low season to around $500 in summer.

The USA

Direct flights between major US and Canadian cities are abundant. Air Canada and Canadian Airlines link Newark and New York City with Montréal. The lowest return fares, often matched by major US carriers, start at US$220. From Boston, roundtrip fares as low as US$160 are available. Royal Air Maroc flights from New York to Montréal start at around US$126.

From Chicago, United Airlines offers roundtrip tickets starting at US$270, as do Air Canada, Canadian Airlines, Northwest and Continental.

Los Angeles is usually the cheapest West Coast gateway to Montréal. Air Canada, Canadian Airlines and many US carriers have roundtrip fares starting at US$450 from Los Angeles and US$500 from San Francisco or Seattle. Student travel agencies such as Council Travel (☎ 1-800-226-8624)

> ### Warning
>
> The information in this chapter is particularly vulnerable to change: prices for international travel are volatile, routes are introduced and canceled, schedules change and special deals come and go. Check directly with the airline or a travel agent to make sure you understand how a fare (and any ticket you may buy) works.
>
> You should also get opinions, quotes and advice from as many airlines and travel agents as possible before parting with your hard-earned cash. The details given in this chapter should be regarded as pointers and are not a substitute for careful, up-to-date research.

Air Travel Glossary

Cancellation Penalties If you have to cancel or change a discounted ticket, heavy penalties are often involved; insurance can sometimes be taken out against these penalties. Some airlines impose penalties on regular tickets as well, particularly against 'no-show' passengers.

Courier Fares Businesses often need to send urgent documents or freight securely and quickly. Courier companies hire people to accompany the package through customs and, in return, offer a discount ticket that is sometimes a phenomenal bargain. However, you may have to surrender all of your baggage allowance and take only carry-on luggage.

Full Fares Airlines traditionally offer 1st-class (coded F), business-class (coded J) and economy-class (coded Y) tickets. These days, so many promotional and discounted fares are available that few passengers pay full fare.

Lost Tickets If you lose your airline ticket, an airline will usually treat it like a traveler's check and, after inquiries, issue you another one. Legally, however, an airline is entitled to treat it like cash: If you lose it, it's gone forever. Take good care of your tickets.

Onward Tickets An entry requirement for many countries is a ticket out of the country. If you're unsure of your next move, the easiest solution is to buy the cheapest onward ticket to a neighboring country or a ticket from a reliable airline that can later be refunded if you do not use it.

Open-Jaw Tickets These are return tickets that permit you to fly into one place but return from another. If available, these tickets can save you from having to backtrack to your arrival point.

Overbooking Because almost every flight has some passengers who fail to show up, airlines often book more passengers than they have seats. Usually, excess passengers make up for the no-shows, but occasionally, somebody gets bumped onto the next available flight. Guess who it is most likely to be? The passengers who check in late.

Promotional Fares These are officially discounted fares, available from travel agencies or directly from the airline.

Reconfirmation If you don't reconfirm your flight at least 72 hours prior to departure, the airline may delete your name from the passenger list. Call to find out if your airline requires reconfirmation.

Restrictions Discounted tickets often have various restrictions – for example, they may need to be paid for in advance, or altering them may incur a penalty. Other restrictions include minimum and maximum periods you must be away.

Round-the-World Tickets RTW tickets give you a limited period (usually a year) in which to circumnavigate the globe. You can go anywhere the carrying airlines go as long as you don't backtrack. The number of stopovers or total number of separate flights is decided before you set off, and these tickets usually cost a bit more than a basic return flight.

Transferred Tickets Airline tickets cannot be transferred from one person to another. Travelers sometimes try to sell the return half of a ticket, but officials can ask you to prove that you are the person named on the ticket. On an international flight, tickets are compared with passports.

Travel Periods Ticket prices vary with the time of year. There is a low (off-peak) season and a high (peak) season, and often a low-shoulder season and a high-shoulder season as well. Usually the fare depends on your outward flight – if you depart in the high season and return in the low season, you pay the high-season fare.

and STA Travel (☎ 1-800-781-4040) have offices in major cities across the US. People younger than 26, students and teachers save up to 50% on many routes. Purchase tickets as far in advance as possible. In Canada, Travel CUTS (see Travel Agencies in the Facts for the Visitor chapter) offers competitive roundtrip student fares.

Weekly travel sections of the *New York Times, Chicago Tribune, San Francisco Chronicle* and *LA Times* are great sources of cut-rate airfares. Air Canada and many US airlines advertise cheap Internet fares that are available only on their respective Web sites; these fares are often posted midweek.

Cuba

Many visitors to Canada make a side trip to Cuba, especially those from the US (whose citizens are forbidden from visiting Castro's realm). Air Transat offers good deals from Montréal to Havana, with fares starting at $500 return. Cubana and Air Canada are also competitive.

Australia & New Zealand

Canadian Airlines, Air New Zealand, Qantas and United Airlines all have regular flights from Australia, most with a stopover in Hawaii or the US. For a return flight, expect to pay A$2350 to A$2750 in the high season and A$2250 to A$2450 in the low season.

Flights from New Zealand to Montréal are limited, with only American Airlines offering direct service. Expect to pay NZ$2466/2607 for a return ticket from Auckland in the low/high season.

In Australia, STA Travel (☎ 131-776 Australia-wide) is a major dealer in budget fares. Web site: www.statravel.com.au. Flight Centre (☎ 131-600 Australia-wide) is another option. Web site: www.flightcentre .com.au. Smaller agencies often advertise in the Saturday travel sections of the *Sydney Morning Herald* and the Melbourne *Age*.

In New Zealand, STA Travel (☎ 09-309-0458) and Flight Centre (☎ 09-309-6171) are popular travel agents. Ads for other agencies can be found in the travel section of the *New Zealand Herald*.

UK & Continental Europe

Montréal is well served from Europe's main airports. Air Canada and Canadian Airlines offer the most flights, but there's plenty of competition, including Air France, British Airways, Continental, KLM, SAS, United Airlines and US Airways.

From London, return fares start as low as £231/280 in the low/high season, taxes included. Canada 3000, US Airways and British Airways often offer good deals. Prices shoot up during peak periods – standard fares around £500 aren't uncommon. Stopover privileges in Canada, such as London-Montréal-Toronto-Vancouver-London, are offered on some tickets.

Cheap airfares appear in the travel pages of the weekend broadsheet newspapers, as well as in *Time Out,* the *Evening Standard* and the free magazine *TNT.* Popular discount travel agencies geared toward students (but not exclusively) include STA Travel (☎ 020-7361-6161), which has many offices, including one at 86 Old Brompton Rd, London SW7. Web site: www.statravel.co.uk. Another is usit Campus (☎ 020-7730-3402), which has a branch at 52 Grosvenor Gardens, London SW1. Web site: www.usitcampus.co.uk.

You can also fly to the eastern US and travel by bus or train to Montréal (an eight-to 10-hour journey from New York City). A bevy of airlines offer heavily discounted flights to New York from Europe's air hubs. Roundtrips from London to NYC can be picked up for as low as £150 to £175 in the low season; from Paris, fares start at 1800FF.

Frankfurt, continental Europe's busiest airport, is a good departure point, as many flights on route from Asia to London make a stopover there. Return tickets to Montréal can cost as little as DM595/1249 in the low/high season.

Return flights from Paris range from 2400FF to 4500FF; tickets from Amsterdam cost about f600 to f1100.

If your schedule is flexible, flying standby can be very reasonable. Airhitch (☎ 01 47 00 16 30 in Paris, ☎ 1-800-326-2009 in the US) specializes in this sort of thing and can get you to or from the northeastern US for US$169 plus taxes. Web site: www.airhitch.org.

Asia

Flights from Asia to Canada are either east-bound, connecting through Vancouver or major US gateway cities (Detroit, Chicago, New York City), or westbound, via Europe and connecting through London, Frankfurt or Paris.

Air Canada, Canadian Airlines, Japan Airlines, Northwest and American Airlines offer some of the lowest fares from Japan, starting at ¥91,000 return, excluding taxes. Asiana and Korean Air fly roundtrip from Bangkok for as low as B41,600. Fares jump if you're flying from Hong Kong (HK$13,250) or Singapore (S$3270) – try Asiana, China Airlines, Eva Air, Korean Air or Thai Airways.

Bucket shops in Bangkok, Hong Kong and Singapore undercut the airlines by far. One-way fares are steeply discounted; a flight from Bangkok to Toronto, sometimes with a stopover in the US, might cost only B15,000. Some travel agencies are of the cut-and-run variety, so ask around before you buy.

From Asia, it's often cheaper to fly first to the US rather than directly to Canada. Northwest Airlines often offers special 'Cybersaver' fares from Tokyo to Detroit on its Web site for as little as US$450 return (see Airlines, next).

Airlines

The following is a list of airlines that serve Montréal. Also see 'Air Line Companies' in the English section of the yellow pages.

You can call airport information (☎ 394-7377) 6 am to 10 pm daily for details on departures and arrivals at Dorval and Mirabel Airports.

Air Canada (☎ 393-3333) www.aircanada.ca
Air France (☎ 847-1106) www.airfrance.com
Air Transat (☎ 1-877-872-6728) www.airtransat.com
American Airlines (☎ 1-800-433-7300)
British Airways (☎ 287-9282) www.britishairways.com
Canada 3000 (☎ 450-476-9500) www.canada3000.com
Canadian Airlines (☎ 847-2211) www.aircanada.ca
Continental Airlines (☎ 1-800-231-0856) www.continental.com
Delta Air Lines (☎ 1-800-325-1999) www.delta.com
Japan Airlines (☎ 1-800-525-3663) www.japanairlines.com
KLM (☎ 397-0775) www.klm.com
Lufthansa (☎ 1-800-563-5954) www.lufthansa.com
Northwest Airlines (☎ 1-800-361-5073) www.nwa.com

Buying Tickets Online

Most airlines have their own Web sites with online ticket sales (see the Airlines section), but you can also buy from a number of Internet-based ticket services. You'll need to use a credit card. Networks include the following:

American Express Travel
    www.americanexpress.com/travel
Atevo Travel
    www.atevo.com
Biztravel.com Inc
    www.biztravel.com
CNN Interactive Travel Guide
    www.cnn.com/Travel
Excite Travel by City.Net
    www.city.net
Microsoft Expedia
    www.expedia.com
Preview.Travel
    www.previewtravel.com
Priceline
    www.priceline.com
Travelocity
    www.travelocity.com

There are also online travel agencies that specialize in cheap fares:

1-800-Airfare
    www.1800airfare.com
Cheap Tickets
    www.cheaptickets.com
LowestFare.com
    www.lowestfare.com
Yahoo Travel
    travel.yahoo.com

Royal Airlines (☎ 1-888-828-9797) www.royalairlines
.com

Sabena (☎ 1-800-955-2000) www.sabena.com

Singapore Airlines (☎ 748-2769)
www.singapore-airlines.com

Swissair (☎ 636-6663) www.swissair.com

United Airlines (☎ 1-800-241-6522) www.unitedairlines
.com

US Airways (☎ 1-800-428-4322) www.usairways
.com

BUS

Buses are cheaper than trains, but they're also less comfortable and usually slower. Allow about 45 minutes before departure to buy a ticket – don't assume the automated ticket vendors will work. Most advance tickets don't guarantee a seat, so show up early to line up at the counter. Note that buses get extremely full around holidays.

The Station Centrale de l'Autobus (Central Bus Station; Map 6; ☎ 842-2281) is at 505 Rue de Maisonneuve Est. Most major lines for Canadian and US destinations depart from there. ⓜ Berri-UQAM.

On Greyhound (☎ 842-2281 or 1-800-231-2222), long-distance routes stretch west to Ottawa ($29.50, 2½ hours, six daily departures), Toronto ($86, 6¾ hours, seven daily departures) and Vancouver ($337, 71 to 75 hours, two daily departures).

Services to the US include New York City ($103, 7¾ to 8½ hours, eight daily departures) and Boston ($84, 7½ hours, five daily departures). Overnight buses leave Montréal between 10 pm and midnight. Greyhound Ameripass holders travel free between Montréal and Boston or New York.

Prices quoted here are regular one-way adult fares; roundtrip tickets are usually discounted no more than 20%. Prices drop sharply if you buy one to two weeks in advance. Discounts are given to students with an ISIC card (25%), youths and seniors (10%); tickets must be bought at least a week in advance. Companion Fares entitle two adults to purchase one full-price ticket and the other at half-price. For cross-country journeys, Greyhound also offers the Canada

Coach Pass, which comes in seven- ($249), 15- ($379), 30- ($449) and 60-day ($599) variations (all prices do not include a 7% tax). Web site: www.greyhound.ca.

Of the regional bus companies serving Québec, the Orléans Express (☎ 842-2281) makes the three-hour run between Montréal and Québec City every hour from 6 am until midnight. Tickets cost $40/30, including tax, for adults/students. The same company serves the Gaspé Peninsula and La Tuque in the Laurentians, via Trois Rivières.

Voyageur (☎ 842-2281) also travels the Montréal-Ottawa route but is marginally cheaper than Greyhound ($29 one-way, $55 return, including tax). There's also a special return fare for students ($42).

Moose Travel (☎ 287-1220 or 1-888-816-6673) runs jump-on, jump-off adventure-hostel circuits in Québec and Ontario. Major pickup points are Montréal, Québec, Ottawa and Toronto. A Québec circuit ($219) runs northeast to Québec City and Tadoussac, and also north to Mont Tremblant in the Laurentians via Val David. Trips run from May to October. Web site: www.moosenetwork.com.

In winter, some companies provide day trips to the Laurentians for downhill and cross-country skiing. One to try is Limocar (☎ 450-435-8899), which has cheap trips to Mont Gabriel (with links to nearby resorts) from the main bus station. Tickets include lift passes.

TRAIN

Canadians feel a special attachment to their 'ribbons of steel' – even though they don't take the train very often. These passenger services, operated by VIA Rail Canada, arguably remain Canada's most enjoyable (and romantic) way to travel.

Long-distance train travel is more expensive than the bus, and reservations are

GETTING THERE & AWAY

important, especially for weekend and holiday travel. Five days' notice drops the fares by as much as 40%, except on Friday and Sunday. Students, seniors and children also get discounts, but there are usually no special return or excursion fares.

Montréal's Gare Centrale (Central Station; Map 5) is the local hub of VIA Rail (☎ 366-8411). Ⓜ Bonaventure. Service is best along the so-called Québec City-Windsor corridor, which includes Montréal, Ottawa, Kingston, Toronto and Niagara Falls. Drinks and snacks are served from aisle carts, and some trains have a dining and bar car.

VIA Rail's overnight service between Montréal and Toronto is a treat. Trains leave at 11:30 pm nightly except Saturday, arriving at 8 am with a complimentary breakfast the next morning. Standard one-way fares in a sleeper cabin start at $90, tax included.

One-way, high-season fares to other cities, tax included, are Ottawa ($46, two hours), Toronto ($112, five hours), Québec City ($59, three hours) and Niagara Falls ($59, 6½ hours, with a change at Toronto). For train schedules and routes, pick up the *National Timetable* booklet at any VIA Rail station. Note that VIA Rail fares vary with the phone call, even within the hour. It's worth trying several times for a day or two and then booking in when you hit a representative giving a low fare. On long trips, you can save literally hundreds of dollars. Web site: www.viarail.ca.

The GO commuter network (☎ 869-3200) serves the suburbs of Montréal from Gare Centrale. Ticket inspection is random, and service is fast but infrequent (eg, a two-hour wait between some trains). Gare Windsor, at the corner of Rue Peel and Rue de la Gauchetière Ouest, is a lesser-used hub for commuter trains. Ⓜ Bonaventure.

Canrailpass

For those who are traveling a lot, VIA Rail offers the Canrailpass, which is good for 12 days of coach-class travel within a 30-consecutive-day period. You can buy it in Canada or Europe at travel agents or VIA Rail outlets, but the price is the same.

The Canrailpass costs $399 plus tax in the low season for adults and $359 for those ages two to 24, students and people over 60. From June to mid-October, the pass costs $639/575. Up to three extra days can be purchased.

Canrailpass holders may be entitled to discounts at car rental agencies, at Gray Line for bus tours and at some hotels.

Amtrak

This railway, which is the US equivalent of VIA Rail, offers cut-rate passes and information on its services at many Canadian train stations.

Amtrak has four routes between the US and Canada. Three of them enter through the east, including New York City to Montréal (US$52 to US$65, 10 hours), New York City to Toronto via Niagara Falls (US$65 to US$99, 12 hours) and Chicago to Toronto (US$86 to US$98, 11½ hours). Reservations are needed for all trains. For information about fares and schedules, contact Amtrak (☎ 215-824-1600 or 1-800-872-7245). Web site: www.amtrak.com.

CAR & MOTORCYCLE

Continental US highways link directly with their Canadian counterparts along the border at numerous points. These roads meet up with the Trans-Canada Highway, which runs directly through Montréal. From Boston to Montréal, it's about 490km, or about 4½ hours; from Toronto, it's 540km, or a little over five hours. Québec City is 2½ hours away.

During the summer and on holiday weekends, waits of several hours are common at major US/Canada border crossings. If possible, avoid Detroit (Michigan); Windsor (Ontario); Fort Erie (Ontario); Buffalo (New York State); Niagara Falls on both sides of the border; and Rouse's Point (New York State). The smaller crossings are almost always quiet.

In Québec, non-French speakers may have some difficulty with the French-only signs. Pick up a decent provincial highway map, which is usually free at tourist offices and sold at service stations.

Visitors with US or British passports are allowed to bring their vehicles into Canada for six months. For information on car rental and parking, see the Getting Around chapter.

Driveaways

One of the best driving deals in North America is Driveaway. Basically, you drive someone's car to a specific destination because the owner has had to fly or doesn't have the time, patience or ability to drive a long distance.

In Montréal, Driveaway (not mapped) is located at 345 Victoria Ave (☎ 489-3861). Once you're matched with a car, you put down a deposit of $200 to $300 and get a certain number of days to deliver the vehicle. Call them three to four days before your planned departure. Ask about what happens if the car breaks down, and get this information in writing. Most cars offered are fairly new and in good working order. Driveaway is open 9 am to 5 pm weekdays. Web site: www.driveaway.com.

Ride Sharing

ecoRide (☎ 1-877-326-7433), an Internet-based service, unites people looking for rides with drivers looking to share gasoline expenses. You can get some unbeatable deals, for example $20/30 to Ottawa/Toronto one-way (plus a $6 fee to ecoRide). Drivers and passengers can give descriptions of their preferences and their vehicles on the Web, and passengers can rate drivers after a trip. Unfortunately, lawsuits from Ontario-based bus companies – who claim ecoRide is competing unfairly – may lead the Ontario government to ban the service in that province. This means that Ottawa, Toronto and other Ontario cities may be unreachable via ecoRide by the time you read this. Web site: www.ecoRide.com.

Allo Stop (☎ 985-3032), the Canadian pioneer among the ride-sharing services, offers lots of rides to destinations in Québec and to the US. However, it no longer operates in Ontario due to a competition court ruling (similar to the ecoRide situation). Web site: www.allostop.com.

Expect a wait at the border crossing during summer weekends and holidays.

JEFF GREENBERG

Autotaxi is a Québec-based bulletin board for ride sharing. Because it doesn't charge a commission, the service won't be hit by the legal complaints that have affected ecoRide and Allo Stop. Web site: www.autotaxi.com.

HITCHHIKING

Hitching is never entirely safe in any country, and we don't recommend it. Travelers who decide to hitchhike should understand that they are taking a small but potentially serious risk. All the same, hitchhiking is relatively popular in Canada, and many budget travelers do it for part of their trip.

People who do choose to hitchhike will be safer if they travel in pairs and let someone know where they are planning to go. Two people, one of each gender, is ideal; if you're three or more, or a single woman, forget it. A cardboard sign with large clear letters naming your destination can be useful.

Stick to the main highways (it's illegal to hitch from the intercity expressways but not from the feeder ramps). To get to Toronto from Montréal, you might try the corner of Blvd René Lévesque and Rue du Fort.

BOAT

Cruise vessels ply the St Lawrence River, but there are no frequent and affordable passenger services to Montréal. AML Cruises (☎ 842-3871 or 1-800-562-4643) links Montréal and Québec City via a daylong cruise once a week during the summer. The boat leaves at 8 am from Quai de l'Horloge and arrives in Québec City at 5 pm, and there is a return trip by bus at 10 pm the same night. Tickets cost $130 per person, including breakfast and lunch – slightly cheaper without the return coach. Reserve ahead of time.

Les Dauphins du St Laurent (☎ 288-4499 or 1-877-648-4499) run weekend hydrofoils in the summer from Montréal to Québec City (five hours). One-way/return tickets cost $69/129; departures are in the late afternoon (call for times) Friday to Sunday from the Quai de l'Horloge. They also make the hop to Trois Rivières daily in the late afternoon (one-way $39/35/19.50 for adults/students/children, 2¼ hours).

If you're cashed-up and have time on your hands, passenger lines cruise the St Lawrence and nearby rivers and the US, especially from New York and New England. Canadian Connection Cruises (☎ 203-254-3339 or 1-800-277-5218) offers four- to six-day luxury cruises between Kingston, Ontario and Québec City, including meals, accommodations and onboard entertainment. Four-night cruises cost $1118/997 in high/low season; bank on at least twice that for US cruises.

ORGANIZED TOURS

Suntrek (☎ 707-523-1800 or 1-800-786-8735) offers two- to five-week trips – most are city-and-sights oriented, but there are also a few geared toward outdoor activities. Web site: www.suntrek.com.

TrekAmerica (☎ 973-983-1144 or 1-800-221-0596, in the UK ☎ 01295-256777) runs three-week Canada Frontier tours starting in New York or Seattle and hitting Montréal, Toronto and Vancouver along their transcontinental route (US$1119). Web site: www.trekamerica.com.

Voyages Campus (Map 6; ☎ 843-8511), 1613 Rue St Denis, runs various trips that include hiking, cycling and canoeing. It can also arrange ski- and sun-destination holidays. The HI youth hostels also run tours and special-event trips year-round.

Tour companies operating from Montréal include Globe-Trotter Aventure Canada (☎ 849-8768), which offers one- to three-day tours in Québec year-round. The tours can include canoeing, horseback riding, rafting, dog-sledding, snowmobiling or other activities. Trips include transportation, accommodations, equipment, meals and a tour guide. One-day canoeing or rafting tours cost $79 or $89, respectively. Web site: www.aventurecanada.com.

Aventure Boréale (☎ 271-1230 or 1-877-271-1230) organizes one-day nature outings, such as bird-watching, canoeing, trekking, fishing, cycling, dog-sledding and ice-fishing. Tours depart daily from downtown Montréal.

Getting Around

Montréal is a pleasant city to experience on foot, but in the North American tradition of sprawl, things are pretty spread out. Notable exceptions are in parts of certain districts – Vieux Montréal, the lower Plateau and the Village, for example. In between, blocks can seem interminable, and you're better off using the city's excellent public transportation system.

When seeking an address, remember that Blvd St Laurent is the dividing point for streets with appendages of *Est* and *Ouest* (East and West). Although the city's grid pattern makes it difficult to get lost, it's slightly off kilter with regard to the compass: What inhabitants refer to as east, for instance, is in fact closer to north.

TO/FROM THE AIRPORT
The cheapest way downtown from Dorval Airport is via the bus and Métro (subway) networks. Outside the Dorval arrivals hall, catch bus No 204 Est to the Dorval Bus Transfer Station and switch to No 211 Est, which delivers you 20 minutes later at Métro station Lionel Groulx (Map 5). You'll wait no more than half an hour between buses, although for most of the day, it's 15 minutes, and the entire journey should take about an hour. Both buses run 5 am to 1 am. To get to the airport from downtown, simply reverse the journey (which costs $2, including transfers).

The Québécois Bus Company (☎ 931-9002) runs Aérobus shuttles from Dorval to downtown, stopping at Station Aérobus, 777 Rue de la Gauchetière Est (Map 4; Ⓜ Champ de Mars), and Station Centrale de l'Autobus (Central Bus Station; Map 6), 505 Blvd de Maisonneuve Est. Ⓜ Berri-UQAM. The 20-minute trip is offered about every 15 minutes on weekdays 7 am to 11 pm and every 30 minutes from 11 pm to 1 am. On weekends, the bus goes from 7 am to 1 pm every half-hour. One-way/return tickets cost $12/22. At the Station Aérobus, a smaller shuttle will pick you up

and drop you anywhere in central downtown, free of charge – an excellent service.

Aérobus shuttles also serve Mirabel Airport; tickets for the one-hour journey downtown are $18/25 for one-way/return tickets. If you've got legions of luggage, taxis are a better alternative (see Taxi, later).

BUS & MÉTRO
Montréal has an extremely modern and convenient bus and Métro system run by STCUM (☎ 280-5653). The Métro is the city's subway system, which runs quickly and quietly on rubber tires, just like the one in Paris. It runs until at least 12:30 am, and some buses run even later. Métro stops are indicated above ground by large blue signs with a white arrow pointing down. Berri-UQAM (Map 6) is the main intersecting station, where three lines converge, and city buses also roll in all directions from there.

One ticket can get you anywhere in the city with a connecting bus or Métro train. On the buses, get a transfer from the driver, and on the Métro, get one from the machines just past the turnstiles. A strip of six tickets (a *lisière* in French) costs $8.25, and single tickets cost $2 each. Buses take tickets, transfers or exact cash only – drivers won't give change.

Tourists can purchase day passes for $7 or three-day passes for $14. However, a weekly card (valid from Monday to Sunday) is a better deal ($12.50). If you're going to be in town for a calendar month and plan to use public transit frequently, buy a monthly pass ($47). It can be shared, as no picture identification is required.

Tickets have magnetic strips, and in the Métro stations, you must insert them into the turnstiles before you can pass (strip tickets go into a simple slot at the ticket booth). Attendants aren't always attentive, so it's not difficult to skip the fare, but keep in mind that there are spot checks, and you'll incur a fine of $500 if you're caught.

Métro for the Common Man

Some Métro stations shine with works by local artists (such as the Place d'Armes station, which is full of stained glass), but one aesthetic pleasure you can enjoy at every station is musical: Whenever a train pulls out, it rings three ascending tones that sound very much like the opening to Aaron Copeland's famous folk symphony *Fanfare to the Common Man* (1944). This performance is completely unintentional and comes from the gear shifts in the electrical compressor of the carriages.

For a map of the Métro, see Map 3 at the back of this book. Routes for the buses and Métro are shown on the Infocentre's standard tourist map. For a detailed map of bus and Métro stops for all of Montréal, pick up the STCUM's *Plan du Réseau* (Network Map) from any Métro station. You can also call STCUM's itinerary service (☎ 288-6287) to find out the best route to anywhere using the bus, Métro or commuter train.

If something goes missing on a bus or train, contact the lost & found department on the mezzanine level of the Berri-UQAM Métro station (Map 6; ☎ 280-4637) from 8:30 am to 6 pm daily.

For information on long-distance buses, see the Getting There & Away chapter.

TRAIN

GO commuter trains (☎ 869-3200) serve the suburbs of Montréal from the Gare Centrale (Map 5) and Gare Windsor (Map 5). Fares in Zone 1 (which includes Dorval Airport) are covered by all Métro and bus tickets; for destinations in other zones, buy a supplement at the ticket counters or at automated ticket machines. Note that commuter trains to Dorval Airport are infrequent, and services end in the early evening.

CAR & MOTORCYCLE

Montréal drivers possess nerves of steel, and you should too if you wish to drive in this town. The rush hours are horrible, lane markings suddenly vanish, and all too often, it's like the qualifying heat for Montréal's Grand Prix. Driving the 'Metropolitan' (the Trans-Canada Hwy, the No 40, which goes through central Montréal) can be a harrowing experience. Vieux Montréal, much of downtown and the more popular parts of the Plateau can get very, very busy – so take the bus or Métro whenever possible.

Road Rules

Whether it's for speeding or not wearing seat belts, fines for traffic violations are stiff in Québec. Although you may see few police cars on the roads, remember that radar traps are common. Motorcyclists are required to wear helmets and to drive with their lights on.

Traffic in both directions must stop when school buses stop to let children off and on. At the white-striped pedestrian crosswalks, cars must stop to allow pedestrians to cross. Turning right at red lights is *not* permitted in Québec, but it is in all other Canadian provinces.

For information on driver's licenses and permits, see Documents, in the Facts for the Visitor chapter.

Gasoline

Canada's prices for gasoline ('gaz' in Québec) are much higher than in the US. The most expensive provinces are Québec, Newfoundland and Labrador; drivers coming from Ontario should fill up before the Québec border.

Service stations in the big cities have the best prices – avoid smaller towns and highway service stations. A liter of gasoline – give or take oil crises or fuel-tax hikes – will cost about 80¢, or about $3 per US gallon. The Canadian (imperial) gallon is one-fifth larger than the US gallon.

Parking

If you absolutely must drive to town, there are pay parking lots downtown and in Vieux Montréal. Most charge $2.50 to $3 per half-hour and a maximum of $10 to $15 per day. One of the largest lots is at the Vieux Port, where you'll pay $2 per half-hour for up to 2½ hours, $12 for 2½ to 12 hours and $15 for 12 to 24 hours.

Street parking, where available, is cheaper for short stays. In central downtown, the best parking rates are in the Place Montréal Trust parking garage (Map 5), northeast of Square Dorchester. It's a flat $4 after 5 pm.

Rental

To rent a car in Québec, you have to be at least 21 years old and have had a driver's license for at least one year. Drivers between the ages of 21 and 25 might have to provide a deposit of up to $500. As a rule, rentals will be cheaper on the weekends,

ROBERT REID

although lively competition means that good deals can be had during the week.

At Dorval Airport, there's a counter in the arrivals hall with car rental companies, including Alamo, Avis, Budget, Hertz, National and Thrifty. Budget (☎ 938-1000) also has several locations in town, including the Gare Centrale (Map 5). You should be able to get a subcompact for around $50 per day with unlimited mileage, taxes and insurance. Similar rates are available at National Tilden (☎ 878-2771), 1200 Rue Stanley. Hertz (☎ 842-8537), 1475 Rue Aylmer, and Avis (☎ 288-9934), 505 Blvd de Maisonneuve, tend to charge more.

Some local agencies offer competitive rates but with limited free mileage. Auto-Rentwise (☎ 722-5678), 3850 Rue Masson, charges $40/245 per day/week in high season, including tax and collision-damage waiver ($500 deductible), for the smallest automatic Honda, Toyota or Chrysler with air-conditioning. You get 250km/1400km free per day/week (12¢ per extra kilometer). It's open 9 am to 7 pm daily. Male drivers must be at least 23 years of age, females 21. Call ahead and they'll pick you up at the Pie IX Métro stop.

Rent-a-Wreck (☎ 328-9419), 10625 Rue St Gertrude, in North Montréal, charges

$46/284 per day/week for its most basic models (stickshift or automatic), all inclusive and with a $500 deductible ($750 if you're under 25). You get 250km/1500km free per day/week and must pay 10¢ per additional kilometer. Despite the name, the firm rents out recent models. They'll pick you up at the Sauvé or St Michel Métro stops.

TAXI

Flag fall is a standard $2.50, plus another $1.20 per kilometer (or 44¢ per kilometer if less than 30km). Waiting time is charged at 44¢ per minute. The minimum fare is $12. From Dorval Airport to downtown Montréal, the fare is a flat $28; from Mirabel, you're looking at about $60.

Taxi services abound, but ones to try include Taxi Diamond (☎ 273-6331) or Taxi Co-Op (☎ 725-9885). Add 10% to 15% to the fare as a tip.

BICYCLE & INLINE SKATES

City authorities never tire of pointing out that Montréal was voted North America's most bicycle-friendly city in 1999 by the US magazine *Bicycling*. While you won't find the same concentration of two-wheelers that you would, say, in Amsterdam, the Island of Montréal does enjoy more than 400km of bike paths, a network that is constantly being expanded. As if to applaud this development, the Tour de l'Île attracts nearly 50,000 cyclists to jockey for position over 65km of paths on the first Sunday in June.

Maps of the city's bicycle paths, including a 12km circuit that runs along the Canal de Lachine, are available from the tourist offices and bicycle rental shops. Helmets and padlocks are provided for free. For virtually any type of bicycle advice pertaining to Montréal and the region, contact Vélo Québec at the bicycle shop La Maison des Cyclistes (Map 8; ☎ 521-8356 or 1-800-567-8356), 1251 Rue Rachel Est. Web site: www.velo.qc.ca. ⓜ Mont Royal.

Vélo-Tour (Map 4; ☎ 236-8356), 99 Rue de la Commune Est, charges $8/12/15/20 per 1/2/4/24 hours for mountain bikes in good condition. Inline skates are available

for similar rates (but cost $30 per day). Web site: www.velo.qc.ca.

Vélo Aventure (Map 4; ☎ 847-0666), at the Vieux Port, charges $7/22 per hour/day for bicycles ($8/25 on weekends). Children's trailers and inline skates are also on offer. There's a major bike path going for miles from right near the shop. ⓜ Champ de Mars.

On Île Sainte Hélène, Plaisirs et Santé (☎ 954-0738), at the kiosk close to the island's only Métro station, charges $7.50/12.50/20 per 1/2/24 hours for bicycles. Inline skates are also available.

Bicycles can be taken on the Métro in the last two carriages of the train from 10 am to 3 pm and after 7 pm weekdays, as well as throughout the weekend. The water shuttles to Parc des Îles also take bicycles at no extra charge.

Also see Bicycling, under Organized Tours, later.

CALÈCHE

These picturesque horse-drawn carriages seen meandering around Vieux Montréal and up on Mont Royal charge about $35 per half-hour or $60 an hour for four to five people. Calèches line up, among other places, at the Vieux Port and at Place d'Armes. In winter, sleighs are used for trips up and around Mont Royal; they charge similar rates. Drivers usually provide running commentary, which can serve as a pretty good historical tour.

BOAT

Regular ferries connect Vieux Montréal with the Parc des Îles and Longueuil on the southern bank of the St Lawrence River. See those sections in the Things to See & Do chapter for details.

ORGANIZED TOURS
Walking

Guidatour (☎ 844-4021) offers tours of Vieux Montréal at 11 am and 1:30 pm daily from late June through September. The bilingual guides go into great detail, adding witty anecdotes about the history and architecture of the old commercial district and old town. Tickets ($12/10/10/5 for adults/

seniors/students/children) go on sale at the gift shop outside Basilique Notre Dame (Map 4) 15 minutes before departure.

For something a bit more theatrical, the Old Montréal Ghost Trail (☎ 868-0303) offers evening tours focused on crimes and ghost themes and led by guides in period costume (read: hard-up local actors). It may sound hokey, but it's actually a lot of fun. Tickets cost $12/10/5 for adults/students/children; they are sold 11 am to 8:20 pm daily in the summer at the booth in the elongated park near Pavilion Jacques Cartier. Tours depart at 8:30 pm from the Pavillon du Bassin Bonsecours, in the Vieux Port.

There are also a number of theme tours dealing with the culture and history of Montréal neighborhoods. Among them, Tourisme Plateau Mont Royal (☎ 524-8767, ext 40 or 1-888-449-9944) conducts circuits (starting at $12 per adult) around the Plateau from different departure points. Call ahead for details.

Les Gens d'Air (☎ 521-9978) conducts walking tours of the Village and the history of gay life in Montréal. The tours last 1½ or three hours and cost $15/20. They depart from the little park at the corner of Rue Ste Catherine Est and Rue Amherst (Map 6) at 12:30 and 4 pm Tuesday, Thursday, Saturday and Sunday from May to September. Reservations are necessary. Ⓜ Beaudry.

Bicycling
La Maison des Cyclistes (Map 8; ☎ 521-8356), 1251 Rue Rachel Est, off Parc La Fontaine, offers three-hour guided bicycling tours of Montréal for groups of five to 20 people, from May to September. It costs $25 ($15 if you have your own bike). The shop, open 9 am to 6 pm, has a good selection of guidebooks and maps for cyclists and rents out bikes ($25 per day; hourly and weekly rates are also available). Ⓜ Mont Royal or Sherbrooke.

Vélo-Tour (Map 4; ☎ 876-3660), 99 Rue de la Commune Est, offers guided and self-guided bike tours. www.velo.qc.ca.

Tourisme Plateau Mont Royal also offers two-wheeled tours of the area (see the preceding Walking section).

Bus & Boat
Gray Line (☎ 934-1222), at the tourist office on Square Dorchester (Map 5), operates 11 sightseeing tours. The basic city-orientation tour takes 1½ hours, costs $18.50/10 for adults/children and takes in Vieux Montréal, the Mont Royal lookout and some other principal sights. There are also tours of town aboard pseudotrolleys. The deluxe bus trip ($45/25 for adults/children, six hours) is a better value and includes admission to the Montréal Tower, Biodôme and Jardin Botanique. An eight-hour trip including Vieux Montréal and the Parc des Îles also costs $45/25. Yet another trip goes to the Laurentian Mountains north of Montréal ($69/47). Buses depart from Square Dorchester (Map 5).

Impérial Autocar (☎ 871-4733) offers narrated tours on board an open-top double-decker bus. This hop-on, hop-off tour goes seven times a day and can take up to six hours with stops (just wait for the next bus to hop on). Tickets are $15/12/8 for adults/students/children. There's a more expensive three-hour tour on an air-conditioned bus (no stops). Buses depart from Square Dorchester (Map 5).

Royal Tours (☎ 871-4733) offers a lot of flexibility, and you can choose from a number of options to customize the tour. Here, too, you can hop on and off the bus at different sights and take advantage of reduced admissions to some attractions. Prices are similar to Impérial's. Buses depart from Square Dorchester (Map 5).

The Amphi Tour (☎ 849-5181) offers a surprise: Fitted with a backboard propeller, this bus tours the Old Port area for half an hour and then drives into the river. It then cruises the port area for another half-hour. The tour ($18/15 for adults/children) departs from Quai King Edward (Map 4) daily from May to October. Reservations are essential.

A couple of companies offer bouncing, soaking jet-boat trips through the nearby Lachine Rapids. Lachine Rapids Tours (☎ 284-9607) has 90-minute trips leaving from Vieux Montréal. Prices are $49/39/29 for adults/youth 13 to 18/children six to 12.

Smaller, faster, less expensive but shorter speedboat trips are also available. Rafting Hydrojet (☎ 767-2230) has rubber-raft trips through the rapids for $34.

AML Cruises (☎ 842-3871) runs river tours from the Quai de l'Horloge (Map 4), known in English as the Clock Tower Pier, at the foot of Rue Berri in Vieux Montréal. The basic two-hour trip around the port, Île Ste Hélène (Map 10) and the Îles de Boucherville (Map 1) leaves at noon and 2:30 pm and costs $22/20/10 for adults/students/children. The 1½-hour sunset trip departs at 7:30 pm and costs $14/12/7. Longer sunset trips and later weekend night cruises with a band, dancing and drinks are other options.

Another popular choice is the 1½ hour cruise aboard the *Nouvelle Orleans*, a Mississippi-style paddle-wheeler, from Quai King Edward (Map 4). It leaves at noon, 2 and 4 pm daily and costs $20/18/10.

Tours are also good aboard *Le Bateau Mouche* (☎ 849-9952), a smaller, comfortable and climate-controlled sightseeing boat with a glass roof. These 1½-hour narrated cruises depart from Quai Jacques Cartier (Map 4) at 10 am, noon, 2 and 4 pm in the summer. Prices are $19/16/9. Dinner cruises are also available. Call for reservations.

Things to See & Do

When it comes down to it, Montréal's charm doesn't lie so much in its official attractions as it does in the wonderfully relaxed atmosphere of the place. Fortunately, the city does boast a good selection of museums, churches, historic sites, parks and other draws. The vast majority of these sights are concentrated in or near downtown, in Old Montreal, in the Parc des Îles and in Olympic Park – but the experience of just wandering through the more enchanting districts is just as memorable. (See Montréal on Foot for walking tours of Vieux Montréal, Downtown and Quartier Latin.)

VIEUX MONTRÉAL (Map 4)

This is the oldest section of the city, dating mainly from the 18th century. The main streets are Rue Notre Dame, which runs past the Basilique Notre Dame, and Rue St Paul. The narrow cobblestone streets divide old stone houses and buildings, many of which are now home to intimate restaurants and clubs. Throughout the area are squares and churches, and the waterfront is never far away.

Vieux Montréal is a must for romantics, although it's unfortunately a bit crowded in the peak season. With all the activity and history, it's a perfect area for just wandering on foot. Do yourself a favor and don't bring your car – it's too busy, and you won't find a parking spot. One oddity to look out for is the peregrine falcons that have been nesting on high ledges around Vieux Montréal since the mid-1980s (see the boxed text 'The Precarious Peregrine,' later in this chapter).

The Vieux Montréal tourist office is at the top of Place Jacques Cartier. Ask there for the 36-page *Old Montréal Walking Tour* booklet (in English or French, $6), which points out noteworthy spots and contains all sorts of interesting factoids.

To get to Vieux Montréal by Métro, get off at the Square Victoria, Place d'Armes or Champ de Mars stop.

Place Jacques Cartier

This square, now the area's focal point, is filled in summer with visitors, vendors, horse-drawn carriages and musicians. The plaza was laid out after 1803, the year a château on the site burned down and city elders decided to set up a public market. At its north end stands the Colonne Nelson (Nelson's Column), a monument erected by the British to the general who defeated the French and Spanish fleet at Trafalgar (it's actually a fiberglass replica).

One little oddity is the statue of an obscure French admiral, Jean Vauquelin, in the square north across Rue Notre Dame; it was put there later by the French as an answer to the Nelson statue.

Highlights

- Place Jacques Cartier and Rue St Paul in Vieux Montréal, with its street performers and lovely stone buildings

- The Paris-style cafés and bars along Rue St Denis and Blvd St Laurent

- Virtually any summertime festival (eg, the Montréal Jazz Festival or Just for Laughs)

- The ultrahip atmosphere of Plateau Mont Royal

- Bicycling in the Vieux Port and on Île St Hélène and Île Notre Dame

- The hustle and bustle at the Atwater or Jean Talon Markets

- Watching a film chosen by the robot at the Cinérobothèque, in the Quartier Latin

- Catching an Alouettes football match in the Molson Stadium

- The intricate wood carvings at Basilique Notre Dame, in Vieux Montréal

- The frolicking penguins at Olympic Park's Biodôme

Hôtel de Ville

The Hôtel de Ville (City Hall) towers over Place Jacques Cartier to the east. It was here, in 1967, that French leader Charles de Gaulle cried *'Vive le Québec libre!'* ('Freedom for Québec!') to the masses from the balcony, fueling the fires of the Québec separatist movement (and straining relations with Canada for years).

The design is pure Second Empire from 1878, but a fire destroyed the building in 1922; there's a famous story of how the major fought the flames to retrieve precious documents. The structure was restored in 1926, after the model of the city hall in Tours, France.

Château de Ramezay

Opposite the Hôtel de Ville is the Château de Ramezay (☎ 861-3708), which was the home of the city's French governors for about 40 years in the early 18th century. Benjamin Franklin stayed here during the American Revolution while fruitlessly attempting to convince the Canadians to join the cause.

The building has housed a great variety of things since, but it is now a museum with

---

Districts in a Nutshell

Vieux Montréal (Map 4)

Vieux Montréal (Old Montréal), with its pretty stone buildings and cobblestone streets, lies south of downtown. The focal points are Place Jacques Cartier, with its buskers and tourist restaurants, and narrow Rue St Paul, with its art galleries, bars and eateries. The park-lined Vieux Port (Old Port) has numerous attractions and is great for a stroll. You can take a tour of town via horse-drawn *calèche* (carriage) from here.

Downtown & Chinatown (Map 5)

This forest of skyscrapers, shops, restaurants and luxury hotels forms the core of Montréal. Rue Ste Catherine is the main shopping artery, with the big department stores, and it passes the Place des Arts, a huge performing arts complex. Blvd de Maisonneuve and Rue Sherbrooke are the two other main east-west streets. Ave McGill College presents some of the city's flashiest corporate buildings and, as it runs north into the McGill University campus, stunning views of Mont Royal.

At the foot of the mountain is a wealthy residential area still known as the 'Golden Square Mile' by some. Rue Crescent and Rue Bishop are the traditional Anglophone centers of nightlife, with an array of bars, clubs and restaurants. The western segment of Rue Sherbrooke features upscale shops and residences, which have an English flavor.

The tiny but well-entrenched Chinatown has oodles of eateries clustered along the pedestrian mall of Rue de la Gauchetière, between Rue St Urbain and Blvd St Laurent.

Quartier Latin & the Village (Map 6)

Undeniably French in character, this is the Paris-style student district along lower Rue St Denis, with the Université du Québec à Montréal (UQAM) at its heart. Here you'll find row upon row of trendy bars, open-air cafés, bistros and music clubs.

The Village is the area around Rue Ste Catherine Est and is the hub of the gay community. Bars, clubs and cafés have a rougher edge here, and the atmosphere is 'anything goes' – especially during the Gay Pride Festival in early August.

Mont Royal Area (Map 7)

Montréal's central neighborhoods are scattered around Mont Royal, a 232m-high extinct volcano that locals grandly refer to as 'the mountain.' The leafy, masterfully planned Parc Mont Royal

a collection of 20,000 objects – paintings, engravings, costumes, photos, tools and other miscellany from Québec's early history. The house is open 10 am to 6 pm daily in summer (closed Monday the rest of the year). Admission is $6/5/4/3 for adults/seniors/students/children up to five.

Three Courthouses

Along the north side of Rue Notre Dame Est near Place Jacques Cartier, no fewer than three courthouses stand bunched together. The most fetching is the neoclassical **Vieux Palais de Justice** (Old Palace of Justice), Montréal's oldest courthouse (1856) and now an annex of the nearby Hôtel de Ville. It's a popular backdrop for wedding photos.

Built in the 1920s, the **Édifice Ernest Cormier** was used for criminal trials before being turned into a conservatory.

The ugliest of the lot is the oversized **Palais de Justice**. It was built in 1971, when sinister glass cubes were still in fashion.

Bonsecours Market

Designed by architect William Footner and inaugurated in 1847, this imposing old

---

Districts in a Nutshell

affords terrific views of the city and teems with nature-lovers year-round. On the north side of the park lie two enormous cemeteries, the (Protestant) Cimetière Mont Royal and the (Catholic) Cimetière de Notre Dame des Neiges.

Plateau Mont Royal (Map 8)
Ignored until a few years ago, this famously hip district, located between Rue Sherbrooke and Blvd St Joseph, charms visitors with its hopping bars and nightclubs, funky shops and droves of eateries.

The chief commercial strips are Blvd St Laurent (also known as 'The Main') and Rue St Denis; in between, the shady Carré St Louis and the restaurant-filled streets Rue Prince Arthur and Ave Duluth are alive with activity. There's a wealth of stylish 19th-century homes with ornate wooden or wrought-iron balconies, pointy Victorian roofs and exterior staircases. Despite this, housing is inexpensive. To the north, Ave du Mont Royal is known for its vintage and offbeat clothing stores, as well as for its nightlife.

Little Italy & Mile End (Map 9)
The small but bustling Little Italy district has several good restaurants and cafés along Blvd St Laurent. The tiny, manicured Parc Martel is the main square, and the colorful Jean Talon Market is a must-see on Saturdays.

Mile End, the alluring quarter between Ave Laurier and Rue Bernard, contrasts tradition with chic – upper-class French live there, but so do communities of Greeks, Italians, Portuguese and Hasidic Jews. Upscale cafés, restaurants and boutiques can be found in the yuppified sections along eastern Ave Laurier and Rue Bernard.

Parc des Îles (Map 10)
In the midst of the mighty St Lawrence lies the Parc des Îles, consisting of the pleasure islands Île St Hélène and Île Notre Dame. Here you'll find La Ronde amusement park, the Casino de Montréal, the Grand Prix racetrack, an Olympic rowing basin and miles of lush parkscape.

Olympic Park (Map on page 73)
The home complex of the 1976 Olympic Games, with its inclined tower, stadium and other sports facilities, is about 3km east of downtown, in Parc Maisonneuve. It shares the site with the Jardin Botanique, the Biodôme and the Insectarium.

What's Free

It's easy to spend a fortune entertaining yourself in Montréal, but some of the best things are free. Here are some suggestions:

- Soaking up the atmosphere in Vieux Montréal and the Vieux Port
- Wandering along Rue St Denis and Blvd St Laurent, day or night
- Fireworks displays on weekends in summer
- Admission to art museums some evenings
- Admiring the panorama over town from Mont Royal
- Tam tam concerts at the Georges Étienne Cartier monument in Parc du Mont Royal
- Cycling along the Canal de Lachine
- The observation deck over the St Lawrence Seaway
- Lunchtime concerts at McGill University's Musée Redpath

market (☎ 872-7730), on Rue St Paul Est, was the main market hall until the 1960s, when local supermarkets effectively drove it out of business. For a while, this silver-domed hall housed municipal offices and a concert hall; in 1992, it reopened as a hall for exhibitions and shops selling arts and crafts, leather goods, designer clothing and other items. It's open 9 am to 6 pm daily.

Place d'Armes & Basilique Notre Dame

The other major square in the area is Place d'Armes, which has a monument to the city's founder – Paul de Chomedey, sieur de Maisonneuve – in the middle. On the south side of the square stands the famous Basilique Notre Dame, a magnet to the visiting multitudes.

In 1823, the Sulpicians decided to enlarge the small parish church on the site as an answer to the much larger Anglican cathedral on Rue Notre Dame (which was destroyed by fire in 1856). They commissioned

James O'Donnell, a New York architect of Irish Protestant background, to design what became, for a while, the largest church north of Mexico. (O'Donnell converted to Catholicism before he died so he could be buried in the church.)

Big enough to hold 5000 people, the church has a magnificently rich interior, with oodles of wood carvings and gilt stars painted in the ceiling vaults. The altar is backlit in weird and wonderful colors. The massive Casavant organ, with 5772 pipes, is used for concerts throughout the year, particularly during Christmastime.

In the back, there's the small **Chapelle du Sacré Coeur** (Sacred Heart Chapel), which was added in 1888. It's also called the Wedding Chapel because of the countless nuptials held there – there's a waiting list of up to two years. The original was damaged by fire in 1978, after which it was rebuilt with a modern altar.

There's a small museum, the **Musée de la Basilique**, that has religious artifacts ($1). Admission to the basilica costs $2/1 for adults/students. Hours are 7 am to 8 pm daily (to 6 pm in winter). You can also get a combination ticket for the basilica and the museum in the Bonsecours church (described later) for $5/4 for adults/students.

Vieux Séminaire de St Sulpice

Just east of the basilica, in the city's oldest building, is the Vieux Séminaire de St Sulpice, which was built by the Catholic order of Sulpicians after they arrived in 1657. The clock, which has wooden innards, was a gift from Louis XIV in 1701 and is believed to be the oldest working clock in North America. The seminary is closed to the public.

Chapelle Notre Dame de Bonsecours

This church on Rue St Paul is also known as the Sailors' Church because of the several models of wooden ships hanging from the ceiling. In the neighboring **Musée Marguerite Bourgeoys**, the fascinating vignettes tell the story of Montréal's first teacher and the founder of the Congregation of Notre

Outdoor stairs typical of Montréal's abodes

Sunday 'tam-tam jam' in Parc du Mont Royal

MARK LIGHTBODY

COLEEN KENNEDY

The Plateau, one of the hippest 'hoods in Canada

MARK LIGHTBODY

Oratoire St Joseph, a place to stay, pray and say 'Wow, would you look at that view?!'

Beautiful architecture abounds in Montréal.

Skaters on a frozen section of the St Lawrence River

Dame order of nuns. From the church tower (reachable via the museum), there's an excellent view of the port.

Entry to the church is free; entry to the museum costs $5/3/2 for adults/seniors and students/children. Hours are 10 am to 5 pm Tuesday to Sunday.

Maison Pierre du Calvet
Opposite the Sailor's Church (see the preceding section), the Pierre Calvet House (☎ 282-1725), at 405 Rue Bonsecours, dates from 1725. The interior has been restored, and the building is now a hotel and restaurant with some lovely antique furnishings.

Centre d'Histoire de Montréal
The Montréal History Centre (☎ 872-3207), in the handsome old fire hall on Place d'Youville, has audiovisual displays, models and reconstructions related to the city's past. It's pretty tame stuff, but the section on the development of the Métro and railway is worth a look.

Hours are 10 am to 5 pm daily May to September (closed Monday the rest of the year). Admission is $4.50/3 for adults/seniors, students and children.

Musée Marc-Aurèle Fortin
Close by is the Musée Marc-Aurèle Fortin (☎ 845-6108), 118 Rue St Pierre, which is less of a museum than a gallery dedicated to this Québec landscape painter, who lived from 1888 to 1970. His depictions of trees are especially famous. Works of other painters also appear in the changing exhibitions. Hours are 11 am to 5 pm Tuesday to Sunday. Admission costs $4/2 for adults/students.

Lieu Historique de Sir George Étienne Cartier
The Sir George Étienne Cartier National Historic Site (☎ 283-2282) consists of two historic houses owned by the Cartier family. One house details the life of Sir George Étienne, a prominent 19th-century lawyer and politician, and how society changed in his lifetime. The other house is a faithful reconstruction of his home during the

Victorian era. Staff dress up in period costume and run guided tours throughout the day.

Hours are 10 am to 6 pm daily in the summer and 10 am to 5 pm Wednesday to Sunday the rest of the year. Admission is $5/2.50/1.50 for adults/seniors/children.

Place Royale
In the west end of Vieux Montréal is the square where Ville Marie, Montréal's first small fort town, was built at a time when the fighting with the Iroquois Confederacy was lengthy and fierce. During the 17th and 18th centuries, this was a marketplace; it's now the forecourt of the Veille Douane (Old Customs House) and is linked to the Pointe à Callière Museum, opposite (see the following entry).

Musée Pointe à Callière
Built on the very spot where Maisonneuve and Jeanne Mance founded the first European settlement, on the south side of Place Royale, the Pointe à Callière Museum of Archaeology & History (☎ 872-9150) provides a good archeological and historical study of the beginnings of Montréal.

For the most part, the museum is underground, in the actual ruins of buildings and an ancient sewage/river system. The first European cemetery is here, established just a few years after the settlement itself. Gravesites are presented like a working dig.

Artifacts are cleverly laid out on levels of shelving according to their time period just as they would be unearthed – the oldest items from Montréal's prehistory are on the bottom. There are also a few interactive exhibits, including video monitors that allow visitors to have a ghostlike 'conversation' with some of the original inhabitants. The lookout at the top of the tower in the new building provides an excellent view of the Vieux Port. The tower can be visited without paying the museum's entry fee.

Hours are 10 am to 5 pm Tuesday to Friday and 11 am to 5 pm weekends. Admission is $8.50/6/5.50/3 for adults/seniors/students/children.

Vieux Port

The Old Port waterfront is a district of riverside redevelopment that is still evolving and changing as construction and ideas continue. It covers 2.5km of riverfront and is based around four *quais* (quays) or piers. The **Promenade du Vieux Port** is a recreational path along the river from Rue Berri west to Rue McGill.

A tourist information booth (☎ 496-7678 or 1-800-971-7678) can be found at the entrance to Quai King Edward – pretty much in the center of things. It's open 10 am to 7 pm daily in the summer. A number of permanent features are listed here, but each year, the port features a range of temporary exhibits, shows and events. Cruise boats, ferries, jet boats and speedboats all depart for tours of the river from the various docks.

Quai Alexandra At this easternmost pier is the huge present-day port and container terminal. Also located here is the Iberville Passenger Terminal, the dock for cruise ships, which ply the St Lawrence River as far as the Magdalen Islands, out in the Gulf of St Lawrence. Nearby is the **Parc des Écluses** (literally, Park of Locks), the site of open-air exhibitions from where a bicycle path leads southeast along the pretty Canal de Lachine.

Quai King Edward This pier is home to the **IMAX cinema** (☎ 496-4629 or 1-800-349-4629) and the latest addition, the sparkling new **Centre iSci** (☎ 496-4724), a science and entertainment center. Something of a cross between a workshop and a video arcade, the iSci has interactive games (eg, a 'fight' with a computer virus), a high-tech 'life lab' and lots of educational screen-based displays.

Hours are 10 am to 6 pm Sunday to Thursday and to 9 pm Friday and Saturday. Admission is $10/9/8 for adults/seniors and students/children. Combined tickets with the IMAX are also available.

Also at Quai King Edward, at the foot of Blvd St Laurent, is a large **flea market** (called a *marché aux puces* in French).

Quai Jacques Cartier & Around This pier features restaurants, an open-air stage and a handicraft center. The Cirque du Soleil, Montréal's phenomenally skilled troupe of acrobats, performs here on occasion (see the Entertainment chapter for details). Trolley tours of the port area depart from here. Also from Quai Jacques Cartier, a ferry goes over to Parc des Îles, which is popular with cyclists (bikes can be taken on the ferry) and has a number of its own attractions (listed later in this chapter). If requested, a stop is made at **Parc de la Cité du Havre**, where there's a restaurant and some picnic tables.

At Cité du Havre, a narrow promontory between Vieux Montréal and Île Ste Hélène connected with the island by the Pont de la Concorde, is a residential complex known as **Habitat 67**. It was designed by Moshe Safdie for the World's Fair as an example of a futuristic, more livable apartment block. The modular design is a bit dated now, but it remains a popular, if not cheap, place to live.

Just east of Quai Jacques Cartier is the **Parc Bassin du Bonsecours**, a grassy expanse enclosed by a waterway crisscrossed with footbridges. In the summer, you can rent the cute paddleboats (equipped with a mock steamboat funnel) by the half-hour for $4; in winter, it's full of ice skaters. Remote-control model sailboats are available for rental at the **Pavillon du Bassin Bonsecours**.

Quai de l'Horloge At the northeastern edge of the historic port on this pier stands the striking white **Sailors' Memorial Clock Tower** (Tour de l'Horloge), now used as an observation tower and open to the public. It also has a history exhibit. Opening hours vary with the season; it is open 10 am to 9 pm daily from late June to late August.

DOWNTOWN (Map 5)

Nestled among the skyscrapers of downtown Montréal are the city's finest museums and several grand churches, many of which are within easy walking distance of each other and accessible via the Métro.

Beware of sightseeing fatigue: Visits to the Musée des Beaux Arts, the McGill University grounds and the Cathédrale Basilique Marie Reine du Monde (in that order) will easily fill an afternoon.

Museums

Musée des Beaux Arts The Museum of Fine Arts ('beaux arts' is pronounced 'bose-ar') is the city's main art gallery (☎ 285-2000), with both modern and pre-Columbian works. The main building, at 1379 Rue Sherbrooke Ouest, is the **Benaiah Gibb Pavilion**, which is devoted largely to Inuit and Amerindian art. The newer annex across the street, the **Jean Noël Desmarais Pavilion**, houses mainly European and American works from all epochs, from medieval to contemporary. Works by some of the great painters (such as Rembrandt, Picasso or Matisse) and sculptors (Henry Moore, Alberto Giacometti or Alexander Calder) are always on display.

Hours are 11 am to 6 pm daily except Wednesday, when it closes at 9 pm. Like many of Montréal's museums, this one is closed Monday. Admission to the general permanent exhibits is free, but there is often some sort of special show on too. Admission to those costs around $10/5 for adults/seniors and students.

The **Musée des Arts Décoratifs** (☎ 284-1252), opposite and part of the Beaux Arts museum, features decorative art displays and handicrafts from the 20th century. The substantial collection includes glass, metal and furniture, as well as industrial and graphic design. It's open 11 am to 6 pm Tuesday to Sunday and to 9 pm on Wednesday. Admission is $6/3 for adults/seniors and students; after 5:30 pm on Wednesday, it's free to everyone. There are also guided tours in English on Wednesday at 2:30 and 5:30 pm. ⓜ Peel or Guy-Concordia.

Musée d'Art Contemporain Located in the Place des Arts complex, the Museum of Contemporary Art (☎ 847-6226) displays works from 1939 to the present, with a permanent collection of more than 6000 works. It's the country's only major gallery that focuses on contemporary art, and about two-thirds of displays are dedicated to Québec artists, such as Paul Émile Borduas. Some of the experimental works are fun – look for items such as a bedstead made out of rifle parts and a motion-activated robot.

Famous artists, such as Picasso, Max Ernst, Andy Warhol, or Piet Mondriaan, make up the remainder of the exhibits, which change regularly. Hours are 11 am to 6 pm Tuesday to Sunday. On Wednesday, it stays open to 9 pm and is free after 6 pm (with a free English-language tour at 6:30 pm). Tours are also given in English at 1 and 3 pm on Saturday and Sunday. Admission is $6/4 for adults/seniors and students. There's a pleasant **restaurant**, La Rotonde, upstairs with terrace dining, and the **sculpture garden** is worth a look. ⓜ Place des Arts.

Centre Canadien d'Architecture The Canadian Centre of Architecture (☎ 939-7026), on Rue Baile, is both a museum and working organization promoting architecture, its history and its future in an impressive modern complex.

The exhibition rooms feature changing shows of local and international architecture, urban planning and landscape design. It may sound dry, but most people will find at least some of the displays (incorporating models, drawings or photographs) of interest.

Part of the building has been created around **Shaughnessy House**, a wealthy businessman's residence built in 1874 (get a good view of the gray limestone annex from Blvd Réne Lévesque out back). Highlights in this section include the solarium and a wonderfully ornate room with intricate woodwork and a fireplace. There's also a busy, well-stocked bookstore with titles on famous architects, styles and photography.

Don't miss the **sculpture garden** on the south side of Blvd René Lévesque. More than a dozen sculptures of varying styles and sizes – even more impressive at night – are scattered about a terrace overlooking parts of south Montréal.

The center is open 11 am to 6 pm Tuesday to Sunday and to 9 pm Thursday from

June to September. It closes at 5 pm the rest of the year. Admission is $6/4/3 for adults/seniors/students. On Thursday, it's free all day for students, and for everybody else, it's free 5:30 to 8 pm. There's parking available. ⓜ Atwater.

Musée McCord The McCord Museum of Canadian History is the city's main history museum (☎ 398-7100), but it's not large; budget 60 to 90 minutes for a visit. Located on the McGill University campus, the two-level museum is well laid out, with exhibits dealing, for the most part, with eastern Canada's early European settlement from 1700. One room exhibits the history of Québec's indigenous people; another displays highlights of the museum's collection, including Canadian costumes, textiles, decorative and folk art. There are changing and permanent exhibits. Sunday workshops at 2 pm are geared toward children ($5).

A highlight of the huge **photograph collection** are those by William Notman, who, with his sons, photographed Canadian people, places and activities from 1850 to 1930.

The 2nd-floor room entitled 'Turning Point: Québec 1900' neatly encapsulates French-Canadian history in Québec. The gift shop has some quality items and interesting reading material. If you tire before seeing the entire photo collection, there's a **tearoom**.

Admission is $8.50/6/5/2 for adults/seniors/students/children, and it's free 10 am to noon Saturday. Hours are 10 am to 6 pm Tuesday to Friday, to 5 pm weekends.

Musée Redpath The Redpath Museum (☎ 398-4086), also on the McGill University campus, houses a natural-history collection that includes lots of stuffed animals and birds, rocks and fossils (including a life-size dinosaur skeleton), as well as a jumble of Egyptian artifacts. Free lunchtime concerts by McGill's faculty and student music groups are also held here in summer. It's free and open from 9 am to 5 pm Monday to Thursday and 1 to 5 pm Sunday. In the winter, it is also open 9 am to 5 pm Friday. ⓜ McGill.

Musée de Soeurs Grises Mentioned more for the building itself, the Grey Nuns Museum (☎ 937-9501), on Rue Guy, is a fine example of early Québec stone architecture, particularly of the numerous convents seen across the province. Founded by Ste Marguerite d'Youville, this is home to the Grey Nuns, an active and hardy group from the colonial era. Inside are Marguerite's tomb and some religious artifacts from the late 17th century.

The Grey Nuns set out by canoe for what was to become Manitoba and founded a mission in St Boniface in 1850. The mission is now a museum in the middle of the largest French community in western Canada. Hours are 1:30 to 4:30 pm Wednesday to Sunday (free). ⓜ Guy-Concordia.

Musée Juste Pour Rire The Just for Laughs Museum (☎ 845-4000), 2111 Blvd St Laurent, is meant to be a useful addition to the Quartier Latin, the seat of the summer comedy festival. You'll see thigh-slapping film clips, and there's a humor hall of fame – but unless you enjoy slapstick, forget it. There are frequent special events and shows in the cabaret theater. Hours are 11 am to 6 pm Tuesday to Sunday (to 9 pm Wednesday). Admission is $8. ⓜ St Laurent.

Churches

For a description of the Basilique Notre Dame, see the Vieux Montréal section, earlier in this chapter.

Cathédrale Basilique Marie Reine du Monde The Cathedral of Mary, Queen of the World is a smaller but still magnificent version of St Peter's Basilica in Rome – scaled down to one-quarter size because of the structural risks of Montréal's severe winters. Built between the years 1870 and 1894, this landmark provided another symbol of Catholic power in what was the heart of Protestant Montréal.

Inside, the neobaroque altar canopy is the main attraction, fashioned of copper and gold leaf and with fantastic swirled roof supports. This too is a replica of Gian Lorenzo Bernini's masterpiece in St Peter's.

The overall impression, including the decoration of the vaults and their support, is far more elegant than that of the more famous Basilique Notre Dame. The 13 sculptures of Christ and the apostles over the entrance are sculpted in wood and covered with copper, and they are brilliantly illuminated at night. Admission is free. Ⓜ Bonaventure.

Cathédrale Christ Church Next to La Baie department store, the Christ Church Cathedral provides a much-needed dash of Victorian style (and a green lawn) on busy Rue Ste Catherine Ouest. Built from 1857 to 1859, the church was modeled on the Protestant cathedral in Salisbury, England – architect Frank Will's hometown. The interior is sober, but the stained-glass windows by William Morris' workshops are cheery relief. Ⓜ McGill.

St James United Church Perhaps it's fitting that this Gothic-style church is fronted by gaudy neon signs in the thick of the shopping district. Otherwise you'd easily miss this house of worship, because stores and offices are built into the façade – only a narrow passageway from Rue Ste Catherine Ouest leads into the church itself. This place shows how Montréal has grown: The entrance once overlooked a garden where traffic now crawls by. Free organ concerts are held at 12:30 pm on Tuesday in the summer. Ⓜ McGill.

Basilique St Patrick St Patrick's Basilica, on Rue St Alexandre just south of Blvd René Lévesque Ouest, was built in 1847 for Montréal's burgeoning Irish population. Rather plain outside, the interior (the work of Brooklyn architect Alexander Locke) contains some interesting details, such as huge columns from single pine trunks, an ornate baptismal font and nectar-colored stained-glass windows. Oddly, this cathedral is more an example of French-Gothic than any Irish-inspired style. The Irish-Canadian patriot D'Arcy McGee was buried here after his assassination in 1868; his pew (No 240) is marked with a small Canadian flag. Ⓜ Square Victoria.

McGill University

On the corner of Rue University and Rue Sherbrooke is McGill University, one of Canada's most prestigious learning institutions, with 15,000 students. Founded in 1828 by James McGill, a rich Scottish fur trader, the university has a fine reputation, especially for its medical and engineering programs. Many campus buildings are showcases of Victorian architecture. The campus is rather nice to stroll around, as it sits at the foot of the mountain. Ⓜ McGill.

Mt Stephen Club

Dating from 1880 and funded entirely by the George Stephen House Foundation, the Mt Stephen Club (☎ 849-7338), at 1440 Rue Drummond, was an exclusive businessmen's club named for the first president of the Canadian Pacific Railway. The 15 rooms inside this Renaissance-style mansion are rich with quality materials and skillful artistry, including a splendid mahogany staircase, marble mantelpieces and other swanky furnishings. Long the home of the private Mt Stephen Club, it's open to the public noon to 4 pm Sunday (except from mid-July to September). Entry costs $3. For an incredible brunch, stop by Sunday morning for duck à l'orange and roast beef ($25). Ⓜ Peel.

Bourse de Montréal

Although once a powerhouse of Canada's stock and bond trading, the Bourse de Montréal (Montréal Stock Exchange) has now been relegated to derivatives (ie, futures and options) – but it still provides a rough-and-tumble trading floor. There are interactive displays and presentations, and guides are on hand in the gallery to explain the secret sign language used by traders. Hours are 8:30 am to 4:30 pm weekdays (free). You may be surprised to find a falcon information center in the lobby (see the boxed text 'The Precarious Peregrine'). Ⓜ Square Victoria.

Dow Planetarium

The Dow Planetarium (☎ 872-4530), 1000 Rue St Jacques, also known as the Montréal

Planetarium, is in a 20m-high dome and offers 50-minute programs on the stars, space and solar system via a celestial projector. Morning shows are geared toward kids, afternoon shows are for all ages, and evenings are meant more for adults. There are special Christmas and other seasonal

The Precarious Peregrine

As you explore Montréal, you may be treated to a rare ornithological sight. Nests of the peregrine falcon, which faced extinction in the 1960s, have appeared on ledges of downtown skyscrapers and in Vieux Montréal.

A good place to find out more about this is at the Peregrine Falcon Information Centre (☎ 871-3582), in the lobby of the Bourse de Montréal. It has good displays and brochures, knowledgeable staff and pictures from a live camera pointed at a peregrine nest, usually occupied in summer, on the 32nd floor of the building. Fewer than 20 pairs of the species survive in Québec, although their numbers are slowly recovering – much to the relief of Montréalers, as the falcons help to curb the local pigeon population. The center is open 9:30 am to 4 pm weekdays, and entry is free, but donations are encouraged.

A roost with a view

programs. Admission costs $6/4.50/3 for adults/seniors/students; free for children under six. Ⓜ Bonaventure.

MONT ROYAL AREA
Parc du Mont Royal (Map 7)

Known as 'the mountain,' this charming, leafy expanse was laid out between 1873 and 1881 by Frederick Law Olmsted, the architect of New York's Central Park. The impetus came from bourgeois residents in the Golden Square Mile to the south who fretted about the vanishing greenery in their neighborhood.

The result is the city's best and biggest park, with 60,000 trees spread over 100 hectares (and more friendly squirrels than you can count). The lush rolling landscape is great in the summer for jogging, picnicking, horseback riding, bicycling and playing Frisbee; in the winter, there's skating, tobogganing and cross-country skiing. Some of the walking trails have stunning views.

The **Chalet du Mont Royal** and the lookout opposite have great views of the city and are about a half-hour walk from downtown. Built in 1932, this grand white villa with bay windows has canvases inside depicting scenes of Canadian history. Big bands play on the huge balcony in summer, reminiscent of the 1930s.

About a kilometer northeast of the lookout stands Montréal's famous steel **Cross of Montréal**, erected in 1924 on the very same spot as the one set up in 1643 by city founder Maisonneuve. It's lit up at night and visible from all over the city.

The parking lot to the north at the **Observatoire de l'Est**, a second major lookout also known as the Belvédère Camillien Houde, is a popular spot for amorous couples (the parking lot fills up on summer nights). You can walk between the two lookouts via the park trail in about half an hour.

From the parking lot at Observatoire de l'Est, take the stairs uphill. If you don't want to go all the way up, walk a few meters east after the first set of stairs to an unofficial lookout point – a protruding boulder with

Views of Montréal

On the north side of downtown where Rue Peel meets Ave des Pins is a staircase that leads to Parc du Mont Royal (Map 7). The lookout at the top, across from the Chalet du Mont Royal, provides excellent views of the city, the river and the surroundings to the south.

Another lookout is at a small park called Parc Summit, just to the northwest of Parc Mont Royal; if you're driving, take Rue Guy from the downtown area to Chemin de la Côte des Neiges and look for the signs. You'll enjoy stunning views of the western residential districts.

Other good vantage points for panoramas are the Montéal Tower (see the Olympic Park map in this chapter) and the Tour de Ville Bar (Map 5). There are also pretty good views from Oratoire St Joseph (see that section) and from various points along the road around Mont Royal.

In Vieux Montréal (Map 4), the Chapelle Notre Dame de Bonsecours (Sailors' Church) and the clock tower on the Quai de l'Horloge afford fine views of the Parc des Îles and the Vieux Port.

Along the northern shore of Île Ste Hélène (Map 10), a good spot for a fantastic view of downtown Montréal is from Alexander Calder's sculpture *L'Homme,* near the ferry docks.

---

no guard rails that provides a fantastic panorama.

Also within the park is **Lac aux Castors** (Beaver Lake), laid out in 1948 in a former marsh as part of a work-creation project. You can rent paddleboats on the lake, and in winter, it freezes over for skating. The slope above has a ski lift that operates when it snows.

Cemeteries (Map 7)

To the north of Parc du Mont Royal lie two enormous cemeteries: the Catholic **Cimetière de Notre Dame des Neiges** and its smaller Protestant counterpart to the east, **Cimetière Mont Royal**. The former has a fascinating bunch of mausoleums that emit solemn music – including that of Marguerite Bourgeoys, a nun and teacher who was beatified in 1982 (see Chapelle Notre Dame de Bonsecours, under Vieux Montréal, earlier). The office of the Cimetière de Notre Dame des Neiges (see the map signs at the entrances) has brochures for self-guided tours around that cemetery. The office is open 8 am to 5 pm weekdays and 9 am to 3 pm weekends. The cemeteries are open during daylight hours.

Oratoire St Joseph (Map 2)

The gigantic St Joseph's Oratory (☎ 733-8211), completed in 1960 and based on and

around a 1916 church, honors St Joseph, Canada's patron saint. The size of the Renaissance-style building is a marvel in itself and commands wonderful views on the northern slope of Mont Royal (the highest point in the city, at 263m). It's also a tribute to Brother André, a monk said to have healing powers, and piles of crutches testify to this belief. Brother André's heart, which is on view here (a display ranking up there with the weirdest) was stolen some years ago but later returned intact. Film buffs will know that scenes of *Jésus of Montréal* were shot here along the Way of the Cross outside the oratory.

The site is open 6 am to 9 pm daily; there's a small museum dedicated to Brother André, who was beatified in 1982 (open 10 am to 5 pm). Admission is free to both. There are free guided tours in several languages at 10 am and 2 pm daily in the summer. Sundays feature organ concerts at 2:30 pm.

The oratory dome, visible from anywhere in the southwestern part of Montréal, is at 3800 Ch Queen Mary, off the western slope of Mont Royal. From downtown, take the Métro to Côtes des Neiges and bus No 16 to the oratory, or walk. For those seeking a quiet night, there are also rooms here (see the Places to Stay chapter). Ⓜ Côte des Neiges.

Holocaust Memorial Centre (Map 2)

Northwest of the cemeteries, the small Montréal Holocaust Memorial Centre (☎ 345-2605), 5151 Ch de la Côte Ste Catherine, provides a record of Jewish history and culture from pre-WWII Europe and holds seminars, exhibitions and other events. There's also a small Jewish library. The center is open 10 am to 4 pm weekdays (free). **Ⓜ** Côte Ste Catherine.

Centre Saidye Bronfman (Map 2)

Next door to the Holocaust Memorial Centre, at No 5170, the Centre Saidye Bronfman (☎ 739-2301) is a Jewish art and performing arts center. It has a gallery of contemporary art that is usually open Sunday to Thursday (call for times). See also Theaters, in the Entertainment chapter. **Ⓜ** Côte Ste Catherine.

Getting There & Away

It's easy to reach Parc du Mont Royal. From downtown, you can walk via the staircase at the top of Rue Peel, or from the Georges Étienne Cartier monument, on Ave du Parc, to the east. Second, you can drive most of the way, park your car and walk the rest (have your coins ready for the parking meters). A third way up the mountain is via bus No 11, which runs through the park and stops near the Observatoire de l'Est. Take the Métro to Mont Royal station and switch (don't forget your transfer slip) to the bus outside. As another option, calèches can be hired (about $60 per hour) for rides up to the lookouts or around the park's trails.

OLYMPIC PARK

Ask any Montréaler and you'll find that scandal, indignation and tales of corruption surround the buildings of Olympic Park. Still, the sports complex (☎ 252-8687), built for more than $1 billion for the 1976 Olympic Games, is magnificent.

The showpiece is the multipurpose **Stade Olympique** (Olympic Stadium), which has a capacity of 80,000 and is often referred to as the 'Big O' – or, more recently, 'The Big Owe.' Finally completed in 1990, the complex has required a laughable litany of repairs (only a year later, a beam collapsed during a football game). In theory, the 65-ton roof can be lifted via the tower cables, but you won't see it in action: High winds have torn holes in the roofing fabric, and the system is plagued by mechanical problems. The stadium still manages to host games of the Montréal Expos baseball team, concerts and trade shows.

A cable car runs up the **Montréal Tower** (Tour de Montréal, also called the Olympic Tower), which overhangs the stadium and is the world's tallest inclined structure (190m). Up top is a glassed-in observation deck, which affords outstanding views of the city and beyond for a distance of 80km. Tickets cost $9/5.50 for adults/students, seniors and children. Combination tickets including a tour cost $12/8.

The **Centre Aquatique** is an impressive swimming complex with six pools, diving towers and a 20m-deep scuba pool (see the Activities section, later, for opening times and admission).

The **Tourist Hall**, at the cable-car boarding station, is a three-story information center with a ticket office, restaurant and souvenir shop. Guided tours of the stadium (☎ 252-8687) leave from there daily; the tours in English take place at 12:40 and 3:40 pm. Tickets cost $5.25/4.25 for adults/ seniors, students and children. It's worth it for those with a special interest in architecture or sports.

If you're seeing several attractions at Olympic Park, a combination ticket is the best value. It covers the Biodôme, Jardin Botanique, Insectarium and the Montréal Tower and costs $15.25/11.25/7.75 for adults/ seniors and students/children. The entire site is in huge Parc Maisonneuve, on the extreme eastern side of the city, off Rue Sherbrooke Est and on the corner of Blvd Pie IX. **Ⓜ** Viau (pronounced 'vee-o') or Pie IX.

Biodôme

Housed in the former Velodrome cycling stadium in the Olympic complex, the Biodôme (☎ 868-3000) is a captivating museum that re-creates four ecosystems and houses approximately 4000 animals and 5000 plants. Under one roof, you can amble through a rainforest, polar regions, the Laurentian Shield woodlands and the ocean environment of the Gulf of St Lawrence.

The rainforest is particularly realistic, with monkeys hanging from trees and alligators lurking in rivers. Other highlights include the underwater views of riverscapes (where ducks may be seen competing with fish for food) and the ocean microcosm and tidal pools (with anemones and sea urchins). The Biodôme's penguins are a perennial favorite, too.

It's a popular attraction, far exceeding attendance expectations. You should plan to go on a weekday if possible, and avoid going midday. Count on around two hours for a visit. You can bring your own lunch, and there are picnic tables near the cafeteria. The gift/bookshop is quite tempting – beware.

Admission is $10/7/5 for adults/seniors/children; free for children under six. A free shuttle runs between the Biodôme and the Jardin Botanique.

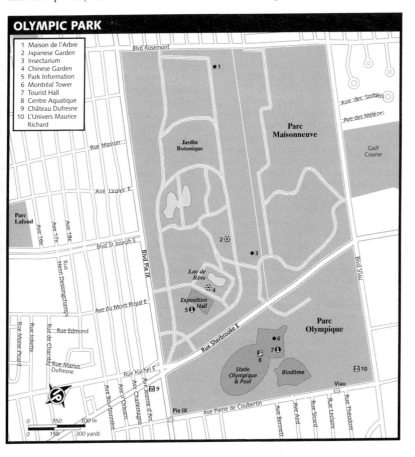

OLYMPIC PARK

1 Maison de l'Arbre
2 Japanese Garden
3 Insectarium
4 Chinese Garden
5 Park Information
6 Montréal Tower
7 Tourist Hall
8 Centre Aquatique
9 Château Dufresne
10 L'Univers Maurice Richard

Blvd Rosemont
Ave des Sorbiers
Ave des Mélèzes
Parc Maisonneuve
Golf Course
Rue Masson
Jardin Botanique
Ave Laurier E
Parc Lafond
Ave 16e
Ave 17e
Ave 18e
Blvd St Joseph E
Blvd Pie IX
Rue Henri Desjongchamps
Lac de Rêve
Blvd Viau
Ave du Mont Royal E
Exposition Hall
Rue Moïse Picard
Rue Joliette
Rue de Charnby
Rue Edmond
Rue Marius Dufresne
Ave Bourbonnière
Ave d'Orléans
Ave Charlemagne
Ave Jeanne d'Arc
Rue Kachel E
Rue Sherbrooke E
Parc Olympique
Stade Olympique & Pool
Biodôme
Viau
Pie IX
Ave Pierre de Coubertin
Ave Bennett
Ave Aird
Rue Sicard
Rue Leclaire
Rue Théodore

0   150   300 m
0   150   300 yards

ROBERT REID

Penguin party at the Biodôme

Jardin Botanique

Opened in 1931, the 81-hectare Jardin Botanique (☎ 872-1400) is now the world's third-largest botanical garden after those in London and Berlin. Some 21,000 types of plants are grown in 30 outdoor gardens and 10 climate-controlled greenhouses (which house cacti, banana trees, 700 species of orchid and more). Flowers bloom in carefully planned stages throughout the warm season, and the huge rosebeds are a blaze of color from June to September. Birdwatchers should bring their binoculars.

The landscaped **Japanese Garden**, with its traditional pavilions, tearoom and art gallery, is a popular draw; the grouping of bonsai is the largest outside Asia. The city of Montréal is twinned with Shanghai, so there's a large and varied **Chinese Garden**, with Hong Kong penjings (a type of ornamental tree) up to 100 years old and a Ming Dynasty–style garden around **Lac de Rêve** (Dream Lake).

In the northern section of the Jardin Botanique, you'll find the **Maison de l'Arbre** (Tree House), a permanent exhibit on life in the 40-hectare arboretum. Displays include the yellow birch, which appears on Québec's official emblem. Other displays change with the seasons, and there are often special temporary exhibits.

Whether you love or hate creepy crawlies, the collection of bugs from around the world at the **Insectarium** (☎ 872-8753) will fascinate you. Some popular ones include the tarantulas and scorpions, but don't miss the dazzling outdoor Butterfly House, which includes some of Québec's native species. In February, biologists don chef hats for a popular taste-testing session (see the boxed text 'Potato Chips with Wings').

Hours are 9 am to 7 pm daily (5 pm in winter). Tickets cost $9.50/7/4.75 for adults/seniors and students/children. The price includes the gardens, the greenhouses and the Insectarium. In the low season, prices drop a couple of dollars.

A free hop-on, hop-off shuttle runs every 10 to 15 minutes to attractions around the gardens.

Château Dufresne

Built for the Dufresne brothers in 1916, this lavish hotel (☎ 259-9201), 2929 Ave Jeanne d'Arc, is inspired by the Petit Trianon at the Versailles palace in France. Restored in 1976, this national monument has a stunning interior, including furniture, art and other decorative objects collected by its owners. Exhibitions are also held here. Hours are 10 am to 5 pm Thursday to Sunday, and entry costs $5/4/2 for adults/seniors and students/children.

L'Univers Maurice Richard

Located at a small arena within Olympic Park, the World of Maurice 'Rocket' Richard is a shrine to the life and achievements of the legendary Canadian hockey star. Visitors will get insights into the nation's obsession with this sport (many thousands of fans turned out for Richard's funeral in 2000). It's open noon to 6 pm Monday to Saturday (free).

PARC LA FONTAINE (Map 8)

One great municipal park not covered elsewhere in this chapter is the Parc La Fontaine, the city's third-largest after Parc du Mont Royal and Parc Maisonneuve. In the warmer months, weary urbanites flock to leafy La Fontaine to enjoy the walking and bicycle paths, the attractive ponds and the general air of relaxation that pervades

Potato Chips with Wings

In late February and early March, the Insectarium in Olympic Park hosts a two-week taste test of its most delectable creepy crawlers. It's a popular event, attracting more than 20,000 people every year to savor a menu that might include walking sticks, crickets, mealworms, caterpillars and locusts. Don't knock it until you've tried it: Visitors remark that wax-moth larvae taste like bacon, and that munching African locusts (baked to a crunchy perfection) is something like eating 'potato chips with wings.' Admission to the Insectarium includes the tasting, but it's a good idea to reserve ahead (see the Jardin Botanique section in this chapter).

the park. The view down the steep banks from Ave du Parc La Fontaine is stunning, especially if the fountains are on. You can rent paddleboats in the summer and ice skate in winter. Something's going on at the open-air Théâtre de Verdure most summer evenings (see Theaters, in the Entertainment chapter).

PARC DES ÎLES (Map 10)

South of the city in the St Lawrence River is this park (☎ 872-4537 or 1-800-797-4537), one of Québec's biggest attractions. Also called Island Park, it consists of Île Ste Hélène and Île Notre Dame, the sites of the immensely successful 1967 World's Fair: 'Man & His World.' For the event, Île Ste

Hélène was considerably enlarged, and Île Notre Dame was completely created with landfill. This park-filled expanse retains some vestiges of the fair and has a number of other attractions. There is an information kiosk near the park's only Métro stop. Ⓜ Île Ste Hélène.

Île Ste Hélène

At the northern end of this island is **Tour de la Ronde** (☎ 872-4537 or 1-800-797-4537), the largest amusement park in the province. It has an assortment of bone-shaking rides, including the 'Monstre,' an impressive big dipper. For the less adventurous, the gentle minirail offers good views of the river and city. A variety of concerts and shows are held throughout the summer, including circuses and high-platform diving. Excellent fireworks displays are held weekend evenings in July and August.

Full admission to La Ronde is $29. Also available is a half-price ticket to the grounds and shows, which includes a limited number of rides (not the major ones). There's a variety of bars and restaurants, too. During the last two weeks of May, La Ronde is open 10 am to 9 pm weekends only; in the summer, hours are 10:30 am to 11 pm. It's closed October to mid-May.

Near La Ronde there's also an old fort where the British garrison was stationed in the 19th century. Inside the remaining stone ramparts is the **Musée Stewart** (☎ 861-6701), with artifacts and tools from Canada's past. Demonstrations are given by uniformed soldiers and others in period dress, and military parades are held daily in summer. Admission is $6/4/4 for adults/students/seniors; free for children under seven. Hours are 10 am to 6 pm daily in summer (to 5 pm the rest of the year). It's a 15-minute walk from the island's Métro station; parking is free.

Walkways meander around the island, past gardens and among the old pavilions from the World's Fair. One of them, the American pavilion, in the spherical Buckminster Fuller dome, is now the **Biosphère** (☎ 283-5000). Using a range of exhibits and interactive displays, this center explains the

Great Lakes–St Lawrence River ecosystem, which makes up 20% of the globe's water reserves. It also tackles pollution and other environmental issues. There's a great view of the river from the upstairs Visions Hall. Hours are 10 am to 6 pm (closed Monday); admission costs $9/7/5 for adults/seniors and students/children.

Île Notre Dame

Created from 15 million tons of earth and rock excavated when the Métro was built, this artificial island is laced with canals and pretty garden walkways.

The main draw here is the huge, spaceship-like **Casino de Montréal** (☎ 392-2746), the former French pavilion from the World's Fair. Opened in 1993, the casino was so popular (and earned so much money) that expansion occurred almost instantly (see the Entertainment chapter for details). The casino is linked by bridges to an attractive garden called the **Jardin des Floralies**, a wonderful place to stroll.

Also popular is the artificial **Plage des Îles** (☎ 872-6093), a sandy beach with room for 5000 people. The water is filtered and treated with chemicals. There are picnic facilities and snack bars at the site. It's open 10 am to 7 pm daily from June 24 to Labour Day, weather permitting. The beach is closed on 'bad days,' but be sure to call to check if it's open – their idea of a bad day may not be the same as yours. Tickets cost $7.50/3.75 for adults/children. To get there, take the bus from the Île Ste Hélène Métro station.

Île Notre Dame is also home to the **Centre Nautique et de Plein Air** (☎ 392-9761), based around the former Olympic rowing basin. Events held here include the Dragonboat rowing races in late July. You can rent sailboards and paddleboats; in winter, the area becomes a huge skating rink. Facilities include a snack bar, lockers and a shop for renting inline skates. There's also some cross-country skiing; equipment can be rented. The center is open to 9 pm daily.

Much of the surrounding grounds are parklands, which you can stroll around in

for free. The annual Formula 1 Grand Prix race is held every June at the **Circuit Gilles Villeneuve**, the racetrack named after the Québec racecar driver. The rest of the year, it's popular with inline skaters.

Getting There & Away

If you're driving to the islands, one bridge, the Pont Jacques Cartier, leads to Île Ste Hélène, and another, the Pont de la Concorde, to Île Notre Dame. Consider taking the Métro to the Île Ste Hélène stop instead, as they hit you pretty hard for parking on the islands. From the Métro stop, there are buses (use a transfer) to attractions on both islands – but walking is almost as fast.

Another option is the Water Shuttle (☎ 281-8000) across the river from the Vieux Port at Quai Jacques Cartier. The shuttle ($3.50 one-way) takes pedestrians and bikes on the 15-minute trip. The first crossing from Quai Jacques Cartier is at 10:35 am, with more departures on the hour; the last from Île Ste Hélène is 7:10 pm daily. (In the summer from Friday to Sunday, the last boat leaves at 11:10 pm.)

Alternatively, you could bike all the way from Vieux Montréal on the bike path for free, via Pont de la Concorde.

LACHINE (Map 2)

The suburb of Lachine, which surrounds the Canal de Lachine, is worth a visit for its history, architecture and general ambience. It's not touristy, it reveals a little of Montréal's roots and culture, and it makes a very good day trip. The attractions listed below are along Lac St Louis, a bulge in the river about 10km from downtown Montréal. The side streets behind the impressive College Ste Anne nunnery and the City Hall, both along Blvd St Joseph, make for good wandering.

Built between 1821 and 1825, the **Canal de Lachine**, to the southwest of Montréal, allowed boats to circumvent the Lachine Rapids of the St Lawrence River. It was closed in 1970, but the area has been transformed into a 14km-long park that's terrific for cycling and walking. The city of Montréal is also building a marina along the canal near downtown, at the bottom of Rue Peel.

The Lachine waterfront is accessible from Vieux Montréal along the cycling route beside the canal. You can also take the Métro to Angrignon and then the No 195 bus to 12th Ave.

Fur Trade in Lachine National Historic Site

This historic site (☎ 637-7433), 1255 Blvd St Joseph, is in an old stone house on the waterfront. The museum tells the story of the fur trade in Canada. Trading was done right there because the rapids made further river navigation impossible. Check out the bales and canoes schlepped by the native trappers, or *voyageurs*. Hours are from 10 am to 12:30 pm and 1 to 6 pm daily from April to mid-October (closed Monday morning). In the fall, it's open Wednesday to Sunday. Tickets cost $2.50/2/1.50 for adults/students/children.

Lachine Canal National Historic Site

This site (☎ 637-7433), located near the Fur Trade, relates the history of the Canal de Lachine. It's open from 10 am to noon and 1 to 6 pm (closed Monday morning) from mid-May to Labour Day. Guided visits are conducted along the canal – you should call ahead to confirm. A nearby shop on the canalfront, Claude Brière (☎ 639-7466), 833 Blvd St Joseph, rents out canoes and paddleboats for $12 and $8 per hour, respectively.

Lachine Museum

This museum (☎ 634-3471), 110 Ch LaSalle, is in the oldest house in Montréal (from 1669). Here you'll see (and smell) the old fur-storage building from the original trading days. Adjacent to the museum is a huge waterfront garden containing around 30 sculptures. Hours are 11:30 am to 4:30 pm Wednesday to Sunday from April to December. Admission is similar to the Fur Trade in Lachine National Historic Site (see earlier).

OTHER ATTRACTIONS
Kahnawake Indian Reserve (Map 1)

South of Lachine, where the Pont Honoré Mercier meets the south shore of the St Lawrence, there's the Kahnawake (pronounced 'gon-a-wok-ee') Indian Reserve, home of (☎ 638-9699) 6000 Mohawks. Kahnawake Tourism (☎ 638-9699) has information on sites and events, including powwows. Located about 18km southwest from downtown Montréal, the reserve has a few things to see but looks not unlike something from a Hollywood western.

In the summer of 1990, the reserve was the site of a standoff between the Mohawks and the Québec and federal governments in a bitter territorial dispute – it made headlines around the world. The residents' support of the Mohawks in Oka exploded into a symbolic stand against the continuing mistreatment of indigenous people across the country.

The **cultural center** (☎ 450-638-0880), with an extensive library relating to the Six Nations of the Iroquois Confederacy, has a small display dealing principally with this reserve and its history. A $3 donation is suggested. It's open weekdays.

The **St Francis Xavier Church** (☎ 450-632-6031), dating from 1717, has a small museum on the early Catholic missions. It's open 10 am to noon and 1 to 5 pm daily (free). Sunday Mass, at 11 am, is sung in Mohawk.

You can also take a three-hour **guided tour** of the reserve at 10 am on Friday, Saturday and Sunday ($12). In the Old Indian Village, open daily in summer, you can see crafts being done and try some Indian food. There are also several gift shops and galleries with arts and crafts.

To get there from Montréal, take Hwy 138 west and cross the Mercier bridge. The reserve is below and to the right, on the riverbank. Then take Hwy 132 and turn off at Old Malone, the main road. You can also take the Métro to the Agrignon station and have a taxi pick you up ($9 one-way; call Kahnawake Tourism at ☎ 638-9699 to book).

Cosmodôme (Map 1)

North of the Island of Montréal is the Cosmodôme Space Science Centre (☎ 450-978-3600 or 1-800-565-2267), 2150 Autoroute des Laurentides in Laval, an interactive museum of space and new technologies. Multimedia exhibits focus on the solar system, satellite communications, teledetection and space travel. You'll find lots of models of rockets, space shuttles and planets. A multimedia show, 'Reach for the Stars,' simulates space travel with stunning special effects on a 360-degree screen.

Admission is $9.75 for adults, $6.50 for students and seniors, and $25 for families of four. From 24 June to Labour Day, it's open 10 am to 6 pm daily, but it's closed Monday the rest of the year. The center also runs well-regarded youth 'space camps' for one to five days of a sort of mini-NASA training.

The center is about a 20-minute drive from downtown Montréal. By public transportation, take the Métro to Henri Bourassa station, go to the Laval bus station outside and take bus Nos 60 or 61 (ask the driver to let you off at the Cosmodôme).

St Lawrence Seaway (Map 2)

This system of locks, canals and dams that opened in 1959 along the St Lawrence River enables oceangoing vessels to sail 3200km inland via the Great Lakes. Across Victoria Bridge from the city is an observation tower over the first locks of the system, the St Lambert Locks, where ships are raised/lowered 5m.

The observation area, which includes explanatory displays, is open 9 am to 9:30 pm April to December (free). From January to March, the locks are closed – they're frozen like the river itself until the spring thaw. The site can be reached by a bike trail.

Musée Ferroviaire Canadien (Map 1)

The Canadian Railway Museum (☎ 450-632-2410) has more than 100 historic vehicles, ranging from locomotives, steam engines and passenger cars to snow plows and Montréal's famous Golden Chariot streetcars.

Admission is $6/5/3.50/3 for adults/seniors/students/children. It's open 9 am to 5 pm daily May to September, and only on weekends and holidays until mid-October.

The museum is a 20-minute drive from Montréal, at 122a Rue St Pierre in St Constant, a district on the south shore near Châteauguay. To get there, take Champlain Bridge from town to Hwy 15, then Hwy 137 at the Châteauguay cutoff to Hwy 209.

ACTIVITIES
Boating

One of the most beautiful spots for boating, canoeing and kayaking is at the Parc Mille Îles (Map 1; ☎ 450-622-1020), in Laval, the town on Île Jésus, north of Montréal. This park on the Rivière des Mille Îles has 10 islands where you can disembark on self-guided water tours, and about 10km of the river (including calm inner channels) are open for paddling.

It's open 9 am to 6 pm mid-May to September. Canoe rentals cost $8/25 per hour/day, two-person kayaks cost $12/40, and rowboats cost $9/35. You can even rent 20-seat *rabaska* canoes, like those used by the fur trappers.

To get there, take the Métro to Henri Bourassa and transfer to the STL bus No 72, which takes you to the park entrance. By car, take Hwy 15 north and exit at Ste Rose Blvd – the park is four blocks east.

High-speed jet-boat tours are available up to the Lachine Rapids (see Organized Tours, in the Getting Around chapter, for more details).

Cycling

Montréal has about 350km of bike paths. Cycling maps can be bought at bookshops, but also ask at tourist offices for freebies. One very fine 13km route leads southwest from the edge of Vieux Montréal all the way to Lachine along the old canal, with a lot of history en route. Picnic tables are scattered along the way, so pack a lunch. Another route covers the Vieux Port area, and yet another the Parc des Îles. All three are connected.

In the river northeast of downtown at Parc de Récréation des Îles de Boucherville (Map 1), there are 22km of trails around this string of island parks connected by bridges. A ferry going there departs from Quai Jacques Cartier in the Vieux Port hourly in the summer.

The lighthearted, good-time Tour de l'Île, on the first Sunday in June, is a major event that attracts about 45,000 cyclists. Some riders wear wacky costumes for this long ride around the city. A week earlier, some 10,000 children participate in the Tour des Enfants. For more information, contact La Maison des Cyclistes (☎ 521-8356), 1251 Rue Rachel Est, or check Vélo-Tour's Web site at www.velo.qc.ca.

Fitness Centers

Nautilus Plus (☎ 843-5993) has the usual barrage of weight-lifting, cycling and climbing machines. It also offers good aerobics and total-fitness programs. Hours and class schedules vary, so call ahead. Nonmembers pay $10 per session. There are 17 branches around town, including the central one (Map 5), at 1231 Rue Ste Catherine Ouest. Ⓜ Peel.

Golf

The Olympic Village (☎ 872-4653), in the Olympic Park (see the Olympic Park map in this chapter), maintains a convenient, straightforward course. It costs $20 for nine holes. Hours are 6:30 am to 7 pm daily throughout the year.

The well-tended greens at Golf Dorval (Map 1; ☎ 631-6624), 2000 Rue Reverchen, include two 18-hole courses. It's open May to October, sunup to dusk, and costs $30 for 18 holes and $25 for nine. To get there, take Autoroute 20 Ouest to exit 53, Blvd des Sources Nord. It's a 15-minute drive northwest of downtown, close to Dorval Airport, on Hwy 520.

Ice & Inline Skating

There is year-round indoor ice skating at the gigantic Atrium (Map 5; ☎ 395-0555), 1000 Rue de La Gauchetière Ouest. Admission is $5 for adults and $3 for seniors and children. Skate rental costs $4. Hours are 11:30 am to 6 pm Tuesday to Friday and Sunday, and 10 am to 10 pm Saturday (various children's and adult sessions). The Bonaventure Métro station leads up into the building.

The YMCA (Map 2; ☎ 255-4651), 4567 Rue Hochelaga, has a good-size rink that's used for hockey, ice ball, *ringuette* (a type of hockey played with a ring instead of a puck) and other frigid sports. Admission is $8/5 for adults/children. You can skate for free at 5 pm on Tuesday and 1:30 pm on Saturday. The rink is open daily, 24 hours a day.

The Parc du Bassin Bonsecours, at the Vieux Port, has one of Montréal's most popular outdoor skating rinks (Map 4; ☎ 496-7678). There's a nativity scene at Christmastime. Skating costs $2, and skate rentals cost $6.

The Lac aux Castors (Map 7; ☎ 872-6559), in Parc du Mont Royal, is another excellent place – it's nestled in the woods near the large parking lot and pavilion. Skating is free, and rentals cost $6.

The Tazmahal Roulodôme and Skate Park (☎ 284-0051), at 1650 Rue Berri, is an indoor center and the city's inline skating temple (not mapped). It's open 9 am to 10 pm daily, and rentals cost $6. As we went to press, the Tazmahal was preparing to close to make way for the construction of a library. In April 2001, the center hopes to reopen in a new location – check the center's Web site at www.taz.qc.ca for details.

Inline rentals are also available at the Centre Nautique et de Plein Air (☎ 392-9761), on Île Notre Dame. Most bicycle shops offer skate rentals (see Bicycle & Inline Skates, in the Getting Around chapter).

Swimming

The best place to do laps is at Olympic Park's Centre Aquatique (☎ 252-4622), which has six indoor pools, wading and diving pools and a waterslide. Hours are 9:15 am to 10 pm weekdays and 1 to 4 pm weekends. Admission costs around $3 or $4. See the Olympic Park map in this chapter.

The CÉGEP du Vieux Montréal (☎ 982-3457), 255 Rue Ontario Est, has a smaller indoor pool (free). It's open from 7:30 am to 9:30 pm Tuesday to Friday and 9 am to 4:30 pm Saturday. Ⓜ St Laurent.

Île Ste Hélène has three large outdoor pools that are open daily from June to Labour Day. Adults/children pay $1/75¢. There's also swimming at the pretty artificial beach Plage des Îles (☎ 872-6093), on Île Notre Dame. Hours are 10 am to 7 pm. Admission is $7.50/5 for adults/children.

Tennis

There are 60 public tennis courts, in Parc La Fontaine and other municipal parks, that are free and open during the day; the tourist offices and the city parks and recreation department (☎ 872-1111) can supply more information.

The Jarry Park Tennis Centre (☎ 273-1234), 285 Rue Faillon Ouest, is a modern complex northwest of downtown. It is home to indoor and outdoor courts that host the Du Maurier Open, Canada's international tennis championships. Courts cost $35 an hour, and equipment rental is available. Hours are 9 am to 9 pm daily. Ⓜ De Castelnau.

COURSES

For an overview of what's on offer, also consult the classified sections of the free entertainment weeklies, such as the *Mirror* or *Hour*.

Dance & Self-Defense

Montréal is a city of dancers, and there are plenty of schools to choose from. The Dance Gallery (Map 5; ☎ 846-6456), 1090 Ave Greene, offers group classes in salsa, ballroom, Latin, swing and other styles regularly throughout the year. Every first Friday of the month, there's a free 'practice party' – a hoot, even if you don't dance. A 10-hour group course that embraces several styles (eg, tango, merengue, waltz and swing) costs $100. Ⓜ Atwater or Lionel Groulx.

Academy Porta da Barra (Map 5; ☎ 214-3099), 372 Rue Ste Catherine Ouest, offers courses in Capoeira, a blend of Brazilian acrobatic dance, combat, music and improvised play. There are two-hour classes three

times a week; you can sit in on one for $9. A month of classes costs $75. Ⓜ Place des Arts.

Cooking

The prestigious Académies Culinaires du Québec (Map 4; ☎ 393-8111), at 360 Champ de Mars, offers a range of excellent courses (French and other cuisines) taught in English or French, year-round. Prices vary, but a one-week course with 10 hours of instruction should cost roughly $200. Ⓜ Champ de Mars.

The Institut de Tourisme et Hôtellerie du Québec (☎ 282-5120) offers short cooking courses in French only several times a year. A five-day course costs $95. Courses are held at the Hôtel de l'Institut, at 3535 Rue St Denis.

The Natural Foods Cooking School (☎ 482-1508), 4865 Rue Harvard, focuses on vegetarian cuisine. It's run by Bonnie Tees, an experienced chef who has worked in Europe and is a graduate of the Natural Gourmet Cooking School in New York. A five-session course costs $175.

Language

The YMCA (Map 5; ☎ 849-8393), 1450 Rue Stanley, offers day courses (four weeks, 68 hours of instruction) for six levels of French for $440. There are also evening courses (seven weeks, 42 hours) for $250. Foreign students pay a $100 registration fee for the courses, which begin once or twice a month (except in March, June, August and December). There's a free placement test every Wednesday afternoon. Ⓜ Peel.

If you're visiting during the spring or fall, the local universities offer courses in French and other major languages. Concordia University (Map 5; ☎ 848-3600), 1600 Rue Ste Catherine Ouest, Suite 117, runs 10-week courses in conversational and written French starting at $190, plus a $15 registration fee. Web site: www.concordia.ca/cont_ed. Ⓜ Guy-Concordia.

McGill University (Map 5; ☎ 398-6160), 688 Rue Sherbrooke Ouest, Room 1199, runs similar but more expensive courses. Web site: www.mcgill.ca/conted. Ⓜ McGill.

MONTRÉAL ON FOOT

Montréal's wealth of historic buildings and its lively, café-filled streets are marvelous to experience on foot. We've provided several walking tours of 1 to 1½ hours in length, but be prepared to take longer if you want to really soak up the ambience and architectural details of these historic districts.

Vieux Montréal Walking Tour

This 2.5km circuit covering the western part of Old Montréal takes just over an hour. The starting point is the **Place d'Armes**. Paul de Chomedey, sieur de Maisonneuve, is believed to have met the Iroquois in battle here, and the clash is depicted at the base of the monument (he won). The fountain-filled square is a refreshing place to cool your heels in summer. At the side of the square stands the **Vieux Séminaire de St Sulpice** (No 1), constructed in 1865 for the Montréal chapter of the Sulpicians, a Catholic order. Just next to the Old Seminary is the **Basilique Notre Dame** (No 2), designed in 1823 – by an Irish protestant, oddly enough.

On the east border of the square stand two considerably newer buildings. The **Aldred Building** (No 3), which was started in 1929 and finished after the Great Crash, emulates the Empire State Building with its setbacks to allow more sunlight into city streets. Features in the L-shaped lobby recall a power and water company – whose president was JE Aldred.

The smaller, eight-story **New York Life Insurance Building** (No 4) to the north is unusual for its red Scottish sandstone and clock tower, which is illuminated at night. Built in 1888, it was Montréal's first skyscraper, and it had the city's first elevator.

Rue St Jacques, which extends north of Place d'Armes, was named after Jean Jacques Olier, founder of the Sulpicians' order. It was known as the Wall Street of Canada until the 1930s, thanks to its many insurance companies, banks and other financial firms. Some of these buildings are veritable temples to capitalism.

The **Banque de Montréal** (No 5) is the country's oldest bank, founded in 1817. This grand, colonnaded edifice (1847) was designed by John Wells along Italian neo-classical lines – its dome and Corinthian portico are modeled after the Pantheon in Rome. Take a closer look at the coat of arms above the entrance: One Amerindian wears an uncharacteristic mustache (Scottish sculptor John Steele didn't know any better).

Heading along Rue St Jacques, the defunct **Royal Bank of Canada Building** (No 6) still bears four lovely Roman columns from 1907, although the female sculptures atop them have long since vanished. Several forlorn-looking lions remain. Nearby, the **Montréal Star Building** (No 7) is a sterling example of Art Deco style. It has been occupied by the *Gazette* newspaper since the *Montréal Star* folded in 1979.

VIEUX MONTRÉAL WALKING TOUR

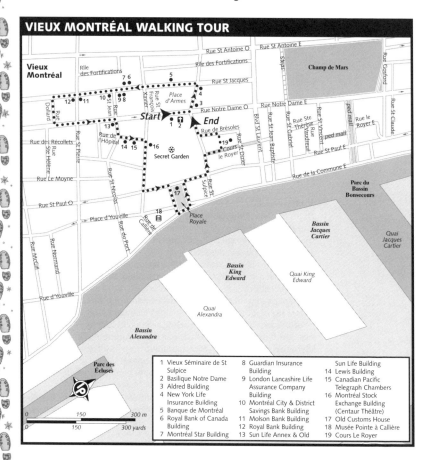

1 Vieux Séminaire de St Sulpice
2 Basilique Notre Dame
3 Aldred Building
4 New York Life Insurance Building
5 Banque de Montréal
6 Royal Bank of Canada Building
7 Montréal Star Building
8 Guardian Insurance Building
9 London Lancashire Life Assurance Company Building
10 Montréal City & District Savings Bank Building
11 Molson Bank Building
12 Royal Bank Building
13 Sun Life Annex & Old Sun Life Building
14 Lewis Building
15 Canadian Pacific Telegraph Chambers
16 Montréal Stock Exchange Building (Centaur Théâtre)
17 Old Customs House
18 Musée Pointe à Callière
19 Cours Le Royer

Opposite the Star Building, the **Guardian Insurance Building** (No 8) is laden with decoration: helmeted women guarding the entrance and lions and greenish mermaids on the 2nd floor. It was built in 1902. Here, the one-upmanship of the owners really becomes apparent. One door farther west, on the corner to Rue St Jean, stands the turn-of-the-century **London & Lancashire Life Assurance Company Building** (No 9), which has a remarkably detailed coat of arms. The designer, Edward Maxwell, was also the one behind the Musée des Beaux Arts.

Across Rue St Jean stands the **Montréal City & District Savings Bank Building** (No 10), which is covered with a delicate floral pattern. Founded in 1846, this good-hearted institution gave part of its profits to municipal charities.

Built in Second Empire style, the **Molson Bank Building** (No 11) looks more like a royal residence than a financial institution. It was established by the Molson brewing family in 1866, and you can still see the heads of founder William and two of his children over the entrance. The Banque de Montréal took the place over in 1925.

The greatest temple of mercantilism around here is the **Royal Bank Building** (No 12), designed by American skyscraper architects York and Sawer. It was built in 1928 after the city relaxed the 335m height limit on buildings, and for a while, the 22-story structure was the city's tallest. Pass under the bronze coat of arms into its stunning banking hall, which resembles a Renaissance Florentine palace or cathedral (sadly, photos aren't allowed). The walls display the insignias of eight of Canada's 10 provinces, as well as that of Montréal (St George's cross) and of Halifax (a yellow bird), where the bank was founded in 1861.

Our circuit turns back toward the Vieux Port. At the corner of Rue Notre Dame and Rue St Jean, you'll find the **Sun Life Annex & Old Sun Life Building** (No 13), which moved here after outgrowing its offices on Rue St Jacques in 1871. The ornate annex is covered with beautiful granite, while its more sober sibling from the 1920s has Corinthian columns and a picturesque colonnade on the upper floors. During WWII, its safes stored gold reserves of some European countries, as well as the British crown jewels.

Dragons and mischievous gargoyles adorn the **Lewis Building** (No 14), at the southeast corner of Rue de l'Hôpital, which was built as the head office of the Cunard Shipping Lines. One satisfied-looking character on the façade is holding a bag full of loot; a more scholarly colleague is taking notes. Moving down Rue de l'Hôpital, note the **Canadian Pacific Telegraph Chambers** (No 15), at the corner of Rue St François Xavier. It houses condos today, but the company's wild-eyed keystone remains above the entrance.

Across the street, the magnificent **Montréal Stock Exchange Building** (No 16), which opened in 1903, recalls imperial Rome with its stately columns and sumptuous marble-and-wood interior. It was vacated in 1965 and later became the home of the Centaur Théâtre (see Theaters, in the Entertainment chapter). The exchange backs onto the enclosed Secret Garden of the Sulpicians' seminary to the north, once a vegetable garden. Forget about trying to see it – the Sulpicians are a secretive bunch.

Heading south down Rue St François Xavier leads to Rue St Paul, where you make a dogleg left to get to the **Old Customs House** (No 17), on Place Royale, the square believed to be where the city's founders first landed. Dating from 1836, the austere neoclassical structure has an Albion figure over the entrance that is a replica of the original. The house is connected by tunnel to the **Musée Pointe à Callière** (No 18), the city's mazelike museum of history and archeology (see the Vieux Montréal section of this chapter).

Turning back, you'll return to Rue St Paul, where you'll make a right and stroll on to Rue St Sulpice. Turn left, and you'll encounter the lovely **Cours Le Royer** (No 19). A religious hospital was located here until 1861, and warehouses built on the same site were leased by the enterprising nuns of St Joseph, who sold them for renovation as condos in the 1970s. In between is a pedestrian mall – a tranquil spot with fountains and lush greenery. Peer into the passageway on the north side to find a stained glass showing Jérôme Le Royer, one of the founders of Montréal, as well as a quaint skyline of the city.

Continue through the passage to Rue des Brésoles and take a left back out onto Rue St Sulpice, where you'll make a right – and you're nearly back at the Basilique Notre Dame.

Downtown Walking Tour

Depending on your pace, this architecture-filled jaunt of 3km should take no more than 1½ hours, including stops. The starting point is **Square Dorchester**, the official center of town once known as Dominion Square. A Catholic cemetery was once located here, and it was well used during the 1832 cholera epidemic before being moved to the north side of Mont Royal. The grassy expanse was remodeled as a public square in 1872. The stern-looking statue on the northern side is of Lord Strathcona, a local philanthropist who helped to sponsor Canada's efforts in the South African Boer War. There's a monument to Scottish poet Robert Burns close by.

The square has several historic buildings, including the aristocratic rump of the **Windsor Hotel** (No 1), opened in 1878 and inspired by New York's Waldorf Astoria. This grand old place closed in 1981, and all that remains is the annex, called Le Windsor, the ballrooms of which are rented for receptions. Take a peek inside at the crystal chandeliers, buffed wooden floors and high windows to recall the splendor of the 1920s.

On the square's north side stands the **Dominion Square Building** (No 2, 1928–29), now home to the Centre Infotouriste office. Have a look in the plush central hall and at the two main entrances, on the east and west sides. The carved arches feature dragons, gargoyles and demons.

Exit the Dominion Square Building from the north, cross bustling Rue Ste Catherine and walk a few meters north up Rue Metcalfe to the shopping complex **Les Cours Mont Royal** (No 3). This place used to be the Mount Royal Hotel (1922), once the biggest in the British Empire. In the mid-1980s, it was converted into an office and shopping complex. The central atrium is impressive, featuring some modern art (check out the birds with human heads), elegant winding staircases and a chandelier from a Monte Carlo casino.

Opposite the west entrance of the complex is the **Seagram House** (No 4, 1929), a faux castle built to house the distilleries company (sorry, no tasting tours are available). Note the rugged stone gallery, sloping roof and the scary imp in the entrance arch.

Make your way back to Rue Ste Catherine and walk a couple of blocks west, enjoying the eclectic mix of characters and businesses on Montréal's busiest shopping street. At Rue Drummond, turn right, and on your left side, you'll see the **Drummond Medical Building** (No 5, 1929). Designed by Percy Nobbs, the structure combines Art Deco with the Arts and Crafts school popular in the 1920s. The branches, pine cones and flowers on the façade are good, but don't miss the lacy artwork on the lobby ceiling either.

Moving north, the next building is the **Mt Stephen House** (No 6, 1884). Its owner, George Stephen, was one of the biggest cheeses in town – chairman of the Bank of Montréal and president of the Canadian Pacific Railway. This Renaissance structure now houses the private Mt Stephen Club; you can view the mahogany staircase, marble mantelpieces and its other swanky furnishings.

Cross Blvd de Maisonneuve going north, and you'll come to the **Emmanuel Congregation Church** (No 7, 1907), on the eastern side of Rue Drummond. It's now property of the Salvation Army and is located on the grounds of **Maison Alcan**, a mélange of carefully restored 19th- and 20th-century buildings. This architectural wonder is the headquarters

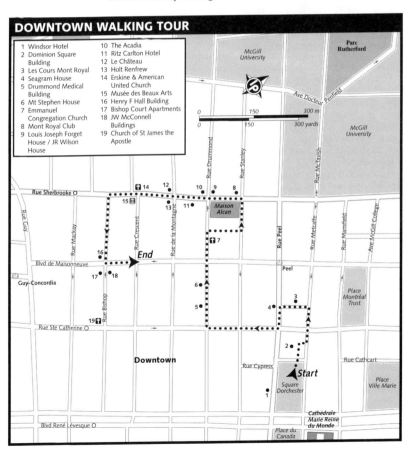

DOWNTOWN WALKING TOUR

1 Windsor Hotel
2 Dominion Square Building
3 Les Cours Mont Royal
4 Seagram House
5 Drummond Medical Building
6 Mt Stephen House
7 Emmanuel Congregation Church
8 Mont Royal Club
9 Louis Joseph Forget House / JR Wilson House
10 The Acadia
11 Ritz Carlton Hotel
12 Le Château
13 Holt Renfrew
14 Erskine & American United Church
15 Musée des Beaux Arts
16 Henry F Hall Building
17 Bishop Court Apartments
18 JW McConnell Buildings
19 Church of St James the Apostle

ROBERT REID

of the aluminum company Alcan, and it has an intriguing atrium with a garden at the back; to get there, turn east into the little passageway leading to Rue Stanley.

Continuing north on Rue Stanley will soon take you to Rue Sherbrooke, Montréal's most prestigious residential street in the early 20th century. On the north corner with Rue Stanley is the **Mont Royal Club** (No 8, 1906), founded as an exclusive men's club. It used to be located in the former house of Prime Minister John Abbott, which burned down in 1904. Its members sought to one-up the older Beaver Club (a dining club across town founded in 1785 by prominent Northwest Company fur traders).

Next door is the **Louis Joseph Forget House** (No 9), a Victorian mansion built in the late 19th century for the first Francophone chairman of the Montréal Stock Exchange. Forget was also a founding member of the Mont Royal Club and ran the Canadian Pacific Railway – much like George Stephen, an earlier CPR president who founded the Mt Stephen Club (see both clubs, earlier). Also worth a look is the adjacent **JR Wilson House** (No 9), rebuilt in 1902 and still one of Montréal's finest residential mansions. There's an old coach house out back.

As apartment living came into fashion in the early 20th century, **The Acadia** (No 10) was built in 1924 as a showcase for wealthy Montréalers. The 12-story structure has a striking colonnaded façade – look for the sculpted medallions on each side.

Across the street, the imposing **Ritz Carlton Hotel** (No 11) was opened on New Year's Day of 1912 in a blaze of publicity. Built in an opulent Beaux Arts style with a terra-cotta finish, it's the only grand hotel in Montréal to survive the era (unlike the Mount Royal and Windsor). The owners spared no expense, making sure that every room had a private bathroom. Pass the liveried flunkies for a look inside, and you'll see why Richard Burton and Elizabeth Taylor chose to be married here in 1964.

One block westward stands the aptly named **Le Château** (No 12). This fortresslike apartment complex was designed by famed Montréal architects George Allen Ross and Robert Henry MacDonald in Scottish and French Renaissance style. It was built a few years after the Acadia. Demons were definitely in mode as ornaments in the early 20th century – just take a look at the façade.

Ross and MacDonald also did the blueprints for **Holt Renfrew** (No 13), opposite Le Château, in Art Deco style, with lots of flowing lines and faunal motifs. The copper and brass doors opened in 1937

Left: Inside the Maison Alcan.

to celebrate the store's centennial. Holt's, as it is known, is an official supplier of furs to Queen Elizabeth. (Also see Department Stores, in the Shopping chapter.)

At the top of Rue Crescent stands the **Erskine & American United Church** (No 14), built in the 1890s. The solid neo-Romanesque structure was adapted to accommodate the beautiful Tiffany stained glass from the American Presbyterian Church in the 1930s, when the two congregations merged.

The **Musée des Beaux Arts** (No 15) was first located at Phillips Square before moving to Rue Sherbrooke in 1912. Huge Ionic columns frame the grand staircase at the entrance, where a cherub frolics amid symbols of the arts. The design is by Edward and William Maxwell; the latter studied at the Paris École des Beaux Arts. The west façade of the new annex, across the street, is a remnant of the New Sherbrooke apartment building, designed in the early 20th century.

Turning south down Rue Bishop takes you past several important structures, including the **Henry F Hall Building** (No 16), the core of Montréal's English-language Concordia University. With no real campus to speak of, the university has acquired buildings around town as it expands. Just southeast and also on Blvd de Maisonneuve are the **Bishop Court Apartments** (No 17), the onetime luxury flats that now house Concordia offices. Built in 1904, this neo-Gothic sandstone gem has some fantastic carvings and limestone decorations, and the garden is nicely manicured.

The contrast with the **JW McConnell Buildings** (No 18), across the street, could hardly be greater. The modern structure with screaming pink tiles (1992) has a terrific atrium, where scattered extracts of literary works (some of them under glass) simulate an intellectual 'whirlwind' – the trick almost works. The X-braces were designed to withstand an earthquake (the last one was in 1988, although a major quake hasn't occurred since 1732). The warm terra-cotta high-rise next door (1912) is in attractive Beaux Arts style.

The last stop on our tour is the **Church of St James the Apostle** (No 19), built in 1864 on a sports field for the British military (for a while, it was called St Crickets in the Fields). The stained glass is worth a look, especially the Regimental Window in the east transept, which was donated in memory of the WWI fallen.

From here, you could sample the myriad pubs, restaurants and clubs in lower Rue Bishop and Rue Crescent. The closest Métro stop is Guy-Concordia, a couple of blocks to the northeast.

Quartier Latin Walking Tour

Expect to spend about an hour on this 2km amble through the student-filled Latin Quarter, which on its north side overlaps with the Plateau. Much of its charm lies not in official sights but in soaking up the laid-back atmosphere – allow yourself to linger.

Our starting point is near Carré St Louis, at the **Institut de Tourisme et d'Hotellerie du Québec** (No 1), the hotels and tourism school on the east side of Rue St Denis. It's a great place to take a course in French cooking (they'll let you peer in the kitchen if you ask). Cross over into

Carré St Louis, surrounded by houses built for wealthy French in the Second Empire period. The site of a reservoir until 1879, this green oasis has a fountain and diminutive café that are popular spots to relax and people-watch.

Turn south on Ave Laval, which is filled with onetime bourgeois homes that feature the exterior staircases so typical of Montréal homes. More recently, this street has attracted writers and artists as tenants (the Québec writers' association is located at No 3492).

At the south end of Ave Laval, on the opposite side of Rue Sherbrooke, is the former boys' school **Mont St Louis** (No 2), a sober, French-style structure with gray stone walls and a mansard roof that has been reinvented as an apartment complex. A few doors to the east is the **Maison Fréchette** (No 3), another charming house built in French

QUARTIER LATIN WALKING TOUR

Second Empire style and the former home of Louis Fréchette, the 19th-century Québec poet. Sarah Bernhardt, the famous actress, stayed here during her North American tours in the 1880s and '90s.

Turn right onto Rue St Denis, and you're in the heart of the Quartier Latin. Many festivities are based here, notably the popular Just for Laughs festival. On your right, amid a tangle of alternative shops and pubs, is the little street **Terrasse St Denis**, a meeting place of Montréal's bohemians at the turn of the 20th century. If you're looking for a place to turn off from stress, this is still it.

Heading farther south will take you to the Université de Québec à Montréal and the **Bibliothèque Nationale** (No 4), a branch of the Québec national library (see the Libraries section of the Facts for the Visitor chapter). Originally built for the Catholic order of Sulpicians, the library was designed by architect Eugène Payette in 1914 in a wonderful blend of Beaux Arts and French Renaissance style. Take a look at the beautiful stained glass inside.

One block south, an important venue for Just for Laughs is the **Théâtre St Denis** (No 5), which was opened in 1914. It's the city's second-largest theater and was renovated in 1989. Immediately next door is the **National Film Board** (No 6), which is in an ultramodern complex and has a robot-activated film menu that enables about 100 people to watch different movies at once. (See the Entertainment chapter for details).

The modern, generic buildings of the **Université du Québec à Montréal**, abbreviated as UQAM, are at the corner of Rue St Denis and Rue Ste Catherine. They've been integrated into the cityscape and are linked to the underground city and the Berri-UQAM Métro station (where three of the city's four lines converge). The most attractive building here is the **Église St Jacques** (No 7), which has a Gothic steeple that has become the university's symbol.

Turn east on Rue Ste Catherine, and tucked among the university buildings on the right, you'll find the **Chapelle Notre Dame de Lourdes** (No 8), which was commissioned by the Sulpicians – effectively to secure their influence in eastern Montréal. Built in 1876, this Romanesque gem was designed by Napoléon Bourassa, who lived on Rue St Denis. It's filled with the artist's imaginative frescoes and is regarded as his crowning glory.

From here, you could continue your walk to **Place Émelie Gamelin**, the site of spontaneous concerts and some wacky metal sculptures, and on to the Village, farther east.

Places to Stay

A silver lining of Montréal's deep recession of the 1990s was a slowdown in price rises for accommodations. The glitzy hotels tend to claim their customary arm and leg, but the rest of the spectrum is very reasonable by international standards – or compared to Toronto, for that matter. You'll find a good range of budget accommodations, including hostels, guesthouses, B&Bs and university housing. Rooms in a respectable B&B can cost $50 or less, and there are plenty of mid-range hotels charging $70 to $90 for doubles, even in summer.

That said, Montréal's growing popularity with tourists means that rooms can be hard to find, especially during the major summer events. The weeks of the Grand Prix (mid-June) and the Montréal Jazz Festival (late June to early July) are considered the peak periods, and conventions held in late summer can also crimp availability. From October to April (excluding the Christmas and New Year holidays), rates are something like 20% to 30% lower.

Although there are scores of restaurants in Vieux Montréal, the range of accommodations in this historic, cobblestoned quarter is decidedly thin. The city's hoteliers recently decided to install several boutique hotels, some of which will be new and sparkling when you visit. These places are tuned for a splurge, housed in renovated 17th-century manors along narrow lanes and decorated with Gallic flair. Otherwise, if you're looking for cozy atmosphere or 'olde worlde' character, look for B&Bs and small hotels on the edges of downtown, in the Plateau, in the Village or in other outlying districts.

Downtown itself is strewn with top-end places that cater to business travelers, but as in most every category, you can often find discounts on the standard rack rates – even for guests who arrive without a reservation. Special deals are often offered on weekends, and some four- and five-star places may be included in package deals by travel agencies in your home country.

Discounts of 10% or more are commonly granted to members of the Canadian or American automobile associations (CAA and AAA), as well as to senior citizens, students, military personnel, journalists, government employees and those with some corporate affiliation. It never hurts to ask, even if you're unsure if you qualify. You might be able to walk in off the street and negotiate a good deal if you know that occupancy is down.

For B&B deals, many budget and mid-range places serve continental breakfasts – typically croissants and/or rolls, jam, coffee and maybe cereals. More upscale hotels will offer hot, English-style breakfasts, with eggs, bacon, sausage etc.

Additional charges include sales and provincial taxes (15% in total), plus a $2 accommodations tax per room per night. Watch your use of telephones, minibars and in-house movies, which can inflate your bill considerably. All prices given in this chapter are summer (ie, high-season) rates, unless otherwise mentioned.

Booking Agencies

Hotels If you arrive in town without reservations, the Centre Infotouriste (☎ 873-2015 or 1-877-266-5687) will make bookings for free. You might have to provide a credit-card number, and bear in mind that some places will charge you a fee if you don't cancel within, say, two days before your arrival. For reservations throughout Québec, call Hospitalité Canada (☎ 287-9049 or 1-800-665-1528), 405 Rue Sherbrooke Est.

B&Bs One alternative to hotels are Montréal's well-priced B&Bs. Most are listed by agencies; if you're staying a while, ask about a weekly rate. Also inquire if the breakfast is full or continental.

B&B Downtown Network (☎ 289-9749 or 1-800-267-5180) is an agency run by Bob and Mariko Finkelstein. It has been operating successfully for years. They have checked over 50 private homes, most of them downtown and in the Quartier Latin, for quality and hospitality beyond minimum requirements. Hosts range from students to lawyers; the places range from mansions with fireplaces in the bedrooms to Victorian homes and apartments filled with antiques. Rates are quite reasonable, starting at $40 for singles, $50 for doubles and $65 for triples. For details and reservations, call or write to 3458 Laval Ave, Montréal, H2X 3C8. Apart from French and English, the staff also speaks Japanese.

A similar organization is Montréal Oasis (☎ 935-2312), 3000 Ch de Bresley, run by Lena Blondel, a Swede, out of her own B&B. Most participant homes are in older houses in the central core, and they pride themselves on the quality of their breakfasts. Ask about the places on quiet, attractive Rue Souvenir, which is perfectly located near Rue Ste Catherine, or about the historic home in Vieux Montréal. Prices range from $40 to $70 for a single and $55 to $90 for a double; triples are also available. Most of the places welcome children.

Bienvenue B&B (☎ 844-5897 or 1-800-227-5897), 3950 Ave Laval, is a smaller agency that specializes in late 19th- and early 20th-century places around the lively French area of Rue St Denis and Carré St Louis. Rates range from $50/60 to $95/110 for singles/doubles. The owners, Carole Sirois and Allard Coté, operate a B&B themselves at the above address – it's in a great location, very close to the Prince Arthur restaurant district. Web site: www.bienvenuebb.com. **Ⓜ** Sherbrooke.

Another agency worth recommending is Relais Montréal Hospitalité (☎ 287-9635 or 1-800-363-9635), 3977 Ave Laval, which provides referrals to B&Bs downtown near Vieux Montréal. Web site: pages.infinit.net/pearson/B_B.

BUDGET
Camping
There's no camping on the island of Montréal, although several sites are within an hour's drive. The Centre Infotouriste (Map 5; ☎ 873-2015) at Square Dorchester can also provide you with a list of campsites.

As you come from the west, before you actually get on the island of Montréal, on Hwy 338 in Coteaux du Lac (exit 17 from Hwy 20), is *Seigneurie de Soulanges (☎ 450-763-5344 or 1-800-263-5344)*. It's about a kilometer off the highway around Dorion and a 45-minute drive to downtown. Sites are $24, with a night's stay thrown in free from the seventh night. It's open May to mid-September.

Also at Coteaux du Lac, there's a *KOA (☎ 450-763-5625 or 1-800-562-9395, 171 Hwy 338 Est)*. It is similarly equipped but cheaper – sites cost $17. Take exit 14 from Hwy 20, and drive on the 210 south till you reach the 338 Est. It's open April 20 to October 20.

South of the city, there is another *KOA (☎ 450-659-8626, 130 Blvd Monette)* in St Phillippe. Take exit 38 off Hwy 15. A tent site costs $23, tax included. It operates from May to October 10. A shuttle links the site with Square Dorchester in Montréal twice daily, departing at 8:30 am and 1:50 pm and returning at 1 and 6 pm. Tickets for the one-hour trip cost $10 one-way.

Nearly an hour's drive west of Montréal is the bucolic *Camping Daoust (☎ 450-458-7301, 3844 Route Harwood)*, on Hwy 342 in Hudson Vaudreuil. Hiking is good around the site, which encompasses a small farm. Take exit 26 coming from Montréal, or exit 22 coming from Ottawa from Hwy 40 (the Trans Canada Hwy); then it's 3km down the road on the right (which is also called Hwy 342). A tent site costs $22. It's open mid-May to mid-October.

Hostels
There is an abundance of good hostels in Montréal. Though aimed mainly at young people and students, hostels also have accommodations for couples and even families. Some offer single and double rooms that are an excellent value, considering what you'd pay in many hotels.

Vieux Montréal (Map 4) Located in a quiet street, *Alternative Backpackers*

(☎ 282-8069, info@Auberge-Alternative .qc.ca, 358 Rue St Pierre) is about a 10-minute walk from the Vieux Port. There are 48 beds spread over two very colorful, un-usually laid-out floors in this converted commercial space. Rates are $17, dropping to $15 in the off-season. If required, a sheet is $2. Double rooms are $50, and there are cooking facilities. Ⓜ Square Victoria.

Downtown (Map 5) The large, central and well-organized *HI Auberge de Mon-tréal* (☎ 843-3317, 1030 Rue Mackay) is south of Blvd René Lévesque. Shared rooms (all air-conditioned) cost $16 and have any-where from four to 10 beds. Private rooms

cost $52/57 for members/nonmembers, and some are for families. Breakfast is offered in the summer, and there are two Internet ter-minals. Check-in is 9:30 am to 2 am; reser-vations are strongly recommended. The hostel organizes activities, such as trips to a local sugar shack or walking tours of town. There's also a free daily shuttle to the Mont Tremblant hostel (see Mont Tremblant, under Les Laurentides in the Excursions chapter). Ⓜ Lucien L'Alllier.

The 420-bed *YMCA* (☎ 849-8393, 1450 Rue Stanley) is a good budget option down-town. Singles/doubles with common bath-rooms cost $40/50, including taxes and breakfast, and both sexes are welcome. The

University Lodging

Most of the city's universities throw open their residences to tourists from mid-May to late August. Prices are competitive, and the standard of accommodations rivals that of the smaller hotels.

McGill University Residence Halls (Map 7; ☎ 398-8299, email reserve@residences.Lan .McGill.ca, 3935 Rue University) charges $40 for one of its 600 smallish singles (which is all there is), $33 for students, taxes included. There are cafeterias and laundry rooms. Rates go down with stays of more than one night, and the weekly rates are good. The residence halls are at the top of a steep hill by Mont Royal. For an extra fee, guests can use the university's pool, gym and tennis courts. Ⓜ McGill.

With 230 rooms of its own, *Royal Victoria College* (Map 5; ☎ 398-6378, email reserve@ residences.Lan.McGill.ca, 3425 Rue University) has single rooms for $36/$43 for students/non-students. Doubles cost a flat $59. It's wheelchair accessible, and there's a shuttle to the airport. Ⓜ McGill.

The *UQAM Residences* (Map 5; ☎ 987-6669 or 1-888-987-6699, 303 Blvd René Lévesque) offer beautiful, modern rooms in a great location. Rates for rooms with shared bath are $35/45 for both students and nonstudents; studio apartments cost $50. Readers have given them rave reviews. Web site: www.residences-uqam.qc.ca. Ⓜ Place d'Armes.

The coed residences of the *Loyola Campus* (☎ 848-4756, 7141 Rue Sherbrooke Ouest) of Con-cordia University are cheaper. This campus is in Montréal Ouest, well away from downtown (not mapped), but rates are cheap: students pay $25/50 for singles/doubles, and the weekly rate is $136/270. Nonstudents pay $35/56, or $182/280 (rates are likely to drop in 2001). Monthly rates are also available. There are common kitchens with a stove and microwave. From the Vendôme Métro stop, take Bus No 105 west (10 to 15 minutes) and alight at the university. Hingston Resi-dence Hall is directly behind the main building. It's open May 15 to August 15.

To the west of Mont Royal (not mapped), the *Université de Montréal* (☎ 343-6531, 2350 Blvd Édouard Montpetit) has singles/doubles with a sink for $23/33 per day or $87.50 per week (singles only, with minimum of three weeks). There are lounges with a TV and microwave. Towels and linen are included. Some rooms are equipped for the disabled. Web site: www.resid.uMontreal.ca. Ⓜ Edouard Montpetit.

cheap cafeteria is open 8 am to 8 pm week-days and until 2 pm weekends, and for a fee, you can use the exercise facilities (swim-ming pool, squash courts, gym and more). This was incidentally the one of the first YMCAs in North America, founded in 1851. Reserve well ahead in summer. Web site: www.ymcamontreal.qc.ca. Ⓜ Peel.

At the women-only *YWCA* (☎ 866-9941, *1355 Blvd René Lévesque Ouest*), singles/doubles without bath or air-conditioning start at $49/66; there's a kitchen on every floor. Good weekly rates are available. A spot in a four-bed dorm costs $22. There's also a small restaurant, a pool and a fitness center. Web site: www.ywca-mtl.qc.ca. Ⓜ Lucien L'Allier.

The people who run Le Gîte du Parc La-fontaine (see Quartier Latin & the Village, next) also operate the new *Le Gîte du Plateau Mont-Royal* (☎ 284-1276, *185 Rue Sherbrooke Est*). It's equally good, very clean and closer to the downtown core; it offers some self-contained units with cooking facilities. Prices are the same as Le Gîte du Parc Lafontaine.

Quartier Latin & the Village (Map 6)
In the Quartier Latin is the *Auberge de Paris* (☎ 522-6861 or 1-800-567-7217, email hdeparis@microtec.net, *901 Rue Sherbrooke Est*). It's in front of Hôtel de Paris (see European-Style Hotels & Mid-Range B&Bs, later). The hostel is somewhat cramped, but it has beds for $18, which includes the use of cooking and laundry fa-cilities. There is a good little café with a patio on the premises. Forty other hostel beds and self-contained apartment rooms are available across the street in a second property.

Even thought it's a hostel, the Village's *Le Gîte du Parc Lafontaine* (☎ 522-3910 or 1-877-350-4483, *1250 Rue Sherbrooke Est*) has an atmosphere more like that of a guesthouse or inn. The location, in a con-verted Victorian house, is a 10-minute walk from the main bus station and close to bar-filled Rue St Denis. Dorm beds are $19, private rooms are $45 to $65 with tax, and there are family rooms. Weekly rates are

offered. Sheets, blankets and a continental breakfast are included, and there's a kitchen and laundry. The owners also run Le Gîte du Plateau Mont-Royal (see Downtown, earlier). It's open May to early September (but reception is closed 11 am to 3 pm). Ⓜ Sherbrooke.

Mont Royal Area West of Mont Royal (Map 7), pretty, inexpensive rooms are available at the *Oratoire St Joseph* (☎ 733-8211, ext 2640, *4300 Ch Queen Mary*), one of the largest churches you'll ever visit (Map 2; see Mont Royal Area in the Things to See & Do chapter). Singles/doubles cost $33/52 with breakfast. Only 13 rooms are available, so reserve ahead. Ⓜ Côte des Neiges.

The Plateau (Map 8) Operated in Jean's private apartment home, *Auberge Chez Jean* (☎ 843-8279, *4136 Ave Henri Julien*) is a very casual place. It charges $17 a night, including breakfast. Guests share the small, busy sleeping space and kitchen. In the off-season, visitors might have a room to themselves. There's also a little garden and courtyard. Look for 'Jean' on the mail-box – it's the only sign. Ⓜ Mont Royal or Sherbrooke.

Mile End (Map 9) The *Collège Français* (☎ 270-4459, *5155 Ave de Gaspé*), also called Vacances Canada, has a range of cheap beds in an institution-like atmosphere. Dorm beds cost $11.50; spots in four-bed rooms with a toilet, shower and sink are $12.50; and double rooms go for $15.50 per person. There are a few singles for $19.50. Cheap breakfasts are offered in the cafeteria, and parking is available. Efficiency studios start at $300 per month. It's busy in the sum-mer, so call ahead. Web site: www.bcity.com/vacancecanada. Ⓜ Laurier.

MID-RANGE
For your money, European-style hotels and B&Bs are the best places to stay in this cat-egory – they have more character than the standard hotels and motels (if fewer com-forts), and you'll often come into direct contact with the owners, who can offer a

PLACES TO STAY

wealth of local tips. For B&Bs in addition to those listed here, see the Booking Agencies section in the beginning of this chapter.

Motels

Motels aren't really a good choice in Montréal, as they're located in uninteresting areas and are rather costly. Most are equipped with TV, swimming pool, free parking and a laundry.

You'll find a knot of them along Rue St Jacques, south and parallel to Rue Sherbrooke and just a 10-minute drive west from the center. Be aware that some of the motels are short-stay only – as in, by the hour.

The best of the lot is the large, modern *Motel Le Chablis* (Map 2; ☎ 488-9561, 6951 Rue St Jacques Ouest), which charges $70, single or double. Quads (two double beds) in a large suite cost $122. All facilities are top notch, and there's a big, inviting swimming pool. Web site: www.chablis.qc.ca. ◍ Montréal Ouest.

The unpretentious *Motel Colibri* (Map 2; ☎ 486-1167 or 1-800-369-4401, fax 486-1160, 6960 Rue St Jacques Ouest) charges $52/59, taxes included. It's the gray place behind Harvey's hamburger restaurant. ◍ Montréal Ouest.

The aging *Motel Raphaël* (Map 2; ☎ 485-3344, fax 489-4258, 7455 Rue St Jacques Ouest) has been around forever but is still serviceable at $48.50 for doubles. It has a swimming pool and restaurant. ◍ Montréal Ouest.

In the east end of Montréal, *Le Paysan* (Map 1; ☎ 640-1415, email maurice.bouffard@sympatico.ca, 12400 Rue Sherbrooke Est), near Olympic Park, charges $54/65 and offers cheaper weekly rates.

Other motels can be found on the south shore, across the river on the mainland. Pont (bridge) Jacques Cartier leads into Blvd Taschereau, also known as Hwy 134 Ouest. *La Parisienne* (Map 2; ☎ 450-674-8899, fax 450-674-8620, 1277 Blvd Taschereau), close to the bridge, charges $49 for its basement singles/doubles; nicer ones that are upstairs and have more light cost $59. ◍ Longueuil. There are others much farther out, in the 8000-number addresses.

At the foot of Pont (bridge) Champlain, there are motels along Blvd Marie Victorin. *Motel Champlain* (☎ 450-671-2299, fax 450-671-0066, 7600 Blvd Marie Victorin) has rooms starting at $59 and fairly comfy suites (for four people) starting at $150.

Airport Hotels

If you need to catch an early-morning flight, there are a couple of charmless but convenient options in the vicinity of Dorval Airport, which serves the bulk of passenger traffic to Montréal.

The most palatable place is the *Best Western Hotel International* (Map 2; ☎ 631-4811 or 1-800-361-2254, email info@bwdorval.com, 13000 Ch Côte de Liesse). It is a pleasant mid-range place with a passable restaurant. Doubles with the usual chain-hotel amenities start at $89, jumping to $99 or $109 during busy periods. If you're flying in and out of town, you can park your car here free for three weeks with one night's stay. ◍ Lionel Groulx, then take bus No 211.

Standard Hotels

If you prefer a more conventional, modern hotel to a B&B but don't care for the prices accompanying the usual luxury choices, there are plenty of options. Check to see if lower weekend rates are on offer.

Downtown & Chinatown (Map 5) In

the western part of downtown, *Hôtel Le St Malo* (☎ 931-7366, email stmalo@colba.net, 1455 Rue du Fort) offers a good deal. The smallest doubles, which are pleasant and modernly furnished, cost $45 in the high season. Larger ones go for $65 and $75, or $85 for rooms with two double beds. ◍ Guy-Concordia or Atwater.

Comfort Suites (☎ 878-2711, 1214 Rue Crescent) charges $125 to $165 for two people weekdays or $90 on weekends. Rooms are decorated in cheery mauve and cornflower hues, and the balconies toward the east afford a nice view of downtown (and, if you're missing your Irish stout, check out the terrace of Hurley's Irish Pub). Web site: www.comfortinn.com. ◍ Lucien L'Allier or Guy-Concordia.

Other mid-range hotels include *Montréal Crescent* (☎ 938-9797 or 1-800-361-5064, 1366 Blvd René Lévesque), which has prices of $85 to $120. Rooms are comfortably furnished and modern, with the exception of some TVs, which appear to have been lifted from a 1960s time capsule. Ⓜ Lucien L'Allier.

The central *Le Riche-Bourg* (☎ 935-9224 or 1-800-678-6323, 2170 Ave Lincoln) has good-value studio apartments and one- and two-bedroom suites with kitchen. Small studio singles or doubles, all with kitchenettes, are $94, or $79 on weekends. Although not much to look at outside, the hotel is equipped with a pool, rooftop balcony, restaurant and grocery store. Weekly rates are available. Ⓜ Atwater.

La Tour Centre Ville (☎ 866-8861 or 1-800-361-2790, fax 866-7257, 400 Blvd René Lévesque Ouest) rents out apartments, from studios ($82) to small and large suites ($92 and $102). All types are equipped with a kitchenette, and some rooms have a great view over Montréal. The hotel also has an indoor swimming pool, sauna and a gym with a panorama of the city. Ⓜ Square Victoria or Place d'Armes.

In Chinatown, *Hôtel Travelodge* (☎ 874-9090 or 1-800-363-6535, 50 Blvd René Lévesque) is centrally located and has 242 standard rooms, all with air-conditioning. Singles/doubles cost $89/99 including continental breakfast, even for walk-ins without a reservation. Youth under 18 with parents stay free. Web site: www.travelodge.com. Ⓜ Place d'Armes.

The four-star *Holiday Inn* (☎ 878-9888, 99 Ave Viger Ouest) is on the edge of Chinatown – you can't miss the fake pagodas on the rooftop. Singles/doubles start at $129 in the summer. It offers above-average luxury for the price, with a health club, indoor pool and sauna. Web site: www.hiselect-yul.com. Ⓜ Place d'Armes.

Quartier Latin (Map 6) Near the eastern edge of the Old Town, the newly renovated *Hôtel Le Roberval* (☎ 286-5215 or 1-877-552-2992, 1167 Rue Berri) has nicely appointed doubles for $80 and suites with a kitchenette for $95. Web site: www.pagel.com/roberval.

European-Style Hotels & Mid-Range B&Bs

Small, independent tourist hotels are the alternative to the costlier standard hotels. There's a good, central assortment, with most in the eastern portion of the downtown area, including the Quartier Latin – an area worth considering is the convenient St Denis bus station area, where there are quite a few places offering a good value.

Nearly all places are in older houses and buildings with 10 to 20 rooms – quality ranges from the plain and functional to the comfy and charming. Price is the best indicator of quality, but sometimes just a few dollars can make quite a difference.

Practically all the smaller ones have a variety of rooms, with price differences depending on facilities – whether it has a sink or toilet or a full bathroom. Air-conditioning adds a few dollars too. Prices are highest June to October.

Vieux Montréal (Map 4) One particularly good value can be had at *Le Beau Soleil B&B* (☎ 871-0299, 355 Rue St Paul Est), which features a lovely upstairs view of Bonsecours Market. The owners are friendly and personable. Homey, if small, singles/doubles/triples cost $65/80/90. It's tough to find anything comparable in the Old Town at these prices. Ⓜ Champ de Mars.

Not far from the Quartier Latin and the Village, the southern end of Rue St Hubert features some cut-rate tourist hotels. The garrulous owner of the *Maison Brunet* (☎ 845-6351, fax 848-7061, 1035 Rue St Hubert) can be found behind the counter amid old-fashioned decor, with touches of sugary rococo. Spacious rooms without/with private bath start at $54/64. Breakfast is served in the garden, next to a cute little fountain. Ⓜ Champs de Mars.

Nearby, cheaper rooms ($30) can be found at such places as *Hôtel de la Couronne* (☎ 845-0901, 1029 Rue St Denis). Ⓜ Champ de Mars.

Les Passants du Sans Soucy B&B (☎ 842-2634, 171 Rue St Paul Ouest) is a B&B with inn atmosphere. Built in 1723, it has comfy rooms furnished with tasteful antiques in

PLACES TO STAY

the heart of Vieux Montréal. The breakfast room is a treat – there is a stained-glass skylight above the dining table – and the entrance hall doubles as an art gallery. Doubles cost $110 to $145, and you'll need to reserve well ahead. **Ⓜ** Place d'Armes.

Hôtel du Vieux Port (☎ 844-0767 or 1-888-977-0767, email hotelvieuxport@qc.aira.com, 756 Rue Berri) is a modish, 27-room inn lodged in an 1882 warehouse. It's above a fine pub/restaurant in the heart of Vieux Montréal. Buffed floors, original wooden beams and views of the Vieux Port set the tone. Some bathrooms have whirlpools. There are special rates for long stays. **Ⓜ** Champ de Mars.

L'Auberge Bonaparte (☎ 844-1448, email bonaparte@securenet.net, 447 Rue St François Xavier) exudes an air of conviviality and relaxation. Its wrought-iron beds and Louis Philippe furnishings lend a suitably Napoleonic touch to the surprisingly spacious rooms, which cost $135 to $185 including breakfast. The suites, decorated in the same vein, start at $325. Most rooms overlook gardens and have a view of the Basilique Notre Dame. **Ⓜ** Place d'Armes.

In the northern part of Vieux Montréal, the inexpensive but good **Hôtel Viger Centre Ville** (☎ 845-6058 or 1-800-845-6058, 1001 Rue St Hubert) has a Victorian shell but a modern interior. Its wide variety of rooms cost $45/49 for singles/doubles in July and August ($3 less in the other summer months). The cheapest rooms have a color TV, sink and fan; doubles cost $55 to $64 and have air-conditioning and a private bathroom. A continental breakfast is included in the prices. Reserve ahead, as it's popular. Web site: www.hotel-viger.com. **Ⓜ** Champ de Mars.

Downtown (Map 5) Several European-style hotels and B&Bs can be found along Rue Ste Catherine near Blvd St Laurent, where the men, painted ladies and some in-betweens appear at about 6 pm.

Hebergement l'Abri du Voyageur (☎ 849-2922, 9 Rue Ste Catherine Ouest) is one of the best low-budget places in the province. The totally renovated hotel with origi-

nal pine floors and exposed brick has 30 rooms – each with a sink, fan and TV. High-season rates are $40/50, and low-season rates are $35/40, all including taxes. Additional guests are $10. The front desk has a binder full of good information for visitors. Web site: www.abri-voyageur.ca. **Ⓜ** St Laurent.

La Villa de France (☎ 849-5043, fax 849-5803, 57 Rue Ste Catherine Est) is also a well-kept, friendly place that is quite OK if you're really on a budget (even if they do rent by the hour). Singles/doubles with shared bath cost $30/40; with bath, they cost $45/55. **Ⓜ** St Laurent.

Manoir Ambrose (☎ 288-6922, 3422 Rue Stanley) is a fine place in a quiet, central residential area. Singles range from $45 all the way up to $70, and doubles range from $50 to $75. Compared to the sterile international hotels, its 22 rooms (some of which are air-conditioned) are a real bargain, even if the decor borders on kitsch. A continental breakfast is included. Web site: www.manoirambrose.com. **Ⓜ** Peel.

Armor Manoir Sherbrooke (☎ 845-0915 or 1-800-203-5485, 157 Rue Sherbrooke Est) is the conversion of two fine Victorian houses into a hotel with 30 rooms. Prices change with the season and vary with the features (some rooms have a Jacuzzi and sumptuous woodwork). In summer, singles/doubles without bath are $50/65, continental breakfast included. Web site: www.armormanoir.com. **Ⓜ** Sherbrooke.

Hôtel Pierre (☎ 288-8519, 169 Rue Sherbooke Est) offers sober, utilitarian rooms for $65 to $85; others with peppier colors and antique furniture cost $75 to $85. There's also a lovely paneled room with a kitchenette and two double beds that are split by a partition ($125). **Ⓜ** Sherbrooke.

The most radical thing about **B&B Revolution** (☎ 842-0938, 2091 Rue St Urbain) is its splendid rates – they start at $45/$60 for decent, air-conditioned singles/doubles. Fancier quarters cost up to $75/120. Rooms have TVs, and there's a kitchen and laundry. Staff are personable, and there's no curfew. Web site: www3.sympatico.ca/christian.alacoque. **Ⓜ** Place des Arts or St Laurent.

All signs in French, even Poulet Frit Kentucky

A sign that works for all languages

Sidewalk cafés along Rue Prince Arthur

ROBERT REID

W WALTON

JEFF GREENBERG

MARK E GIBSON

The immense *ville souterrain* is a great place to escape from Montréal's harsh winters.

LEE FOSTER

Shopping for the art of Montréal in the heart of it

NEIL SETCHFIELD

Henry Birk & Sons window display

MARK LIGHTBODY

Above all souvenirs: a 'Habs' hockey jersey!

West of Rue Jeanne Mance is the 20-room, upgraded stone *Hôtel Casa Bella* (☎ 849-2777 or 1-888-453-2777, 264 Rue Sherbrooke Ouest). The price range at this central hotel is quite wide, with singles from $50 to $65 and doubles from $50 to $85, including continental breakfast, air-conditioning and parking. Web site: www .hotelcasabella.com. Ⓜ Place des Arts.

Hôtel du Nouveau Forum (☎ 989-0300 or 1-888-989-0300, 1320 Rue St Antoine Ouest) occupies a historic house next to the Molson Centre. Behind the drab stone façade are cheery, newly renovated rooms, all with air-conditioning and disabled access (but no telephones). The staff is exceedingly friendly. Single/double rooms with shower (no bathtubs) cost $65/70 in summer (add $5 on weekends). Ⓜ Lucien L'Allier.

Among B&Bs, *Le Gîte Touristique du Centre Ville* (☎ 845-0431, email app@sympatico .ca, 3523 Rue Jeanne Mance) comprises three rooms with shared bath for $60 to $75, including a copious breakfast. The salon, with its piano and fireplace, is an oasis of calm. Owner Bruno Bernard also rents out apartments at 3463 Rue Ste Famille, to the southwest; the places have a pretty view of the city, are well-equipped and afford access to a swimming pool and sauna. Ⓜ Place des Arts or Sherbrooke.

Another good bet is *Montréal Oasis* (☎ 935-2312, 3000 Ch de Breslay), a B&B in a comfy residential area off Rue Sherbrooke Ouest. It's decked out in furniture collected from Asia, Africa, Sweden and Québec. Double rooms are $55 with shared bath and $90 with private facilities. Its host also runs a B&B agency (see Booking Agencies, earlier). Ⓜ Atwater.

Castel Durocher (☎ 282-1697, 3488 Rue Durocher) is in a tall, turreted stone house a couple of blocks east of McGill University. The two cheapest rooms of this B&B (singles/doubles $85/95) have access to a kitchen and a private living and dining room, and there's free Internet service for guests. A larger suite with terrace costs $145. Breakfast includes fresh croissants, cheese and pastries from the nearby Belgian bakery. Web site: www.openface.ca/~durocher. Ⓜ McGill.

Farther south, on Rue St Denis between Blvd René Lévesque and Vieux Montréal, the sprawling *L'Américain* (☎ 849-0616, 1042 Rue St Denis) has 60 rooms in a range of configurations. The basic ones with sink and TV are just $30/40; with private bath, the cost rises to $45/55. Triples and quads are also available. None has air-conditioning. The rooms on the top floor are reminiscent of those in tryst scenes in French movies. Ⓜ Champ de Mars.

Quartier Latin (Map 6) At the northern end of the Quartier Latin, *Castel St Denis* (☎ 842-9719, 2099 Rue St Denis) has a brilliant location. Renovated and redecorated a couple of times, this place is a good value, if not grand. Singles/doubles with private bath cost $50/60 before taxes. Rooms have TV and air-conditioning. Web site: www .castelsaintdenis.qc.ca. Ⓜ Sherbrooke.

La Maison Jaune (☎ 524-8851, 2017 Rue St Hubert) is a B&B with five rooms appointed in different colors in a pretty yellow Victorian-era building. The quietest room has a balcony overlooking the garden. Rooms with shared bath cost $45/65. Ⓜ Sherbrooke.

Hôtel de Paris (☎ 522-6861 or 1-800-567-7217, email hdeparis@microtec.net, 901 Rue Sherbrooke Est) is a turreted mansion with a wide range of upgraded rooms ($60 to $80) and suites with kitchens ($120 to $140). The good standard rooms are $80, all with private bath. Additional people cost $7, and some rooms can accommodate six people. There is a fine little café on the premises, and the location is excellent. In another building across the street, apartments are rented by the week. There's also a hostel on site; see the Hostel section, earlier, for details. Ⓜ Sherbrooke.

West of Rue St Denis, there are places to stay on Rue Ontario. *Hôtel Villard* (☎ 845-9730 or 1-800-394-9730, 307 Rue Ontario Est) has 14 rooms with good prices: doubles range from $47 to $57; singles are about $10 less. Ⓜ Berri-UQAM.

Romantic Victorian decor is the main selling point at *Hôtel Le Jardin d'Antoine* (☎ 843-4506, 2024 Rue St Denis). Simple singles or doubles with private bathroom range from $90 to $98. Deluxe rooms (including whirlpool baths) cost $135 to $155, while the suites will set you back $145 to $180. Web site: www.hotel-jardin-antoine .qc.ca. Ⓜ Berri-UQAM or Sherbrooke.

In the café district, there's the larger, more modern *Hôtel St Denis* (☎ 849-4526 or 1-800-363-3364, 1254 Rue St Denis), which has 60 clean rooms starting at $69 for a double. Prices drop $10 in the off-season. It's got air-conditioning and a restaurant. Ⓜ Berri-UQAM.

The Village (Map 6) On the western end of the Village, in an excellent location near the bus station, there's *Hôtel Le Breton* (☎ 524-7273, 1609 Rue St Hubert). Singles or doubles range from $45 to $70, depending on size and amenities. Some rooms come with a TV, shower or bath. Web site: www .contact.net/publix/breton. Ⓜ Berri-UQAM or Beaudry.

Close by, *Hôtel Louisbourg* (☎ 598-8544 or 1-800-466-1949, fax 524-8796, 1649 Rue St Hubert) posts a price of just $25 for well-kept rooms; most of them, however, cost $40/45 to $59/64 for singles/doubles. Ⓜ Berri-UQAM or Beaudry.

The Plateau (Map 8) While there are a few hotels in this district, the well-priced, atmospheric B&Bs are generally a better bet.

Gay-Friendly Accommodations

The establishments listed here welcome both sexes (unless specifically mentioned) and aren't exclusively gay. For gay-friendly bookings, contact the Cachet Accommodations Network (☎ 254-1250, ext 2, email can4rsvp@fido.ca); the line is staffed from 10 am to 10 pm.

Chez Roger Bontemps B&B (Map 6; ☎/fax 598-9587, chezrogerbontemps@qc.aira.com, 1441 Rue Wolfe) has 10 nicely furnished, if somewhat cramped, rooms on two levels around a pleasant courtyard close to the Village action. Prices start at $55/65 for singles/doubles ($35/55 in the low season). All have fans (no air-conditioning). Ⓜ Beaudry.

Bed & Breakfast du Village (Map 6; ☎ 522-4771, 1279 Rue Montcalm) is a pleasant, well-run place with a Jacuzzi, an enclosed courtyard and balconies, as well as a resident masseur. Year-round prices are $65 for a small double, $75 to $85 for larger ones with TV and private bathroom, and $120 for a self-contained apartment. All have air-conditioning. Web site: www.bbv.qc.ca. Ⓜ Beaudry.

Turquoise B&B (Map 6; ☎ 523-9943, 1576 Alexandre de Sève) looks like something out of *Better Homes & Gardens*. Each bedroom is individually appointed with Victorian ceiling moldings, buffed wood floors, and carved faux gables (yes, indoors). Breakfast is served outdoors, next to the fishpond. It charges $50/70 in the low season and $70/90 during the high season. Ⓜ Beaudry or Papineau.

Ruta Bagage B&B (Map 6; ☎ 598-1586, 1345 Rue Ste Rose) is a B&B with wonderful Italianate rooms, each with television and sink. Many have a balcony, and there's a Jacuzzi. Singles/doubles cost $60/70. Web site: www.rutabagage.qc.ca. Ⓜ Beaudry.

Aux Berges (Map 5; ☎ 938-9393, 1070 Rue Mackay) is a classy men-only hotel with a bar, sauna, Jacuzzi and rooftop sundeck. Check out the tasteful backlighting in the bathrooms. It charges $75/92 for singles/doubles with shared bathroom and $83/100 with private facilities. Continental breakfast is included. Web site: www.auxberges.ca. Ⓜ Lucien L'Allier.

Hôtel Le Bourbon (Map 6; ☎ 523-4679, 1574 Rue Ste Catherine Est) is a popular place built into the huge Bourbon entertainment complex. The hall carpets have seen better days, but the rooms are very comfy, with a minibar, cable TV and room service. Suites ($120 for four people) have a sunken Jacuzzi and a sound system. Standard doubles/triples/quads cost $85/95/115 in the high season ($10 less from mid-October to April). Web site: www.bourbon.qc.ca. Ⓜ Beaudry or Papineau.

Many of them are set in attractive, 19th-century stone houses close to the bars, clubs and restaurants on Blvd St Laurent and Rue St Denis.

Bienvenue B&B (☎ 844-5897 or 1-800-227-5897, 3950 Ave Laval), has 12 nicely furnished rooms in a lovely stone Victorian house with wrought-iron balconies. It's located in a quiet street three blocks north of pretty Carré St Louis. Singles/doubles with sink and shared bath start at $55/65; rooms with private bathroom start at $65/75. Web site: www.bienvenuebb.com.

À la Dormance B&B (☎ 529-0179, email dormance@microtec.net, 4425 Rue St Hubert) has five spacious, pleasant rooms with shared bath that cost $50 to $70, including taxes and breakfast. It's a great value, and hosts Chantal and Eddy are full of good humor. ☯ Mont Royal.

Not far away, **Shézelles B&B** (☎ 849-8694, 4272 Rue Berri) is a bastion of warmth and hospitality, with its paneled walls and large fireplace. The studio apartment ($100 for two) is superb, occupying the entire ground floor. The beds are huge, and there's a spacious bathroom with a whirlpool. Upstairs are two rooms for $75, as well as a smaller 'love nest' behind a Japanese sliding door for $65 (the bed is directly under a skylight). Web site: www.bbcanada.com/2469.html. ☯ Mont Royal.

There are several inviting B&Bs on Carré St Louis, the charming little plaza between Rue St Denis and Ave Laval. **Pierre & Dominique B&B** (☎ 286-0307, 271 Carré St Louis) is in a row of stone Victorian houses. The light, airy bedrooms are decked out in Swedish-style furniture and have a washbasin. Singles/doubles with a shared bathroom cost $40/85. Web site: www.pierdom.qc.ca/acceuill.html. ☯ Sherbrooke.

Virtually next door, **À La Belle Victorienne B&B** (☎ 288-2014, 259 Carré St Louis) has spacious, if plain, bedrooms with washbasin. It's a superb price for the location, with rooms for $40/65. Web site: www.bbcanada.com/4342.html. ☯ Sherbrooke.

La Maison du Jardin (☎ 598-8862, 3744 Rue St André) is in a charming, 19th-century house with tasteful decor. As the name implies, the main feature is the impre well-tended garden. The double with cony costs $65, while the larger mansard room goes for $85 and the sprawling garden room for $105. Web site: www.openface .ca/~durocher/jardin. ☯ Sherbrooke.

Run as a training center for the Québec tourism and hotel board, **Hôtel de l'Institut** (☎ 282-5120, 3535 Rue St Denis) offers top-end luxury at mid-range prices. Decked out in cheery oranges and greens, their spacious, comfortable singles/doubles range from $80/115 to $88/135. The two suites cost $140 and $187, which is quite a deal for a salon with a massive oak table and huge double room. The only drawback is the smallish bathrooms. Web site: www.ithq .qc.ca. ☯ Sherbrooke.

East Montréal (Map 1) If you've got wheels and are in the mood for something a touch bucolic, try **La Victorienne** (☎ 645-8328, fax 255-3493, 12560 Rue Notre Dame Est), a 20-minute drive from downtown. This charming B&B, surrounded by gardens on the banks of the St Lawrence, has spacious, high-ceiling rooms and a swimming pool with stunning views of the river. Breakfast is served on the rear patio. Rates are $40/50/65 for singles/doubles/triples. It's open May to mid-October.

TOP END

Geared mainly toward the business traveler, these places tend to charge hefty fees for parking, telephone calls, the minibar and every other time you turn around. But keep an eye out for cut-rate weekend specials; you may also get a surprisingly cheap booking through a package deal from your travel agent. Prices are generally lower in the summer, when there's less commercial traffic.

Vieux Montréal (Map 4) Between a new high-rise and a restored annex in the 19th-century Nordheimer building sits the **Inter-Continental Montréal** (☎ 987-9900 or 1-800-361-3600, 360 Rue St Antoine Ouest). The entire complex is linked to the World Trade Centre and upmarket shops. The guest rooms are stylish, with photos and paintings by local artists, and the turret suites ooze character. Doubles cost $180 to $310, and suites start at $350.  Square Victoria.

Several swanky boutique hotels have invaded heritage buildings in Old Town. Among them, ***Hôtel Place d'Armes*** (☎ 842-1887 or 1-800-450-1887, 701 Côte de la Place d'Armes) is housed in the former Canadian head office of a large life-insurance company. The lobby is quite a sight, with charcoal tile floors, white marble countertops and pistachio paint. Even the smallest rooms seem airy, thanks to large windows and views up to Mont Royal or of the Basilique Notre Dame. Singles/doubles cost $175/275, and junior suites start at $350. Web site: www .hotelplacedarmes.com.  Place d'Armes.

Downtown (Map 5) There are 227 sleek, newly renovated rooms at ***Novotel*** (☎ 861-6000 or 1-800-668-6835, email novomtl@ aol.com, 1180 Rue de la Montagne), as well as some useful business extras, such as large desks and modem outlets. Two children under 16 who share their parents' room stay free and get a complimentary breakfast. There are also special rooms designed for disabled guests. Rooms start at $180/200 for singles/doubles.  Lucien L'Allier.

Hotel Le Germain (☎ 849-2050 or 1-877-333-2050, 2050 Rue Mansfield) is a gem of refinement and serenity. The mahogany furniture contrasts nicely with the blanched walls, which are lined with photo exhibits. You'll find all the usual creature comforts, including modem hookups and sumptuous bathrooms with lots of chrome. Single/ double rooms run from $210 to $230; the duplex apartments cost $400 to $550. Web site: www.hotelgermain.com.  Peel or McGill.

The ***Marriott Château Champlain*** (☎ 878-9000 or 1-800-200-5909, 1 Place du Canada), next to the Molson Centre, has skyscraper rooms starting at $200. Ask for quarters facing Square Dorchester for a stunning view. Amenities include an indoor pool, health club and sauna. Las Vegas-style revues are often presented.  Bonaventure.

The ***Château & Hôtel Versailles*** (☎ 933-8111 or 1-888-933-8111, 1808 Rue Sherbrooke Ouest) is a renovated onetime European-style pension with old-world touches and spacious rooms. It consists of two buildings, the Edwardian-era Château and the more modern Hôtel. The former links four turn-of-the-century townhouses, which have very comfy (if slightly outdated) decor and furnishings. Standard rooms cost $120/140, but lookout for special weekend rates. There's a French restaurant in the tower. Web site: www.versailleshotels.com.  Guy-Concordia.

The ***Hilton Montréal Bonaventure*** (☎ 878-2332 or 1-800-445-8667, 1 Place Bonaventure) is your standard Hilton with more facilities than you can shake a bankroll at. A highlight is the sprawling rooftop garden with a duck pond and heated pool

---

⸎ Montréal's Closest Encounter

On the evening of November 7, 1990, at least 75 people witnessed a bizarre array of lights floating in a cloudless sky above the Hilton Montréal Bonaventure hotel in downtown Montréal – the largest mass sighting of a UFO in Canadian history. It was first reported at 7:15 pm, several hours after sunset. According to eyewitness accounts, the object consisted of six globes of light, apparently larger than three football fields, and emitted bluish and yellowish beams.

At 9:30 pm, a Montréal police officer at the scene contacted the superintendent of a high-rise under construction across from the hotel and had him turn off the bright spotlights on a building crane; this had no effect on the luminous globes.

Between 10:30 and 11 pm, the UFO began to move eastward and was reported over an electrical power station at Longue Point; shortly thereafter, there was a blackout at the same station, and the mysterious lights disappeared. To date, no one is sure whether the cause was natural, manmade or extraterrestrial in origin. The Canadian government – which denied any military operations took place in the area at the time – has no plans to investigate further.

⚜ ⚜ ⚜ ⚜ ⚜ ⚜ ⚜ ⚜ ⚜ ⚜ ⚜

(see the boxed text, 'Montréal's Closest Encounter'). Standard guest rooms start at $195 in the summer. Web site: www.hilton .com/hotels/YULBHHF/index.html.  Bonaventure or Square Victoria.

The **Ritz Carlton** (☎ 842-4212 or 1-800-363-0366, 1228 Rue Sherbrooke Ouest), with standard rooms from $160 to $275, has long been *the* place in Montréal for the ultimate splurge. Suites start at $395. Following a face-lift a few years back, the marble-floored bathrooms are wired for TV and radio sound. If you catch the right moment, the limos out front will disgorge big-shot entertainers and politicians. Web site: www.ritzcarlton.com.  Peel.

LONG-TERM RENTALS

Most long-term options will require you to guarantee your stay by check or money order, with a cancellation period of two days or more.

The universities (see the boxed text 'University Lodging') are excellent choices May to August. Info-McGill is a cyber bulletin board of students, ex-students and others seeking roommates, flatmates and tenants to let or sublet accommodations. See the Classified Ads section on the Web site, at gopher://vm1.mcgill.ca.

The classifieds of the *Montréal Gazette* list some places that rent out rooms by the week to, shall we say, a varied clientele. One such establishment is **Chambres à Louer** *(Map 5; ☎ 933-2046, 2105 Rue Tupper),* tested by your author for $77 a *week.* Prices range from $65 to $85 per week, with your basic kitchenette, sink and double bed. Bring your own sheets. If you just need a place merely to flop, this is it.  Guy-Concordia.

Hotel Apartments A-1 *(Map 6; ☎ 524-0694, fax 524-5695, 1701 Rue St Hubert)* offers standard, if unexciting rooms with TV, air-conditioning, private bath and a kitchenette. Prices start at $39 per day and $189/499 per week/month.  Berri-UQAM.

Studios du Quartier Latin *(Map 6; ☎ 845-6335, 1273 Rue St André)* has efficiency apartments in the Quartier Latin and Plateau areas. Residences have a fully equipped kitchenette, TV, private telephone and bed linen. Bathrooms are private or shared. Rents start at around $50/280/730 for two people per day/week/month, June to October. Prices drop sharply in the low season.  Beaudry.

From $850 per month, you can stay in a swish 1½ room apartment in the **Tour Trylon** *(Map 5; ☎ 843-3971, 3463 Rue Ste Famille).* Each room has an alcove with a view, and there's a pool and sauna at street level. Web site: www.trylon.qc.ca.  Place des Arts.

PLACES TO STAY

Places to Eat

Some people say it's the French background, others put it down to a sin-and-repent mentality of a predominantly Catholic city; whatever the reason, Montréalers do love to eat out. The city's reputation for culinary excellence has Gallic roots, but its more recent cosmopolitanism makes for a veritable United Nations of cuisine.

The downtown and Plateau areas have the greatest concentration of restaurants. Spanning the two districts are two major dining strips along Blvd St Laurent and Rue St Denis, both of which enjoy a wide range of reasonably priced, high-quality food. The farther north you go, the smaller and more innovative the establishments become. Two smaller streets, Rue Prince Arthur Est and Ave Duluth Est, intersect those two major strips and have a lot of 'bring your own wine' restaurants. Mile End, particularly along Ave Bernard and the north end of Ave Du Parc, has some top-end places worthy of note.

Montréal has a bewildering array of ethnic restaurants. Among them, Chinatown has a bevy of low-cost eateries bunched close together. To the north and a bit out of the way, vibrant Little Italy has a decent choice of Italian restaurants (but there are desirable Italian places elsewhere, too). Greek places seem ubiquitous and specialize in *brochettes*, a Montréal favorite otherwise known as kebabs. Portuguese cuisine, with its wonderful roasted meats and seafood, is well represented, especially in the Plateau around the western end of Ave Mont Royal.

Until a decade or so ago, all haute cuisine was indubitably French, while the lower reaches of the culinary firmament were left to Québécois and ethnic eateries. How things have changed. After the recession of the early 1990s, the scene was transformed by the waves of immigrants who established themselves as restaurateurs. Dozens of foreign cuisines are now represented, from Antillean to Zambian, and there never seem to be too many restaurants: at last count,

there were over 4,500 – more per capita than anywhere else on the continent, except for New York.

Many places have lunch specials, and at dinner, there is often a table d'hôte (a fixed-price meal including dessert or coffee). If you're flexible about what you eat, these tend to be incredible bargains – a table d'hôte costing $10 to $15 isn't uncommon for dinner at the cheaper restaurants.

The main drawbacks to eating out are the taxes and tip, which can add about 30% to the cost of your meal. (Although tourists can get a tax refund on merchandise and lodging, food and entertainment aren't covered.) Tipping is conducted American-style, with the customary 15% of the pretax amount to be left on the table after you've settled the bill.

Many restaurants have a policy of *apportez vôtre vin* (bring your own wine) – we've included the acronym BYOW where it applies. The waiters will refer you to a neighborhood *dépanneur* (convenience store) if there's no government outlet of the alcohol retailers, known as SAQs, open and close by (convenience stores stay open longer than SAQs but charge considerably more for alcohol).

Better establishments don't start to get busy until around 8 pm and will stay that way for a couple of hours. Just as in France, if you're an early eater, you may have the place to yourself. That said, the less opulent eateries (and that doesn't mean the food's not just as good) open their doors at 5 or 6 pm. After 11 pm or so, the options for a sit-down meal narrow considerably. See the boxed text 'Late-Night Eateries' for guidance.

An increasing number of restaurants have bilingual menus, but some are written only in French. Don't be bashful about asking for a translation – the waiters are used to it. One important tip: in French, an entrée is a starter, not a main course – the latter is *le plat principal*. For more menu terms, see the Language chapter.

FOOD

The most famous local specialties are smoked meat and bagels. Different altogether from pastrami, Montréal smoked meat is sold in countless delicatessens, including the city's uncrowned king of curers, Schwartz's (see Smoked Meat under The Plateau, later). More than a health-food fad, bagels enjoy an equally wide following (see the boxed text 'The Great Bagel Debate').

Oddly, genuine Québécois cuisine is relatively rare in Montréal, overshadowed by more popular (and let's admit it, refined) French dishes. A Québécois meal tends to be a hearty, cholesterol-filled affair, and might include stews with some form of potatoes, carrots or turnips; game (especially caribou); or *tourtière* (meat pie). Until the early 20th century, the tourtière was prepared exclusively from the meat of the wood pigeon, which explains why the latter is all but extinct in Québec.

You won't miss signs for *poutine,* french fries covered in cheddar curds and brown gravy and served with chicken or sausage. A favorite dessert is *pudding chômeur* (literally, 'pudding for the unemployed'), a kind of sponge cake doused in a gooey, brown-sugar sauce.

Montréal tends to be behind the curve on international food fads, but many of them have stuck around: sushi bars, Tex-Mex, fondue restaurants, fusion cuisine, designer pizzas and pasta bars are all still popular, as are gourmet coffee bars. Lasting plagues include the 99-cent pizza joints – which are a bit of a con, as only plain cheese slices cost that little. Fortunately, you shouldn't have to fall back on them, given the abundance of cheap, tasty eats.

DRINKS

In the area of nonalcoholic drinks, anyone familiar with other North American cities will find few surprises. Québecers tend to favor strong, dark coffees of the type popular in France, although the gourmet coffee craze (some say it started in Montréal) has diluted any regional trend.

Beer is a different story. Apart from the mainstream Canadian lagers such as Molson or Labatt's, Québec is home to a number of good regional and microbrewers with limited distribution. Some of the tastier brews include Boréale, St Ambroise and Belle Geule; for a doomsday kick, try Fin du Monde (End of the World), which is 9% alcohol. Expect to pay $3 to $5 at a bar or pub (around $6 per pint).

Wine is expensive by comparison, with bottles costing from around $8 in the supermarket and $20 in restaurants for a basic, drinkable vintage. You'll find plenty of Californian, French, Italian, Chilean and other New World wines, but you'd better know your stuff if Québec wine is on offer: the industry is young, and much of the tipple tastes like it.

RESTAURANTS
Vieux Montréal (Map 4)

Old Montréal is a fine place to splurge. The charm of many of these establishments is in some measure the location and restaurant decor rather than purely gastronomic excellence. Also, because this is a major tourist area, prices tend to be a little high. Nonetheless, it is such a great area that a meal out should not be resisted too strongly.

Cafés The small *Café St Paul* (143 Rue St Paul Ouest) serves burgers and sandwiches for under $5, but the club sandwich, at $7.25, is really good. It's a great place to cool your heels after a jaunt round the Old Town. **Ⓜ** Place d'Armes.

For deli sandwiches to die for, try *Olive & Gourmando Boulangerie* (☎ 872-4920, 351 Rue St Paul Ouest). These mouthwatering creations, served on the place's own crisp baguettes, include grilled grain-fed chicken with guacamole, *chipotle* (smoked chile) and mango ($7). Juices are pressed to order. Hours are 8 am to 6 pm (closed Sunday and Monday). **Ⓜ** Square Victoria.

The highly recommended *Titanic* (☎ 849-0894, 445 Rue St Pierre) is tucked in a basement. Catering to an established local clientele, the staff and atmosphere are friendly and casual, with artsy exhibits alongside the diner counter and wooden tables.

Choose from an excellent array of salads, creative sandwiches and pastas. A cream-of-vegetable soup, half-baguette brie and tomato sandwich and a coffee is $8. It's open 8 am to 4 pm weekdays. **Ⓜ** Square Victoria.

Kilimanjaro (☎ 875-2332, 39 Rue de la Commune Est) is probably the nicest café at portside, and the food's a good value too. Grab one of the shaded terrace tables and launch into one of their tasty, oversized sandwiches or burger spreads with side salad ($6 to $9). Service is friendly and quick. **Ⓜ** Place d'Armes.

French & Québécois Run by the former chef of Toqué, *Chez L'Épicier (☎ 878-2232, 311 Rue St Paul Est)* combines fine French/international dining with a gourmet grocery store. A three-course dinner – including quirky dishes such as corn and lobster oil soup, guinea hen seasoned with balsamic vinegar, and a layered chocolate dessert with orange zest, grapefruit and Campari granité – runs about $40. Cheaper one-course meals (nachos and the like, $5 to $8) are available in the wine bar. Yummy ready-to-heat dishes for two can be had from the glass case for $6 to $10. The grocery operates 11 am to 6 pm, but the restaurant opens at 5 pm. **Ⓜ** Champ de Mars.

Whether it's hearthside on an icy winter day or on the flower-filled terrace, *Le Claude Postel (☎ 875-5067, 443 Rue St Vincent)* offers top-notch atmosphere and dining, even in the heart of the tourist district. The specialty is fish, as its delectable Dover sole attests, but Québécois specialties such as grilled caribou are equally excellent. The desserts alone justify a trip. Reckon on spending $26 to $60 per head, including wine. It's open 11:30 am to 11 pm daily (closed at lunchtime on weekends). **Ⓜ** Place d'Armes or Champ de Mars.

Le Père St Vincent (☎ 397-9610, 431 Rue St Vincent) has fine multicourse meals from soup to dessert priced at $19 to $27. The tables are arranged in a series of small, intimate rooms in a 16th-century stone house, one of the oldest in Vieux Montréal. Service is incredibly friendly, and there's a good wine list. **Ⓜ** Place d'Armes or Champ de Mars.

Good for lingering over a meal is *La Sauvagine (☎ 861-3210, 115 Rue St Paul Est)*, at the corner of Rue St Vincent. Lunch prices range from $5 to $10, dinners from $15 to $23. The Dover sole is good and comes with lobster soup and escargot on the prix fixe menu. The menu includes game. Beware of the price of the wine. **Ⓜ** Place d'Armes or Champ de Mars.

Late-Night Eateries

Boustan (Map 5; ☎ 843-3576, 2020a Rue Crescent) is a Lebanese place that makes fantastic shwarma sandwiches, *shishtou* (grilled marinated beef on a skewer), dishes rolled in *takula* (a spicy red powder) and other tasty delights. Nothing like a garlicky jolt of *tsatsiki* (cucumber yogurt sauce) to bring the clubbers back to their senses. It's open till at least 2 am daily. **Ⓜ** Peel or Guy-Concordia.

Just a block south, *Arahova Souvlaki (☎ 499-0262, 1425 Rue Crescent)* has a plethora of Greek specialties in earthy surroundings. It's open until 2 am (5 am Friday and Saturday). **Ⓜ** Lucien L'Allier.

In the thick of the Plateau's nightclub district, *Restaurant Rapido du Plateau (Map 8; ☎ 284-2188, 4494 Rue St Denis)* is a café/diner that does fantastic poutine ($3.50), burgers ($5 to $8) and chicken ($8 for a half). Best of all, it's open 24 hours, seven days a week. **Ⓜ** Mont Royal.

In the Village, *Resto du Village (Map 6; ☎ 524-5404, 1310 Rue Wolfe)* serves snacks and hot meals around the clock in homey surroundings (give or take the Christmas lights). The cuisine is Canadian – minute steak, rib eye, chicken and smoked meat. Daily specials cost $7 to $8 (BYOW). **Ⓜ** Beaudry.

International The main fare is a touch pedestrian at *Les Jardins Nelson (☎ 861-5731, 407 Place Jacques Cartier)* – crêpes ($10 to $15) and pizzas ($10 to $13), but there's live classical music at lunchtime and a jazz group every evening. The place has a charming inner courtyard behind the hollow façade of a 19th-century building. Ⓜ Champ de Mars.

Cheap eats with atmosphere can be had at *Usine de Spaghetti Parisienne (☎ 866-0963, 273 Rue St Paul Est)*. Meals include fettucine with baby clams or curried beef-filet medallions (both $14). Prices include all the bread and salad you can eat. Ⓜ Champ de Mars.

For omelettes, crêpes or burgers around $8, try *EggSpectation (☎ 282-0119, 201 Rue St Jacques)*. It closes at 5 pm. Ⓜ Place d'Armes.

Chez Better (☎ 861-2617, 160 Notre Dame Est) is a branch of a European sausage house. Varieties range from mild to singeing, served with a generous dollop of sauerkraut for $8.50. The imported beer list is among the best in town, and the excellent meats remind us that the place's founder was a German immigrant who missed the good wurst back home. Ⓜ Place d'Armes or Champ de Mars.

Gibby's (☎ 282-1837, 298 Place d'Youville) is a snazzy, popular place in a 200-year-old converted stable. The specialties are steak and roast beef, although the lobster and scampi also warrant a visit. A meal costs $30 to $50 per person. Reservations are suggested, especially on weekends. If you're going all the way, you could try top wines (up to $300). Hours are 4:30 to 11 pm daily. Ⓜ Square Victoria.

Polish The *Stash Café (☎ 845-6611, 200 Rue St Paul Ouest)* serves hearty Polish cuisine in an intimate setting featuring church pews and low-hanging ceiling lamps. Don't be surprised if a customer jumps up and starts to dance with the waiters. Most mains run $11 to $18; a good set meal including standards such as pirogi and borsch costs $14. It's open daily for lunch and dinner.

Seafood Visiting *Chez Delmo (☎ 849-4061, 211 Rue Notre Dame Ouest)* is a blast from the past. The dim entrance hall is lined with two bars, 20 seats each, for the lunch crowd eager to pick up a lobster sandwich or bowl of clams (under $10) and ponder the motto on the old-fashioned tiles: 'From Wine What Sudden Friendship Springs.' Main dishes run around $28 in the evening and are served in the rather ordinary rear dining room. It's closed Monday and during lunchtime on weekends. Ⓜ Place d'Armes.

Downtown (Map 5)

Asian The tasty dishes of *Phaya Tai (☎ 933-9949, 1235 Rue Guy)* are full of color, seductive scents and the skilled use of herbs. The decor may be a touch sobering, but the incendiary peppers provide all the warmth necessary. Vegetarian main dishes are $7, and seafood and meat dishes cost $8 to $12. It's open daily for lunch and dinner. Ⓜ Guy-Concordia.

Amid a blaze of kimonos and stylish decor, *Katsura (☎ 849-1172, 2170 Rue de la Montagne)* regularly welcomes film stars, CEOs and grateful tourists to sample its excellent lunches ($8 to $14). Best take an evening table d'hôte ($27 to $37) at the monumental sushi bar. The Nipponese delicacies are prepared with the greatest care, but the ambience is glacial. It's open lunch and dinner (evening only on weekends). Ⓜ Peel or Guy-Concordia.

Cafés & Bistros The sophisticated yet cozy *Bistro Rock Détente (☎ 847-9117, 1410 Rue Peel)* is an eatery with a bar and a split-level dining room. The music is tasteful pop and rock via an excellent sound system. *Panini* (Italian sandwiches) cost $9, salads run $5 to $10 and fixed menus start at $14. It's a great place to decompress after a shopping trek. It's open until 10 pm Monday to Wednesday and until 11 pm Thursday to Saturday (closed Sunday). Ⓜ Peel.

Fast Food Just south of Rue Ste Catherine, on Blvd St Laurent, are several of the city's best-known places for french fries and hot dogs, such as *Frites Dorées (1212 Blvd St*

Laurent). Montréalers take these pedestrian items seriously. Ask for 'toasté all dress,' and you'll get the full Québec dog treatment – relish, mustard and onion, topped with chopped cabbage and on a toasted bun.

French & Québécois Montréal is renowned for its French food, and *Chez La Mère Michel (☎ 934-0473, 1209 Rue Guy)* is a fine place to confirm this reputation. This place has been around so long, an entire generation knows it as Mother Michael's. Dinner for two will set you back roughly $120, including wine, tax and tip. The three-course lunches are a treat at $17. The service, the food, the style – everything is 1st-class. It's closed Sunday and at lunchtime Saturday to Tuesday. Ⓜ Guy-Concordia.

Splurging never felt so good as at *Guy & Dodo Morali (☎ 842-3636, 1444 Rue Metcalfe).* This is a gourmet restaurant with a timeless style – leather-back chairs, wainscoting, oil paintings and black-vested waiters. Mains ($29 to $40) include a tender duck with refried potatoes and sautéed oyster mushrooms ($34.50). It's open 11:30 am to 10:30 pm daily (Saturday from 5:30 pm, closed Sunday). Ⓜ Peel.

Nestled amid a forest of skyscrapers, the Victorian villa that houses *Le Caveau (☎ 843-3661, 2063 Rue Victoria)* is like a weird apparition. You'll enjoy the table d'hôte ($12 to $15 at lunch, $16 to $20 at dinner), which may include fine courses such as glazed snails or marinated salmon. The upper dining floors are filled with French paintings and antiques. It's open for lunch and dinner weekdays and for dinner only on weekends. Ⓜ McGill.

For great French cuisine with Québécois innovations, the *Restaurant Globe (☎ 284-3823, 3451 Blvd St Laurent)* is just the ticket. Try the crisp Fundy salmon with roasted artichokes and black trumpet mushrooms ($26). The fine waiters provide impeccable but unobtrusive service, which is unusual in this touristy part of town. Add a fine wine, and you're looking at $40 per person. It's open 6 to 11 pm (until midnight from Thursday to Saturday). Ⓜ St Laurent.

Indian Part of the Bombay House chain, *Pique-Assiette (☎ 932-7141, 2051 Rue Ste Catherine Ouest)* is one of the oldest Indian restaurants in town. A few years ago, a famous Indian TV chef was brought in to revamp the menu, and his efforts paid off. The meats and vegetable curries are sublime (have a peek at the clay pots in the kitchen), and the midday buffet ($8) is a treat. Ⓜ Atwater or Guy-Concordia.

Maison de Cari (☎ 845-0326, 1433 Rue Bishop) dishes up excellent curry dinners in its cozy, casual basement quarters for $8 to $12. The Persian-style chicken dhansah is a popular item. It's open until 10 pm daily. Ⓜ Guy-Concordia.

International In an attractive converted warehouse, *EggSpectation (☎ 842-3447, 1313 Blvd de Maisonneuve Ouest)* has excellent coffees and huge, delicious lunches of omelettes, crêpes or elaborate burgers for about $8. It's open all day until 10 pm. Ⓜ Peel or Guy-Concordia.

An unexpected find for budget eaters is *Chez Parée (☎ 866-0495, 1258 Rue Stanley),* a strip joint frequented by hard-up students for the *free* buffet. All you have to do is buy a drink, sit back and enjoy the food. It's open from 11:45 am (1 pm on weekends) to 3 am daily. Ⓜ Peel or Lucien L'Allier.

Because you BYOW to the downtown branch of *Bazou (☎ 982-0853, 2004 Ave l'Hôtel de Ville)*, it's cheaper than the more opulent branch in the Village (see that section, later). It's open 11 am to 11 pm Monday to Saturday. Ⓜ St Laurent.

Italian Budget-conscious eaters should take note of *Café Presto (☎ 879-5877, 1244 Rue Stanley).* It's a cozy little bistro catering to the downtown lunch crowd. The decor is out-of-the-box Italian, with checkered tablecloths. The menu is mostly pasta – linguine, farfalle and penne, with various sauces – and all mains cost $4. Chef Rino Massironi will come out in his smock to chat and make you feel at home. It's open for lunch and dinner (closed Sunday). Ⓜ Peel or Lucien L'Allier.

Il Facolaio (☎ 879-1045, 1223 Square Phillips) fires scrumptious pizzas in its wood-burning oven with every conceivable topping for $8 to $10. The terrace is a terrific place for watching passersby and buskers on Square Phillips. Hours are 11 am to 11 pm daily. Ⓜ McGill.

In the heart of the so-called 'McGill ghetto,' *Amelio's* (☎ 845-8396, 201 Rue Milton) has been a popular student draw for decades. The generous portions of pizza and pasta cost mostly $6 to $12; a medium pizza with salad ($11) is enough to stuff two people. Lineups outside the plain flattop structure aren't unusual at 6 pm. It's open daily until 10 pm (closed Sunday). Ⓜ Place des Arts.

More often than not, the elegant *Bueno Notte* (☎ 848-0644, 3518 Blvd St Laurent) is filled with fashion victims doing the see-and-be-seen thing on the Main. Because of – or perhaps despite – its posing clientele, the chefs serve up excellent Italian and international fare, from delicate, savory pastas to sizzling Angus steaks. The table d'hôte is $12 to $18 at lunchtime, $25 to $30 in the evening. Reservations are a must on weekends. Ⓜ St Laurent, then take bus No 55.

Portuguese There's a superb seafood menu at *Ferreira Café Trattoria* (☎ 848-0988, 1446 Rue Peel), a swanky Mediterranean place with Portuguese cuisine and hand-painted porcelain tiles. It's pricey but worth it, with mains costing $18 to $39. Hours are 5 to 11 pm daily (closed Saturday at lunchtime and all day Sunday). Ⓜ Peel.

North African Run by Moroccan owner and chef Khalil, *La Maison du Bedouin* (☎ 935-0236, 1616 Rue Ste Catherine Ouest) is a great place for lunch on the 3rd floor of the Le Faubourg complex. It has a diverse and authentic North African menu, including a scrumptious *pastilla* (pastry) with almonds, chicken and a dash of rosewater ($6). Offerings also include chicken or veal *tagine* (stew) and couscous. Daily specials generally cost $4 to $6. Don't miss the sticky pastries for dessert, such as the donuts with honey ($1). Ⓜ Guy-Concordia.

In the southern end of downtown, *Le Relais des Sultans* (☎ 934-4655, 1520 Rue Notre Dame Ouest) is a highly recommended little eatery that serves great Tunisian and Italian fare. Apart from *brik* (flaky pastry pockets, deep-fried with various fillings), its brochettes are spicy and succulent. A dinner for two costs about $25 to $30. It's open lunch and dinner daily (closed Sunday). Ⓜ Lucien L'Allier, then walk or take bus No 36 west from Rue St Antoine Ouest.

Pub Food Throughout Québec, there was a long tradition of 'men only' grubby drinking establishments known as taverns. These have often been reincarnated as larger, brighter and cleaner establishments known as brasseries, with little hint of their mono-sexual past. The central area contains several such places, which are busy at noon weekdays with office and retail workers.

One to try is the old, wood-paneled *McLean's Pub* (☎ 393-3132, 1210 Rue Peel), with meals around $6. It does an excellent Reuben with a mountain of fries for $7. There's live music some evenings. Ⓜ Peel.

The *Bar-B-Barn* (☎ 931-3811, 1201 Rue Guy), usually packed at dinner and with a queue out the front – serves the best and biggest spareribs you've ever had. It's a comfortable, if small, place decked out like a barn-pub, with a zillion business cards of visitors stuck in the rafters. It also does good chicken – the only other thing on the menu. Meals cost $8 to $19, and there's parking around the back. Hours are 7 to 11 pm daily. Ⓜ Guy-Concordia.

The *Peel Pub* (☎ 844-6769, 1107 Ste Catherine Ouest) is a favored hangout of McGill students – indeed, it feels big enough to accommodate the entire student body. The atmosphere is nothing special, but its bargain-basement food (eg, a quarter chicken and ribs with salad for $7) pulls in the crowds. Pizzas start at $5 and burgers at $3. Ⓜ Peel.

Smoked Meat Hollywood stars have been known to have sandwiches flown in from *Ben's* (☎ 844-1000, 990 Blvd de Maisonneuve Ouest), an informal deli where time, if not the prices, stood still around 1950. It's full of office workers at lunchtime, and the waiters are creaking old wisecrackers. We had no regrets, however, about our basic smoked-meat sandwich – a two-inch-high pile of succulence, served with French mustard ($4.25). Bigger numbers run $7 to $8, with french fries, pickle and coffee. Peel.

Dunn's (☎ 393-3866, 1219 Square Phillips) has a pleasant covered terrace overlooking the goings-on at Square Phillips (forget about the chain-style interior). Sandwiches run $4 to $9, steaks start at $15, and snacks (chicken wings, nachos, *poutine* and so on) cost $4 to $7. Hours are 11 to midnight daily. McGill.

Reuben's (☎ 866-1029, 1116 Rue Ste Catherine Ouest), with the rows of pickled peppers in the window, does its eponymous sandwich (smoked meat, sauerkraut and melted cheese) for $7. Peel or McGill.

Steakhouses One renowned steak house is *Joe's* (☎ 842-4638, 1430 Rue Stanley). It serves dinners ranging from $11 to $18, including a baked potato or french fries and an excellent all-you-can-eat salad bar. For $8, you can have just the salad bar. The filet mignon special is an especially good value. It's open 11 am to 11 pm daily (Saturday until midnight). Peel.

Mr Steer (☎ 866-3233, 1198 Rue Ste Catherine Ouest) has been serving burgers and steaks for nearly half a century. The Mr Steer special (costing precisely $6.72) includes your choice of a quarter chicken, burger, hotdog or chili – plus a salad, fries and drink. The meat is 1st-class, but the Suzy Q fries are something special, too – crazy curly and deep-fried to perfection. The place also does big, cheap breakfasts. Hours are 7 am to 11 pm daily. Peel.

At the top end, *Queue de Cheval* (☎ 390-0090, 1221 Ave René Lévesque Ouest) serves up prime beef that's dry-aged on the premises and broiled over charcoal. Although it's not pretension-free, this place has 12 varieties of delectable steaks that span filet mignon, T-bone and thick slabs of marbled tenderloin for $28 to $40. The atmosphere is a stable-cum-wine-cellar, and despite the name, horsemeat doesn't actually appear on the menu. Lucien L'Allier.

Chinatown (Map 5)

Montréal's Chinatown is small but well entrenched, with a portion of the main street, Rue de la Gauchetière, closed to traffic (Place d'Armes). The food is mainly Cantonese, although spicier Szechuan dishes show up, and several Vietnamese places can be found. Many offer lunch specials as cheap as $6.

Cristal de Saigon (☎ 875-4275, 1068 Blvd St Laurent) is a Vietnamese diner specializing in satisfying Tonkinoise soups (meals in themselves) for about $6. It's often packed with local Chinatown residents. Across the street, *Hoang Oanh* (1071 Blvd St Laurent) serves Vietnamese submarine sandwiches.

Jardin de Jade (☎ 866-3127, 67 Rue de la Gauchetière Ouest) has an immense buffet to match its enormous seating capacity spread over several rooms. The food isn't gourmet class, but it certainly is plentiful, ranging from dim sum to Szechuan to Western pastries, and it's an all-you-can-eat bargain. Prices vary with the time of day: after

lunch, it costs $5.50; after 9 pm, it's $7.50. The food is the freshest on Saturday, which is very busy.

Sing Ping (☎ 397-9598, *74 Rue de la Gauchetière Ouest*) enjoys an excellent reputation, with its huge tables ideal for a good meal with friends before hitting the clubs along Rue St Denis. Mains average $8 to $12, with multicourse meals starting at $15.

Quartier Latin (Map 6)

Asian Soup-lovers wax lyrical at *Zyng* (☎ 284-2016, *1748 Rue St Denis*), where a bowl of delicious noodle, meat or veggie costs $5 (your choice of ingredients). The peppy interior (all bright greens and oranges) make the flavors even more vivid. Mains cost $10 to $15. It's open lunch and dinner until 10 pm weekdays and until 11 pm on weekends). ⓂBerri-UQAM.

Diners Frequently credited with the thickest, juiciest burgers in town, *La Paryse* (☎ 842-2040, *302 Rue Ontario Est*) serves them with a dazzling assortment of toppings. One favorite is the 'special' burger, with bacon and mozzarella ($5.50). The homemade fries ($2) and vegetable soups ($2.50) are terrific. It's a classic diner with neo-retro flair and is next door to the jazz club Jazzons. Hours are 11 am to 11 pm weekdays and 2 to 10:30 pm weekends. Ⓜ Berri-UQAM or Sherbrooke.

Italian A colorful working-class restaurant is *Da Giovanni* (*572 Rue Ste Catherine Est*). Spaghetti with garlic bread and Caesar salad costs less than $9. It's open until 11 pm (1 am on Saturday), but arrive before 5:30 pm to avoid lines. Ⓜ Berri-UQAM. There's another outlet (not mapped) at 690 Ste Catherine Ouest.

Vegetarian The food is priced by weight at *Le Commensal* (☎ 845-2627, *1720 Rue St Denis*), which offers good self-serve vegetarian meals, salads and desserts. The hot and cold buffet costs $1.55 per 100g. An average meal is about $9, including drink, but let yourself get carried away and your

bill will balloon. It's open 11 am to 11 pm daily (until 11:30 pm on Friday and Saturday). Ⓜ Berri-UQAM. Other outlets are at 5043 Rue St Denis and 1204 Rue McGill College (not mapped).

The Village (Map 6)

Asian Because of its excellent Vietnamese food at affordable prices, *Pho Viet* (☎ 522-4116, *1663 Rue Amherst*) is a screamingly popular place. Soups and starters cost anywhere from $2 to $4, vegetarian and grilled dishes run $7 to $9, and fixed three-course meals are $10 to $14. A Vietnamese fondue (with spiced and citronella-perfumed chicken, shrimp, and veggies) for two will set you back just $21. It's open 11 am to 3 pm and 5 to 9 pm daily (closed Saturday morning and Sunday). Ⓜ Beaudry.

Like many Japanese restaurants in North America, *Miyako* (☎ 521-5329, *1439 Rue Amherst*) has a sushi bar at the entrance, a tiny salon at the rear, lots of screens and light-colored wood, and waiters in kimonos. The sushi and sashimi (squid, lobster, mackerel, tuna and more) are blended with Californian flavors, all impeccably prepared. Figure on spending $25 per head, including sake. It's open 11:30 am (5:30 pm on Sunday) to at least 9:30 pm daily. Ⓜ Beaudry.

As for Thai food, the ever-fresh ingredients and boat-shaped bar at *Bato Thai* (☎ 524-6705, *1310 Rue Ste Catherine Est*) get it rave reviews. Daily specials cost $7 to $8, and all mains are under $10 (eg, beef curry with coconut milk and basil leaves for $9). It's hard to shake the tourist feel about the place, but the food's so good, it hardly matters. Hours are 11 am to 3 pm and 5 to 10 pm daily (closed at lunchtime on weekends). Ⓜ Beaudry.

Brazilian The bright-yellow *Bijú* (☎ 522-1554, *1257 Rue Amherst*) serves up spicy Brazilian, Mexican and Cajun lunches starting at $9 and dinners from $13 to $22 (BYOW). You might try the alligator in coconut sauce and *feijoada*, a Brazilian national dish (a bean, pork and beef stew served with collards). Hours are 5 to 11 pm daily (closed Sunday). Ⓜ Beaudry.

Cafés & Bistros With huge pasty faces on its façade, *Kilo* (☎ 596-3933, 1495 Rue Ste Catherine Est) does creamy cakes and tarts to die for ($3.50 to $6.25), usually baked with a shot of Grand Marnier or some other liquid decadence. It also does hot sandwiches, snacks and salads for $6 to $8. This is a great place to people-watch through the ceiling-high windows. Beaudry.

Girly's (☎ 598-7070, 1271 Rue Amherst) is a café for lesbians – nothing but. Its standard fare includes burgers and salads (both $6 to $8), as well as breakfast. Hours are 10 am to 10 pm daily (closed Monday). Beaudry.

French An excellent restaurant with the air of a Parisian bistro can be found at *Au Petit Extra* (☎ 527-5552, 1690 Rue Ontario Est). Dishes tend to be simple, but the flavors and textures are distinct. Fixed menus run about $14 to $21 (such as the filet de mahi-mahi vinaigrette in champagne sauce for $17.25). Service is professional and the wine list copious. If you can still move afterward, check out the attached club Lion d'Or.

Papineau, and then take bus No 45 north to Rue Ontario Est.

In the thick of the Village action, *Resto Bisous* (☎ 526-2552, 1327 Rue Ste Catherine Est) exudes an air of unhurried elegance, with the soft lighting of Japanese lamps and artwork on the bare brick walls. A fixed three-course menu costs $10 to $19. The duck à l'orange ($18) couldn't be more tender. Hours are 11:30 am to 3 pm and 5 to 11 pm daily (open at 9 am for breakfast on weekends). Beaudry.

International Based on an automobile theme, *Bazou* (☎ 526-4940, 1310 Blvd de Maisonneuve Est) is a fusion restaurant with stylish decor (the high-backed sofas are actually comfy) and a huge dining terrace. The menu spans French, Mexican, Indian and Asian cuisine. The name means 'wreck,' but there's nothing broken-down about the food – eg, the blackened swordfish with pineapple and fresh coriander salsa ($19). Fixed menus run $6.50 to $10 at lunchtime and $14.50 to $26 in the evening. It's open 11 am to 11 pm Monday to Saturday. Beaudry.

Kilo café in the Village

The Plateau (Map 8)

Your first encounter with the Plateau is as you move north from downtown. As you cross Rue Sherbrooke, the slightly seedy, bohemian air of the Quartier Latin gives way to the chichi crowd of upper Rue St Denis and Blvd St Laurent, where you'll find some of the city's slickest dining establishments. Just north of there, around where Rue Prince Arthur intersects those two streets, the Plateau begins in earnest.

Rue Prince Arthur Est is a small, old residential street that has been converted into a dining and entertainment enclave. The restaurant segment runs west from Carré St Louis (just north of Rue Sherbrooke) to a block west of Blvd St Laurent. Many small, inexpensive and mostly ethnic restaurants line the pedestrian street. Greek and Vietnamese restaurants are most prominent, but the selection includes French and Polish too. Most of the restaurants here aren't licensed, so BYOW.

Farther north, around the 4000 block of Blvd St Laurent, Ave Duluth is a narrow old street (once a red-light district) that has been redone as a restaurant center, much like Rue Prince Arthur. From just east of Blvd St Laurent, running east to Rue St Denis and beyond, there are numerous good-value Greek, Italian and Asian eateries. A complete dinner at many of them runs $12 to $18.

For eateries within easy walking distance of Rue St Denis, we've provided Métro stations. For ones closer to Blvd St Laurent, take bus No 55 north along that street (the same line runs south along Rue St Urbain, the next main street to the west). Out-of-the-way places have Métro and bus links in the listings.

Asian The small, unpretentious Japanese eatery *Sushi et Boulettes* (℡ 848-9474, 3681 Blvd St Laurent) dishes up lunch specials such as soup and beef teriyaki ($7) and a dazzling array of sushi and sashimi for $3.25 to $4.25. Combination plates cost under $10. Hours are 11 am to 11 pm daily (until 3 am Thursday to Saturday).

Like Malaysian food? Run by a former barkeeper of Blvd St Laurent, *Nantha's*

University Cafeterias

If you're out of pocket, Montréal's half-dozen universities all have student cafeterias where you can easily eat for $5 or less. You may need to show a student ID, although some counters don't check. Among them, *McGill University Student Union* (Map 5; 3480 McTavish) is open until 8 pm daily. Ⓜ Peel. The *École de Technologie Superieur* (Map 5; 1100 Rue Notre Dame Ouest) has cheap eats in the foyer café, behind the exhibits of race cars and planes (open at lunchtime only). Ⓜ Bonaventure.

Kitchen (℡ 845-4717, 9 Ave Duluth Est) is an experience. The mix of flavors and textures is subtle, with ingredients such as basil, ginger, lemon grass, tumeric root and fresh coriander. The chilis can be incendiary, especially if you venture into the curries. You'll pay about $15 to $18 per head. It's open until 9:30 pm daily.

L' Harmonie d'Asie (℡ 289-9972, 65 Ave Duluth Est) serves up good-value Vietnamese dishes between $8 and $15. For an idea of what's at best, try the chop suey with okra soup and vermicelli or the crispy grilled duck. The spicy soups and starters are also excellent ($4 to $6). On weekends, the tiny place gets intimate or cramped, depending on your point of view. Hours are 5 to 10 pm daily.

Bagels Superb hot bagels can be bought at two authentic open-fire bakeries, both of which are open 24 hours a day, seven days a week. It's more exciting once you realize you're buying into an institution (see the boxed text).

The *St Viateur Bagel & Cie* (℡ 528-6361, 1127 Ave du Mont Royal Est) is a splendid café that serves up grilled bagels with soup or salad. The most popular are the traditional smoked lox with cream cheese ($8) and roast beef with Swiss cheese, olive oil and tomato ($7). The fillings are generous and the Italian coffee sublime. It's open 6 am to midnight daily. Ⓜ Mont Royal.

PLACES TO EAT

Cafés & Bistros Throbbing with techno, *Caffé Elektra* (☎ 288-0853, *24 Ave des Pins Est*) is a tiny diner that serves awesome roast-beef salads ($8) and sandwiches ($5 to $7) prepared with great care. The creamy cakes and Italian coffees are just as good. It's open until 11 pm daily.

Café Santropol (☎ 842-3110, *3990 Rue St Urbain*) is the ideal spot for reading, writing postcards or just plain procrastinating. It's also known for its utterly bizarre sandwiches – peanut butter and roast beef, for example. The hearty soups are good, too, and the beautiful rear garden is a choice spot when the weather's nice. The owners run a Meals-on-Wheels program for senior citizens, and a portion of profits goes to charity. You can easily have a meal and drink

The Great Bagel Debate

The Montréal bagel has a long and venerable history. It all started in 1915 when Isadore and Fanny Shlafman, Jews from the Ukraine, opened a tiny bakery on Roy Street in the Plateau district. They made the yeast bread rings according to a recipe they'd brought from Kiev, where Isadore Shlafman's father was a baker. By 1919, they started the Montréal Bagel Bakery in a wooden shack in a lane just off Blvd St Laurent, a few doors from Schwartz's delicatessen.

After WWII, many Holocaust survivors emigrated to Montréal, and the market for bagels boomed. Isadore Schlafman decided to build a bakery in the living room of his house at 74 Ave Fairmount, where he opened Fairmount Bagel in 1950 (see the Mile End section of this chapter). Meanwhile, Myer Lemkowicz, a Polish Jew who survived the concentration camp at Auschwitz, went on to establish the competing St Viateur bakery – also known as La Maison du Bagel – in 1957 (see that listing under Mile End). A legendary rivalry was born, and a score of other bagel bakeries sprang up in their wake.

Ask any Montréaler whose bagel is the best, and passions will flare. Year-in and year-out, critics visit the main bagel bakeries to chat, chew and cogitate; in recent years, La Maison du Bagel had tended to edge out Fairmount for the No 1 slot. Lesser entries are dismissed with scorn – 'hockey puck' is a common assessment.

One thing locals do agree on: Montréal's bagels are superior to their New York cousins. Montréal bagels are lighter, sweeter and crustier, chewy but not dense, thanks to the use of an enriched eggy dough that looks almost like batter. The dough doesn't rise much before cooking, and the bagels are formed by hand and boiled in a honey-and-water solution before baking (ideally, in a wood-burning oven). The dry heat and the wood smoke cook the bagels to a crusty, near-charred perfection.

But are they really tastier than New York bagels? When it comes down to it, the standards are entirely different. Montréalers tout lightness, while natives of the Big Apple often complain that their own bagels aren't dense enough. Nonetheless, it's telling that your author met a Manhattan resident schlepping a dozen Montréal bagels back home to compare – and plenty of other New Yorkers apparently do the same.

for under $10. Take bus No 55 north on Blvd St Laurent to Ave des Pins, and walk two blocks west, then north on Rue St Urbain.

The shady, wraparound terrace at *Café Cherrier* (☎ 843-4308, 3635 Rue St Denis) is filled to bursting in the summer. This classic Paris-style bistro café serves snacks and light meals for $7 to $12; it also has a good table d'hôte for $13 to $17. Its most popular item, however, is atmosphere. It's open all day and serves breakfast from 8 am (9 am on weekends), as well as brunch. Ⓜ Sherbrooke.

Brûlerie St Denis (☎ 286-9158, 3967 Rue St Denis) makes superb coffees, roasting the beans on the premises. Try the strawberry cheesecake ($4). The terrace is a great place to nurse a cup of java and plan your day. Ⓜ Sherbrooke.

Bookworms will love *Porté Disparu* (☎ 524-0271, 957 Rue Mont Royal Est), with shelves of volumes against a bare brick wall. Patrons play chess, scrabble or cards against a background of Québec music and (in winter) poetry and philosophy readings. Its café fare has a philosophical twist (sandwiches with names such as 'Optimist' and 'Libertine'). It's open lunchtime till late. Ⓜ Mont Royal.

Fast Food The delicious smell of *Coco Rico* (☎ 849-5554, 3907 Blvd St Laurent) bathes the entire area around its little abode. It has a variety of salads, but its fame comes from its superb broiled chicken ($4.50 for a quarter, with broiled potatoes and salad). There's only a long counter and flimsy bar stools inside, but most people just pick up their orders while cruising the Main.

French & Québécois One of the hottest, trendiest places in town is *Toqué!* (☎ 499-2084, 3842 Rue St Denis). Québec chefs Normand Laprise and Christin La Marche get rave reviews for their superfresh, innovative fusion menu that blends organic ingredients into eclectic dishes (the name, incidentally, means 'crazy'). It's elegant, with minimalist decor resembling an exhibition room, and expensive – in the $100-for-two

range, with wine. Main dishes average $29 to $32. Ⓜ Sherbrooke.

To savor authentic Québécois cuisine in typical Montréal atmosphere, try *La Binerie Mont Royal* (☎ 285-9078, 367 Rue Mont Royal Est). The pork and beans and pudding chômeur are the great specialties. A meal shouldn't cost more than $7, and takeouts are even cheaper. It's open 6 am to 9 pm (closed at dinnertime on weekends). Ⓜ Mont Royal.

Ma-am-m Bolduc (☎ 527-3884, 4351 Ave de Lorimier) is a neighborhood eatery serving plenty of mainstays of Québécois cuisine: meatball stew, tourtière, and more poutines than you can shake a chicken leg at. Most mains cost $6 to $7. This comfortable joint is run by Martin Bolduc, son of the famous founder Madame. It's open 7 am to at least 9 pm (8 am to 10 pm Saturday and from 9 am Sunday). Ⓜ Papineau, then walk one block east to Ave de Lorimier; then take bus No 10 north to Ave Marie Anne.

Greek Rue Prince Arthur Est has several cut-rate Greek places that offer excellent value, both at lunch and dinner. Tasty, if unadventurous, dinners can be had at *La Casa Grècque* (☎ 842-6098, 200 Rue Prince Arthur Est) for about $20 for two. Ⓜ Sherbrooke.

A couple of blocks north, *La Maison Grècque* (☎ 842-0969, 450 Ave Duluth Est) is a sprawling, busy eatery with a popular outdoor area. Its cheap fixed meals include chicken oregano filet, rainbow trout or filet mignon ($8 to $11). It's BYOW, and there's a dépanneur nearby. Ⓜ Sherbrooke or Mont Royal.

Comfortably urbane *Ouzeri* (☎ 845-1336, 4690 Rue St Denis) is recommended for its contemporary twist on traditional Greek food. Considering its oh-so-cool decor and multiple patrons dressed in black, dinner for two before wine isn't that expensive (about $35). There's an extensive wine list, including French, Chilean and Italian vintages. Ⓜ Mont Royal.

Latin American The little *Chez José Boulangerie* (☎ 845-0603, 173 Ave Duluth Est) serves up fresh Latin American and

Provençal empanadas for just $3. The place is known for its brunchtime fruit crêpes and omelettes, but the daily soups ($3) are a real treat (eg, tomato and blue cheese, or gazpacho). Ask for José's homemade salsa – some customers even put it on their sandwiches. It's open for lunch only. **Ⓜ** Sherbrooke or Mont Royal; or take bus No 55 north along Blvd St Laurent and get off near Ave Duluth.

North African An inviting little eatery with a split personality, *Kamela Couscous* (☎ 526-0881, 1227 Rue Marie Anne Est) specializes in Algerian/Tunisian and Italian cuisine. Its 30-odd varieties of pizza ($6 to $8) come with a delicious thin crust – don't miss the spicy *merguez* (beef and mutton sausage). Pastas cost $7 to $8 and are nicely complemented with homemade sauces. The tasty couscous ($7 to $14) comes in vegetarian, merguez and grilled-chicken varieties. Hours are 4 to 11 pm daily. **Ⓜ** Mont Royal.

Polish Some of the best comfort food in the Plateau can be had at *Mazurka* (☎ 844-3539, 64 Rue Prince Arthur Est), and it's dirt cheap. The daily specials are around $6, featuring pierogi and meat or cheese blintzes (filled pancake rolls), or Polish sausage. The set meals include homemade soup and coffee or tea. It's a sprawling place, with nearly 200 seats over four levels and down-home paintings from the Old Country on the walls. Hours are 11:30 am to midnight daily.

Portuguese Step up to the charcoal grill at the counter of *Rotisserie Portugalia* (☎ 282-1519, 34 Rue Rachel Ouest), a meatlover's mecca. Its wonderful *churrasco* chicken (ie, marinated and grilled Portuguese-style) costs $16, including french fries and salad ($9.50 for takeout). The menu is brief, but everything's succulent, including ribs ($6.50), cod ($10) or steak ($6). This is a quintessential corner eatery, with pictures of locals and knickknacks from the owner's stays in Angola. It's open for lunch and dinner until 8 pm daily.
  Bistro Duluth (☎ 287-9096, 121 Ave Duluth Est) is another place renowned for its excellent chicken dishes ($7 to $17). There's also an impressive selection of port and whiskey. It's open for lunch and dinner – grab a patio seat in summer across from the graffiti-filled wall. **Ⓜ** Sherbrooke or Mont Royal.

Seafood Run by a friendly French/Italian couple, *Il Sole* (☎ 282-4996, 3627 Blvd St Laurent) is an ideal spot for a candlelight dinner. The focus is fish and traditional pasta, simple but well-prepared, with little touches such as an *amuse bouche* (a prestarter) of *bruschetta* (garlic toast with tomatoes). Our veal with prosciutto was cooked to perfection, but the sole stuffed with salmon also looked tempting. Mains average $20 to $25; count on paying $80 for two, including wine. It's open evenings only.

Smoked Meat Patrons talk in hushed tones about *Schwartz's* (☎ 842-4813, 3895 Blvd St Laurent), which is widely considered to serve the best smoked meat in Montréal, if not in all of Canada. It's an old-time Hebrew deli staffed by veteran waiters, and lineups are common for its fantastic sandwiches – smoked brisket, duck, chicken and turkey, all piled high on sourdough rye bread ($6 to $9). The Romanian-style meat is cured on the premises and aged without chemicals. Don't bother with the lean grade, which is like drinking light beer – ask for medium fat, and you'll come away smiling. Hours are 9 am to 12:30 am (1:30 am on Friday, 2:30 am on Saturday).

ROBERT REID

Dream sandwich: smoked meat and bread

Vegetarian Macrobiotic (ie, made with ingredients that are locally grown and minimally processed) can be had at *Bio Délices Inc* (☎ 528-8843, 1327a Ave du Mont Royal Est). Soups are $2, and the mains cost $3 to $5.50. The changing menu features veggie items such as ratatouille, pastas and quiches, but there's also a remarkable grain-fed chicken. The excellent desserts ($1 to $3) are favorite takeouts. There are only two small tables and a small serving counter, and the decor is determinedly simple. It's open until 5 pm (7 pm on Thursday and Friday, 5 pm on Saturday, closed Sunday). Ⓜ Mont Royal, then bus No 97 east to Rue de Brébeuf.

Little Italy (Map 9)

Good Italian restaurants can be found throughout Montréal, but few emulate the Old Country with as much determination as those in tiny, bustling Little Italy. On summer evenings, crowds fill the eateries and sidewalk cafes along the main artery, Blvd St Laurent, and a festive mood prevails into the wee hours. Atmosphere tends to come first, but a few establishments dish up excellent food to boot.

Italian On the main drag, *Café International* (☎ 495-0067, 6714 Blvd St Laurent) does fantastic panini, salads and pizzas (all $6 to $9). The coffees are expectedly good and freshly ground. As the day progresses, the patrons who come to read a newspaper or meet with friends and family melt away, and the place becomes a stage for the see-and-be-seen, especially at streetside. It's open 7 am to 1 am (3 am on Friday and Saturday). Ⓜ Jean Talon.

Il Mulino (☎ 273-5776, 236 Rue St Zotique Est) is perhaps the top Italian restaurant in town, offering a breathtaking array of specialties in the range of $20 to $35. Try the vegetarian starter plate ($10), which includes the likes of sautéed peppers and olives, stuffed eggplant and grilled mushrooms, before moving on to baby lamb chops, which are so tender they practically cut themselves. Service is impeccable. The only shortcoming is the decor, which is rather anonymous. Meals are served for lunch and dinner (evenings only on Saturday, closed Sunday). Ⓜ Jean Talon.

Lebanese The bistro ambience and unbeatable prices make *Le Petit Alep* (☎ 270-9361, 191 Rue Jean Talon Est) a student favorite. The hummus, salads and *muhammara* (spread made of walnuts, garlic, bread crumbs, pomegranate syrup and cumin) are all full of color and startling flavors. Most mains are under $10, and everything tastes better on the cozy dining terrace. It's open daily until 11 pm. Ⓜ Jean Talon.

Mile End (Map 9)

This district boasts some of the city's most expensive homes, so little surprise that it's also a hub of swanky restaurants, especially along Rue Bernard and Ave Laurier. However, there are a few good, cheap eateries and cafés if you look hard. And while you're up here, do not, under any circumstances, miss sampling some of Montréal's legendary bagels.

Bagels The *Fairmount Bagel* (☎ 272-0667, 74 Ave Fairmount Ouest) carries oodles of modern bagel variations, including pumpernickel and cumin, sun-dried tomato and cinnamon raisin. They also make their own matzo boards and have some New York–style creations such as the 'bozo bagel,' which is triple the normal size. Ⓜ Laurier.

Seek out *La Maison du Bagel* (☎ 276-8044, 263 Ave St Viateur Ouest) for the real deal. A dozen freshly made plain, poppy-seed or sesame-seed bagels cost $4.25, and they are perfectly crusty, chewy and slightly sweet. Also known as the St Viateur bagel shop, this place has a reputation stretching across Canada and beyond – check out the posted newspaper articles from places around the world. Take the No 55 bus north along Blvd St Laurent to Ave St Viateur.

Cafés For a touch of history, seek out *Wilensky's Light Lunch* (☎ 271-0247, 34 Ave Fairmount Ouest). It's a neighborhood fixture immortalized in Mordecai Richler's novel *The Apprenticeship of Duddy Kravitz.* Check out the photos from 1932 to the present. It's famous for its rickety wooden stools and daily specials (mainly grilled sandwiches and burgers) for just a couple of bucks. There's no liquor license, so you can go for a hand-pumped soda. It closes at 4 pm weekdays (closed weekends). Ⓜ Laurier.

French In the most fashionable part of Mile End, *La Chronique* (☎ *271-3095, 99 Ave Laurier Ouest)* tempts the trendy set with innovative dishes and a spirited yellow decor. Enjoy tender scallops on fried yam or spiced salmon ($8) before launching into a delicious main, such as blackened

Breakfast Favorites

Breakfast falls broadly into two camps: continental and the more voluminous Québécois or English variety. A continental breakfast will set you back a couple of bucks and typically consists of croissants or crusty bread and butter, jam and a mug of stiff coffee. For more variety – and bulk – the Québécois breakfast can include eggs, toast, bacon, sausage, potatoes, baked beans, fruit and coffee, on a sliding scale of about $3 to $8. Countless other breakfast styles are available, of course – you won't have to look far for bagels, pancakes or French toast. Many places in this chapter serve breakfast, but we've listed a few personal favorites here.

A sleek, retro '50s diner, *Beauty's (Map 8; ☎ 849-8883, 93 Ave Mont Royal Ouest)* cooks what is possibly Montréal's best breakfast in an atmosphere that's all New York. Ask for 'The Special' – a toasted bagel with lox, cream cheese, tomato and onion ($6). From the freshly squeezed juice to the piping hot eggs, sausage and pancakes, it'll be hard to go anyplace else once you've tried it. The Sunday brunch is legendary. Hours are 7 am to 5 pm daily (Sunday from 8 am). Ⓜ Mont Royal, or take bus No 55 north up Blvd St Laurent and get off at Ave du Mont Royal.

A popular student hangout a few blocks east of McGill University, *Place Milton (Map 5; ☎ 285-0011, 220 Rue Milton)* is great value. The breakfast – $3 for two eggs, toast and coffee – goes down well in this relaxed diner or out back on the garden patio. Have a peek from the street entrance at the flour-dusted chefs in the kitchen. It's open 7 am to 5 pm. Ⓜ Place des Arts.

In the Quartier Latin, *Café Croissant de Lune (Map 6; ☎ 843-8146, 1765 Rue St Denis)* is a great place for breakfast. A café au lait and one or two of the fresh sweet buns or croissants, served in the sun on the street-front terrace, will hold you over for hours. It's open all day until 9 pm. Ⓜ Berri-UQAM.

Le Toasteur (Map 8; ☎ 527-8500, 950 Rue Roy Est) does a variety of huge, straightforward breakfasts all day that will keep you going through the afternoon. Try the Toasteur Special: two eggs, two meats, baked beans, French toast and a pancake for $8. The stained glass, flowers and mirrors provide a suitable olde-worlde ambience. It's open 7 am to 4 pm (to 5 pm on weekends). Ⓜ Sherbrooke.

The *Green Spot (Map 5; ☎ 932-2340, 3041 Rue Notre Dame Ouest)*, near Atwater Market, resembles a classic truck stop, with miniature jukeboxes at your booth and waiters who talk like they've heard it all. The fantastic breakfast specials run until 11 am (later on weekends), eg, two eggs with sausage, fried potatoes, toast, baked beans and melon slices ($3). It is open 5 am to midnight (continuously from Friday morning until Sunday midnight). Ⓜ Lionel Groulx.

The down-home Québécois place Ma-am-m Bolduc does breakfasts all day – a great value for two eggs, toast and coffee ($3) or French toast with fruit, maple syrup and coffee ($4.60). See French & Québécois, under The Plateau, for the listing.

EggSpectation serves up cheap, belt-busting breakfasts starting at $4. Not that you won't be tempted to spend more: the French-toast special with fruit and English cream is tough to beat ($8). For listings, see International under Vieux Montréal and Downtown & Chinatown.

breast of duck with shrimps ($22). It's top-end food at mid-range prices; expect to pay at least $30 per head, plus wine. It's open for lunch and dinner Tuesday to Saturday. Ⓜ Laurier.

Greek On Ave du Parc, running north up beyond the mountain, there are numerous more traditional-style Greek restaurants (no kebabs), many specializing in fish.

Madonna is among the stars who've dined at *Milos* (☎ 272-3522, 5357 Ave du Parc), a casual but expensive place, with stucco walls, starched tablecloths and refrigerated counters of mouthwatering fish and fruits. A dinner for two is around $110, including a range of Greek appetizers. More economical meals can be had by groups of four or more, because you select and order a whole fish, which is priced by the pound (generally $24 to $34). Ⓜ Laurier, or take bus No 80 on Ave du Parc toward Ave St Viateur.

Japanese Even local Japanese flock to *Kotori* (☎ 270-0355, 5468 Ave du Parc), which serves up authentic Japanese food at great prices in simple, tasteful surroundings. The sushi and sashimi are as delectable as the starters ($2.25 to $4) and the combination plates ($5.50 to $11.50). Its fish wholesaler also supplies Japanese restaurants in Montréal. It's open for lunch and dinner until 10 pm Tuesday to Saturday, and for dinner on Sunday (closed Monday). Ⓜ Laurier, or take bus No 80 on Ave du Parc toward Ave St Viateur.

Seafood For terrific mussels ($9 to $11) in a very French place, try *Le Troquet* (☎ 271-6789, 106 Ave Laurier Ouest). The Neapolitain, which consists of sausages and mussels in beer sauce, is great. They also serve panini, soups and salads, and there's a good selection of imported beers. There is live music, mostly jazz and blues, on weekends. Hours are 10 am to midnight (until 3 am Thursday to Saturday). Ⓜ Laurier.

Mussels are also the star at *La Moulerie* (☎ 273-8132, 1249 Rue Bernard Ouest), which is renowned for its 20-odd ways of serving the mollusks. Main dishes including fish and meats are about $15 and there's a pleasant patio. It's open lunch and dinner to at least 11 pm daily. Ⓜ Outremont, then bus No 160 east to Rue Bernard.

SELF-CATERING
Supermarkets
For a meal or making up your own, try shopping around *Le Faubourg* (Map 5; ☎ 939-3663, 1606 Rue Ste Catherine Ouest). This Parisian-style mall-cum-market includes a bakery, liquor store and a fabulous food court on the 3rd floor. It's open 9 am to 9 pm daily. Ⓜ Guy-Concordia.

Among the supermarkets in town, *Provigo Supermarket* (Map 5; ☎ 932-3756, 1953 Rue Ste Catherine Ouest) is huge and well stocked and has wonderful deli counters with fried chicken and smoked-meat sandwiches. It's open 8 am to 2:30 am daily. Ⓜ Guy-Concordia.

In the Village, there's a large outlet of *Metro* (Map 6; ☎ 525-5090, 1955 Rue Ste Catherine Est), a supermarket open 7:30 am to 2 am daily.

In Little Italy (Map 9), you'll find loads of well-stocked groceries, butchers and cheese shops on Blvd St Laurent, a few blocks south of Jean Talon. In the Plateau (Map 8), the section of Blvd St Laurent between Ave des Pins and Ave Mont Royal is another segment that's chockablock with grocery stores. The neighborhood is mainly Portuguese, but there are plenty of Latin American restaurants, music shops and newspaper stores, as well as European delis, kosher stores and Middle Eastern shops – all shoulder-to-shoulder and vying for business.

Toward the West Island is the *National Cheese Factory Outlet* (Map 2; ☎ 364-5353, 9001 Salley), in LaSalle. It sells meats and olive oil, as well as a huge selection of cheeses. It's open Saturday only.

Markets
There are three fresh markets where farmers sell their produce directly, and you can get meat, cheese, fish and just about anything else. Most sites have indoor sections that stay open all winter. Hours are uniformly 8 am to 6 pm Monday to Wednesday (until

PLACES TO EAT

Montréal is home to many fantastic fresh farmers markets.

Moisson (☎ 931-6540), on the ground floor and with dozens of bread varieties stowed in huge baskets and wall racks. Its cheery café has unbeatable cakes and lovely French wrought-iron chairs.

The **Marché de Maisonneuve** *(Map 2; ☎ 253-3993, 4445 Rue Ontario Est)* is in the east end of the city, outside the original market center, in the beautiful Beaux Arts building girded by pretty gardens. There are about 20 farm stalls and a new building housing a dozen vendors of meat, cheese, fresh vegetables, tasty pastries and pastas.

Located in the heart of Little Italy, the **Jean Talon Market** *(Map 9; ☎ 277-1588, 7075 Rue Casgrain)* is more ethnically varied and is the city's largest market. There are some 250 market stalls on a huge square ringed by shops stocking produce year-round. The selection is overwhelming, and you're expected to haggle over the fruits, vegetables, eggs, potted plants, herbs and (of course) maple syrup.

For fresh fish, there's no beating **Waldman Plus** *(Map 8; ☎ 285-8747, 76 Rue Roy Est)*. This Montréal landmark supplies many of the city's hotels and restaurants, but you'll still find some extremely good buys. The volume and variety will make your head spin, with tanks of lobsters, fresh shrimp, oysters, skate, cod both fresh and salted, crab and smoked fish from around the world. It also runs a little restaurant serving fish delicacies next door. The market is open daily until 6 pm (9 pm on Thursday and Friday); the restaurant closes at 11 pm.

9 pm Thursday and Friday, until 6 pm Saturday and until 5 pm Sunday).

Atwater Market (Map 5; ☎ 935-5716, 138 Atwater), near the Canal de Lachine, has scores of vendors outside and high-class delis and specialty shops inside, in the tiled, vaulted hall under the clock tower. You'll find some of Montréal's best butchers and cheese merchants here. There's also a fantastic *boulangerie* (bakery), Premiere

Entertainment

Even rival Torontonians will admit it: Montréal's nightlife is the liveliest in Canada. Nightclubs serve alcohol until 3 am – the longest opening hours in the country – and the variety of these establishments is astounding. Most places don't start humming until after 11 pm, and expect to line up and be mustered. The dress code may not be as strict as in New York or Los Angeles, but ripped denims and sneakers won't do at the smarter *boites* (clubs).

Montréal is also a good place for raves – some people even drive up from New England to catch one. Check the flyers in record stores, or do a basic search on the Web. Details of venues are usually announced at the last minute.

Many establishments are multifaceted. Pubs with traditional British or Irish names may have a great dance floor, while some clubs have bars that are attractions in themselves. For live music, many bars and clubs have eclectic programs featuring rock, pop, folk and alternative groups. For blues and jazz clubs, see the Montréal Jazz special section.

The Downtown area around Rue Crescent, Rue de la Montagne and Rue Bishop tends to be Anglo-Saxon oriented, whereas the French crowd parties on Rue St Denis and Blvd St Laurent. It's fun to wander either district at night, maybe have a beer and people-watch. A lot of the action has shifted from downtown to the Plateau, to the many clubs on upper Blvd St Laurent and upper Rue St Denis.

Rue Ste Catherine, especially in the segment between Rue St Urbain and Rue St Denis, has quite an array of straight and gay strip clubs where staff dancers, even couples, take it all off. They're tolerated as part of the landscape – remember that Montréal was known as 'Sin City' in the 1920s.

The *Mirror* and *Hour* are free weeklies focused on culture, arts and entertainment, with reviews of films and restaurants, listings of what's on and some humorous columns. The French-language equivalents are *Voir* and *Ici*. All these publications are laid out in public places, bars and restaurants. Places des Arts also publishes the monthly *Calendrier des Spectacles* of performing arts events. *Montréal Scope* is published every two months, with listings among reams of advertisements. The monthly *Nightlife* is good for hot clubs and music trends.

The Friday and Saturday editions of the Montréal *Gazette* also have club and entertainment listings, as does the French-language *La Presse*. An agenda of gay and lesbian events appears in the bilingual *Village*. *Fugues* is a free monthly booklet for the gay and lesbian scene (in French, but with easy-to-read club listings).

Call Info-Arts Bell (☎ 790-2787) for details of theater, shows and other events. For major pop and rock concerts, shows, festivals and sporting events, purchase tickets from the box office or call Admission (☎ 790-1245 or 1-800-361-4595). Ticketmaster (☎ 790-1111) sells tickets to Théâtre St Denis (see the Theater section, later). For Place des Arts events, call or visit the box office next to the Place des Arts Métro station. You can pay by credit card at all of these venues.

Tam-Tam Jam

On Sunday afternoons in summer, 'hippie' crowds collect for the legendary 'tam tam' concerts at the edge of Parc du Mont Royal (Map 7). Go to the Georges Étienne Cartier monument, opposite Parc Jeanne Mance, at Ave du Parc and Ave Duluth. There'll be droves of percussionists – tireless in their dedication, as some riffs go on for an hour or more – as well as snack vendors, alternative handicrafts and a fantastic atmosphere.

DISCOS & CLUBS
Vieux Montréal (Map 4)

***Les Deux Pierrots** (☎ 861-1686, 104 Rue St Paul Est)* is a huge two-story club that's been around for the best part of three decades. The public is encouraged to sing along in the French chansons. The cover charge is usually around $3. It's open Thursday to Saturday and occasionally on other nights.

Its sister club next door, ***Le Pierrot***, features live rock bands on Friday and Saturday nights in summer. Ⓜ Champ de Mars or Place d'Armes.

Downtown (Map 5)

You'll find a jet stream of yuppies at ***737 Altitude** (☎ 397-0737, 1 Place Ville Marie)*, on the 43rd floor. Try pre-dinner drinks on the two terraces – the skyline won't disappoint. One floor up, there's a dance floor, and an overpriced club restaurant is a level above that. There's a Latin American dance contest every Monday night ($8). It's closed Wednesday. Ⓜ McGill.

***Sphinx** (☎ 843-5775, 1426 Rue Stanley)*, an alternative/gothic/retro dance bar, has varied recorded music nightly (which is also broadcast on the Web). There may be a line, which is usually staged to make the place look even more popular than it already is. Some nongoths mix with the standard *Night of the Living Dead* clientele. The cover is $6. Ⓜ Peel.

Students, alternafreaks and all manner of trendies go to ***Foufounes Electriques** (☎ 844-5538, 87 Rue Ste Catherine Est)*, a renowned bastion of underground music (the name means 'electric buttocks'). There's a massive terrace, two floors with lots of TV screens and some pool tables. The place has some bizarre touches – Egypto/sci-fi art, weird backlighting in the aquarium room and a pit (don't ask). The café-bar is open 3 pm to 3 am daily; the dance floor opens at 10 pm. Ⓜ St Laurent.

***Salsathèque** (1220 Rue Peel)* is a bright, busy, dressy place featuring large live Latin bands who pump out infectious music – some patrons are phenomenal dancers. It's open Wednesday to Sunday. There are free salsa lessons on Wednesday nights, and the cover is $5 on Friday and Saturday. In the summer, it's a hangout for the more mobile members of the Montréal Expos. Ⓜ Peel.

To shake with the multitudes, visit ***Metropolis** (☎ 844-3500, 59 Rue Ste Catherine Est)*, which has Canada's largest dance floor (capacity 2500). Housed in a former Art Deco cinema, this place features live bands and DJs, bars spread over three floors and dazzling sound and light shows. There's no set schedule, so check the listings for what's on. It's open Friday and Saturday only, until 3 am – expect lines from 11 pm. Buy tickets at the box office around the corner at 1413 Rue St Dominique. Ⓜ St Laurent.

***Isotori** (☎ 396-2298, 486 Rue Ste Catherine Ouest, Suite 100)* is Montréal's hip-hop palace on Saturday nights, with R&B other nights. It's good for pool, too. Ⓜ McGill.

Wearing black? Well, then ***Loft** (☎ 281-8158, 1405 Blvd St Laurent)* is just your ticket. It has two dance floors (one for mainstream rock and another for alternative music), rough murals of bands on the walls and a great rooftop terrace. The target crowd is 18 to 25, but the odd 30-something slips in from time to time. It's open Tuesday to Saturday. Ⓜ St Laurent.

The spirit of the '80s lives on at ***Electric Avenue** (☎ 285-8885, 1469 Rue Crescent)*, which is chock-a-block with a 30s and 40s crowd dressed to kill. Next door to Winnies (see Pubs & Bars, later), it's open Thursday to Saturday and charges a cover (usually $5). Ⓜ Guy-Concordia.

***Club Zone** (☎ 398-9875, 1186 Rue Crescent)* serves up an eclectic mix of pop to jazz to New Wave lounge – you name it. This is a stage venue with table service and a bar, and there's live music most nights. It is open 4 pm to 3 am daily. Ⓜ Lucien L'Allier.

***Club Soda** (☎ 790-1111, 1225 Blvd St Laurent)* is equally varied, hosting top jazz acts (such as Ranee Lee, a Sarah Vaughan-style singer) but also avant-garde, heavy metal and other artists in a hall that seats several hundred. It has a view for new faces and new talent. Call for a recorded schedule. Ⓜ St Laurent.

The Village (Map 6)

Lion d'Or (☎ 598-0709, 1676 Rue Ontario Est) is a classy 1930s-style club aimed at beautiful people (such as visiting film-production crews). It has a spacious wooden dance floor and some killer party bands – mostly sophisticated rock and retro. It's often used for private events, so check the listings. Ⓜ Papineau.

The Plateau (Map 8)

There are plenty of clubs along Blvd St Laurent, particularly in the 4000 and 5000 blocks, around Ave du Mont Royal. The crowds tend to be young and hipper-than-thou. For clubs near Blvd St Laurent, you can take bus No 55 up that street and get off at your nearest cross street (as an alternative to walking from a distant Métro stop).

The **Café Campus** (☎ 844-1010, 57 Rue Prince Arthur Est) is one of the most popular student clubs, with '80s hits, French rock and live Québécois bands. Happy hour ($1 a beer) is 8:30 to 10:30 pm. It's closed Sunday. Ⓜ Sherbrooke.

Belmont (☎ 845-8443, 4483 Blvd St Laurent) is a great place to meet people, with a couple of DJ-run dance floors, pool tables, cheap beer and big-screen sports. It attracts a mixture of yuppies, jeans and leather jackets, and it gets really packed on weekends for the laser light shows. Hours are 8 pm to 3 am Wednesday to Sunday. The cover is $3 to $4. Ⓜ Mont Royal.

Le Ballatou (☎ 845-5447, 4372 Blvd St Laurent) is dark, smoky and the most popular Afro-Caribbean nightclub in Montréal (check out the happy faces in the photo gallery out front). The clientele are multiethnic and the better dancers double-jointed, judging by the sophisticated swings of their hips. Shows are presented only during the week, when the cover varies. On weekends, the cover is $7 and includes one drink. It's closed Monday. Ⓜ Mont Royal.

College posers will love **Angels** (☎ 282-9944, 3604 Blvd St Laurent), a fun spot for just hanging out. There are funky projections, big-screen movies and scary works of wall art out front; the bar area looks like something from a Jules Verne novel. The upstairs dance floor is technoland and opens at midnight sharp. It's open Thursday to Saturday and Tuesday. Ⓜ Sherbrooke.

Across the street, **Jaï Bar** (☎ 284-1114, 3603 Blvd St Laurent) specializes in ethnic rhythms and reggae.

Tokyo Bar (☎ 842-6838, 3709 Blvd St Laurent) is dead chic, with a water-filled backlit bar and sunken circular sofas that dwarf their occupants. The crowd is oh-so-sophisticated types in their late 20s and early 30s; one dance floor features rock, pop, hip-hop, funk and Motown, and '80s classics. The rooftop bar gets going around midnight. It's open 10 pm to 3 am daily. Ⓜ Sherbrooke.

A landmark of Montréal house music, **Jingxi** (☎ 985-5464, 410 Rue Rachel Est) attracts legions of 20-somethings to be freeze-framed by the terrific light shows. It's open Wednesday to Saturday and sometimes Sunday. Ⓜ Mont Royal.

The **Jailhouse** (☎ 844-9696, 30 Ave Mont Royal Ouest) is a raucous place for down-and-dirty rock, hosting bands with intriguing names such as 'Alabama Thunder Pussy' and 'Hacksaw.' Watch out for flying underwear from enthused fans. Ⓜ Mont Royal.

There's no sign out front, but **Blizzarts** (☎ 843-4860, 3956a Blvd St Laurent) is a cool, discreet music bar with teams of popular DJs (up to four at once) from the local club scene who serve up jazz, funk, hip-hop, roots and dub. There's a small dance floor here. Hours are 8 pm to 3 am daily. Ⓜ Sherbrooke.

A clothing store by day, **Passeport** (☎ 842-6063, 4156 Rue St Denis) changes identity after dark and spins New Wave, gothic and techno for its small but intimate dance floor. Beer starts at just $1.75, but the price changes by the hour, gradually rising to $3.50 after midnight. Hours are 10 pm to 3 am Wednesday to Saturday. Ⓜ Mont Royal.

Get lost in the minimalist space at **Laïka** (☎ 842-8088, 4040 Blvd St Laurent), an intimate lounge bar that plays New Wave, house, techno and alternative music (DJs only). It's open 9 am to 3 am and serves a good continental breakfast (brunch on weekends). Ⓜ Sherbrooke or Mont Royal.

ENTERTAINMENT

PUBS & BARS
Vieux Montréal (Map 4)

The old town isn't a great place for a pub crawl, as most places are pretty touristy and expensive. One exception is the **Pub St Paul** (☎ 874-0485, 124 Rue St Paul Est). It affords a terrific view of the port, which you can enjoy while dancing or playing pool. The cover charge is $5. **Ⓜ** Place d'Armes or Champ de Mars.

Downtown (Map 5)

Rue Crescent has plenty of bars and clubs whose patrons aren't averse to instant companionship. The sprawling, split-level **Winnies** (☎ 288-0623, 1455 Rue Crescent) draws crowds with its multiple bars, pool tables, and thumping disco music. Local author Mordecai Richler used to knock back cold ones in the **Sir Winston Churchill Pub** upstairs. It serves so-so food all day (mains cost $10 to $16), and drinks are half-price from 5 to 8 pm. **Ⓜ** Guy-Concordia.

Thursday's (☎ 288-5656, 1449 Rue Crescent), right next door to Winnie's, is another lively singles place with mammoth bars and a dance floor over two levels. It is open 11:30 am to 3 pm and 6:30 pm to 2 am daily.

Hurley's Irish Pub (☎ 861-4111, 1125 Rue Crescent) is a cozy place with live music (usually rock and folk, with great Celtic fiddlers) most nights starting at 9 pm. As in many pubs, football and soccer matches are shown on big screens – prepare to join in. Hours are noon to 3 am daily. **Ⓜ** Guy-Concordia.

Le Vieux Dublin Pub & Restaurant (☎ 861-4448, 1219a Rue University) has a good selection of English and Irish beers (about $6 per pint) and live Celtic or pop music nightly. Hours are 11:30 am to 3 pm and 5 pm to 3 am daily. **Ⓜ** McGill or Square Victoria.

With its garage-sale furniture, **McKibbin's** (☎ 288-1580, 1426 Rue Bishop) cultivates a familiar, down-at-the-heels pub atmosphere. Live entertainment varies from Celtic, pop and punk music to informal drinking contests. Hours are 10 am to 3 am Wednesday to Saturday. **Ⓜ** Guy-Concordia.

The cozy **Le Swimming** (☎ 282-0005, 3643 Blvd St Laurent) has pool tables (thus the name of the place), which are free until 5 pm if you order at least one drink per hour. From Thursday to Saturday, there's live music (jazz, pop, rock and rockabilly). It's open noon to 3 am daily. **Ⓜ** St Laurent.

Pub Ste Élisabeth (☎ 286-4302, 1412 Rue Ste Élisabeth) has an expansive drink menu – including some good imported beers and Scotch – and a lovely vine-covered courtyard. If plans to demolish the pub come to pass, the city will lose a fine place. **Ⓜ** Berri-UQAM or St Laurent.

The **Mad Hatter** (☎ 982-1955, 1230 Blvd de Maisonneuve Ouest) is a screamingly popular student bar with foosball tables, sports banners and cheap beer specials (eg, a 60oz pitcher for $8.50). It bills itself as a library bar, but reading is low on the agenda here. **Ⓜ** Peel.

O'Donnell's (☎ 877-3128, 1224 Rue Bishop) is another sprawling Irish pub with live folk music from Wednesday to Saturday. There are two-for-one drinks from 4 to 8 pm. **Ⓜ** Guy-Concordia or Lucien L'Allier.

Gerts (☎ 398-3319, 3840 McTavish), in the McGill University student union building, plays DJ-driven R&B, hip-hop, blues and house, with an 'oldies night' thrown in for good measure. Hours are 9 am to 1 am weekdays (until 3 am Thursday and Friday) and 5 pm to 3 am on Saturday (closed Sunday). **Ⓜ** Peel.

Among the better brewpubs is **Brutopia** (☎ 323-9277, 1219 Rue Crescent), with eight varieties of suds on tap (including honey beer and the evil-sounding raspberry blonde). Pints cost $4, but they're half-price until 8 pm (and all night Monday). The bare brick walls and wood paneling are conducive for chats among this relaxed student crowd. It's open 3:30 pm to 3 am (from noon on Saturday), with live blues Wednesday to Saturday nights. **Ⓜ** Lucien L'Allier.

For a drink with a view, try the **Tour de Ville Bar** (☎ 879-1370, 777 Rue University), at the top of the Delta Hotel. Cocktails are particularly costly, but nursing one is kind of fun.

For barn-size fun, the **Peel Pub** (☎ 844-6769, 1107 Rue Ste Catherine Ouest) is an institution with students for its cheap beer and grub. During televised sporting events, it gets crowded (read: impossible to move). See also the Places to Eat chapter. Ⓜ Peel.

Quartier Latin (Map 6)
Le Saint Sulpice (☎ 844-9458, 1680 Rue St Denis) is *the* student place of the second. It's spread over four levels, with a café, several terraces, a disco and a huge back garden for drinks. It is open 11 am to 3 am (the dance floor opens at 10 pm). The DJ spins everything from hip-hop and ambient to mainstream rock and jazz. Ⓜ Berri-UQAM.

The cozy **Bar Les Conneries** (☎ 845-3889, 2033 Rue St Denis), in the basement, is known for its Wednesday oldies evening ('60s and '70s classics). Ⓜ Sherbrooke or Berri-UQAM.

The **Quartier Latin Pub** (☎ 845-3301, 318 Rue Ontario Est) is a cool bar with 1950s lounge-style decor, a small dance floor and a DJ playing New Wave. The front terrace is a great place to watch the world go by. Ⓜ Berri-UQAM.

Next door, **Le Magellan Bar** (☎ 845-0909, 330 Rue Ontario Est) plays canned jazz and chansons amid a sprinkling of maritime doodads. Look for the mock lighthouse out front. Ⓜ Berri-UQAM.

The Plateau (Map 8)
Quai Des Brumes (4481 Rue St Denis) is a fine place for live blues, rock and jazz. The interior is in dark Parisian café style, with framed mirrors, ceiling moldings and lots of paneling. Ⓜ Mont Royal.

Barfly (☎ 993-5154, 4026a Blvd St Laurent), two doors north of Laïka (see Discos & Clubs, earlier), has cheap beer, pool tables and some gritty, itinerant clientele – it's a bit like Tom Waits meets Jack Kerouac. Ⓜ Mont Royal or Sherbrooke.

Bières et Compagnie (☎ 844-4394, 4350 Rue St Denis) is a relaxed pub with an excellent choice of European and local microbrews. They serve standard pub grub and mussels with fries. Ⓜ Mont Royal or Sherbrooke.

Lounge Bars

The lounge – once a seedy dive whose patrons might shun photographers – has been given a new lease on life in Montréal. The reincarnation has a relaxed and languorous atmosphere, stuffed leather seats (designer products, mind you) and the stogies that remain a fad in Canada. Some of the more popular lounges include the following:

The **Jello Bar** (Map 5; ☎ 285-2621, 151 Rue Ontario Est) is the quintessential lava lounge, with live music and dancing most nights. Prearranged jam sessions produce some great talent – close your eyes, order one of 20 martinis and listen to Marvin Gaye. It's open 9 pm to 3 am daily (cover $5). Ⓜ St Laurent.

Sofa (Map 8; ☎ 285-1011, 451 Rue Rachel Est) is often standing room only on the weekends; grab one of the comfortable leather booths before 9 pm, sit back and enjoy the vibes – mainly live soul and jazz. Hot snacks are served. Hours are 4 pm to 3 am daily. Ⓜ Mont Royal.

At the ultrahip **Go-Go Lounge** (Map 8; ☎ 286-0882, 3682 Blvd St Laurent), the decor looks like a stage set from an Austin Powers movie, with its '60s psychedelics and flower-power motifs. It's open 7 pm to 3 am daily (Thursday and Friday from 5 pm). Ⓜ Sherbrooke.

Mile End (Map 9)

Fûtenbulle (☎ 276-0473, 273 Rue Bernard Ouest) is a neighborhood fixture featuring dozens of fine brews from around the world. The half-dozen 'beers of the day' cost just $3 on tap, and there's a good dinner menu of burgers, mussels, pastas and steak. Most dishes cost $6 to $12. It's open for lunch and dinner and stays open until 3 am (midnight on Sunday). Ⓜ Rosemont.

Mondexo (☎ 273-5015, 400 Ave Laurier Ouest) is a stylish, upmarket place with pleasant jazz from Thursday to Saturday in the summer. The balcony lounge above the ground floor is a great place to sit – padded wicker seats under African elephant tusks. There's an upscale restaurant, too. Ⓜ Laurier.

The brewing gizmo in the window gives some idea of what **Dieu du Ciel** (☎ 490-9555, 29 Ave Laurier Ouest) is about. The food's nothing special (pizza, nachos and other bar snacks), but this brewpub does serve great suds. It's next door to a wonderful late-19th-century fire station (now a dullish museum). Ⓜ Laurier.

POOL & BILLIARDS

Sharx (Map 5; ☎ 934-3105, 1606 Rue Ste Catherine Ouest) has pool and billiard tables everywhere you look (several dozen in total), rows of TV screens and a post-apocalyptic feel. An hour of play costs $9. Hours are 11 am to 3 am daily. Ⓜ Guy-Concordia.

Isotori (see Discos & Clubs) has 24 pool tables, while Le Swimming (see Pubs & Bars) has 10 pool tables and a billiard table. Some other places listed in this chapter have a pool table or three.

GAY & LESBIAN VENUES (Map 6)

The majority of gay and lesbian entertainment is in the Village, especially along Rue Ste Catherine Est, with a smattering of venues elsewhere in the city. For event listings, check the bilingual publication Village. Also, Fugues is a free monthly booklet for the gay and lesbian scene – it's in French, but it has easy-to-read club listings.

Unity (☎ 523-4429, 1400 Rue Montcalm) is a mixed gay and lesbian club spread over four levels: The mezzanine light shows attract hordes of ravers, muscle queens go for techno on the top floor, and two floors are devoted to '80s classics and hip-hop. The rooftop terrace is great for the Benson & Hedges fireworks displays on summer nights. It is open 10 pm to 3 am Thursday to Sunday, and the cover is $5 to $7. Ⓜ Beaudry.

The **Sky Pub** (☎ 529-6969, 1474 Rue Ste Catherine Est), which has a pub on the 1st floor, is a fixture in the gay community. One floor is dedicated to disco, another to house. There's a pretty terrace, elegant decor, lots of wood and intimate lighting. Don't miss the drag show on Tuesday night – it's the event in the Village. Ⓜ Papineau or Beaudry.

Cabaret l'Entre-Peau (☎ 525-7566, 1115 Rue Ste Catherine Est) puts on drag shows for a mixed crowd. (The name means 'between skin' – you figure it out.) The shows, which include standup comedy routines in drag, take place nightly at 11:30 pm and 1:30 am. Ⓜ Beaudry.

Le Drugstore (☎ 524-1960, 1366 Rue Ste Catherine Est) is a cavernous, six-level Western-style bar with lots of neon big-city props, nine theme bars, boutiques, a large delicatessen and a dance club in the basement. For bad hair days, there's even a hairdresser. Lesbians and gays have staked out their terrain on different floors. It's open 8 am to 3 am. Ⓜ Beaudry.

In the nearby multipurpose Bourbon entertainment complex (see Places to Stay on the map), **Le Track** (☎ 268-4679, 1574 Rue Ste Catherine Est) is a popular disco-bar with a leather boutique. Hours are 3 pm to 3 am daily. The complex is quite an attraction and incorporates the **Mississippi Club** (same telephone number) with dancing, live cabaret and drag shows. It's open 10 pm to 3 am daily. Ⓜ Papineau or Beaudry.

The **Stud Bar** (☎ 598-8243, Rue Ste Catherine Est) is a leather bar with poor visibility, '80s music and lots of guys with no hair. It's open 6 pm to 3 am daily. Ⓜ Papineau.

Apart from Le Drugstore, lesbians should check out **Sisters** (☎ 522-8357, 1456 Rue Ste Catherine Est). It's got some rough edges – grrrlz belting out Britney Spears tunes – but it's sizzling with 20-somethings looking for fun. Hours are 9 pm to 3 am. Ⓜ Beaudry.

MONTRÉAL JAZZ

Montréalers (and Québecers in general) have enormous respect for jazz musicians, and there's generous state support for jazz concerts and education programs. The city also possesses an ever-expanding array of jazz clubs that attract top-notch talent, including local musicians such as Oliver Jones, Alain Caron and Yannick Rieu. The scene, in a word, is excellent – thanks in no small measure to North America's biggest jazz festival, which is held here every year.

International Jazz Festival

I sing at many jazz festivals around the world, but this one is the most magnificent – the best jazz festival I have ever encountered.

– Tony Bennett

COURTESY OF MONTRÉAL INTERNATIONAL JAZZ FESTIVAL

Back in 1978, the idea of a jazz festival in Montréal was no more than the pipe dream of Alain Simard, a young local music producer. He'd already brought *la crème de la crème* of jazz to local concerts – Chick Corea, Weather Report and Dave Brubeck among them – and he wanted to create a festival that would attract the lucrative American tourist trade. After a false start in 1979, he co-founded the first festival a year later, which brought 12,000 visitors together on Île Ste Hélène for a dozen shows, featuring Chick Corea, Ray Charles, the Vic Vogel Big Band and Gary Burton.

The festival was judged as hip – thanks to its laid-back atmosphere, quality acts and free street concerts – and became a regular event in the Quartier Latin. The event soon outgrew that neighborhood and moved to the Place des Arts in 1989. In 2000, it drew more than 1.6 million visitors. On offer were 2000-odd musicians playing 350 free outdoor shows, 100 indoor concerts, 30 concert cruises on the St Lawrence aboard the paddle-steamer *Nouvelle Orléans* and numerous jam sessions.

St Cat, the blue saxophone-playing feline, is the mascot of the festival, which in turn attracts some of the biggest cats in jazz – Sonny Rollins, Al Jarreau, Herbie Hancock, Wayne Shorter, Al Dimeola, John Scofield and Jim Hall are among recent guests, as well as Montréal's own Oscar Peterson. Big pop 'crossover' artists also put in an appearance (eg, Sting and Rickee Lee Jones), and you'll hear just about everything under the sun, including blues, Latin, Cajun, Dixieland and reggae. Every year, the festival focuses on a single theme, and a significant section is dedicated to it – Louisiana jazz, for example. So far, the organizers have drawn the line at inviting more than a few pop artists to ensure the flavor remains firmly jazzy.

Right: Local jazz bassist Alain Caron plays that funky music.

There's no mistaking Montréal's distinct Latin American flavor. The presence of Brazilian, Caribbean and other Latin American bands; ethnic parades; and of course, the thumping nightlife of the Quartier Latin make the label 'Latin Capital of the North' almost believable. During the Jazz Festival of 2000, the Brazilian group Timbalada drew an incredible 225,000 visitors to its free concert at Place des Arts – and that wasn't just because it was Brazil's 500th birthday. Latecomers were lucky to get within a block of the stage. Still, it wasn't too bad – even several streets away, the silhouettes of the band's grass-skirted singers were visible, thanks to giant projections around the square.

Practicalities

The organization of the festival is impeccable and gets slicker every year. The vast majority of concerts are held at Place des Arts on Rue Ste Catherine (Map 5), and several blocks are closed to traffic. That part of downtown effectively shuts down for the festival – something that would be unthinkable in New York, another great jazz hub.

Info Jazz Bell (☎ 871-1881 or 1-888-515-0515) provides events information and hands out free festival programs and maps at its kiosks around Place des Arts. Concerts are held from midday until late evening, when artists also play at local clubs (some of which are listed later in this section).

The 1½-week festival is held in late June and early July. Tickets go on sale in mid-May and are available from the Places des Arts box office and the Admission ticket agency (☎ 790-1245 or 1-800-361-4595) via credit card. Tickets for the biggest acts, some of which play at the Centre Molson (Map 5), generally cost $30 to $70, but there are also great concerts on offer for just a few dollars. The free concerts take place daily from around noon to 8 pm. Web site: www.admission.com (tickets) or www.montrealjazzfest.com (festival schedule and details).

Refreshment and food stands abound, but expect to pay dearly for a smallish beer or hot dog. There are pay parking garages at the Complexe Desjardins and Place des Arts, but they fill up quickly, and traffic is dreadful – it's better to take the Métro. Hotels tend to raise their prices during the festival, and rooms can be hard to come by, so reserve early. Lawn chairs (as well as

COURTESY OF MONTRÉAL INT'L JAZZ FESTIVAL

Left: Local jazz pianist Oliver Jones

bicycles, dogs and your own alcohol) aren't allowed on the site, but there's often seating space on the steps at the Place des Arts.

Jazz & Blues Clubs

l'Air du Temps (Map 4; ☎ 842-2003, 191 Rue St Paul Ouest), in Vieux Montréal, is a Montréal institution, with a smoky, spotlit stage girded by a wooden balcony and bar. Furnishings include part of an early Paris Métro carriage and a spiral staircase from a London double-decker bus. Small groups or solos start around 5 pm (there's usually no cover charge), and big groups start after 9:30 pm (the standard cover is $5). Performers are mostly local musicians, but some big names turn up, too. Call for a bilingual message and schedule. **Ⓜ** Place d'Armes.

Biddles (Map 5; ☎ 842-8656, 2060 Rue Aylmer) is another fixture on the scene, run by venerable bassist Charlie Biddle (who also performs at the festival). It's a tad touristy but fun, with *fin-de-siècle* decor and musical paraphernalia hanging from the ceiling. There's no cover charge, and you can eat ribs or chicken for about $15 per head, including drink. Prepare to stand in line if you haven't reserved. It opens at 6 pm. **Ⓜ** McGill.

Descend the few steps into **Upstairs** (Map 5; ☎ 931-6808, 1254 Rue Mackay), which recently expanded but still hosts quality jazz and blues acts nightly (except Sunday) starting at about 9:30 pm. The walled terrace behind the bar is an enchanting place at sunset, and the food isn't bad either. **Ⓜ** Guy-Concordia.

Jazzons (Map 6; ☎ 843-9818, 300 Rue Ontario Est) is situated in a cramped but cozy venue on the north edge of the Village. In summer, the owners open the windows and spill the riffs for free (closed Tuesday). **Ⓜ** Berri-UQAM or Sherbrooke.

The hub of Afro-Cuban and Latin jazz is **Cubano's Club** (Map 5; ☎ 252-9749, 381 Rue Ste Catherine Ouest). A highlight is the big Cuban orchestras and the mambo competitions during the jazz festival. It's open 10 pm to 3 am nightly. **Ⓜ** Place des Arts.

The **Bistrot à Jojo** (Map 6; ☎ 843-5015, 1627 Rue St Denis) is a smoky place for rough diamonds in the thick of the Quartier Latin. It serves up some excellent blues and rock groups nightly. The cover charge is generally $2 to $5. **Ⓜ** Berri-UQAM.

Jazzi'z (Map 8; ☎ 287-0004, 4075b Rue St Denis) is a brand-new upstairs club with lounge atmosphere; it hosts lively Latin, blues and jazz bands. The cover is generally $5. **Ⓜ** Sherbrooke.

For big bands and combos, **Jazz & Blues** (Map 5; ☎ 398-3319, 3840 McTavish), in the McGill University student union building, holds regular concerts consisting of its excellent student bands – check the listings or the McGill University Web site at www.mcgill.ca. **Ⓜ** Peel.

FOLK & TRADITIONAL MUSIC

Québec folk and rock music is pretty well integrated into the mainstream bar and club scene. One notable place for French-language folk is Les Deux Pierrots (see Discos & Clubs, earlier). The Irish pubs, of course, regularly feature Celtic musicians.

The *Yellow Door Coffee House (Map 5; ☎ 398-6243, 3625 Rue Aylmer)* has survived from the '60s – US draft dodgers found refuge here. Despite the association with the '60s, it doesn't serve either dope or alcohol. The program is English-language folk music, poetry and literature readings, but the schedule is erratic; call for upcoming events. It's closed in the summer. Ⓜ McGill.

CLASSICAL MUSIC, DANCE & OPERA

The renowned *Orchestre Symphonique de Montréal (☎ 842-9951)*, under the direction of Swiss conductor Charles Dutoit, performs at the Place des Arts (Map 5) when it's not on tour. Check for free summer concerts at the Basilique Notre Dame, Olympic Park and in municipal parks in the Montréal area; its Christmas performance of *The Nutcracker* is legendary.

The *Orchestre Métropolitain de Montréal (☎ 598-0870)*, made up of youngish local musicians, performs in the same complex, as well as in the Église St Jean Baptiste, nearby.

The city has two fine chamber ensembles, the *McGill Chamber Orchestra (☎ 398-4455)* and *I Musici de Montréal (☎ 982-6038)*, both of which perform at McGill's Pollack Concert Hall (listed later), among other venues.

Les Ballets Jazz de Montréal (☎ 982-6771), a Montréal modern-dance troupe, has a sterling reputation in experimental forms, while *Les Grands Ballets Canadiens (☎ 849-8681)* is Québec's leading troupe, performing a classical and modern program throughout the year.

L'Opera Montréal (☎ 985-2258) holds its lavish stage productions at the Place des Arts, with big names and voices from Québec and around the world starring in classics such as *Mefistofele, Aïda* and *Carmen.* Translations (into French or English) are run on a video screen above the stage. Tickets cost $38 to $98 during the week and $40 to $105 on Saturday nights. The box office is open 9 am to 5 pm weekdays.

CONCERT HALLS

The *Place des Arts (Map 5; ☎ 842-2112)*, Montréal's municipal center for the performing arts, opened in 1992 and now presents an array of concerts and dance in five theaters. The city's symphony plays in the 3000-seat Salle Wilfrid-Pelletier, and ballet, opera and other musical troupes often perform here. The eponymous square is the focal point of the Montréal Jazz Festival, held in June and July.

The *Spectrum de Montréal (Map 5; ☎ 861-5851, 318 Rue Ste Catherine)* is an converted cinema with great acoustics that seats about 2000. It hosts comedy, rock and pop concerts, and in the summer, it serves as a stage for the Jazz Festival. The box office is open 10 am to 9 pm (to 5 pm on Sunday), and shows usually start at around 11 pm. Ⓜ Place des Arts.

The *Stade Olympique (☎ 252-8687, 4549 Ave Pierre de Coubertin)* is home to the Montréal Expos baseball team. It also hosts musical happenings, such as Cream – the electronic-music festival that draws more than 15,000 people every September. The stadium is mapped on the Olympic Park map, in the Things to See & Do chapter.

The *Pollack Concert Hall (Map 5; ☎ 398-4547, 555 Rue Sherbrooke Ouest)* is McGill University's main concert hall and features recitals from its students and faculty year-round. It's in the Victorian building behind the statue of Queen Victoria. Ⓜ McGill.

When it's not hosting matches of the Canadiens hockey team, the 21,000-seat *Centre Molson (Map 5; ☎ 932-2582)*, a block south of Blvd René Lévesque, is *the* downtown venue for big concerts. Pavarotti, Céline Dion and touring orchestras usually end up there. The box office is open 10 am to 6 pm weekdays (to 9 pm on days of events). Ⓜ Lucien L'Allier.

Typical architecture of Vieux Montréal

Cathédrale Basilique Marie Reine du Monde

Landscaped grounds of Oratoire St Joseph

Religious building and statue in Lachine

Buckminster Fuller dome, home of the Biosphère, Île de St Hélène

Montréal Tower, Olympic Park

Credit Lyonnaise Building, Downtown

CINEMAS

The trend is toward huge, multiscreen (up to 30) complexes, complete with video games, boutiques and cafés. You can survey what's on offer at www.cinema-montreal .com, which includes reviews and details of discount admissions.

Several repertory film theaters offer double bills and midnight movies on weekends. These cinemas are generally cheaper than the chains showing first-run films, but membership may be required. *Cinéma du Parc (Map 5; ☎ 281-1900, 3575 Ave du Parc)*, at Rue Prince Arthur Ouest, is the last purely English-language repertory cinema in town. Admission is $4.50. ⓜ Place des Arts.

In the Quartier Latin, the *National Film Board (Map 6; ☎ 283-9000, 1564 Rue St Denis)* is worth a visit for serious cinephiles. There are regular screenings, but the real attraction is its **Cinérobothèque** – make your choice, and a robot housed in a huge, glass-roofed archive pulls your selection from one of 6,000 videodiscs. Then settle back into individual, stereo-equipped chair units to watch your personal monitor for $2/3 per hour (students/nonstudents). There's also a huge Canadian-video collection available. It's open noon to 9 pm Tuesday to Sunday. ⓜ Berri-UQAM.

Just south of the NFB, the *Cinémathèque Québécoise (Map 6; ☎ 842-9763, 335 Blvd de Maisonneuve Est)* features French and Québécois avant-garde films and has a permanent exhibition on the history of filmmaking. There's also a TV and new-media section. Entry costs $4. Hours are 1 to 9 pm Tuesday to Sunday. ⓜ Berri-UQAM.

The *Excentris Cinema (Map 5; ☎ 847-3536, 3530 Blvd St Laurent)* is a showcase for independent films from around the world founded by the creator of Softimage, a Montréal special-effects company. Besides several movie halls (including a 3D hall), there are production studios for noncommercial users. The place is full of high-tech film gadgetry – even the box office cashier appears on a screen when you buy a ticket. ⓜ St Laurent.

In the Vieux Port area of Montréal, there's an *IMAX cinema (Map 4; ☎ 496-4629 or 1-800-349-4629)*. On the big screens, watch the Cirque du Soleil, dinosaurs or marine life come tumbling into your lap with the aid of 3D glasses. Tickets cost $11/9 for adults/children. ⓜ Place d'Armes. There's another, the brand-new *Famous Players IMAX (☎ 842-5828, 977 Rue Ste Catherine Ouest)*, in the Paramount complex, which also has regular movies. ⓜ Peel.

The *Café Ciné-Lumière (Map 9; ☎ 495-1796, 5163 Blvd St Laurent)*, up in Mile End, shows old films for free. Don a headset for listening along with your food and drink. The old props and movie paraphernalia make for great ambience. It's open 1 pm to midnight daily (closed Monday). ⓜ Laurier.

THEATERS

The *Centaur Théâtre (Map 4; ☎ 288-3161, 453 Rue St François Xavier)* generally has the best in English presentations, from classics such as *Waiting for Godot* to works by experimental Canadian playwrights. The building itself is spectacular – it's Montréal's former stock exchange (1903). The season runs from October to June, but other groups perform during the summer. ⓜ Place d'Armes.

The *Monument National Theater (Map 5; ☎ 871-2224, 1182 Blvd St Laurent)* holds regular rehearsals of dramatic plays by students of the National Theatre School. The programs are in English or French and cover a range of genres, from Shakespeare to Sam Shephard. There are two stages – one with 800 seats and one with 150 seats. Tickets ($5) go on sale one month before opening. ⓜ Place d'Armes.

Théâtre St Denis (Map 6; ☎ 849-4211, 1594 Rue St Denis) hosts touring companies of Broadway productions but also features rock concerts and comedians. Its two halls also host performances for the Just for Laughs festival, in the summer. The box office is open noon to 9 pm daily. ⓜ Berri-UQAM.

Théâtre de Verdure (Map 8; ☎ 872-2644, Parc La Fontaine) is an open-air theater that hosts musical, dance and drama productions June to August. Movies are also screened there at pondside on summer nights. ⓜ Sherbrooke or Mont Royal.

ENTERTAINMENT

The *Centre Saidye Bronfman (Map 2; ☎ 739-2301, 5170 Côte Ste Catherine)* is the city's chief Jewish theater, with performances in English, Yiddish and Hebrew during the summer. The center also hosts a variety of other events during the year, including dance and musical recitals, puppet shows, readings and plays in English – many are free. The box office is open from 11 am to 8 pm Monday to Thursday and noon to 7 pm Sunday. Ⓜ Côte Ste Catherine.

Among French-language venues, *Théâtre du Rideau Vert (Map 8; ☎ 844-1793, 4664 Rue St Denis)* hosts repertory productions. Ⓜ Mont Royal.

Théâtre de Quat' Sous (Map 8; ☎ 845-7277, 100 Ave des Pins Est) is more a forum for intellectual and experimental drama (Ⓜ Sherbrooke), and *Théâtre du Nouveau Monde (Map 5; ☎ 866-8667, 84 Rue Ste Catherine Ouest)* specializes in French classics. Ⓜ St Laurent.

HIGH-TECH ENTERTAINMENT
Laser Quest (Map 5; ☎ 393-3000, 1226 Rue Ste Catherine Ouest) offers laser games, the most popular being shoot-or-be-shot in a maze spread over three floors. It's open 6 to 10 pm Tuesday to Thursday, 4 pm to mid-

night on Friday and Saturday, and 1 to 9 pm Sunday. You'll have to pay a $20 annual membership unless a special is running (eg, $10 for one night's play). Ⓜ Peel.

Due to open by early 2001, the *Montréal Forum* entertainment center *(Map 5; ☎ 933-6786)*, on the corner of Atwater and Rue Ste Catherine Ouest, is an arena-style entertainment temple built on the site of the old Canadiens hockey rink. Cinemas, restaurants, high-tech games and various free shows are on offer. Web site: www.montrealforum.com. Ⓜ Atwater.

The sparkling new *Metaforia Centre (Map 5; ☎ 868-6382, 698 Rue Ste Catherine Ouest)* offers a barrage of virtual-reality shows, interactive games and whizzbang special effects (the same company was involved in the movies *Apollo 13* and *Titanic*). Regular 'tours' include an undersea trip through an Atlantis-type realm.

It's open 11 am to 11 pm Tuesday and Wednesday, 10 am to midnight Thursday, 10 am to 1 am Friday, 9 am to 1 am Saturday and 9 am to 11 pm Sunday (closed Monday). Admission is $15/12 for adults and seniors/children. Ⓜ McGill.

COMEDY
The upstairs *Comedyworks (Map 5; ☎ 398-9661, 1238 Rue Bishop)* presents standup comics nightly, usually in English. Events include open-mike nights, improvisation and headline acts on weekends. Heckling is encouraged. There's also a full bar, pool and darts. Shows are at 9 pm, and there's an additional 11:15 pm show on Friday and Saturday. Admission prices vary. Ⓜ Guy-Concordia.

The *Comedy Nest (Map 5; ☎ 932-6378, 1740 Blvd René Lévesque)*, in the Nouvel Hotel, features talent from all over North America. There's a dash of cabaret – with singers, dancers, musicians, female impersonators and more. Shows are Wednesday to Saturday at 9 pm, with an additional 11:15 pm set on Friday and Saturday. The cover charge ranges from $3 to $15 (there are discounts for students). It's a comfortable stage venue with bar that seats 200. Ⓜ Lucien L'Allier or Guy-Concordia.

Cirque du Soleil

Don't miss the internationally famed Cirque du Soleil (Map 2; ☎ 722-2324 or 1-800-678-2119), 8400 Second Ave, if it's in town. Founded in Montréal in 1984, the circus is based on acrobatics and a range of astounding acts of dexterity – without the use of animals. The troupe goes on worldwide tours, but its North American tours bring it back to the Vieux Port or its big top in the northern Montréal suburb of St Michel.

Ticket prices vary with the show, but expect to pay at least $45/30 for adults/children. For a sample of what it's like, visit the IMAX cinema's highly acclaimed Cirque du Soleil film *Journey of Man* at the Vieux Port.

GAMBLING

The flashy *Casino de Montréal* *(Map 10;
☎ 392-2746 or 1-800-665-2274)*, on Île Notre
Dame, is one of the 10 largest in the world
and occupies the former French pavilion
from the Expo '67. Methods of separating
yourself from your hard-earned cash include roulette, baccarat, blackjack and a
few thousand slot machines; oddly, alcohol
isn't served in the gambling halls, which are
open 9 am to 5 pm. There's no strict dress
code, but shorts and beachwear are a no-no.
Glitzy Las Vegas–style shows are produced
from time to time, and the view of downtown is stupendous from the upstairs gallery. To get there, take the Métro to Île Ste
Hélène and transfer to bus No 167; there's
underground parking if you absolutely must
drive.

See Spectator Sports for information on
horse racing.

SPECTATOR SPORTS

Hockey and Catholicism are regarded as
national religions in Québec, but baseball
also attracts a fair number of fans. Ironically, although the internationally renowned
Habs and Expos have fallen upon hard
times in their leagues, Montréal's dark-
horse football team is riding an unexpected
wave of popularity (see the boxed text 'The
Alouettes Rise Again').

Tickets for most sporting events are
available from the Admission ticket service
(☎ 790-1245), which has various outlets
around town, including one in the Berri-
UQAM Métro station.

Hockey

The Centre Molson (Map 5; ☎ 932-2582)
replaced the smaller Montréal Forum in
1996 as home to the Canadiens of the National Hockey League (also see Concert
Halls, earlier).

The 'Habs,' as the team is called, have won
the Stanley Cup 24 times, but the last time
was in 1993 – and the Molson family did the
unthinkable by selling the team in 2000. Still,
Montréalers have a soft spot for the Habs,
and if you're in town during the season,
don't miss the opportunity to see a match.

Tickets go on sale in advance during the
season (October to April, with playoffs until
June); call Admission (☎ 790-1245). List
prices range from $17 for a seat in the
rafters (bring your binoculars) to $130 for
rink-side seats. Otherwise, seats are available through the legions of scalpers who
begin lingering about noon on game days.
Buy just after the game starts, and you can
often negotiate the scalpers down to half-
price.

Outdoor hockey games are some of Québec's most memorable sporting affairs –
earsplitting cries of *but* (goal) fueled by
thermoses of mulled wine. During the winter, informal matches take place just about
wherever a pond has frozen over and public
rinks are set up – for example, at Parc La
Fontaine (Map 8) or at the Olympic rowing
basin of Île Notre Dame, in the Parc des Îles
(Map 10).

You can attend matches year-round at
the Sportplex (Map 1; ☎ 626-2500), 15540
Blvd Pierrefonds, a four-rink complex in
the western suburb of Pierrefonds (a 15-
minute drive from downtown Montréal).
In the summer, the Montréal Métro AAA
Summer Hockey League (☎ 338-1543) organizes frequent matches there for the
Montréal Kings, the Lac St Louis Lions and
other local 'midget' teams – call for a schedule. The same people plan the winter season,
too. Tickets cost $5/2.50 for adults/children.
Take Hwy 40 to exit 52 (Blvd St Jean) and
drive 3km north.

Baseball

The major-league baseball team the Montréal Expos, of the National League (☎ 253-3434 or 1-800-463-9767), has fallen on hard times, and few fans bother to attend games at the Stade Olympique anymore.

The owners, led by American art dealer Jeffrey Loria, have considered moving the onetime World Series winners to the US, which may still happen if investors can't agree to build a new stadium downtown. Gone are the days when the crime rate went down when the Expos played – nowadays, the team can only fill a fraction of the Stade Olympique's 62,000 seats (see the Olympic Park map, in the Things to See & Do chapter). Tickets are available from the box office or from Admission (☎ 790-1245) from April to September; they cost $7 to $23.

Football

The Alouettes, the once-defunct football team of the teetering CFL (Canadian Football League), have begun filling the house since it moved to the Molson Stadium at McGill University (Map 5). Rules are a bit different from American football: The field is bigger and there are only three downs. The season runs from late June to November. You can buy advance tickets ($17 to $50) at the Alouettes Billeterie (Map 5; ☎ 254-2400), 646 Rue Ste Catherine, open 9 to 5 pm weekdays. Ⓜ McGill.

Grand Prix Racing

The annual Grand Prix du Canada is held every June at the Circuit Gilles Villeneuve (☎ 350-4731), on Île Notre Dame (Map 10). Formula 1 racing is rare in North America – the only US event is held in Indianapolis, which was relaunched in 2000 after a 10-year break. Tickets are virtually impossible to get unless you purchase well ahead of time, and Montréal's hotels are booked

The Alouettes Rise Again

Montréal's Canadian Football League (CFL) team has risen from the ashes – again. Born as the Alouettes after WWII, the 'Als' won several Grey Cup championships (1949, 1970, 1974, 1979) before their fortunes flagged. The team folded twice in the 1980s, only to re-emerge as the Concordes and later, under US ownership, as the Baltimore Colts. Sold back to Montréal in the late 1990s, the by-now 'hapless Als' faced an uncertain future.

However, as Montréal's famous hockey and baseball teams started losing, sports fans looked to the gridiron for hope. In 1998, the team left the accident-prone Stade Olympique (after a 55-ton beam collapsed over an amazed crowd) and resettled at McGill University, in the more central Molson Stadium (18,000 capacity). The change of venue undoubtedly helped: While Als games regularly sell out, the Montréal Expos – the onetime World Series champions – seldom attract more than 7000 spectators. The Als are winning, too. In 2000, the team made its first Grey Cup appearance since 1979 (though they lost by two points). *Allez* Als!

solid during the event. Expect to pay at least $150 for a grandstand seat. Ⓜ Île Ste Hélène.

Horse Racing

Harness racing can be seen at the Hippodrome de Montréal (Map 2; ☎ 739-2741), 7440 Boulevard Décarie, at 7:30 pm on Wednesday, Friday and Saturday and at 1:30 pm Sunday. Major races include the Coupe de l'Avenir in October, with a total purse of over half a million dollars. Pari-mutuel betting and the snack bar are open 11 am to 11 pm. Admission is free, and there's a free shuttle that runs regularly on race days from the Métro stop. Ⓜ Mamur.

Shopping

There's something for everyone to buy in Montréal. First, it's an excellent center for traditional Canadian gifts and goods: Inuit and Amerindian crafts, country furniture, outdoor and winter clothing and maple syrup are some of the most popular items. The vast majority of Canada's fur companies are based in Montréal, a prime place to pick up a pelt (nonanimal furs are widely available, too). Museum shops such as the one at Musée McCord (Map 5) sell beautiful items, such as wooden toys, handmade jewelry and colorful quilts, at reasonable prices.

Second, as one of the hippest places to live in North America – just ask anyone – the city also has a great choice of vintage clothing, CDs and records and retro/antique furnishings. The plethora of well-stocked bookshops is a treat, too. Clothing deserves special mention: Montréal's designers are trend-setters and their styles have an irrepressible Gallic flair. You won't pay dearly, however, if you buy garments from factory outlets such as those in the Chabanel area (see Shopping Centers under Where to Shop, later).

Most stores are open Monday to Wednesday 9:30 or 10 am to 6 pm and Thursday and Friday until 9 pm; Saturday hours tend to be 10 am to 5 pm. A few shops are also open on Sunday, notably along Rue Ste Catherine and Blvd St Laurent and in the larger malls. All foreigners should keep their receipts for refunds of sales tax. (See Taxes & Refunds in the Facts for the Visitor chapter for more details.)

WHERE TO SHOP

Shopping is a popular pastime in Montréal, and at times you'll find yourself drawn with the herds to certain popular streets and malls, which have their pros and cons. It can be more rewarding, however, to explore

the backstreet shops downtown and in the Plateau, which tend to be cheaper and less picked over. The outlet stores are the most reliable places to get brand names at cut-rate prices.

Streets

Downtown, the east-west-running Rue Ste Catherine is the main shopping strip. It has revived in recent years and is now home to four large department stores, specialist clothing stores and consumer-goods shops. Swanky boutiques, galleries, jewelry and fur merchants can be found along Rue Sherbrooke and, to a lesser extent, the top end of Rue Crescent. A few antique shops are on Rue Sherbooke, but Rue Notre Dame is the place for the serious collector.

Blvd St Laurent and Ave Mont Royal are the meccas of hip fashion, music shops and some budget stores. Rue St Denis has some quirky places, starting with headshops in the Quartier Latin. In Vieux Montréal, Rue St Paul Ouest has a slew of art galleries. Bookshops are scattered throughout downtown and along Blvd St Laurent.

Shopping Centers

Montréal's slew of shopping complexes includes some impressive works of architecture. Les Cours Mont-Royal (Map 5; ☎ 842-7777), at Rue Peel and Blvd de Maisonneuve Ouest, was built into the old Mount Royal Hotel (once the largest hotel in the British Empire) and is good for wandering. The skylit atrium, designer ponds and winding staircases give it a sumptuous, elegant feel. ⓶ Peel. Similarly impressive is the upscale Ruelle des Fortifications (Map 4; ☎ 982-9888), in the Centre Mondial du Commerce, with a sweeping inner concourse and still more fountains. ⓶ Square Victoria.

At some point or another, you'll end up at the Centre Eaton (Map 5; ☎ 288-3708), on Rue Ste Catherine Ouest, a showcase shopping complex with myriad retailers, especially clothing stores – some selling quality stuff, others junk. The Promenade de la Cathédrale is an underground portion of the complex that runs beneath a church. ⓶ McGill.

Not far away is Place Montréal Trust (Map 5; ☎ 843-8000), another modern mall with a big branch of Indigo Books. ⓶ Peel or McGill. Besides housing a hundred-odd shops, the mammoth Complexe Desjardins (Map 5; ☎ 281-1870), opposite Place des Arts, has a pleasant atrium with trees and tinkling waterfalls. ⓶ Place des Arts or St Laurent. The cruciform Place Ville Marie (Map 5; ☎ 861-9393) dates from the 1950s and marks the start of the underground city (see the boxed text).

Bargain-seeking buyers know to flock to the Chabanel, an eight-block expanse of old factory buildings in northern Montréal, just west of Blvd St Laurent (Map 2). Inside them are several hundred 'suites,' effectively warehouse storage rooms stuffed to the gills with locally made and imported items, especially garments. From Buffalo jeans to Monte Calvo coats to Indian skirts, the choice is so big it's almost paralyzing. Just start on a top floor (the buildings have up to nine stories) and work your way down. Bring cash and be prepared to bargain (prices are good even if you don't). Hours are generally 8:30 am to 1 pm Saturday, when something of a fun-fair atmosphere prevails. Some shops also open all day weekdays. ⓶ Crémazie, then walk three blocks north.

Department Stores

Rue Ste Catherine is home to the majority of department stores. It's a window-shopper's paradise, and the displays of the flagship department stores are impressive, even if you just want to browse.

The Hudson Bay Co (Map 5; ☎ 281-4422), 585 Rue Ste Catherine Ouest, known in French as La Baie, became famous three centuries ago for its blankets – the stripes on its main entrance doors mimic the wool blankets once used to measure the size of fur skins. Pass the legions of perfumery stands on the ground floor and take the escalators to its cavernous clothing boutiques. It's good for crystal, china and all things Canadian, including Inuit handicrafts. The 8th floor has tons of reduced-price clothing.

La Maison Simons (Map 5; ☎ 282-1840), 977 Rue Ste Catherine Ouest, fuses French

The Underground City

Montréal's *ville souterrain,* or underground city, was created to alleviate congestion and provide an escape from the harsh winter. It's unique in the world, with 2000 shops in 29km of corridors, with hotels, restaurants, offices, cinemas, banks, convention centers and exhibition halls, all underground. Add climate control and Métro stations throughout, and you've got a self-contained world, shielded from the frigidity (or sweltering heat) above. Stories abound of molelike Montréal residents going for weeks or even months without seeing the light of day.

The first segment, a tunnel from Place Ville Marie to Place Bonaventure, was completed in 1962, and the introduction of the Métro the same decade spurred expansion. The network continues to evolve, with no master blueprint. Other cities (such as Toronto) have similar labyrinths, but they're considerably smaller.

While the notion is functional and innovative, there's really not much to see – the shops are all modern and most of the system looks no different from a contemporary shopping mall, except that it's bigger and has the Métro going through it. The tourist office has a good map of the entire system; it may prove useful on rainy or snowy days.

GEORGI SHABLOVSKY

flair with young, peppy North American fashion for men and women. This fashionable Québec City chain has a mind-boggling selection – from $15 T-shirts to $5000 designer coats. It's next door to Place Montréal Trust. Ⓜ Peel or McGill.

Moving upmarket, Holt Renfrew (Map 5; ☎ 842-5111), 1300 Rue Sherbrooke Ouest, sells clothes to the label-conscious, cashed-up professionals of both genders. The styles of this former furrier are subdued, yet the simplest designs ooze exclusivity. January and August are the big sales months – look for half-price or better. Ⓜ Peel or Guy-Concordia.

Ogilvy (Map 5; ☎ 842-7711), 1307 Rue Ste Catherine Ouest, is more a collection of high-profile boutiques than a department store. Every Christmas, it puts out an ancient mechanical display that's a Montréal fixture. Although now French owned, its heritage is unmistakable: A kilted bagpiper plays at the stroke of noon. Ⓜ Peel or Guy-Concordia.

WHAT TO BUY
Antiques & Memorabilia

Montréal has an excellent range of shops selling collectible furniture and memorabilia. You'll find several dozen of them, sometimes side by side, on 'Antique Alley,' the stretch of Rue Notre Dame Ouest between Ave Atwater and Rue Guy (Map 5). The Village (Map 6) also has a few good places for antique shopping, especially along Rue Amherst.

Lucie Favreau Antiques (Map 5; ☎ 989-5117), 1904 Rue Notre Dame Ouest, is chock-o-block with giggle-inducing housewares, signed baseballs, advertising plaques, toys and other collectibles. It's open 10 am to 6 pm Monday to Friday and to 5 pm Saturday. Ⓜ Georges Vanier.

For more than two decades, Les Antiquités Grand Central (Map 5; ☎ 935-1467), 2448 Rue Notre Dame Ouest, has been the most elegant place on the strip. Get buzzed in to see the Louis IV chairs, full dining room suites and crystal chandeliers. It's closed Sunday. Ⓜ Lionel Groulx.

Lussier Antique (Map 5; ☎ 938-2224), 3645 Rue Notre Dame Ouest, is crammed full of lamps, furniture, china, paintings and silverware, with some good bargains to be had. It opens 10 am to 5 pm Monday to Saturday (to 7 pm Thursday and Friday). Ⓜ Lionel Groulx.

A L'Antiquité Curiosite (Map 6; ☎ 525-8772), 1769 Rue Amherst, has a splendid collection including mahogany tables, chests of drawers and fixtures. Hours are 11 am to 6 pm weekdays (to 7 pm Thursday and Friday) and 11 am to 5 pm weekends. Ⓜ Beaudry.

Cité Deco (Map 6; ☎ 528-0659), next door at 1767 Rue Amherst, is a blast from the past with '30s- to '60s-style furniture, blenders and toasters, and lamps that look like old hairdryers. Hours are 11 am to 6 pm weekdays (to 7 pm Thursday and Friday) and 11 am to 5 pm Saturday. Ⓜ Beaudry.

Art
Vieux Montréal is well-endowed with commercial art galleries – Rue St Paul Ouest has clusters of them.

Gallery 2000 (Map 4; ☎ 844-1812), 45 Rue St Paul Ouest, displays an eclectic mixture in well-lit exhibition halls over two levels, with barely an inch of wallspace to spare, from classic landscapes to neo-Cubist portraits. It's open 10 am to 9 pm daily. Across the street, Galerie Parchemine (☎ 845-3368) has an extensive collection of modernist works and (affordable) sketches and prints. You can get purchases framed on the premises. Hours are 11 am to 6 pm daily (to 9 pm Thursday and Friday).

Galerie St Dizier (Map 4; ☎ 845-8411), 20 Rue St Paul Ouest, has some pretty huge naïve and other modernist artworks. The sculptures are wild: Look for the crazed motorcyclist chasing the chicken near the entrance hall. It's open 10 am to 6 pm daily.

Among museum-type galleries, the Centre de Design (Map 6; ☎ 987-3395), 1440 Rue Sanguinet, has exhibitions of works from graphic and fashion designs as well as architecture. Hours are noon to 6 pm Wednesday to Sunday. Ⓜ Berri-UQAM.

La Galerie de L'UQAM (Map 6; ☎ 987-8421), 1400 Rue Berri, presents contemporary art and works by the university's professors and students (it's always refreshing). It's open noon to 6 pm (closed Monday). Ⓜ Berri-UQAM.

Handicrafts
The Guilde Canadienne des Métier d'Art Québec (Map 5; ☎ 849-6091), 2025 Rue Peel, has a small and somewhat expensive collection of the work of Québec artisans and other Canadiana, as well as Inuit prints and carvings. There are rotating exhibits from the country's best artisans, including prints, sculptures and crafts. It's closed on Monday in winter. Ⓜ Peel.

La Guilde Graphique (Map 4; ☎ 844-3438), 9 Rue St Paul Ouest, exhibits more than 200 contemporary artists in a variety of media and techniques. Most works are on paper – sketches, woodcuts, etchings and lithographs. Have a peek at the artists working in the upstairs studio. Ⓜ Champs de Mars or Place d'Armes.

Galerie Le Chariot (Map 4; ☎ 875-4994), 446 Place Jacques Cartier, has an enormous selection of Inuit and Amerindian art. You'll find prints, walrus tusks, fur hats, mountain goat rugs and more moccasins than you can shake a whalebone at. It's open daily to 6 pm (to 3 pm Sunday). Ⓜ Champ de Mars.

Artisanat Canadien (Map 4; ☎ 873-2839), 301 Rue St Paul Est, concentrates on Amerindian and Inuit crafts – beaded necklaces, snowshoes, drums, dolls and (yes) fur hats and vests. You'll also find carvings galore. It's open 10 am to 7 pm daily (to 11 pm in summer). Ⓜ Champ de Mars.

The shops along Rue Ste Catherine (west of Rue Guy) and Ave du Mont Royal are full of offbeat and at times rare ethnic goods. It's fun to nose around, even if you don't want to buy. Le Souk du Tassili (Map 8; ☎ 287-3988), 50 Ave Duluth Est, has traditional North African art including tall hookah pipes, tea sets, baskets and rugs. It's open daily to 5 pm (to 8 pm Thursday and Friday). Ⓜ Sherbrooke.

Soravy (Map 9; ☎ 277-2391), 97 Ave Laurier Ouest, has Cambodian handmade gifts – statues, chess boards with intricate engravings, brightly colored purses, table-cloths, wood carvings and hangings. Ⓜ Laurier.

China & Porcelain
The Crystal House (Map 2; ☎ 731-1656), 2795 Ch Bates, Suite 101, is a treasure trove of 1st-class crystal, china and tableware. You'll find oodles of swish brand names: Swarovski crystal, Villeroy & Boch china, Hummel figurines, Mont Blanc pens and plenty more. The display rooms are stuffed full and the prices are good. It's open 10 am to 7 pm Monday to Wednesday, to 8 pm Thursday and to 4 pm Friday and Saturday. It's half-hidden in an old factory on an industrial estate. The closest Métro station is Outremont or Acadie, but you're better off taking a commuter train from Gare Centrale to the Canora stop.

Books & Comics
Chapters Bookstore (Map 5; ☎ 849-8825), 1171 Rue Ste Catherine Ouest, has three huge floors of English- and French-language books and a good travel section (lots of Lonely Planet titles). If it's in print, chances are you'll find it here. There's an Internet café, too. It's open to 11 pm daily. Ⓜ Peel.

Indigo (Map 5; ☎ 281-5549), 1500 Ave McGill in the Place Montréal Trust, is almost as big as Chapters and has a good CD section and a coffee bar. Check out the photos of famous Canadians on the 2nd floor. Ⓜ Peel or McGill.

Double Hook Bookshop (Map 5; ☎ 932-5093), 1235a Ave Greene, has been Montréal's specialist in Canadian English-language books for a quarter-century. Staff are extremely helpful and knowledgeable. It also hosts occasional readings. Ⓜ Atwater.

Librairie Russell (Map 4; ☎ 866-0564), 275 Rue St Antoine Ouest, is the largest English-language used-book shop in the city, with about one million titles over two floors. You'll find lots of well-priced publishers' leftovers. It's open weekdays, all day Saturday and 11 am to 5 pm Sunday. Ⓜ Square Victoria or Place d'Armes.

Behind the Art Deco portals of Archambault (Map 6; ☎ 849-6201), 500 Rue Ste Catherine Est, you'll find Montréal's oldest and largest book and record shop. Spread over four floors, this emporium boasts a great selection of CDs and books, apart from assorted musical supplies such as pianos and sheet music. Some recordings sold here are hard to find outside Québec. It's open weekdays and until 5 pm Saturday and Sunday. Ⓜ Berri-UQAM.

Odyssey Books (Map 5; ☎ 844-4843), 1439 Rue Stanley, sells used soft- and hard-cover books as well as records (including good classical and jazz sections). It's strong in mysteries, literature, jazz, philosophy, history, art and cookbooks. Recent arrivals have a special section. It's open to at least 8 pm weekdays and to afternoon Saturday and Sunday. Ⓜ Peel.

Librairie Astro (Map 5; ☎ 932-1139), 1844 Rue Ste Catherine Ouest, has an impressive collection of new, used and collectible comics, books, cards and some CDs. Don't miss the back room – all used books there cost $1 to $2. Hours are 9 am to 9 pm Monday to Saturday. Ⓜ Guy-Concordia.

1.000.000 Comix (Map 5; ☎ 989-9587), 1418 Rue Pierce, could practically document the history of the comic book (both new and used) but also sells toys, T-shirts, cards and more. It's open to 11 pm weekdays, to 6 pm Saturday and to 5 pm Sunday. Ⓜ Guy-Concordia.

Newspapers & Magazines
Canada's oldest news agent (1918), Metropolitan News Agency (Map 5; ☎ 866-9227), 1109 Rue Cypress, carries more than 5,000 newspapers and magazines from across the globe. You'll find obscure Montréal acquisition and sports periodicals, too. It's open daily 8 am to 6:30 pm. Ⓜ Peel.

Maison de la Presse Internationale (Map 5; ☎ 844-4508), 1393 Rue Ste Catherine Ouest, stocks newspapers from a couple dozen countries, magazines on every imaginable subject and best-selling paperbacks. It's open 7:30 am to 11 pm Monday to Wednesday, to midnight Thursday to Saturday and 8 am to 11 pm Sunday. Ⓜ Peel.

Clothing

Contemporary Zulu (Map 5; ☎ 878-3993), 60 Rue Ste Catherine Est, in the skinny, stand-alone building with Roy Lichtenstein cartoon faces on the sides, has the latest street-, surf- and sportswear. The really hip gear is pricey (for example, baggy skating pants for about $70), but keep an eye out for clearance sales. It's open noon to 9 pm daily. Ⓜ St Laurent.

Underworld (Map 6; ☎ 284-6473), 289 Rue Ste Catherine Est, is Montréal's biggest punk supply store, with lots of carefully ripped clothes, a big CD and record store and a crunchy clientele. Hours are 10 am to 7 pm Monday to Saturday (to 11 pm Thursday and Friday) and 11 am to 7 pm Sunday. Ⓜ Berri-UQAM.

Vintage & Off-the-Wall Behind the storefront swarm of plastic cockroaches, Boutique Eva B (Map 5; ☎ 849-8246), 2013 Blvd St Laurent, has a great selection of secondhand women's clothing. You'll probably find that glow-in-the-dark alpaca halter top here. The leather jackets for both sexes are also cheap, and the theatrically minded can borrow costumes, too. It's open 10 am to midnight daily (from noon on Sunday). Ⓜ St Laurent.

For more secondhand items, make a pilgrimage farther up Blvd St Laurent to Ave du Mont Royal Est. This is the hub of hip vintage and home to a dozen stores such as Scarlet O'Hara Boutique (Map 8; ☎ 844-9435) at No 254, Rose Nanane (☎ 289-9833) at No 118 and Rebella (☎ 844-4434) at No 151. Ⓜ Mont Royal. On Blvd St Laurent near here, the Friperie St Laurent (Map 8; ☎ 842-3893), at No 3976, has more good secondhand gear and some screaming 1940s ties. A few doors down, Twist Encore (☎ 842-1308), at No 3972, is another favorite. Ⓜ Sherbrooke.

For those who'd rather go naked than dress poor and don't have a budget for fancy labels, the city's factory outlets are the best bet. The most famous is Le Château (Map 2; ☎ 341-5301), 5255 Rue Jean Talon Est, but there's also a smaller, more conveniently located section in the Eaton Centre.

While it's not the most prestigious label, it's a good el-cheapo imitation of what's hip.

Urban Outfitters (Map 5; ☎ 874-0063), 1246 Rue Ste Catherine Ouest, is an impossibly trendy place with garments ranging from off-the-wall trash to the smart and fashionable. It also stocks President Kennedy GI Joe dolls, solar-powered toothbrushes and other items of the second. Ⓜ Peel.

Gothic slaves will enjoy Diabolik (Map 8; ☎ 849-1049), 257 Ave Mont Royal Est, with some pretty bizarre ready-for-casket wear (for example, low-cut shrouds and tombstone chasers). You can't miss the gargoyles out front. It's open to 6 pm (to 9 pm Thursday and Friday). Ⓜ Mont Royal.

Family Marks & Spencer (Map 5; ☎ 499-8558), 1500 Ave McGill College in the Place Montréal Trust complex, repeats the formula that has made it one of Britain's most-loved clothing stores: well-made, reasonably stylish garments at affordable prices. There's an in-house supermarket with tasty, albeit expensive, ready-to-eat foods. It's open daily. Ⓜ Peel or McGill.

Cohoe's (Map 4; ☎ 849-1341), 409 Rue Notre Dame Ouest, has been flogging low-priced women's, men's and kids' clothing for almost half a century. Prices are slashed on slow-moving items, even up-to-the-minute fashions. Keep your eyes peeled for the clearance racks, which offer some impressive discounts. It's open daily (11 am to 5 pm Sunday). Ⓜ Square Victoria.

Fur & Leather Buying garments made from animal skins is a controversial matter, although it might not seem so in Montréal – more than three-quarters of Canada's fur makers are located here. You'll also find quite a few shops selling Canadian leathers.

Fourrures Dubarry (Map 5; ☎ 844-7483), 370 Rue Sherbooke Ouest, carries oodles of off-the-rack jackets, hats, fur-trim capes and coats. There are no middlemen, which keeps prices low. It's open Monday to Saturday. Ⓜ Place des Arts.

HSG Fur Group (Map 5; ☎ 985-6655), 1449 Rue St Alexandre, handles the furs for a major Montréal store and has a good selection of high-end brands (Guy Laroches, Alfred Sung and others). Expect to pay between $3000 and $10,000 for a full-length sable or mink.  Place des Arts.

Alaska Leather Garments (Map 9; ☎ 277-6259), 71 Ave St Viateur Est, supplies some of Montréal's swankiest boutiques. Men's and women's jackets and coats in up-to-date styles can be had for about half the price of those downtown.  Laurier.

Music

There's a brilliant collection of small, independent record shops in the Plateau, each quirkier than the last, along or near Blvd St Laurent and Rue St Denis. Among them, Musique Noize (Map 8; ☎ 985-9989), 3697 Blvd St Laurent, is good for techno, house, hip-hop, dub and jazz, and has a great stock of '70s and '80s fare, on both vinyl and CD. There's also a recording cabin, rentable by the hour, for writing music and mixing CDs. Also see the Books & Comics section, earlier, for bookstores that carry music.  Sherbrooke.

Rotation (Map 8; ☎ 848-9562), 30 Rue Prince Arthur Ouest, is a record boutique with a chi-chi lounge atmosphere. You can sip an espresso and sit on comfy chairs while absorbing the latest techno, house and minimalist releases.  Sherbrooke.

Cheap Thrills (Map 5; ☎ 844-8988), 2044 Rue Metcalfe, is the oldest used CD and cassette shop in town, with a decent collection of paperbacks and records. The selection covers everything from electronica, noise and indie-rock to jazz, blues and R&B, including hard-to-find imports. Upstairs, you can buy new recordings at a discount, usually several dollars below prices elsewhere. In addition to standard opening hours, it's open Sunday afternoon.  Peel.

Mojo (Map 8; ☎ 282-7730), 3968 Blvd St Laurent, has reggae, soul, jazz and funk and lots of hard-to-find records. If you've been hankering for a late-1960s Recorded at Playboy Mansion jazz album, chances are you'll find it here. Look for the Moorish arches and fan blades outside.  Sherbrooke.

The larger chains include the well-stocked Sam The Record Man (Map 5; ☎ 281-9877),

Shear Delights

Need a trim while you're in ravetown Montréal? The city has droves of modish cutters, including Kenzo Hair (Map 8; ☎ 286-2510), 72 Ave Duluth Est. The billowing curtains, mirror globes and Himalayan murals make for a trip into another dimension, wherever that may be. Count on paying upward of $35. It's closed Sunday.  Sherbrooke or Mont Royal.

399 Rue Ste Catherine Ouest, and the cavernous, multilevel HMV (Map 5; ☎ 875-0765), 1020 Rue Ste Catherine Ouest, which doubles as an entertainment center (it even has a stage for live bands).

Underworld is primarily a clothing shop, but CDs and records are also on offer (see Clothing, Contemporary, earlier).

Sports & Outdoor

For survival, sporting and leisure gear, Le Baron (Map 5; ☎ 866-8848), 932 Rue Notre Dame Ouest, is the top address in town. Backpack buyers should set aside a few hours just to look.  Bonaventure.

Centre de Surplus (Map 8; ☎ 524-6819), 967 Ave Mont Royal Est, carries a wide assortment of camping and outdoor gear, including bicycle accessories. Items are sometimes dusty or faded, as they have been picked up cheap from retailers, but the prices are great.  Mont Royal.

A fixture in Vieux Montréal, the Atelier Boutique de Cerfs Volants (Map 4; ☎ 845-7613), 224 Rue St Paul Ouest, does kites – boxes, multitailed dragons, the Michelin man, you name it. The owner will make creations to order, guaranteed for three years, and leads occasional kite-flying days at the Vieux Port.  Square Victoria or Place d'Armes.

Cameras & Video Supplies

Simon's Camera (Map 4; ☎ 861-5401), 11 Rue St Antoine Ouest, has one of the city's best selections of cameras, cases, tripods, camcorders and other equipment at

The US trade embargo against the Castro regime helps keep the stogie market alive and well in Canada.

competitive prices. They take trade-ins, sell used items and rent equipment. Ⓜ Place d'Armes.

On the main shopping drag, York Photo (Map 5; ☎ 874-0824), 1344 Rue Ste Catherine Ouest, is a cross between a musical instrument and camera store. It carries new and used cameras, videos and lenses. Ⓜ Peel or Guy-Concordia.

AFC Camera Service (Map 5; ☎ 397-9505), 1015 Côte du Beaver Hall, is a good-value camera and video repair service. Its friendly staff will look at your camera and charge $10 if no repair is necessary or desired. It's closed Sunday. Ⓜ Square Victoria.

Electronics

Future Shop (Map 5; ☎ 393-2600), 470 Rue Ste Catherine Ouest, is Canada's one-stop-shop for music systems, computers and software, printers, cellular needs, video cameras and other entertainment gadgets. Its weekly flyers have some pretty good price reductions. It's open 9 am to 9 pm weekdays, 10 am to 9 pm Saturday and noon to 9 pm Sunday. Ⓜ McGill or Place des Arts.

Erotica

Lingerie Romance (Map 5; ☎ 876-3656), 38 Rue Ste Catherine Ouest, displays its seductive trappings over 5000 sq ft of shop space. It also carries swimwear, massage lotions, games and joke items.

Sexe Cité (Map 5; ☎ 937-3678), 1821 Rue Ste Catherine Ouest, has more accessories than you'd think could fit into a sex bou-

tique – videos, latex, vinyl, lingerie, leather and more. It's open to midnight daily. Ⓜ Guy-Concordia.

Cigars

H Poupart (Map 5; ☎ 842-5794), 1385 Rue Ste Catherine Ouest, is the Rolls-Royce of Montréal tobacco shops. Here you'll find the city's largest selection of cigarettes, cigars and pipe tobaccos from the far corners of the earth, stored in old-fashioned walnut drawers. It's open 9 am to 6:30 pm weekdays (to 9 pm Thursday and Friday), to 5:30 pm Saturday and noon to 4 pm Sunday. Ⓜ Guy-Concordia.

La Casa del Habano (Map 5; ☎ 849-0037), 1434 Rue Sherbrooke Ouest, has 50 brands of Cuban cigar, plus cutters, humidors, lighters and other cigaraphernalia. There's a lounge and espresso bar that attracts young puffers. It's open Monday to Saturday plus Sunday afternoon. Ⓜ Guy-Concordia.

Travel Supplies

Instead of buying this stuff in the duty-free shop, visit Jet-Setter (Map 9; ☎ 271-5058), 66 Ave Laurier Ouest, which stocks all the odd gadgets that make travel bearable – credit-card-size knife sets, money pouches, electricity converters, water filters and those pillows that keep you from breaking your neck when you fall asleep. There's a good selection of maps and travel books (lots of Lonely Planet titles). It's open daily (noon to 5 pm Sunday). Ⓜ Laurier.

Excursions

When it comes to short trips from Montréal, you're spoiled for choice. Within an hour's drive, there's a cheese-making monastery, a maple sugar shack, white-water rapids, fabulous skiing and hiking in the Laurentian Mountains, as well as the bucolic Cantons de l'Est (Eastern Townships). Farther afield, plan on spending a couple of days exploring charming Québec City, the only walled town in North America, and Ottawa, the nation's oft-underrated capital.

OKA

About 50km west of Montréal, where the Ottawa River meets the St Lawrence River, this small town is known for its **cheese-making monastery** (☎ 450-479-8361) dating from the 1880s. Some 70 Trappist monks still live there, but it's open to visitors, who come to see the religious artworks, a mountain with the Stages of the Cross and several old stone buildings. The chapel, gardens and boutique are all closed Sunday.

In 1990, Oka was the arena of a major confrontation between Mohawk people and the federal and provincial governments. At first a local land squabble, this issue soon came to represent all the continuing issues such as land claims and self-government that Native Indians across the country would like to see properly resolved.

On the edge of the large Lac des Deux Montagnes, the **Parc d'Oka** (Oka Park; ☎ 514-479-8337) offers a bunch of activities, including bathing on a sandy beach (supervised), sailing, canoeing, kayaking and cycling. You can also rent cross-country skis and snowshoes for the 70km of trails. There's a good campsite, too.

From Montréal, take Hwys 15 or 13 to Hwy 640 (Ouest), which leads to Hwy 344. The monastery and park are signposted.

RIVIÈRE ROUGE

About an hour's drive northwest of Montréal is the Rouge River, one of the best white-water rivers in North America. New World River Expeditions (☎ 819-242-7238 or 1-800-361-5033), based in Calumet, Québec (near Hawkesbury, Ontario), offers

Rivière Rouge offers one of the best white-water adventures in North America.

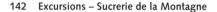

EXCURSIONS

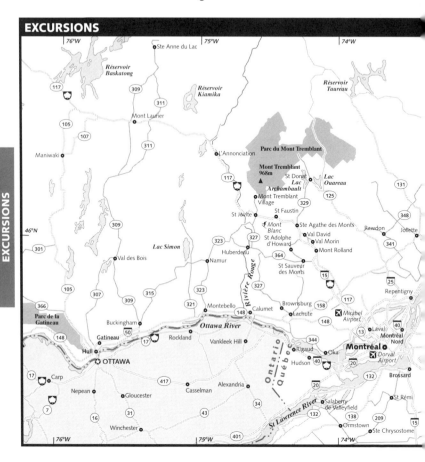

five-hour trips from April to October (reserve ahead), which cost $85 ($89 on Sunday) including a hot dog lunch. Be prepared to go overboard: If your raft doesn't flip in the rapids, the guides will make sure it flips. There's a restaurant-lodge and pool, so you're not exactly roughing it. Two to five-day trips are on offer, too. Staff will fax or tell you directions – the route's a bit tricky.

SUCRERIE DE LA MONTAGNE
Situated in a maple forest, this place (☎ 450-451-0831) depicts a 20th-century Québec sugar shack where sap is converted to maple syrup and sugar. A visit includes a tour and an explanation by the grizzled proprietor, a meal and folk music – a tad staged but fun. The lunch package costs $30, the dinner $40. The shack is open all year.

To get to the site, 70km west from downtown Montréal, take Hwy 40 west to 300 Rang St Georges, Rigaud. Without a car, take the train to Rigaud and take a $16 taxi ride.

There are seasonal sugar shacks throughout the Laurentians; ask at the Montréal tourist office (listed in the Facts for the Visitor chapter).

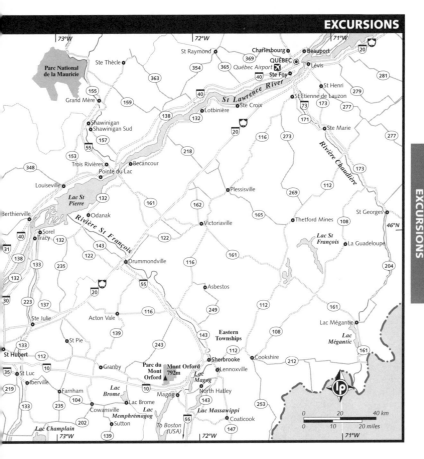

LES LAURENTIDES

Between 80km and 150km north of Montréal, the Laurentian Mountains are a lake-sprinkled playground popular not only for skiing, but also for hiking, camping, fishing and swimming. Cyclists enjoy good distance trails and rougher mountain biking in many areas. The picturesque French towns and scenery make it great for relaxing as well. For an overview, check out the Web site www.laurentides.com.

The Laurentians tourist association (☎ 450-436-8532, 514-990-5625 or 1-800-561-6673) has extensive information on the region, and runs a free lodging reservation service. The office is at 14142 Rue de la Chapelle in Mirabel (about 50km northwest of Montréal, near Mirabel Airport).

St Sauveur des Monts

This first stop-off on the way north, about 60km from Montréal, is a small, pleasant resort town with four nearby ski hills. It's a favorite refuge for weekend day-trippers, especially on Sunday afternoons. The tourist office (☎ 450-229-3729 or 1-800-898-2127) is at 605 Ch des Frênes; from Hwy 15, take exit 60.

Close by, on the other side of Hwy 364 is **Mont St Sauveur**, one of the area's most important centers of Alpine skiing. The first mechanical ski lift in North America was built here in 1934. The cute little Anglican church, **Église Épiscopale St François d'Assise**, on Rue St Denis, is built out of logs; look for the bird motifs on the windows.

Summer or winter, day or night, Rue Principale is always bustling with restaurants, cafés, hotels and shops. The highly recommended *Auberge Victorienne* (☎ 450-227-2328, 119 Rue Principale) is furnished in grand Victorian style, even the bathrooms. It charges from $65/70 for singles/doubles. The charming, tastefully decorated *Aux Petits Oiseaux* (☎ 450-227-6116 or 1-800-227-6116, email auxpetitsoiseaux@sympatico.ca, 342 Rue Principale) has great mountain views and rooms for $75/85.

La Brûlerie des Monts (☎ 450-227-6157, 197 Rue Principale) is a great spot for breakfast, salads and Sunday lunch. Count on paying $8 to $12 per head. There's a good view of the church from upstairs. The *Restaurant des Oliviers* (☎ 450-227-2110, 239 Rue Principale) offers a good French table d'hôte for $11 to $25.

Val David

Close to Ste Agathe (see the next section) but to the east off Hwy 15, Val David is a small town that's become an arts & crafts center. Studios and workshops can be visited, and stores sell a variety of handicrafts. There's a good bike trail and cross-country ski options along the elongated city park.

There's an inn/HI hostel, *Le Chalet Beaumont* (☎ 819-322-1972, 1451 Rue Beaumont), perched on a hill with great views. Hostel beds go from $18 and private rooms cost $35 per person. There are also family rooms. All meals are available, and there is a common kitchen. If you call ahead, you may be able to get picked up from the bus stop. The village also has several B&Bs and motels.

The *Auberge du Vieux Foyer* (☎ 819-322-2686, 3167 1er Rang Doncaster) serves quality, affordable Québec cuisine, from $12 for main courses. In the village, *Le Grand Pas*

(☎ 819-322-3104, 2481 Rue de l'Église) is a convivial place also offering hearty meals from $12. It's closed in April.

Ste Agathe des Monts & St Donat

Sainte Agathe is the largest town in the Laurentians (with about 6000 residents) and a busy resort center with lots of history and atmosphere. Queen Elizabeth took refuge here during WWII, and Jackie Kennedy was among other famous guests.

The tourist office (☎ 819-326-0457 or 1-800-326-0457) is at 24 Rue St Paul and stays open to 8 pm. In town, at the edge of Lac des Sables, there's room for a picnic, and cruises of the lake depart from the wharf. Around the lake are busy sandy beaches (admission $5).

In town at the lakeside, *Chez Girard* (☎ 819-326-5228, 10 Ch Tour du Lac) has elegant, spacious rooms from $45 ($60 with fireplace). It also serves some of the town's Québec-style meals, including game and seafood for $28 to $35. *La Sauvagine* (☎ 819-326-7673 or 1-800-787-7172, 1592 Hwy 329) has rustic rooms and a riverside pool and charges $55/80 for singles/doubles.

The *Kamenbert & Poivre Noir* (☎ 819-326-7968, 133 Rue Principale) is among the cheapest places on the main drag. It's a cheese shop and butcher that serves a good fixed-price lunch for $7.

Northeast of Ste Agathe, the little lakeside town of St Donat is a supply center for Mont Tremblant Park, which lies just to the north. There are beaches on **Lac Archambault** and, in summer, 90-minute cruises around the lake. Bars and cafés along the main streets are lively at night.

St Faustin

Saint Faustin (population 1400) is the base for Mont Blanc. In summer, you can visit the large Centre Educatif, a nature interpretive center at Lac du Cordon with 35km of walking and hiking trails. Guided walks are given, detailing flora and fauna of the area, and there is canoeing and camping. Admission is $5/3.50/2.50 for adults/seniors and students/children six to 12.

There is a maple-sugar shack here open in April and May, where the production can be seen and the results sampled. Cabane à Sucre Millette (☎ 819-688-2101) is at 1357 Rue St Faustin.

The Pisciculture, a trout hatchery in a wooded setting just off Lac Carré at 747 Ch de la Pisciculture, can also be visited. The fish raised here are used to restock the rivers and lakes of the Laurentians. Nearby, on the other side of small Lac Carré, there's a free public beach. North of town, roads lead past Lac Supérieur into Mont Tremblant Park.

Mont Tremblant

Mont Tremblant is a three-part resort and park district that marks the northernmost point of the easily accessible Laurentian destinations.

Mont Tremblant Village is the older, more genuine section with restaurants, accommodations and stores. About 4km to the east is Mont Tremblant itself (968m), the area's highest peak and a major ski center (☎ 819-681-2000 or 1-800-461-8711, 3005 Ch Principal) with more than 60 runs. Web site: www.tremblant.ca.

There are state-of-the-art ski facilities here as well as golf courses, water sports, cycling and tennis. A chair lift runs to the mountain peak year-round. At the foot of the mountain, there's a traditional-looking 'Alpine' township including hotels, condos, bars and restaurants, with walking paths alongside pretty Lac Tremblant.

The tourist office (☎ 819-425-2434) is a few kilometers south of the village on the corner of Ch Principal and Montée Ryan. It's open daily all year.

There's a beach at Lac Mercier at the western edge of the village; admission is $2 (waived if you're staying at the hostel). Bicycles and skates can be rented for the 10km skating/cycling path that goes through town and over to the resort.

Places to Stay & Eat The *HI Tremblant International Hostel* (☎ 819-425-6008, email info@hostellingtremblant.com), is a popular place to stay. Just 1km from the village center, the hostel has 80 dorm beds

The Laurentian Mountains are a haven for outdoor enthusiasts, including skiers.

EXCURSIONS

from $18 (sheets included), up to $58 for doubles. If you stay here and at the Montréal hostel, you can catch a free shuttle bus in the 'peak' season. Web site: www.hostellingtremblant.com.

Within the village, *Le Couvent* (☎ 819-425-8608, 135b Rue du Couvent) offers a great value, with singles/doubles going for $70/80. It has a terrific terrace, too. The *Auberge Sauvignon* (☎ 819-425-5466, email sauvignon@tremblant.com, 2723 Ch Principal) charms with its rural furnishings and charges $80 for a double ($95 in winter).

The tourist office can also help locate a place. Call ☎ 1-800-567-6760 for the reservation service.

If cheese is your thing, try *La Savoie* (☎ 819-681-4573, 3005 Ch Principal) for fondues and raclette costing $15 to $20. They also do excellent grilled meats and fish (from $17). There are other places along Ch Principal, including *Trembagel*, a favorite bagel bakery in the tiny old section of town.

Getting There & Away Limocar Laurentides buses run from Montréal's main bus station to St Jovite, which is a 10-minute drive to Tremblant, from Thursday to Saturday. In ski season, special buses operate to various hills; call the Laurentians tourist center at ☎ 1-800-561-6673 for details. There's no public transport, but the HI hostel (see Places to Stay & Eat, above) operates a shuttle service.

The Autoroute Laurentienne (Hwy 15) is the fastest route north from Montréal. The old Hwy 117 north is slower but more pleasant. A second major route goes northeast of Montréal to Joliette, and then smaller roads continue farther north.

Parc du Mont Tremblant
Opened in 1894, this wild, wooded area (1500 sq km) about 25km from Mont Tremblant features many hiking and biking trails as well as river routes for canoes. There are many campgrounds in the park; some have amenities, but most are basic.

The park is divided into sectors. The most developed is the Diable, close to Mont Tremblant and pretty **Lac Supérieur**. At the lake, there's an information center (☎ 819-688-2281) and canoes for rent. There are numerous trails in the vicinity, including a 30-minute walk to Diable Falls.

Farther east, the Pimbina sector (☎ 819-424-2954) north of St Donat also has an information center, rentals and campgrounds with some amenities. **Lac Provost** nearby is great for swimming and has hiking and biking trails. The wilder interior is accessible by unsurfaced roads, some of which are rough old logging routes.

LES CANTONS DE L'EST (THE EASTERN TOWNSHIPS)
Known as the 'Garden of Québec,' this region is appreciated for its rolling hills, green farmland, woods and lakes – an extension of the US Appalachians. Also called 'L'Estrie' by French-speakers, this 13,100-sq-km area begins 80km southeast of Montréal and extends to the Vermont and New Hampshire borders. Keep an eye out for the remaining covered bridges and round barns.

Spring is the season for 'sugaring off' – the tapping, boiling and preparation of maple syrup (see the boxed text). Summer brings fishing and swimming in the numerous lakes. During fall, the foliage dazzles and apples are harvested, with lots of cider being produced. Skiing is a major winter activity, with centers at Mont Orford and Sutton.

The Eastern Townships were mainly English until the 1970s. Once the homeland of Abenakis Indians, the region became a refuge for Loyalists fleeing the USA after the revolution of 1776. Irish immigrants, and later French settlers, have added to the area's diversity.

The main regional tourist office (☎ 1-800-263-1068) is on the Autoroute (Hwy 10) south from Montréal at exit 68. It's open daily all year. Other offices can be found in Magog, Granby and Sherbrooke.

L'Estrie is a great hiking and cycling region, and rentals are available in Magog, North Hatley and other places. The district also produces some wines and most notably, mead, an ancient nectar made from fermented honey. You can follow a self-guided wine tour through the region. Visit the Web site www.tourisme-cantons.qc.ca for more information on the area.

Note that accommodations in this area tend to be on the expensive side.

Lac Champlain
Although essentially a US lake that divides Vermont from New York State, Lac Champlain protrudes into Québec as well. Steeped in history, the area is popular with Canadian and US holidaymakers.

The lake is good for swimming and fishing and, in places, is scenic. At Plattsburgh, New York, there's a good and busy beach, where you'll find plenty of Québecers on summer weekends. The short, pleasant ferry trip across part of the lake is worth taking if you're traveling through the area.

Granby
The Granby Zoo (☎ 450-372-9113) is known far and wide in Québec. Its displays of a thousand-plus animals include reptiles, an African pavilion with gorillas and a cave of nocturnal animals. The newest crowd-puller is a huge, Amazon-style waterpark equipped with a wave pool, beaches and water slide. Admission is $20/15/9 for adults/seniors, students and children two to four.

Lac Brome (Knowlton)
South of Hwy 10 on Hwy 243 is the town of Lac Brome, on the lake of the same name. Seven former English Loyalist villages, including Knowlton, make up the town of 5000. Many of the main street's Victorian

buildings have been restored, and it's a bit of a tourist center with craft and gift shops. A favorite meal in this area is Lac Brome duck, which shows up frequently on the better menus.

Sutton

Farther south, Sutton is synonymous with its ski hill, one of the area's highest. In summer, there are hiking trails in Sutton Park. Around Sutton and near the village of Dunham, there are a number of Québec's wineries open for visiting, as well as apple orchards open for purchases (or casual fall work). A 10km cycling path runs south to the US border. At the natural environment park, there's the decidedly nonregional llama-breeding farm, where rides on the haughty creatures can be attempted.

Magog

At the northern tip of large Lac Memphré-magog, Magog (population 15,000) is an attractive town with a resort flavor, good for walking and relaxing. The main street, Rue Principale, has a flotilla of cafés, bars, bistros and restaurants. The tourist office (☎ 819-843-2744), 55 Rue Cabana, provides information about the area. Web site: www .magog-orford.qc.ca. Two-hour boat cruises are offered around the lake daily in summer.

Parc du Mont Orford

Just out of Magog, this is a good but relatively small park (though the largest in the Eastern Townships). Dominated by Mont Orford (792m), the park is a skiing center in winter but fills up quickly with campers in summer. You can swim here and walk the trails; the chair lift operates throughout summer.

Each summer, the Orford Art Centre presents the Jeunesses Musicales du Canada music and art festival. The HI hostel *Auberge la Grand Fugue* (☎ 819-843-8595), on the wooded grounds of the center, is open April to November. It's a very comfortable, spacious hostel with some rustic cabins, and it makes a good base for exploring the park. Bicycles can be rented here. Call for transportation details from Magog, where there's a bus station.

Lac Memphrémagog

This is the largest and best-known lake in the Eastern Townships, but most lakefront properties are privately owned. Halfway down the lake at St Benoît du Lac is a **Benedictine monastery**, where, even from a distance, you can still hear the monks performing the ancient Gregorian chants. Visitors can attend services, and there's a hostel for men and another nearby at a nunnery

Québec's Liquid Gold

Québec is the world's largest maker of maple syrup, and the Eastern Townships, with their abundance of sugar-maple forests, is the obvious center of production.

It's believed that the indigenous Indians, who had a spring date known as the sugar-making moon, passed their knowledge onto early pioneers. Production techniques vary, but essentially in spring, when the sap begins to run, the trees are tapped and buckets are hung from them to collect, drop by drop, the clear sap. The liquid is then poured into large kettles and boiled at a 'sugar shack' for days, driving off most of the water. As it thickens, the sap's color becomes more intense and the sugar content rises to around 90%. It's then cooled, graded and bottled.

It's most often spread over vanilla ice cream or pancakes, but many people eat it on just about anything – it's not bad on bacon, for instance. A further refining results in maple sugar. The Montréal or Eastern Townships tourist offices can tell you where to see a demonstration of the process in early spring. Maple syrup is also produced in eastern and central Ontario and in New Brunswick.

Unfortunately, acid rain has seriously damaged the maple forests of Québec, and there's concern over the future of this small-farm industry.

for women, if you want to stay. One of Québec's cheeses – L'Ermite, a blue cheese – is made and sold here. Also try to taste the cider the monks make (call ☎ 819-843-4080 for information). **Rock Island**, at the southern end of the lake, is a busy border crossing.

North Hatley

Just east of Magog, North Hatley sits at the north end of Lac Massawippi, the shape of which can make the waters quickly turn rough. The village was a popular second home for wealthy US citizens who enjoyed the scenery, but even more, they enjoyed the absence of Prohibition during the 1920s. Many of these huge old places are now inns and B&Bs. Try the Massawippi dark beer at *Le Pilsen* pub. There's an English-language theater in town along with galleries and antique and craft stores.

Sherbrooke

Sherbrooke is the region's main commercial center, with several small museums, a wide selection of restaurants and a pleasant central core lying between the Magog and St François Rivers. The city is bilingual.

The tourist office (☎ 819-821-1919) is at 3010 Rue King Ouest. The 18km walking and cycling path along the Magog River, known as Réseau Riverain, makes for an agreeable stroll. It begins at the edge of the Magog River in Blanchard Park.

The **Musée des Beaux Arts**, 241 Rue Dufferin, is a sizable art gallery open every afternoon except Monday. The local fall fair is a big event held each August.

On the outskirts at Bromptonville is the **Shrine of Beauvoir**, dating from 1920, a site of religious pilgrimages with good views over the city and the surrounding area. In **Lennoxville**, there's Bishop's, an English university. Also in Lennoxville are a couple of cottage breweries and some antique and craft shops to browse through. On Hwy 216 toward Stokes is the **Centre d'Interpretation de l'Abeille**, the Honey Bee Interpretive Center, a research facility open to visitors, with displays about the little buzzers and the honey they produce.

Places to Stay & Eat Here, as elsewhere around the Eastern Townships, the motels, hotels and inns are not at all cheap. Alternative B&Bs can be found through the local tourist office, but these are not cheap either.

In summer, rooms are available at low rates at the university. *Motel L' Ermitage* (☎ 1-888-569-5551, 1888 Rue King Ouest) charges from $65 per double.

Two well-established, four-star eateries are *Au Petit Sabot* and *l'Élite*. For simpler fare, there is the *Marie Antoinette (333 Rue King Ouest)*.

Getting There & Away The bus station (☎ 819-569-3656) is at 20 Rue King Ouest. Various small companies run to Montréal, Trois Rivières, Magog, Granby and other regional towns.

Southwest of town, several of the smaller area highways join Hwy 55, which leads south to Rock Island, the major entry point into the USA, close to the states of New York, Vermont and New Hampshire. During summer, particularly on weekends, there can be major waits (as in hours) at this border, as officials check vehicles for goods being imported.

MONTRÉAL TO QUÉBEC CITY

Leaving Montréal behind, traveling east on Hwy 138, you begin to get a sense of what small-town Québec is like. Stone houses with light-blue trim and tin roofs, silver-spired churches, ubiquitous chip (french fry) wagons (called cantines) and main streets with shops built right to the road, are some characteristics. The best section is from Trois Rivières onward to the northeast.

A much quicker route is Hwy 40, a four-lane expressway that can get you from Montréal to Québec City in 2½ to three hours. There are not many services along this route, so watch your fuel levels.

From Montréal, there is also one fast and one slow route along the south shore to Québec City and beyond. The old Hwy 132 edges along the river but isn't as nice as its north shore counterpart (Hwy 138). The Trans Canada (Hwy 40) here is the fastest way to Québec City but is boring until beyond Québec, where it runs a little closer to the water. At Trois Rivières, you can cross the river.

Louiseville

One of Canada's grandest churches is easy to miss if you don't look hard. **St Antoine de Padoue Church** is in Louiseville, on the north side of the St Lawrence River. Topped by a silver steeple typical of Québec, the church has a rather plain interior, but the sheer dimensions of the place are breathtaking.

Odanak

Almost directly across the river from Louiseville is Odanak, a small Abenakis Indian village settled in the early 17th century. A museum (☎ 450-568-5959) on Hwy 226 outlines their history and culture. It's open 10 am to 5 pm weekdays, 1 to 5 pm weekends (closed on weekends from November to April). Admission is $4/2 for adults/seniors and students. An annual powwow is held the first Sunday of July.

Trois Rivières

Trois Rivières, more than 350 years old and the largest town between Québec's two main cities, is a major pulp and paper center. Don't bother looking – there aren't three rivers. The name of the town refers to the way the Maurice River divides as it approaches the St Lawrence.

The attractive **old town**, based around Rue Notre Dame and Rue des Forges with its reminders of a long history, is small but good for a stroll. Cafés and bars are abundant in this lively area. Rue des Ursulines and Rue Radisson are also main streets. There's a year-round tourist office (☎ 819-375-1122) at 1457 Rue Notre Dame. Listen for the Blues Festival in July.

On Rue des Ursulines are several old houses now open to the public as small free museums and examples of various architectural styles. The **Ursuline Museum** (☎ 819-375-7922), at No 734, displays materials relating to the Ursuline Order of nuns who were prominent in the town's development. Admission is $2.50 for adults. The **Manoir Boucher de Niverville** (☎ 819-376-4459), a

historic house at 168 Rue Bonaver, the corner of Rue Hart, has chang plays on the city's past.

The **Cathèdrale de l'Assomption** (1858), at 362 Rue Bonaventure, is the only Westminster-style church on the continent and is open daily.

Two-hour **cruises** along the river aboard the MS *Jacques Cartier* depart from the dock in Parc Portuaire at the foot of Blvd des Forges, in the center of the old town.

There's an HI hostel here, *Auberge la Flotille* (☎ 819-378-8010, 497 Rue Radisson), where dorms cost $18 and single rooms $36. A good $3 breakfast is available, and small tours of local areas of interest are offered. The hostel is about a 10-minute walk from the bus station. Several motels can be found on Blvd Royal.

The old train station at 1075 Rue Champflour is now used solely for buses (☎ 819-374-2944); there's no train service. Voyageur Colonial and Orléans Express go to Montréal and Québec City; Autobus Messier goes to Sherbrooke and elsewhere in the Eastern Townships.

Lotbinière

A stately museum, **La Domaine Joly de Lotbinière**, lies on the south shore of the St Lawrence River, between Lotbinière and Ste Croix, on the way to Québec City from Trois Rivières. It was built for Henri Gustave Joly de Lotbinière (1849–1908), once the premier of Québec. Not only is this one of the most impressive manors built during the seigneurial period of Québec, it remains nearly as it was in the late 19th century. The outbuildings and huge cultivated garden are a treat in themselves. Lunch and afternoon teas are served. It's open June 24 to Labour Day. Admission is $8/6 for adults/seniors, students and children.

QUÉBEC CITY
☎ 418

Québec City, rich in history, culture and beauty, is the heart of French Canada. The old city in particular is an architectural gem, with its centuries-old churches, old stone houses and narrow streets. The district has

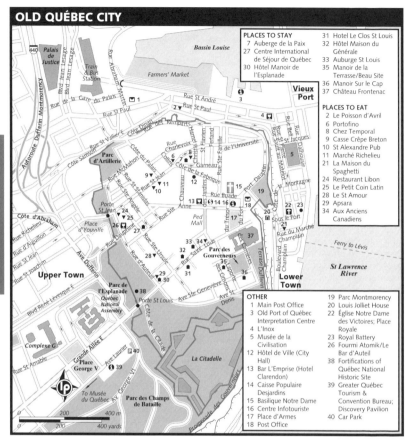

OLD QUÉBEC CITY

PLACES TO STAY
7 Auberge de la Paix
27 Centre International de Séjour de Québec
30 Hôtel Manoir de l'Esplanade
31 Hotel Le Clos St Louis
32 Hôtel Maison du Générale
33 Auberge St Louis
35 Manoir de la Terrasse/Beau Site
36 Manoir Sur le Cap
37 Château Frontenac

PLACES TO EAT
2 Le Poisson d'Avril
6 Portofino
8 Chez Temporal
9 Casse Crêpe Breton
10 St Alexandre Pub
11 Marché Richelieu
21 La Maison du Spaghetti
24 Restaurant Libon
25 Le Petit Coin Latin
28 Le St Amour
29 Apsara
34 Aux Anciens Canadiens

OTHER
1 Main Post Office
3 Old Port of Québec Interpretation Centre
4 L'Inox
5 Musée de la Civilisation
10 Hôtel de Ville (City Hall)
12 Bar L'Emprise (Hotel Clarendon)
14 Caisse Populaire Desjardins
15 Basilique Notre Dame
16 Centre Infotouriste
17 Place d'Armes
18 Post Office
19 Parc Montmorency
20 Louis Jolliet House
22 Église Notre Dame des Victoires; Place Royale
23 Royal Battery
26 Fourmi Atomik/Le Bar d'Auteil
38 Fortifications of Québec National Historic Site
39 Greater Québec Tourism & Convention Bureau; Discovery Pavilion
40 Car Park

been declared a Unesco World Heritage site and remains the only walled city in North America.

The city is also an important port, lying where the St Charles River (Rivière St Charles) meets the St Lawrence River. It sits on top of and around a cliff, a wonderful setting with views over the St Lawrence River and the town of Lévis (pronounced not as in jeans but 'lev-ee') across the river.

Although the vast majority of Québec City's 690,000 residents are French-speaking and have French ancestors, English is spoken around the attractions and in shops.

Exhibits at national sites are bilingual, whereas some provincial attractions are labeled only in French. Before buying any ticket, it's good to ask.

There are good summer and winter attractions, but it must be said that the winters get numbingly cold, much colder than in Montréal. There may be mountains of snow, especially in January and February.

History

One of the continent's earliest settlements, the site of Québec City was an Iroquois Indian village called 'Stadacone' when the

French explorer Jacques Cartier landed here in 1534. The name 'Québec' is derived from an Algonquian Indian word meaning 'the river narrows here.' Explorer Samuel de Champlain founded the city for the French in 1608 and built a fort in 1620.

The English successfully attacked in 1629, but Québec was returned to the French under a treaty and became the center of New France. In 1759, General Wolfe led the British to victory over Montcalm on the Plains of Abraham (see the boxed text 'The Battle of Québec City'). In 1763, the Treaty of Paris gave Canada to Britain. In 1775, the American Revolutionaries had a go at capturing Québec and were promptly turned back.

In 1791, the divisions of Upper Canada (Ontario) and Lower Canada (Québec and the Atlantic Provinces) were created. In the early 19th century, Lower Canada became known as Québec and Québec City was chosen as the provincial capital.

Orientation

The city is surprisingly small, covering 93 sq km, with nearly all things of interest packed into one compact corner. Québec is divided into Upper Town and Lower Town; the Citadelle, a fort and famous landmark, stands on the highest point of Cap Diamant overlooking the city. Together, these historic upper and lower areas form the appealing Old City (Vieux Québec).

A well-known landmark in Old Québec is the copper-topped, castle-style Château Frontenac hotel dating from 1892. Behind the Château, a large boardwalk called the Terrasse Dufferin edges along the cliff providing good views over the river. Here you will also find the statue of Monsieur de Champlain, who started it all.

At the other (south) end is the wooden slide used during the Winter Carnival. From here, the boardwalk leads to the Promenade des Gouverneurs, a path that runs between the cliff's edge and the Citadelle. Beyond the Citadelle, outside the walls, is the huge park called Parc des Champs de Bataille. This is where the battles over Québec took place. The park has several historical monuments and some sites within its boundaries.

Information

The main office is Centre Infotouriste (☎ 649-2608 or 1-800-363-7777), 12 Rue Ste Anne on Place d'Armes, opposite the Château Frontenac hotel. The bilingual staff will supply maps and other information, find accommodations and provide a free walking tour booklet of the old town. It's open 8:30 am to 7:30 pm daily late June to early September; at other times it closes at 5 pm.

A second tourist office is at 215 Rue du Marché Finlay (☎ 643-6631) in Lower Town. It's on a large square, Place de Paris, near the water east of Place Royale, and deals mainly with the Place Royale area.

The Greater Québec Tourism and Convention Bureau (☎ 649-2608), 835 Ave Wilfrid Laurier, near the Plains of Abraham, opens 8:30 am to 7 pm daily June to Labour Day, 9 am to 5:15 pm Labour Day to mid-October and 9 am to 5 pm weekdays the rest of the year. Web site: www.quebecregion.com.

Kiosk Frontenac, a booth on Terrasse Dufferin facing the Château Frontenac,

KEVIN LEVESQUE

Château Frontenac, Old Québéc City

EXCURSIONS

makes reservations for all city activities and is the starting point for some tours.

For money, the Caisse Populaire Desjardins (☎ 694-1774), 19 Rue des Jardins, is open daily in summer 9 am to 6 pm. Transchange (☎ 694-6096), 43 Rue Buade, opens 8:30 am to 10 pm in summer. There's also an ATM in the Centre Infotouriste (see above).

There's a post office (☎ 694-6102) in the walled section of Upper Town, at the bottom of Rue Buade at No 3, opposite Parc Montmorency. The main post office (☎ 694-6175) is at 300 Rue St Paul, next to the train station.

Québec has two French daily newspapers, *Le Soleil* and *Journal du Québec.*

Old Upper Town

Citadelle The French started to build here in 1750 when bastions were constructed for storing gunpowder. The fort (☎ 694-2815) was completed by the British in 1820 after 30 years' work and served as the eastern flank of the city's defense system.

Today, the Citadelle is the home base of Canada's Royal 22s, a French regiment that developed quite a reputation through WWI, WWII and the Korean War. There's a museum outlining its history and a more general military museum containing documents, uniforms and models situated in several buildings, including the old prison at the southeast end.

Tours run April to November. The Changing of the Guard ceremony takes place at 10 am daily in summer. The Beating of the Retreat at 6 pm on Tuesday, Thursday, Saturday and Sunday during July and August is followed by the last tour. The Citadelle is still considered a working military site, so wandering around on your own is not permitted.

The entrance fee ($5.50/4/2.75 for adults/seniors/children) includes admission to these museums and a guided tour. Hours are 9 am to 6 pm July to Labour Day and more restricted the rest of the year.

Parc des Champs de Bataille Battlefields Park is the huge park running southwest from the Citadelle. Its hills, gardens, monuments and trees make it pleasant now; however, the park was once a bloody battleground, the site of a conflict that may have determined the course of Canadian history. The part closest to the cliff is known as the **Plains of Abraham**, and it was here in 1759 that the British finally defeated the French – with both generals, Wolfe of the British and Montcalm of the French, dying in the process (see the boxed text).

Walking or bus tours of the park depart from the new Discovery Pavilion (☎ 648-4071), 835 Ave Wilfred Laurier, in the lower level of the Greater Québec Tourism and Convention Bureau.

The National Battlefields Park Interpretive Centre, housed in the Musée du Québec (see later), focuses on the dramatic history of the park with a multimedia show. The center opens daily in summer but is closed on Monday the rest of the year.

Musée du Québec Toward the southwest end of the park at 1 Ave Wolfe Montcalm, the Québec Museum (☎ 643-2150) has changing exhibits, mainly on Québec's art but with major international touring exhibits, too. Encompassing three buildings, it shows both modern and more traditional art, ceramics and decorative works. The old prison nearby is now part of the gallery.

The museum opens 10 am to 5:45 pm daily in summer (to 9:45 pm Wednesday). During other seasons, it's closed Monday. Admission is $7/6/2.75 for adults/seniors/students.

Fortifications of Québec National Historic Site The largely restored old wall (ramparts) site (☎ 648-7016) can be visited free of charge. In fact, you can walk a complete circuit on top of the walls, 4.6km, all around the Old City. At the old Powder Building beside Porte St Louis, an interpretive center has been set up, which provides a little information on the wall's history. Guided walks, for a fee, leave from the Frontenac Kiosk on Terrasse Dufferin.

Parc d'Artillerie Beside the wall at Porte St Jean, Parc d'Artillerie (☎ 648-4205), a National Historic Site, has been used militarily for centuries. A munitions factory built cartridges for the Canadian forces here until 1964. It's now an interpretive center with a scale model of Québec City the way it was in the early 19th century. In the Dauphine Redoubt, built between 1712 and 1748, there are costumes and displays about the soldiers for whom it was built during the French regime.

Latin Quarter The Latin Quarter refers to a section of Old Upper Town surrounding the large **Québec seminary** complex with its stone and wooden buildings, grassy, quiet quadrangles, chapel and museum. The focus here is the very good **Musée de l'Amerique Française** (North American Francophone Museum; ☎ 692-2843), 2 Côte de la Fabrique. It's open daily in summer

($4/3/2/1 for adults/seniors/students/youth 12 to 16) and contains various artifacts relating to French settlement and culture in the New World. Excellent changing exhibits are mounted in one of the seminary buildings. To enter the seminary grounds, go to 9 Rue de l'Université.

Parc de l'Esplanade Just inside the Old City by Porte St Louis and Rue St Louis is this city park where many of the Québec Winter Carnival's events are held. Calèches, the horse-drawn carts for sightseeing, line up for business along the edge of the park.

Other Sights The small square to the north of the Château Frontenac, **Place d'Armes**, was once a military parade ground and is

EXCURSIONS

The Battle of Québec City

In the French and Indian War, it became quickly apparent that whoever controlled Québec City would also win the rest of 'Nouvelle France.' With the stakes so high, the British and French generals James Wolfe and Louis Joseph Montcalm – two of the era's great military strategists – were called in.

In June 1759, the British landed at Point Levy and built batteries to fire at Québec City. Wolfe saw how difficult it would be to take the town – even though his 20,000 troops outnumbered the French by almost three to one. The settlement was well fortified, flanked by batteries Montcalm had built along the shore to the north.

Wolfe became desperate as the summer wore on, ordering the British to raid villages around Québec City and kill for no real military purpose. From Point Levy, his cannon pounded Québec City and reduced the port area to rubble. Still, Montcalm's men stood firm; he knew the English would have to leave before the harsh Québec winter.

In a last-ditch effort, Wolfe decided to attack at Anse au Foulon, a risky site south of the city. On the morning of September 13, some 4500 British troops scaled the cliffs at Anse au Foulon and surprised the French, who mistook the enemy for their own supply ships.

Wolfe sent his troops ahead to the Plains of Abraham just outside the southern walls, and French soldiers came out to meet them in battle. What unfolded next has an element of comedy: While Wolfe's troops were mostly career soldiers, Montcalm's forces included Indian and Québécois backwoodsmen who had little experience with the European rules of war. When the British opened fire, the Indian and Québécois recruits instinctively dropped to the ground – and the Frenchmen left standing fled, assuming their ranks had thinned. With the French forces in disarray, the British surrounded Québec City, which surrendered a few days later.

Although Wolfe and Montcalm held each other in great esteem, the generals would never meet: Both were mortally wounded in this final battle, which lasted a mere 20 minutes. A monument to the generals stands on Terrasse Dufferin, the only one in the world dedicated to two opponents. Its inscription appears not in English or French but, quite diplomatically, in Latin.

now a handy orientation point. **Rue du Trésor** is up, away from the water, off Place d'Armes. This narrow street, linking Rue Ste Anne with Rue Buade, is jammed with painters and their wares – mostly kitsch stuff but some pretty good work, too. At the end of Buade is the **Hôtel de Ville** (City Hall), dating from 1833. The park next to the Hôtel de Ville is used for shows and performances throughout summer, especially during festival time.

On the corner of Rue Buade and Rue Ste Famille is the **Basilique Notre Dame**, dating from 1647. The interior is ornate and contains paintings and treasures from the early French regime. How times change; there is now a bilingual multimedia historical presentation shown in the cathedral for $7.

Old Lower Town

The oldest section of Québec City is also worth exploring. Get down to it by walking down Côte de la Montagne by Parc Montmorency. About halfway down on the right there is a shortcut – the 'break-neck stair-case' – that leads down to Rue du Petit Champlain. You can also follow the sidewalk beside the Musée du Fort toward the river and take the funicular railway from Terrasse Dufferin down ($1.75). It also goes to Rue du Petit Champlain, to **Louis Jolliet House**. The house dates from 1683, and Jolliet lived in it when he wasn't off exploring the northern Mississippi. Rue du Petit Champlain, a busy, attractive street, is said to be the narrowest in North America and is also one of the oldest.

Place Royale is the 400-year-old principal square of Lower Town, often used to refer to the entire district. When Champlain founded Québec, it was this bit of shoreline that was first settled. Also on the square are many buildings from the 17th and 18th centuries, tourist shops and a stern statue of Louis XIV in the middle.

Dating from 1688, the **Église Notre Dame des Victoires** on Place Royale is the oldest stone church in the province. It's built on the spot where 80 years earlier Champlain set up his 'Habitation,' a small stockade.

BILL BACHMANN

Carriage ride through Old Québec City

Hanging from the ceiling is a replica of a wooden ship, thought to be a good-luck charm for the ocean crossing and early battles with the Iroquois. This place is a favorite with marrying couples.

In 1691, a dozen cannons were set up at the **Royal Battery**, at the foot of Rue Sous le Fort, to protect the growing town. The Lower Town information office is just off the park. The Canadian government has a coast guard base near the ferry terminal across the street.

Vieux Port

Built around the old harbor in Lower Town north and east of Place Royale, Vieux Port (Old Port) is a redeveloped waterfront with government buildings, shops, condominiums and recreational facilities.

Near Place Royale at the river's edge, you'll see the **MV *Louis Jolliet*** and other vessels offering cruises downriver to the waterfalls Chute Montmorency and Île d'Orléans. You'll get good views of the city. (You can also get views from the cheap ferry plying the river between town and Lévis.)

On the waterfront, the large, striking **Musée de la Civilisation** (☎ 643-2158), 85 Rue Dalhousie, deals with both Québec and broader historical and communication topics with the use of permanent and changing exhibits. Human history and culture is explored through new and old artifacts and the creations of humankind. It's definitely worth seeing, and unlike many museums around the province, there are English-speaking guides on hand. Admission is $7/6/4/2 for adults/seniors/students/youth 12 to 16. It's open 10 am to 7 pm daily, late June to Labour Day. The rest of the year, it shuts at 5 pm and is closed Monday – but there's free admission on Tuesday.

A short distance away, housed in a building at 100 Rue St André, is **Old Port of Québec Interpretation Centre** (☎ 648-3300). This National Historic Site is a large, four-story exhibition depicting the local 19th-century shipbuilding and timber industries, with good displays and often live demonstrations. Admission is $3/2.25/2 for adults/seniors and students/children six to 16.

National Assembly

Outside the walls, in Upper Town, the home of the Provincial Legislature (☎ 643-7239) is a castle-style structure dating from 1886. There are free tours of the sumptuous interior from 9 am to 4:30 pm daily in summer, weekdays the rest of the year, with commentaries in English and French. The Assembly sits in the Blue Room. The Red Room, equally impressive, is no longer used as the Upper House.

Special Events

The Carnaval du Québec is a famous event unique to Québec City. Also known as Winter Carnival, it lasts for two weeks in late January and early February. Featured are parades, ice sculptures, a snow slide, boat races, dances, music and lots of drinking. The carnival symbol and mascot is the frequently seen roly-poly snowman figure with a red hat called Bonhomme.

The Summer Festival is a two-week bash in early July with free shows and concerts throughout the town, including drama and dance. In August, the Medieval Festival is a popular five-day event early in the month on odd-numbered years. At the end of the month, Expo Québec features commercial stands, agricultural competitions, handicrafts, a blackjack parlor, horse racing and midway, a large carnival. Nearly 750,000 people visit each year.

Organized Tours

There's a ticket booth on Terrasse Dufferin representing many of the tour companies. Autocars Dupont (☎ 649-9226) runs numerous narrated tours from Place d'Armes and picks up at hotels. A two-hour trip around town costs $25/13 for adults/children.

Adlard Tours (☎ 692-2358) conducts walking tours in English, departing from the tourist office at 12 Rue Ste Anne. The excellent guided walk ($12) takes more than two hours.

There are also interesting 50-minute guided tours of Château Frontenac (☎ 691-2166) every hour, on the hour, from 10 am to 6 pm in summer. It costs $6.50/5.50/3.75 for adults/seniors/children.

A variety of river cruises is offered on the big open-deck MV *Louis Jolliet,* which can carry 800 passengers. Tickets (☎ 692-1159) may be bought at the kiosk on the boardwalk behind the Château or at the booth along the waterfront near Place Royale. The basic trip going downriver to Île d'Orléans and Chute Montmorency with a bilingual guide costs $20, and the boat gets jammed with people. There are also evening trips with music and dancing. Get a ticket early, as the trips are popular.

Le Coudrier (☎ 692-0107) does similar 90-minute cruises on a smaller vessel for $15 and cheaper one-hour trips, too. There are also full-day trips with a meal that include Grosse Île. For information, call or see them at quay No 19 along the Old Port dock opposite the Agora.

The ferry over to Lévis is, in a sense, a short cruise and provides a great view of the Château inexpensively.

Places to Stay

There are many places to stay in Québec City, and generally the competition keeps the prices down to a reasonable level. The bulk of the good-value accommodations are in small European-style hotels. Prices listed here are summer high-season rates.

Camping The *Camping Municipal de Beauport* (☎ 666-2228, 95 Rue Serénité) north of Québec City is green, peaceful and just a 15-minute drive to the Old City. To get there, take Hwy 40 toward Montmorency to exit 321, turn north and follow the blue-and-white signs. Tent sites cost $17.50. There are also a few places on Hwy 138 going east from Québec City through the Ste Anne de Beaupré area, including *Camping Mont Ste Anne* (☎ 826-2323, St Férréol les Neiges).

Hostels The huge HI *Centre International de Séjour de Québec* (☎ 694-0775 or 1-800-461-8585, 19 Rue Ste Ursule) is central, and its 245 beds are usually full in summer. Dorm bunks cost $16, private rooms start at $46, and there are some family rooms. The pleasant, economical cafeteria offers all three meals. Web site: www.tourismej.qc.ca.

Marked by a peace sign outside, *Auberge de la Paix* (☎ 694-0735, 31 Rue Couillard), also well located, is relatively small and quiet. It's open all year and has 60 beds. It charges $19 with breakfast, and $2 extra for sheets. There are two double rooms (also $19 per person), but you can't reserve them. Try to arrive in the morning to secure a bed. It's a short walk from the bus/train station, but it's uphill all the way.

The *YWCA* (☎ 683-2155, 855 Ave Holland) takes couples or single women. Singles/doubles cost $30/52, and there's a cafeteria and pool. Bus No 7 along Ch Ste Foy goes past Ave Holland. Walk south on Ave Holland – it's not far.

The *Université Laval* (☎ 656-5632), between Ch Ste Foy and Blvd Wilfrid Laurier, to the east of Autoroute du Vallon, rents rooms from May to mid-August. Rates are $21.50/30 with a student card, $34/44 without. Bus No 800 from the Old City will get you there. Web site: www.ulaval.ca/sres.

Hotels Many of the hotels listed here have long, convoluted Web addresses via www.quebec.com.

Named after General Montgomery (whose remains were moved here after he was killed during the siege of Québec in 1775), the *Hôtel Maison du Générale* (☎ 694-1905, 72 Rue St Louis) has simple singles and doubles for $33 to $52. The cheapest rooms are on the noisy street side.

One of the best of the cheapies is *Auberge St Louis* (☎ 692-2424, 48 Rue St Louis). The 27 rooms start at a reasonable $55 a single or double, including breakfast, but go up to $95 with private bath. Parking is available but costs extra.

The super-renovated *Hôtel Le Clos St Louis* (☎ 694-1311 or 1-800-461-1311, 71 Rue St Louis) has 29 rooms at $65 to $120 for singles or doubles when it's busy, but prices drop about one-third other times. Breakfast is included.

The *Hôtel Manoir de l'Esplanade* (☎ 694-0834, 83 Rue d'Auteuil) offers 36 spacious, modern rooms inside old brick walls for $70/115 and is in a great location near the Citadelle.

There are numerous places perfectly located by Parc des Gouverneurs to the south of the Château Frontenac. The **Manoir de la Terrasse/Beau Site** (☎ 694-1592, email *beausite@sympatico.ca, 4 and 6 Rue de Laporte*) charges $89 to $105. A continental breakfast is supplied. Many rooms (with wrought-iron beds) have their own balcony, and there's a pleasant garden.

Manoir Sur le Cap (☎ 694-1987, 9 Ave Ste Geneviève) has 15 rooms carved out of the old house, some with views of the park, others of the river and Lévis. Singles and doubles start at $95; large deluxe rooms with fireplaces go for up to $265. Web site: www.manoir-sur-le-cap.com.

If you want to go all the way, **Château Frontenac** (☎ 692-2480, 57 Rue Ste Anne) has 151 singles/doubles from $89/99 to $249/259, with positively regal decor. Room 633 offers an incomparable view through oval windows.

Places to Eat

Restaurants are abundant, but many fall into the upper-end category. Taking a midday fixed-price meal and a light dinner is one way to avoid eating a hole in your budget.

Old Upper Town For French-style breakfast, there's **Le Petit Coin Latin** (8½ Rue Ste Ursule). This small café has croissants, muffins, eggs, café au lait in big bowls and low-price lunch specials. It has an outdoor summer patio with a fixed-price dinner of $12 to $18.

Chez Temporal (☎ 694-1813, 25 Rue Couillard) is a little café that serves coffee, croissants, great salads (from $7) and sandwiches (from $4). It's perfect for snacks, breakfasts and light meals. The café feels very French – a good place to sit in the morning and plan the day. Credit cards aren't accepted here.

Rue St Jean is one of the main streets for restaurants. Near Côte du Palais, **Casse Crêpe Breton** (☎ 692-0438, 1136 Rue St Jean) is a small restaurant specializing in crêpes of many kinds ($3.75 to $6). You can sit right up at the counter and watch them put the tasty crêpes together. The busy **St**

Alexandre Pub (1087 Rue St Jean) has 200 kinds of beer and an array of pub-type grub.

To make your own meal, try **Marché Richelieu** (1097 Rue St Jean), which offers breads from the in-house bakery, fruits, cheeses and even bottles of wine with screw-top lids. It's open daily until 9 pm.

Québec City is a fine place for a special dinner out at a good French restaurant. **Le Saint Amour** (☎ 694-0667, 48a Rue Ste Ursule) has a $30 to $35 dinner table d'hôte, value lunch specials on weekdays and an excellent reputation. The elegant setting includes an inner garden.

Aux Anciens Canadiens (☎ 692-1627, 34 Rue St Louis) is in Jacquet House, Québec City's oldest, dating from 1677. It serves traditional dishes and typically Québécois specialties. Here, one can sample such provincial fare as apple wine, pea soup, duck or trout followed by dessert of maple-syrup pie. The special table d'hôte menu offered from noon to 6 pm is fairly priced from $14, including a glass of wine or a beer.

Apsara (☎ 694-0232, 71 Rue d'Auteuil) has excellent Asian fare. Dishes cost about $12; a complete dinner for two will cost around $42. Down the street, there's a cheap Lebanese spot, **Restaurant Liban** (23 Rue d'Auteuil) with felafel and kebabs for $3 to $5.

A good Italian place is **Portofino** (☎ 692-8888, 54 Rue Couillard), serving very tasty pastas and charcoal-cooked pizzas for $9 to $15 at lunchtime. There's often live music in the evening.

Old Lower Town With an attractive patio beneath the Château Frontenac, **La Maison du Spaghetti** (40 Rue Marche Champlain) is a great bargain with various pasta dishes, including bread and salad, from $10 ($8 at lunch). Don't bother with the indoor salad bar as it's very basic and the atmosphere outside is better.

Le Poisson d'Avril (☎ 692-1010, 115 Quai St Andre), near the port, is renowned for its fish dishes. Expect to pay $40 per person for a captain's meal including lobster, bouillabaisse and fresh mussels. The wall murals and maritime paraphernalia inside are a treat.

EXCURSIONS

The *farmers' market* is near Bassin Louise. In the covered area, you'll find fresh bread, cheeses, fruit and vegetables. It's really humming Saturday morning.

Entertainment

Québec City is small but active after dark. Many of the cafés and restaurants – some mentioned in the last section – have live music at night. Much of the nightlife is in the Old City or just outside the walls. If you just want to sit, Terrasse Dufferin, away from the clubs and behind the Château, is perfect, as is the patio bar in the hotel. *Voir* is a French entertainment paper appearing each Thursday with complete listings.

Rue St Jean is alive at night – this is where people strut. There are good places for just sitting and watching in addition to places with music.

Folk clubs, known as *boîtes à chanson*, come and go along and around Rue St Jean and are generally cheap with a casual, relaxed atmosphere. Try *Chez Son Père* (☎ 692-5308, 24 Rue St Stanislas).

At *Bar Le d'Auteuil* (☎ 692-2263, 35 Rue d'Auteuil) there is often live music. Next door at No 33, *Fourmi Atomik* is also popular. *L'Inox* (☎ 692-2877, 38 Rue St Andre), in the Old Port area, is the city's only brew pub and has a pleasant outdoor patio.

The *Bar L'Emprise* (☎ 692-2480, 57 Rue Ste Anne), at the Hotel Clarendon, has jazz groups playing around its grand piano Friday and Saturday evenings.

The *Grand Théâtre de Québec* (☎ 643-8131, 269 Blvd René Lévesque Est) is the city's main performing arts center, presenting classical concerts, dance and theater among its shows.

Cinema Le Clap (☎ 650-2527, 2360 Ch Ste Foy), in Ste Foy, shows films in English, French and other languages, many with subtitles. *Théâtre IMAX* (☎ 627-4629, 5401 Blvd des Galeries) shows large-format and 3D films featuring digital wraparound sound.

Getting There & Away

The airport is west of town, off Hwy 40, near where Hwy 73 intersects it on its way north. Both Air Canada (☎ 692-0770) and Canadian Airlines (☎ 692-0912) serve Québec City, but fares tend to be steep for the short hop to Montréal (about $300 roundtrip).

The bus station (☎ 525-3000) is at 320 Rue Abraham Martin, at the main train station. Orléans Express (☎ 525-3000) has buses to Montréal nearly every hour during the day and evening ($38). There are no direct buses to or from the USA; most go via Montréal.

Québec City has not one, but three train stations (☎ 692-3940). The beautiful old Gare du Palais in Lower Town is for trains going to/from Montréal. Bus No 800 from Place d'Youville runs to the station. The station in Ste Foy, southwest of the downtown area, by the bridges over to the south shore, is served by the same trains. The third station, on the south shore about 10km from the river in the town of Charny, is used primarily for trains heading eastward to the Gaspé Peninsula or the Maritimes.

Reserve rental cars a few days ahead in the busy periods. Budget (☎ 692-3660) is located at 29 Côte du Palais; there's also an office at the airport. For compact vehicles, the rate is about $63 per weekday for 250km and as low as $27 on a weekend day with 350km free. Ask what the insurance rate is. Montréal is 270km from Québec City, or a 2½-hour drive.

Allo Stop (☎ 522-0056), 467 Rue St Jean, matches up drivers and passengers. It offers good deals in Québec (such as to Montréal for $20) but isn't allowed to operate in Ontario, so Ottawa and Toronto are off-limits. Web site: www.allostop.com. EcoRide (☎ 1-877-326-7433) is a good Web-based alternative. Web site: www.ecoride.com. You can also try Autotaxi's ride-sharing bulletin board at www.autotaxi.com.

The ferry between Québec City and Lévis runs constantly – all day and most of the night. The roundtrip fare is $2, less for kids and seniors, plus $3 for a car. You'll get good views of the river, cliffs, the Québec skyline and Château Frontenac, even if the cruise only lasts 10 minutes. The terminal in Québec City is in Place Royale, Lower Town.

Getting Around
Autobus La Québécoise (☎ 570-5379) shuttles between downtown and the airport for $9. It leaves from major hotels but will make pick-ups around town if you call at least one hour before flight time. A taxi costs about $35.

City buses (☎ 627-2511) charge $1.70 with transfer privileges. The terminal, Gare Centrale d'Autobus, is at 225 Blvd Charest Est in Lower Town. Many buses serving the Old City area stop in at Place d'Youville (known locally as Carré d'Youville) just outside the wall on Rue St Jean. Bus No 800 goes to the central bus and train station.

Driving isn't worth the trouble in town: You can walk just about everywhere, the streets are narrow and crowded, and parking is painful. A good parking lot near the tourist office on Ave Wilfrid Laurier charges $5 per day.

Vélo Passe-sport (☎ 692-3643), 77a Rue Ste Anne in Old Upper Town, has bicycles and inline skates for rent. Bikes cost $24/day, and hourly rates are offered. Cyclo Services (☎ 692-4052), which has an office beside the Agora along the boardwalk close to the river (in front of the Musée de la Civilisation), charges $25/day for bikes.

Horse-drawn carriages (calèches) are nice but cost $50 for about 40 minutes.

OTTAWA
☎ 613
Ottawa, the capital of Canada, arouses mixed emotions. This city of 1.1 million sits majestically on the south bank of the Ottawa River at the confluence with the Rideau River, and the gently rolling Gatineau Hills of Québec are visible to the north. It's not a hugely lively place, but its streets are wide and clean, and there's wonderful parkland in town that acts as a green lung.

The government is the largest employer, and the stately Gothic-style parliament buildings are attractions in their own right. With its abundance of museums and cultural activities, the city draws five million tourists a year. Many enjoy the traditionally garbed Royal Canadian Mounted Police, known as the Mounties, who patrol on horseback.

In 1826, British troops founded the first settlement to build the Rideau Canal, which links the Ottawa River to Lake Ontario. First called Bytown, the name was changed in 1855 and Queen Victoria made it the capital in 1857. Don't be surprised if you hear French spoken – the Québec border isn't far away.

Orientation
Ottawa is dotted with parks, and most of the land along the waterway is for recreational use. Ottawa's central core is quite compact, making walking a good way of getting about. The smaller town of Hull, which has been incorporated into Greater Ottawa, lies on the northern bank of the Ottawa River.

Wellington St, on the western side, is the main east-west street and has Parliament Hill and many government buildings. One block south is Sparks St, a pedestrian mall with shops and fast-food outlets. Bank St runs south and is the main shopping strip, with many restaurants and several theaters. Just to the west of the canal are Elgin St and large Confederation Square, with the National War Memorial at its center. The gigantic French-style palace here is the Château Laurier hotel.

On the other side of the canal is Ottawa East, with Rideau St as its main street. The huge Rideau Centre is here, a three-level shopping mall. To the north lies Byward Market, the hub of the restaurant and nightlife district.

Information
The well-stocked, efficient Capital Info-centre (☎ 239-5000 or 1-800-465-1867) is at 90 Wellington St opposite the parliament buildings. It's open 8:30 am to 9 pm daily, mid-May to early September, and 9 am to 5 pm the rest of the year. Web site: www.capcan.ca.

Several banks can be found along Sparks St. The Accu-Rate Foreign Exchange in the World Exchange Plaza, 111 Albert St, 2nd floor, has longer hours and sells traveler's checks. It's open Saturday, too.

There's a post office (☎ 734-7575) at 59 Sparks St, open 9 am to 5:30 pm weekdays.

EXCURSIONS

EXCURSIONS

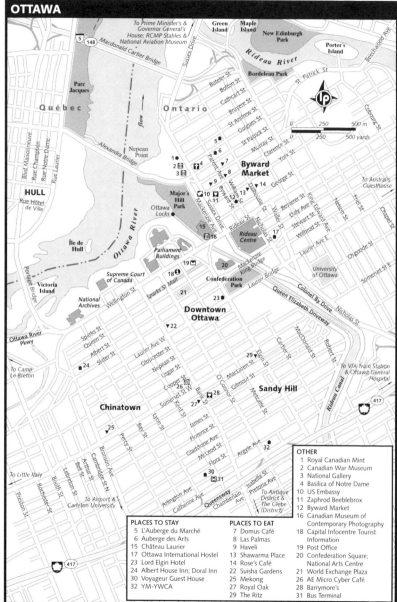

OTTAWA

OTHER
1 Royal Canadian Mint
2 Canadian War Museum
3 National Gallery
4 Basilica of Notre Dame
10 US Embassy
11 Zaphrod Beeblebrox
12 Byward Market
16 Canadian Museum of
   Contemporary Photography
18 Capital Infocentre Tourist
   Information
19 Post Office
20 Confederation Square;
   National Arts Centre
21 World Exchange Plaza
26 AE Micro Cyber Café
28 Barrymore's
31 Bus Terminal

PLACES TO STAY
5 L'Auberge du Marché
6 Auberge des Arts
15 Château Laurier
17 Ottawa International Hostel
23 Lord Elgin Hotel
24 Albert House Inn; Doral Inn
30 Voyageur Guest House
32 YM-YWCA

PLACES TO EAT
7 Domus Café
8 Las Palmas
9 Haveli
13 Shawarma Place
14 Rose's Café
22 Suisha Gardens
25 Mekong
27 Royal Oak
29 The Ritz

Le Château Frontenac on high, Québec City

Ice sculpture in Québec City's Winter Festival

Aerial view of Québec City's Vieux Port and the St Lawrence River

Proud mountie: saddle sore but smiling

Parliament Building, Ottawa

Ottawa's National Gallery of Canada, designed by Moshe Safdie

The AE Micro Cyber Café (☎ 230-9000), 288 Bank St, charges $2 per 15 minutes of Web surfing, or $7 per hour. It's open 11 am to 9 pm weekdays, to midnight Saturday and 8 pm Sunday.

Ottawa General Hospital (☎ 737-7777) is at 501 Smyth Rd. There's also a walk-in clinic, Minto Place (☎ 235-4140), at 344 Slater St between Lyon and Kent Sts.

Parliament Hill

The striking Parliament Building (☎ 239-5000), with its Peace Tower and clock, is home to the Commons and Senate chambers, which can be viewed in session (not during summer). Alongside are the East and West blocks, with their green copper-top roofs.

The interior is all hand-carved limestone and sandstone, and the library is a highlight with its fantastic carved wood and wrought iron. Free 20-minute tours are run twice hourly; you'll have to reserve in the white tent out on the front lawn in summer, or at the indoor desk in winter. Security is tight and includes metal detectors.

At 10 am in summer, you can see the Changing of the Guard on the lawns, and the crowds gather in anticipation. At night in summer, there's a free sound and light show on Parliament Hill – one version in English, the other in French.

Pick up a free copy of *Discover the Hill,* with a self-guided tour in and around the buildings.

Supreme Court of Canada

Completed in 1946, this intimidating structure (☎ 995-5361) at 301 Wellington St has a 12m-high grand entrance hall. It opens its grounds, lobby and courtroom from 9 am to 5 pm weekdays. In summer, a free tour is given by law students – call for a schedule.

National Archives of Canada

This institution (☎ 463-2038) collects and preserves the documentation of Canada, including paintings, maps, photos, diaries, letters, posters and even 60,000 cartoons and caricatures. The exhibition rooms with varying displays are open daily (free admission).

National Gallery

The National Gallery (☎ 990-1985) is Canada's premier art gallery, with an enormous collection of North American and European works in various media. This impressive building is at 380 Sussex Dr, a 15-minute walk from the parliament buildings.

Opened in 1988, the striking glass and pink granite gallery overlooking the Ottawa River was designed by Moshe Safdie, who also created Montréal's Habitat apartment complex and Québec City's Musée de la Civilisation. The numerous galleries display both classical and contemporary pieces, with the emphasis on Canadian artists. The USA and European collections contain works of nearly all the heavyweight artists. One architectural feature nearby is the beautifully restored **Rideau St Chapel** (1888), located between the two courtyards visible from the gallery.

Hours are 10 am to 6 pm daily in summer (to 8 pm Thursday). The rest of the year, it's open 10 am to 5 pm Wednesday to Sunday. Admission to the permanent displays is free; rates vary for changing exhibitions.

Ottawa Locks

This series of locks between the Château Laurier and the parliament buildings mark the north end of the 198km Rideau Canal, which runs to Kingston and the St Lawrence River. Colonel By, who was in charge of building the canal, set up his headquarters here in 1826. The locks are now maintained as heritage parks.

Canadian Museum of Contemporary Photography

On the canal's edge by the Château Laurier, the CMCP (☎ 990-8257) sits in a reconstructed railway tunnel. Originally part of the National Film Board, this museum still houses the photographic research departments and the country's vast photographic archives. The gallery is a bit cramped, but the displays (which change quarterly) are usually outstanding.

Hours are 11 am to 5 pm daily except Wednesday, when it's open 4 to 8 pm. The rest of the year, it's open the same hours Wednesday to Sunday only. Admission is free.

Byward Market

This lively area north of Rideau St teems with restaurants and pubs. The market building itself (between George and York Sts) was opened in the 1840s and is packed with specialty shops selling gourmet meats, seafood, baked goods and cheeses; the periphery is lined with stands of vegetables, fruit and flowers.

Canadian War Museum

This museum (☎ 776-8600), 330 Sussex Dr, contains Canada's largest war-related collection and traces the country's military history. The life-size replica of a WWI trench is good. You'll also find multimedia displays and a huge collection of war art. It's open 9:30 am to 5 pm daily in summer (to 8 pm Thursday), and Tuesday to Sunday in winter. Admission is $4/3/2 for adults/seniors and students/children. Sunday morning it's free until noon.

Royal Canadian Mint

Next door to the War Museum is the mint (☎ 993-8990) at 320 Sussex Dr. Its main job nowadays is to strike special-edition coins, commemorative pieces and bullion investment coins, but this imposing stone building (1908) is also Canada's refiner of gold. Tours of the coin-stamping facility are given by appointment. Summer hours are from 9 am to 8:30 pm weekdays, to 5:30 pm weekends. The rest of the year, it opens 9 am to 5 pm daily. Admission is a flat $2.

Basilica of Notre Dame

This Gothic-style house of worship (1839) contains some stunning carvings, stained-glass windows and vaulted ceilings. Pick up a pamphlet by the door for details of the many features. It's on Guiges Ave opposite the National Gallery.

Prime Minister's & Governor General's Houses

Northeast of downtown, you can view the exterior of the prime minister's ritzy residence at 24 Sussex Dr. The premises is closed to visitors, but you can take a peep from the perimeter.

Rideau Hall (☎ 998-7113), the governor general's pad built in the early 20th century, is around the corner at 1 Sussex Dr. The visitor's center (open April to late October) gives 45-minute tours of the residence throughout the day, with some amusing anecdotes. You can stroll the grounds, and a small Changing of the Guard ceremony takes place on the hour from late June through August.

National Aviation Museum

This collection of more than 100 aircraft is housed in a huge triangular building at Rockcliffe Airport (☎ 993-2010), about 5km northeast of downtown along Rockcliffe Parkway. You'll see planes ranging from a Silver Dart of 1909 and the renowned wartime Spitfire to the most modern aircraft. Displays include aviation-related video games.

Hours are 9 am to 5 pm daily (to 8 pm Thursday); it's closed Monday in winter. Admission is $6/4/2 for adults/seniors and students/children.

RCMP Stables & Practice Ground

Even the Mounties have to practice, and the RCMP Stables & Practice Ground (☎ 993-3751) is where they perfect the musical ride pageant.

Practice sessions, which are interesting and open to the public, take place daily. During the week prior to Canada Day (July 1), the Mounties put on a musical ride in full uniform.

Call for schedule details, as the troops are sometimes away on tour. Free guided tours of the stables take place 8:30 am to 11 am and 1:30 to 3:30 pm Monday to Friday. By car, take Sussex Dr east to Rockcliffe Parkway and turn right into the grounds at Birch St. Bus No 7 also goes there from the center of Ottawa.

Activities

The city has an excellent network of parks and canals, perfect for **jogging**, **cycling** and **walking**. Pick up free maps at the tourist office, including one of a bicycle path that winds all over town. For those interested in

boating, you can rent canoes and rowboats at Dows Lake Pavilion (☎ 232-1001), about 3km south of the Laurier Bridge.

In winter, there's **skiing** as close at 20km from Ottawa, in the Gatineau Hills, and the Rideau Canal opens an **ice-skating** rink along a 5km-long stretch back in town. For bicycle rentals, see the Getting Around section, later.

There's good **white-water rafting** on the Ottawa River from April to October. Ottawa Adventures (☎ 819-648-5200 or 1-800-690-7238) is just over the Québec border a few kilometers from Fort Colonge and has a pick-up service from the Ottawa International Hostel. Day-long trips in bouncy 14-foot rafts cost $75 ($85 on Saturday) and include a barbecue lunch.

Organized Tours

Gray Line (☎ 725-3047) offers a two-hour tour of the city daily from May to November. Tickets ($20/17 for adults/seniors, students and children) are sold at the office in Confederation Square beside the National Arts Centre.

Capital Double Decker & Trolley Tours (☎ 749-3666) does much the same thing but offers hop-on, hop-off privileges at 20 stops. Tickets cost the same as at Gray Line.

Paul's Boat Lines (☎ 235-8409) runs 1½-hour cruises on the Ottawa River and Rideau Canal. Tickets cost $12/10/8/6 for adults/seniors/students/children. The ticket booth is on the Rideau Canal opposite the National Arts Centre.

Places to Stay

Camping *Camp Le Breton* (☎ 236-1251) is an excellent campground close by, west along Wellington St past the parliament buildings, on the corner of Fleet and Booth Sts. It's aimed at hikers and cyclists, with 200 sites costing $7.50 per person without water or electricity. It's open May to Labour Day. A city bus runs right to the campsite; otherwise it's a 25-minute walk from Parliament Hill.

Camp Hither Hills (☎ 822-0509, 5227 Bank St), on Hwy 31, 20km south of Parliament Hill, charges $16 per basic site. The

tourist office has a list of other campgrounds in the area.

Hostels The HI *Ottawa International Hostel* (☎ 235-2595 or 1-800-663-5777, 75 Nicholas St) is in the old Ottawa jail – see the gallows at the back. It's close to the parliament buildings and has 130 beds, mostly in the inmates' old cells. It charges $17/21 for members/nonmembers. Bus No 4 goes from the bus station on the corner of Arlington and Kent Sts to within two blocks of the hostel; from the train station, bus No 95 does the same thing. Web site: hostellingintl.on.ca.

The *YM-YWCA* (☎ 237-1320, 180 Argyle Ave) has good, standard rooms with shared bathroom for $42/50 singles/doubles. More expensive singles with private bath are available. There's a cafeteria and pool for guest use.

The *University of Ottawa* (☎ 564-5400) opens its dormitories for visitors from May to August. Singles/doubles cost $22/35 for students, $33/40 for nonstudents. It has a laundry, swimming pool and cheap cafeteria. Go to Stanton Residence at 100 University St, southeast of the parliament buildings.

B&Bs & Inns The *Voyageur Guest House* (☎ 238-6445, 95 Arlington St), on a quiet residential street right behind the bus terminal, is probably the best low-price option in town. Singles cost $39 to $44, doubles $54 to $64 including breakfast. There are six clean rooms with shared bathrooms. Web site: www.bbcanada.com/1897.html.

The *Auberge des Arts* (☎ 562-0909, 104 Guigues Ave) has singles/doubles at $55/65. English, French and Spanish are spoken here. It serves great breakfasts to order, and its air-conditioned rooms are nicely furnished. Web site: www.members.home.net/aubergedesarts.

L'Auberge du Marché (☎ 241-6610 or 1-800-465-0079, 104 Guigues Ave) is an older, renovated house with three rooms for $60/80 with shared bath and full breakfast. Web site: www.comsearch-can.com/aubmar.htm.

The comfy *Australis Guesthouse* (☎ 235-8461, 35 Marlborough St) is run by a friendly couple and serves bulging breakfasts.

Rooms cost $50/65 with shared bathroom. The owners will pick you up at the station if arranged in advance. Marlborough St is south of Laurier, about a half-hour walk to the parliament buildings. Web site: www .bbcanada.com/1463.html.

On the downtown side of the canal is **Albert House Inn** (☎ 236-4479 or 1-800-267-1982, 478 Albert St), with 17 well-appointed rooms. It's more expensive at $80/90 but has a good location and is a heritage home with all the comforts. The breakfast menu is extensive. Web site: www.albertinn.com.

Hotels & Efficiencies The central **Doral Inn** (☎ 230-8055, 486 Albert St) has decent rooms starting at $109/119, plus a few housekeeping units for $10 more. It runs specials for $89 from time to time.

The stately old **Lord Elgin Hotel** (☎ 235-3333 or 1-800-267-4298, 100 Elgin St) has regular summer rates of $150/155. It, too, runs specials as low as $89. There's free parking. Web site: www.lordelginhotel.ca.

The classic **Château Laurier** (☎ 241-1414 or 1-800-441-1414, 1 Rideau St) is the castlelike place by the canal and a landmark in its own right. Rates start at $149, but look for discounts during quiet periods. There's an indoor swimming pool. Web site: www .cphotels.ca.

There are also motel strips on each side of the downtown area, along Rideau St and its extension, Montréal Road.

Places to Eat

The Byward Market area is very popular and offers a great selection of places, many with outdoor tables; the place is hopping on weekends. The market building has a good gourmet bagel stand inside. For breakfast, **Zak's Diner** (☎ 241-5866, 14 Byward St) is a '50s-style eatery with triple-decker burgers ($9.50). It serves breakfast all day and is open late. For inexpensive, varied pasta dishes, there's **Oregano's** (☎ 241-5100, 74 George St), which serves an all-you-can-eat buffet dinner for around $10. The terrace is the place to be.

Colorful **Las Palmas** (☎ 241-3738, 111 Parent Ave) is a Mexican place with great fajita platters ($17); most dishes cost $9 to $12. The cocktails look good but are watery.

Shawarma Place (☎ 562-3662, 284 Dalhousie St) does felafel, shwarmas and other Lebanese takeouts starting around $4, with good-value platters available.

Excellent Indian food is dished up at the more upscale **Haveli** (☎ 241-1700, 39 Clarence St). Its veggie mains cost $6 to $8; try also the Kadri beef served in a mini-wok ($10). Good, cheap Indian food can also be found at the unlikely named **Roses Café** (☎ 241-8535, 349 Dalhousie), open for lunch and dinner. Its generous lunch buffet costs $8.

The **Domus Café** (☎ 241-6007, 87 Murray St) has excellent Canadian regional dishes with fresh ingredients, such as pan-seared pickerel filet with sweetbutter and mashed potatoes ($19). Lunches cost about $9 to $16 and dinners $17 to $26.

Downtown, Bank St and its side streets have numerous restaurants. **Suisha Gardens** (☎ 236-9602, 208 Slater St) has excellent, if somewhat westernized, Japanese food. Dinner for two costs about $33 before drinks, but lunches are cheaper.

In the Chinatown area, **Mekong** (☎ 237-7717, 637 Somerset St W) does good Vietnamese and Chinese dishes, such as stir-fried scallops and snow peas for $13. Lunches average $6 to $7.

Of the British-style pubs, try the **Royal Oak** (☎ 236-0190, 318 Bank St) for British beer and food. It's friendly and you can play darts.

The **Ritz** (☎ 235-7027, 274 Elgin St) does great Italian food – lines of people outside aren't uncommmon. Lunch specials, such as phyllo stuffed with sauteed beef and portobello mushrooms, cost $10 to $11.

Entertainment

Capital City is the free entertainment weekly; Capital Xtra is geared to gays. Check also Friday's Ottawa Citizen for complete club, cinema and other listings. There are pubs and clubs scattered along Bank St and around Byward Market.

Zaphrod Beeblebrox (☎ 594-3355, 27 York St) is an eclectic place for everything from New Age rock to African music and rhythm and blues. Live bands play Tuesday, Thursday, Friday and Saturday nights. *Barrymore's* (☎ *656-8880, 323 Bank St*) features heavy rock and metal live on weekends.

The *National Arts Centre (NAC;* ☎ *755-1111, 53 Elgin St)* stages dramas and operas and is home to the symphony orchestra. It also presents a range of concerts and films.

Good repertory theaters include the *Mayfair (*☎ *730-3403, 1074 Bank St),* at Confederation Square, which charges $8 for nonmembers for the double bill, and Bytown Cinema (☎ *789-3456, 325 Rideau St),* between King Edward and Nelson Sts.

Getting There & Away

The surprisingly small airport is 20 minutes south of town. Airlines serving Ottawa include Royal Air, Air Canada and Canadian Airlines. See the Getting There & Away chapter for fares to Montréal from out of Canada.

For buses, the Central Station (☎ 238-5900) is at 265 Catherine St. The principal bus lines are Voyageur and Greyhound; some 20 buses go from/to Montréal ($28 or $29). Other one-way fares include Toronto ($87), Kingston ($32) and Sudbury ($80). Students get about one-third off.

The VIA Rail station (☎ 244-8289) is 7km southeast of downtown, at 200 Tremblay Rd near the junction of Alta Vista Rd and Hwy 417, just east of Rideau Canal. There are four daily trains to Montréal ($46) and Toronto ($93). The fare to Kingston is $41. You can save up to one-third by avoiding peak days like Friday.

By car from Montréal, take Hwy 40 Ouest (west), the Trans Canada Hwy, which becomes Hwy 417 in Ontario. It's about 190km, or two hours by car. In Ottawa, there's free parking in the World Exchange Plaza and the Rideau Centre on weekends.

Getting Around

City bus No 97 links the Rideau Centre and Slater St with the airport ($2.35). You can also take the Airport Shuttle bus ($9, 25 minutes), which leaves every half-hour from the Château Laurier hotel from 5 am to midnight.

OC Transpo (☎ 741-4390) runs the Ottawa bus system. One-way tickets cost $2.35 on the bus, but cheaper tickets ($1.60) can be bought from corner stores. Most buses quit about midnight.

Ottawa is an excellent city for bicyclists, with an extensive system of paths in and around town. For rentals, try Cycle Tour Rent-A-Bike behind the Château Laurier, in the parking lot. It's open daily May to September and charges $20/12 per day/half-day. ID is required. The youth hostel also rents two-wheelers.

AROUND OTTAWA

The **Diefenbunker** is an underground fort built in the early 1960s to house up to 300 personnel in case of nuclear attack. It's now the Cold War Museum (☎ 839-0007), with displays including air-raid sirens and (defused) bombs.

Hours are 10 am to 3 pm daily (in winter, weekdays only). Admission, which includes an hour-long tour, is $12/10/5 for adults/seniors and students/children. It's at 3911 Carp Rd in the village of Carp, about a 30-minute drive west of town.

Language

English and French are the two official languages of Canada. You'll notice both on highway signs, maps, tourist brochures and all types of packaging. In the west, French isn't as prevalent, but in Québec, English can be scarce. Indeed, roadside signs and visitor information will often be in French only; in certain regions (such as the Eastern Townships), they're in both languages. Outside Montréal and Québec City, the use of some French, or your own version of sign language, will be necessary at least some of the time.

Many immigrants use their mother tongue, as do some groups of Native Indians and Inuit. In some Native Indian communities, though, only older members retain their original indigenous language. Few non–Native Indian Canadians speak any Native Indian or Inuit language, but some words such as igloo, parka, muskeg and kayak are commonly used.

The Inuit languages are interesting for their specialization and use of many words for what appears to be the same thing; for example, the word for 'seal' depends on whether it's old or young, in or out of the water. There are up to 20 or so words for 'snow,' depending on its consistency and texture.

CANADIAN ENGLISH

Canada inherited English primarily from the British settlers of the early and mid-19th century. This form of British English remains the basis of Canadian English. There are some pronunciation differences; for example, Britons say 'clark' for clerk, Canadians say 'clurk.' Grammatical differences are few. The Canadian vocabulary has been augmented considerably by the need for new words in a new land and the influence of the Native Indian languages as well as the pioneering French.

Canada has never developed a series of easily detectable dialects such as those of England, Germany or even the USA. There are, however, some regional variations in idiom and pronunciation. In Newfoundland, for example, some people speak with an accent reminiscent of the west country of England (Devon and Cornwall) or Ireland, and some use words such as 'screech' (rum) and 'shooneen' (coward).

The spoken English of the Atlantic Provinces, too, has inflections not heard in the west, and in the Ottawa Valley you'll hear a slightly different sound again, due mainly to the large number of Irish who settled there in the mid-19th century. In British Columbia, some expressions reflect that province's history; for example, 'leaverite' (a worthless mineral) is a prospecting word derived from the phrase 'Leave 'er right there.'

Although Canadians and Americans may sound the same to many non–North Americans, there are real differences. Canadian pronunciation of 'ou' is the most notable of these; words like 'out' and 'bout' sound more like 'oat' and 'boat' when spoken by Canadians. Canadian English has been strongly influenced by the USA, particularly in recent years via the mass media and the use of US textbooks and dictionaries in schools. Most spellings follow British English, such as 'centre,' 'harbour' and 'cheque,' but there are some exceptions, such as 'tire' ('tyre') and 'aluminum' ('aluminium'). US spelling is becoming more common – to the consternation of some people. Perhaps the best-known difference between US and Canadian English is in the pronunciation of the last letter of the alphabet. In the USA, it's pronounced 'zee,' while in Canada it's pronounced 'zed' (like both the British and the French).

Canadian English has also developed a few of its own distinctive idioms and expressions. The most recognizable is the interrogative 'eh?' that seems to appear at the end of almost every spoken sentence. Canadian English has also added to the richness of the global English language, with words like kerosene (paraffin), puck (from ice hockey), bushed (exhausted) and moose and muskeg from anglicized Native Indian words.

For those wishing to delve deeper into the topic, there is the excellent *Oxford Dictionary of Canadian English.*

CANADIAN FRENCH (QUÉBÉCOIS)

The French spoken in Québec is not, for the most part, the language of France. At times it can be nearly unintelligible to a Parisian. The local tongue of Québec, where the vast majority of the population is French, is known as *Québécois* or *joual,* but variations on it occur in all parts of the province. However, many English (and most French) students in Québec are still taught the French of France. Despite this, where many around the world schooled in European French would say *Quelle heure est-il?* for 'What time is it?,' on the streets of Québec you're likely to hear *Y'est quelle heure?*

Most Québecers will understand a more formal French – it will just strike them as a little peculiar. Remember, too, that broken French can sound as charming as the French speaker's broken English if said with a friendly attitude. Other differences between Old World French and the Québec version worth remembering (because you don't want to go hungry!) are the terms for breakfast, lunch and dinner. Rather than *petit déjeuner, déjeuner* and *dîner,* you're likely to see and hear *déjeuner, dîner* and *souper.*

If you have any car trouble, you'll be happy to know that generally, English terms are used for parts. Indeed the word *char* for car may be heard. Hitchhiking is known not as *autostop* but as *le pousse* (the thumb).

Announcers and broadcasters on Québec TV and radio tend to speak a more refined, European style of French, as does the upper class. Visitors to the country without much everyday French-speaking experience will have the most luck understanding them. Despite all this, the preservation of French in Québec is a primary concern and fuels the separatist movement. In 1977, the passage of Bill 101 affirmed the primacy of French and effectively made it the official language of Québec. The relative weighting of the Francophone and Anglo-Saxon communities is frequently a front-page item; the percentage of Québecers whose native tongue is English has been dwindling for decades (8.8% at the 1996 census compared to 13% in 1971).

New Brunswick is, perhaps surprisingly, the only officially bilingual province. French is widely spoken, particularly in the north and east. Again, it is somewhat different from the French of Québec. Nova Scotia and Manitoba also have significant French populations, but there are also pockets in most provinces.

The following is a short guide to some French words and phrases that may be useful for the traveler. The combinations 'ohn/ehn/ahn' in the phonetic transcriptions are nasal sounds – the 'n' is not pronounced; 'zh' is pronounced as the 's' in 'measure.' Stress in French is much weaker than in English. All it really does is lengthen the final syllable of the word, so it is important to make an effort to pronounce each syllable with approximately equal stress.

Québec French employs a lot of English words; this may make understanding and speaking the language a little easier.

For a far more comprehensive guide to the language, get a copy of Lonely Planet's *French phrasebook* – it's a handy pocket-size book for travelers.

Civilities & Basics

Yes.	*Oui.*
	wee
No.	*Non.*
	nohn
Please.	*S'il vous plaît.*
	seel voo pleh
Thank you.	*Merci.*
	mehr-see
You're welcome.	*Je vous en prie.*
	zhe voo-zohn pree
Hello. (day)	*Bonjour.*
	bohn-joor
Hello. (evening)	*Bonsoir.*
	bohn-swar
Hello. (informal)	*Salut.*
	sa-lew

Goodbye.	*Au revoir.*		Excuse me.	*Pardon.*
	oh rev-warr			par-dohn
How are you?	*Comment ça va?* (or *Ça va?*)		Pardon/What?	*Comment?*
	com-mohn sa vah?			com-mohn?
I'm fine.	*Ça va bien.*			*Quoi?* (slang)
	sa vah bee-ahn			kwah?
Welcome.	*Bienvenu.*		How much?	*Combien?*
	bee-ahn ven-oo			kom-bee-ahn?

Language Difficulties

I don't understand.
  Je ne comprends pas.
    zhe neh com-prohn pah
I understand.
  Je comprends.
    zhe com-prohn

Do you speak English?
  Parlez-vous anglais?
    par-lay vooz ang-lay?
I don't speak French.
  Je ne parle pas français.
    zhe neh parl pah frohn-say

Getting Around

bicycle	*vélo*		return ticket	*billet aller et retour*
	veh-loh			bee-yay a-lay eh
bus	*autobus*			reh-tour
	oh-toh-booss		boat cruise	*croisière de bateau*
train	*train*			kwa-zyeh de ba-toh
	trahn		petrol (gasoline)	*essence/gaz*
plane	*avion*			eh-sohns/gaz
	a-vee-ohn		lead-free (petrol)	*sans plomb*
train station	*gare*			sohn plom
	gar		self-serve	*service libre*
platform	*quai*			sairvees lee-br
	kay		Where is …?	*Où est …?*
bus station	*station d'autobus*			oo eh …?
	sta-seeyon d'ohtoh-			
	booss			
one-way ticket	*billet simple*			
	bee-yay sam-pluh			

What time does the … leave/arrive?
  A quelle heure part/arrive le …?
    a kel ur pahr/ahreev le …?

Directions

I want to go to …	*Je veux aller à …*		left	*à gauche*
	zhe vur a-lay a			a goshe
			right	*à droit*
				a drwat
			straight ahead	*tout droit*
				too drwat
			near	*proche*
				prosh
			far	*loin*
				lwahn
			here	*ici*
				ee-see
			there	*là*
				lah

Signs

Billeterie	Box/Ticket Office
Complet	Full/No Vacancy
Entrée	Entrance
Halte Routière	Rest Stop
Sortie	Exit
Stationnement	Parking

⚜ ⚜ ⚜ ⚜ ⚜ ⚜ ⚜ ⚜ ⚜ ⚜

LANGUAGE

Around Town

bank	*banque*
	bohnk
beach	*plage*
	plazh
the bill	*l'addition/le reçu*
	la-dis-yohn/
	le reh soo
bridge	*pont*
	pohn
convenience store	*dépanneur*
	day-pahn-nur
department store	*magasin*
	mag-a-zahn
grocery store	*épicerie*
	ay-pee-seh-ree

museum	*musée*
	mew-zay
opening hours	*horaires*
	oh-rair
post office	*bureau de poste*
	bew-roh de post
the police	*la police*
	la po-lees
show/concert	*spectacle*
	spek-tahk'l
toilet	*toilette*
	twah-leh
tourist office	*bureau du tourisme*
	bew-ro doo too-rees-muh
traveler's check	*cheque voyage*
	shek vwoy-yazh

Accommodations

Do you have any rooms available?
  Est-ce que vous avez des chambres libres?
    ehs-ker voo zah-vay day shombr leebr?

with a bathroom	*avec salle de bain*
	ahvek sahl de bahn
with a kitchenette	*avec cuisinette*
	ahvek kwee-zee-net

hotel	*hôtel*
	o-tell
youth hostel	*auberge de jeunesse*
	o-bairzh de zheu-ness
a room	*une chambre*
	oon shombr
a double room	*une chambre double*
	oon shombr doobl

Food & Dining

bakery	*boulangerie*
	boo-lohn-zhe-ree
beer	*bière*
	bee-yair
a bottle of	*une bouteille de*
	oon boo-tay duh
bread	*pain*
	pahn
a cup of	*une tasse de*
	oon tass duh
cheese	*fromage*
	fro-mahzh
a glass of	*un verre de*
	uhn vair duh
bill/check	*l'addition*
	la-dee-see-ohn
breakfast	*le (petit-)déjeuner*
	luh (puh-tee) day-zhuh-nay
lunch	*le dîner*
	luh dee-nay
dinner	*le souper*
	luh soo-pay

dish of the day	*le plat du jour*
	luh plah dew zhoor
fixed-price menu	*le table d'hôte*
	luh tab doht
fresh fish store	*poissonnerie*
	pwa-sohn-e-ree
fruit	*fruit*
	frwee
main course	*le plat principal*
	luh pla pran-see-pal
meat pie	*tourtière*
	tor-tee-air
milk	*lait*
	leh
red wine	*vin rouge*
	vahn roozh
restaurant	*restaurant*
	rest-a-rohn
snack bar	*casse croûte*
	kass krewt
soft drink	*liqueur*
	lee-ker

steak	steack/bavette		wine	vin	
	stayk/bah-vet			vahn	
vegetables	légumes		wine list	la carte des vins	
	lay-gyoom			la cart day van	
Waiter!	Monsieur!/Mademoiselle!				
	muh-syuh/mad-mwa-zel		I would like to order …		
water	eau			je voudrais commander	
	oh			zhe voo-dray ko-mahn-day	
white wine	vin blanc		I'm a vegetarian.		
	vahn blohn			Je suis végétarien/végétarienne (m/f)	
				zhe swee vay-zhay-teh-ryahn/ryen	

Other Useful Words

big	grand	expensive	cher
	grond		share
small	petit	before	avant
	peh-tee		ah-vohn
much/many	beaucoup	after	après
	boh-coo		ah-preh
cheap	bon marché/pas chère	tomorrow	demain
	bohn mar-shay/pa sher		de-mahn
	c'est cheap	yesterday	hier
	seh cheep		yeah

Numbers

1	un	uhn	25	vingt-cinq	vahn sank
2	deux	der	30	trente	tronht
3	trois	twah	40	quarante	car-ohnt
4	quatre	cat	50	cinquante	sank-ohnt
5	cinq	sank	60	soixante	swa-sohnt
6	six	sease	70	soixante-dix	swa-sohnt dees
7	sept	set	80	quatre-vingt	cat-tr' vahn
8	huit	weet	90	quatre-vingt-dix	cat-tr' vahn dees
9	neuf	nerf	100	cent	sohn
10	dix	dees	500	cinq cents	sank sohn
20	vingt	vahn	1000	mille	meel
21	vingt et un	vahn-teh-un			

Emergencies

Help!	Au secours!	Leave me alone!	Laissez-moi tranquille!
	oh say-coor		leh-say-mwa tron-kill!
Call a doctor!	Appelez un médecin!	I'm lost.	Je me suis égaré/égarée.
	a-pay-lay uhn		(m/f)
	med-sahn!		zhe muh swee
Call the police!	Appelez la police!		ay-ga-ray
	a-pay-lay la poh-lees!		

⚜ ⚜

Glossary

Acadians – The first settlers from France who lived in Nova Scotia.

Amerindians – An increasingly acceptable term for North America's Native Indians.

aurora borealis – Also called the northern lights, they are charged particles from the sun that are trapped in the earth's magnetic field. They appear as otherworldly colored, waving beams.

beaver fever (giardiasis) – The bacteria that causes this disease is found in many freshwater streams and lakes. It affects the digestive tract and can be avoided by boiling drinking water.

boîtes à chanson – Cheap, casual and relaxed folk clubs, popular in Québec.

boondoggle – A futile or unnecessary project or work.

boreal – Refers to the Canadian north and its character, as in the boreal forest, the boreal wind etc.

brew pub – A pub that brews and sells its own beer.

cabin fever – A traditional term still used to indicate a stir-crazy, frustrated state of mind due to being cooped up indoors over the long northern winter. It's also used to denote the same feelings that come from being forced to remain in the house, cottage, or tent because of inclement weather or bad health.

calèche – Horse-drawn carriage that can be taken around parts of Montréal and Québec City.

Canadian Shield – Also known as the Precambrian or Laurentian Shield, this is a plateau of rock that was formed 2.5 billion years ago and covers much of the northern region of the country.

clearcut – This is an area where loggers have cut every tree, large and small, leaving nothing standing.

CLSC – Centre Local de Santé Communautaire, or local community health center. You'll see green-and-white CLSC signs in almost every Québec town or urban district.

correspondence – A transfer slip like those used between the Métro and bus networks in Montréal.

côte – This French word for 'side' is also an old Québec term meaning 'hill' (eg, the Montréal street Côte du Beaver Hall).

coulees – Gulches, usually dry.

dépanneur – Called 'dep' for short, this is a Québec term for a convenience store, often one open 24 hours.

dome car – The two-level, glass-top observation car of a train.

l'Estrie – Québécois term for the Cantons de l'Est (Eastern Townships), a former Loyalist region southeast of Montréal toward the US border.

First Nations – A term used to denote Canada's indigenous peoples. It can be used instead of Native Indians or Native people.

flowerpots – Unusual rock formations, these geological forms are created by erosion from waves. Examples can be seen at Tobermory in Ontario and at The Rocks in New Brunswick.

Front de Libération du Québec (FLQ) – A radical, violent political group active in the 1970s that advocated Québec's separation from Canada. In 1970, the FLQ kidnapped and murdered Québec health minister Pierre Laporte.

fruit leather (cuir de fruits) – A blend of fruit purees dried into thin sheets and pressed together, common among backpackers and hikers.

gasoline – Petrol, known as gasoline or simply gas (*gaz* in Québec). Almost all gasoline in Canada is termed unleaded and comes in regular and more costly higher-octane versions.

gîte du passant – A Québec term often used for bed-and-breakfasts (B&Bs).

Grande Noirceur – The term 'Great Darkness' is sometimes used to describe the period of the Duplessis government in Québec (1944–59).

Group of Seven – A group of celebrated Canadian painters from the 1920s.

Haligonians – Residents of Halifax, Nova Scotia.

Hudson Bay Company (Compagnie de la Baie d'Hudson) – An English enterprise created in 1670 to exploit the commercial potential of the Hudson Bay and its waterways. In the 18th century, the Hudson Bay Company and its rival, the Northwest Company, established forts and commercial outlets in a vast region between present-day Québec and Alberta. The companies merged in 1821. The department store The Bay (La Baie) is the last vestige of Canada's oldest enterprise.

igloo – Traditional Inuit houses made from blocks of ice.

Innu – Another name for the Montagnais and Naskapi peoples.

inukshuk – Inuit preferred to trap caribou in water, where they could be hunted from a kayak. For this reason, they built stone figures called 'inukshuks' next to lakes to direct the animals into the water.

interior camping – This refers to usually lone, individual sites accessible only by foot or canoe. You must preregister for those in provincial or national parks (for your own safety).

Je me souviens – This Québec motto with a nationalist ring ('I remember') appears on license plates across the province.

loon – A fish-eating diving bird of the genus *Gavia*.

loonie – Canada's one-dollar coin, so named for the loon stamped on one side.

Lotto 649 – The country's most popular, highest-paying lottery.

Loyalists – Residents of America who maintained their allegiance to Britain during the American Revolution and fled to Canada.

Mennonites – Members of a religious utopian group originating in Europe who are mostly found in the Kitchener-Waterloo region of southern Ontario.

Métis – Canadians of French and Native Indian stock.

Mounties – Royal Canadian Mounted Police (RCMP).

mukluks – Moccasins or boots made from sealskin and often trimmed with fur; usually made by Inuit people.

muskeg – Undrained boggy land most often found in northern Canada.

NAFTA – North American Free Trade Agreement, an accord that eliminated a range of trade barriers among Canada, the USA and Mexico. The French acronym is ALENA.

Naskapi – A group of Native Indians, also called the Innu, found in northeastern Québec.

Newfie – A term applying to residents of Newfoundland, or 'The Rock' as it is sometimes known.

no-see-um – Any of various tiny biting insects that are difficult to see and that can annoy travelers when out in the woods or along some beaches. No-see-um netting, a very fine mesh screen on a tent, is designed to keep the insects out.

Nunavut – Official territory of the Inuits in northern Canada since 1991, a vast area encompassing 350,000 sq km.

permafrost – Permanently frozen subsoil that covers the far north of Canada.

piastre – Québécois term for a Canadian dollar.

portage – The process of transporting boats and supplies overland between navigable waterways. Also the overland route used for such a purpose.

petroglyphs – Ancient paintings or carvings on rock.

pourvoirie – A forest area with lakes and rivers granted by the Québec government to a private group or association for commerce and tourism. They're traditionally used for hunting and fishing, and entry fees are charged. In recent years, some owners have switched to animal protection and observation. There are about 600 pourvoiries in Québec.

public/separate schools – The two basic school systems. Both are free and essentially the same, but the latter is designed for Catholics and offers more religious education.

qiviut – The wool of the musk ox that was traditionally woven into garments by some Inuit groups in the far north.

Québécois – The local tongue of Québec, where the vast majority of the population is French; also known as *joual*. The term also refers to the residents of Québec, although it is applied only to the French, not English Québecers.

Refus Global – The radical manifest of a group of Québec artists and intellectuals during the Duplessis era (1944–59).

ringuette – A sport played on ice, similar to hockey but with a ring instead of a puck and a straight stick with no flat or angled end.

rock hounds – Rock collectors.

rubby – A derelict alcoholic who is often homeless. The term comes from rubbing alcohol, which is often mixed with cheap wine for drinking.

RV – Recreational vehicle (commonly a motor home).

SAQ – Société des Alcools du Québec, a state-run agency whose branches are authorized to sell beer and wine.

screech – A particularly strong rum once available only in Newfoundland but now widely available across Canada in diluted form.

seigneury – Land in Québec originally held by grant from the King of France. A seigneur is thus a holder of a seigneury.

sourdough – Refers to a person who has completed one year's residency in northern Canada.

sous – Québécois currency term sometimes used for cents.

spelunking – The exploration and study of caves.

steamies – Hot dogs in Québec, which get their name from the way they are cooked.

sugar-making moon – A former Native Indian term for the spring date when the maple tree's sap begins to run.

sugar shack – The place where the collected maple sap is distilled in large kettles and boiled as part of the production of maple syrup.

taiga – The coniferous forests extending across much of subarctic North America and Eurasia.

toonie – Sometimes spelled 'twonie,' this is a Canadian two-dollar coin introduced after the 'loonie,' or one-dollar coin.

trailer – In Canada, as well as in the USA, this refers to a caravan or a mobile home (house trailer). Also a vehicle used for transporting goods.

trap line – A marked area along which a trapper will set traps to catch fur-bearing animals.

tundra – The vast, treeless Arctic plains, north of the treeline and with a perpetually frozen subsoil.

voyageur – A boatman employed by one of the early fur-trading companies. He could also fill the function of a woodsman, guide, trapper or explorer.

LONELY PLANET

You already know that Lonely Planet produces more than this one guidebook, but you might not be aware of the other products we have on this region. Here is a selection of titles which you may want to check out as well:

Canada
ISBN 0 86442 752 2
US$24.95 • UK£14.99

Toronto
ISBN 1 86450 217 7
US$15.99 • UK£9.99

Available wherever books are sold.

Index

Text

Places to Stay

Places to Eat

Boxed Text

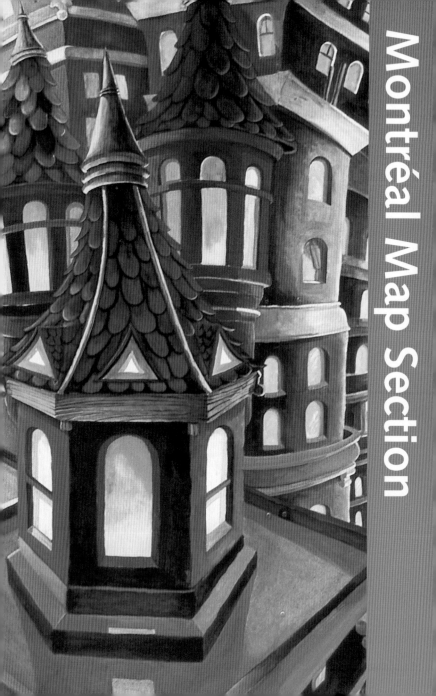

MAP 1 ISLAND OF MONTRÉAL

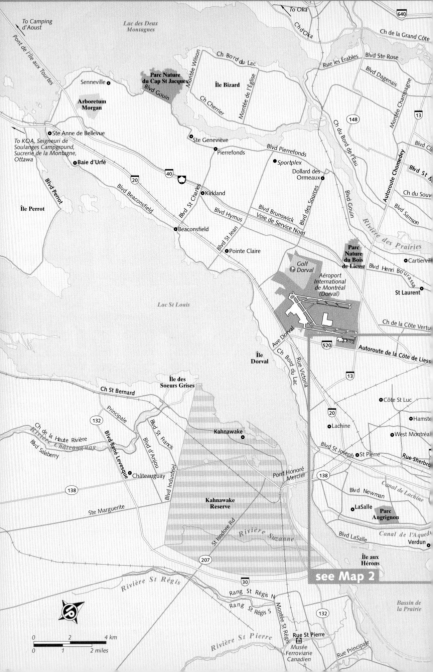

To Camping
d'Aoust

To Oka

Ch d'Oka

640

Ch de la Grand Côte

Lac des Deux
Montagnes

Ch Bord du Lac

Rue les Érables

Blvd Ste Rose

Pont de l'île aux Tourtes

Montée Wilson

Île Bizard

Blvd Dagenais

Senneville

Parc Nature
du Cap St Jacques

Blvd Gouin

Montée Champagne

148

13

Arboretum
Morgan

Ch Cherrier

Montée de l'Église

Ch du Bord de l'eau

Autoroute Chomedey

Blvd Cl

Ste Anne de Bellevue

Ste Geneviève

Blvd St N

To KOA, Seigneuri de
Soulanges Campground,
Sucrerie de la Montagne,
Ottawa

Pierrefonds

Blvd Pierrefonds

Ch du Souv

Baie d'Urfé

Sportplex

Dollard des
Ormeaux

Blvd Samson

40

20

Île Perrot

Blvd Perrot

Blvd Beaconsfield

Blvd St Charles

Kirkland

Blvd Brunswick

Blvd des Sources

Blvd Gouin

Rivière des Prairies

Blvd Hymus
Voie de service Nord

Beaconsfield

Blvd St Jean

Parc
Nature
du Bois
de Liesse

Blvd Henri Bourassa

Cartierville

Pointe Claire

Golf
Dorval

Aéroport
International
de Montréal
(Dorval)

St Laurent

Lac St Louis

Ch de la Côte Vertu

Ave Dorval

Ch Bord du Lac

Rue Victoria

520

Autoroute de la Côte de Liess

Île
Dorval

13

Île des
Soeurs Grises

Ch St Bernard

Côte St Luc

Principale

132

Blvd René Levesque

Blvd St Farès

Blvd d'Anjou

Blvd Industriel

Kahnawake

Hamste

Lachine

West Montréal

Ch de la Haute Rivière

Rivière Châteauguay

Blvd Salaberry

Blvd St Joseph

St Pierre

Rue Sherbro

Châteauguay

Pont Honoré
Mercier

138

138

Ste Marguerite

Blvd Newman

Canal de Lachine

Kahnawake
Reserve

St Isadore Rd

Rivière Suzanne

LaSalle

Parc
Angrignon

207

Blvd LaSalle

Canal de l'Aqued

Verdun

Île aux
Hérons

see Map 2

30

Rang St Régis N

Rang St Régis S

Montée St Rég

132

Bassin de
la Prairie

Rivière St Régis

Rue St Pierre

Rivière St Pierre

Musée
Ferroviaire
Canadien

Rue Principale

0   2   4 km
0   1   2 miles

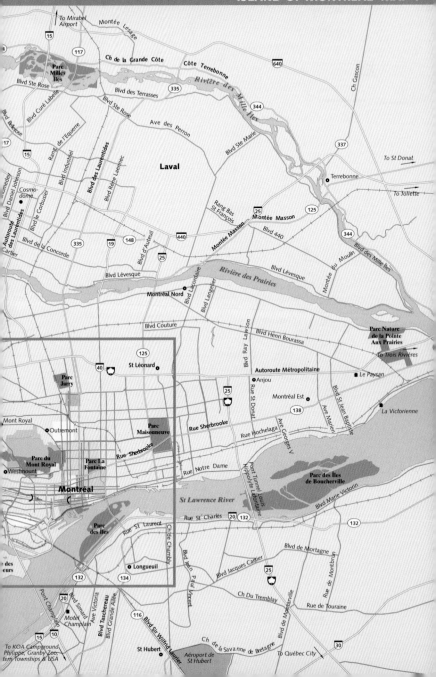

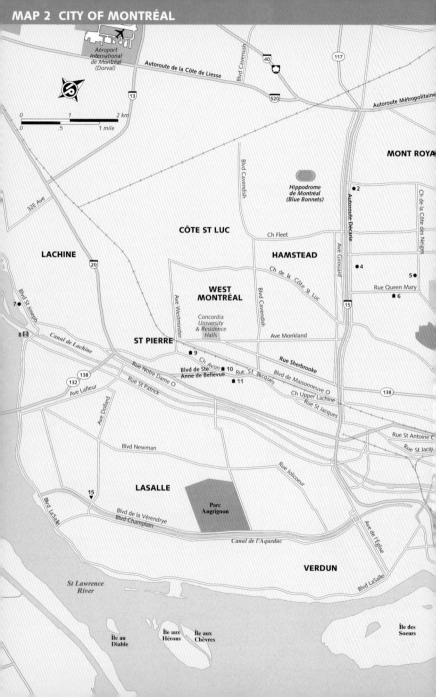

MAP 2 CITY OF MONTRÉAL

Aéroport
International
de Montréal
(Dorval)

Autoroute de la Côte de Liesse

Blvd Cavendish

40

117

520

Autoroute Métropolitaine

13

0   1   2 km

0   .5   1 mile

MONT ROYA

Blvd Cavendish

Hippodrome
de Montréal
(Blue Bonnets)

• 2

Ch de la Côte des Neiges

Autoroute Décarie

32E Ave

CÔTE ST LUC

Ch Fleet

HAMSTEAD

Ave Girouard

• 4

5 •

Rue Queen Mary

LACHINE

20

Ch de la Côte St Luc

WEST
MONTRÉAL

♦ 6

Blvd St Joseph

7 •

Ave Westminster

Blvd Cavendish

15

8 🏛

Canal de Lachine

Concordia
University
& Residence
Halls

Ave Monkland

ST PIERRE

9 ♦

Rue Sherbrooke

Ch Avon   • 10

Blvd de Ste
Anne de Bellevue

Rue St Jacques

Blvd de Maisonneuve O

138

138

132

Ave Lafleur

Rue Notre Dame O

♦ 11

Ch Upper Lachine

Rue St Patrick

Rue St Jacques

Ave Dollard

Rue St Antoine C

Rue St Jacqu

Blvd Newman

Rue Joliceour

15 ♦

LASALLE

Parc
Angrignon

Ave de l'Église

Blvd La Salle

Blvd de la Vérendrye
Blvd Champlain

Canal de l'Aqueduc

VERDUN

Blvd LaSalle

St Lawrence
River

Île des
Soeurs

Île au
Diable

Île aux
Hérons

Île aux
Chèvres

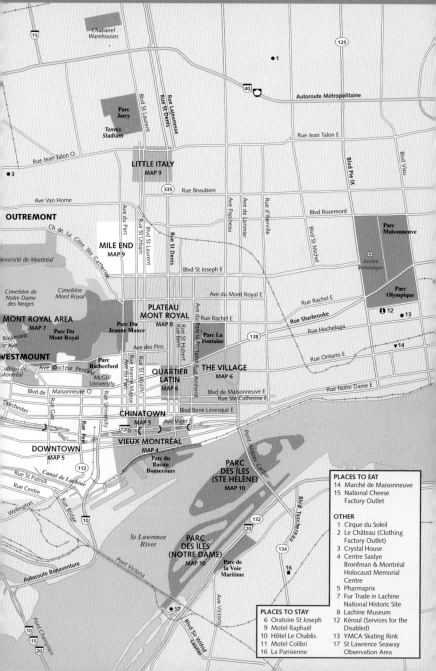

15

125

Chabanel Warehouses

●1

40

Autoroute Métropolitaine

Parc Jarry

Rue Jean Talon E

Tennis Stadium

Rue Jean Talon O

Blvd Pie IX

Blvd Viau

LITTLE ITALY
MAP 9

335   Rue Beaubien

●3

Ave Van Horne

Blvd Rosemont

OUTREMONT

Ch de La Côte Ste Catherine

Université de Montréal

Parc Maisonneuve

MILE END
MAP 9

Blvd St Joseph E

Jardin Botanique

Cimetière de Notre Dame des Neiges

Cimetière Mont Royal

Ave du Mont Royal E

Rue Rachel E

Parc Olympique

MONT ROYAL AREA
MAP 7

Parc Du Mont Royal

Parc Du Jeanne Mance

Rue Rachel E

Rue Sherbrooke

ℹ12   ●13

Boulevard

138

Rue Hochelaga

WESTMOUNT

Parc Rutherford

Ave des Pins

Parc La Fontaine

Ave Docteur Penfield

McGill University

▼14

Rue Ontario E

Collège de Montréal

PLATEAU MONT ROYAL
MAP 8

QUARTIER LATIN
MAP 6

THE VILLAGE
MAP 6

Blvd de Maisonneuve O

Maisonneuve O

Blvd de Maisonneuve E

Rue Notre Dame E

Dorchester

Rue Guy

CHINATOWN
MAP 5

Rue Ste Catherine E

Blvd René Lévesque E

720

Ave Viger E

Rue University

VIEUX MONTRÉAL
MAP 4

DOWNTOWN
MAP 5

112

Parc du Bassin Bonsecours

PARC DES ÎLES (STE HÉLÈNE)
MAP 10

Rue St Patrick

Canal de Lachine

Rue Centre

132

Wellington

Rue Bridge

10

20

St Lawrence River

PARC DES ÎLES (NOTRE DAME)
MAP 10

134

16 ▲

Autoroute Bonaventure

Pont Victoria

Parc de la Voie Maritime

10

15

20

Pont Champlain

●17

Blvd Sir Wilfrid Laurier

Ave Victoria

PLACES TO EAT
14 Marché de Maisonneuve
15 National Cheese Factory Outlet

OTHER
1 Cirque du Soleil
2 Le Château (Clothing Factory Outlet)
3 Crystal House
4 Centre Saidye Bronfman & Montréal Holocaust Memorial Centre
5 Pharmaprix
7 Fur Trade in Lachine National Historic Site
8 Lachine Museum
12 Kéroul (Services for the Disabled)
13 YMCA Skating Rink
17 St Lawrence Seaway Observation Area

PLACES TO STAY
6 Oratoire St Joseph
9 Motel Raphaël
10 Hôtel Le Chablis
11 Motel Colibri
16 La Parisienne

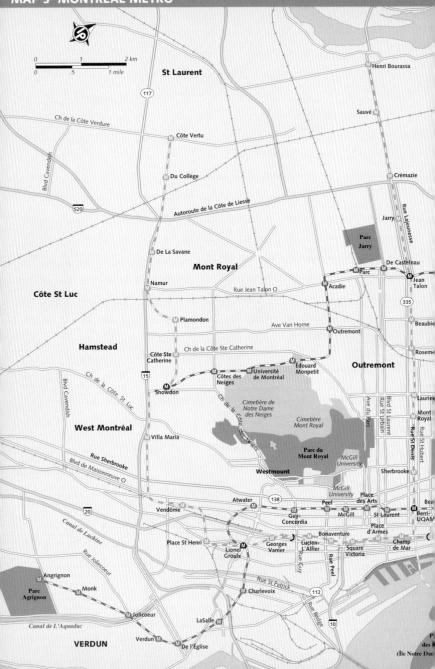

MAP 3 MONTRÉAL METRO

0   1   2 km
0   .5   1 mile

117

St Laurent

Henri Bourassa

Sauvé

Ch de la Côte Verdure

Côte Vertu

Blvd Cavendish

Crémazie

Du Collège

Rue Lajeunesse

520

Autoroute de la Côte de Liesse

Jarry

De La Savane

Parc
Jarry

Mont Royal

De Castelnau

Parc

Namur

Rue Jean Talon O

Acadie

Jean
Talon

335

Côte St Luc

Beaubie

Plamondon

Ave Van Horne

Outremont

Rosem

Hamstead

Côte Ste
Catherine

Ch de la Côte Ste Catherine

Édouard
Monpetit

Outremont

Blvd Cavendish

15

Côtes des
Neiges

Université
de Montréal

Laurie

Mont
Royal

Ch de la Côte St Luc

Snowdon

Cimetière de
Notre Dame
des Neiges

Cimetière
Mont Royal

Ave du Parc
Rue St Urbain
Blvd St Laurent

Rue St Denis
Rue St Hubert

West Montréal

Villa Maria

Parc du
Mont Royal

McGill
University

Rue Sherbrooke

Blvd de Maisonneuve O

Ch de la Côte des Neiges

Westmount

Sherbrooke

20

Atwater

138

Peel

McGill
University

Place
des Arts

Bea
Berri-
UQAM

Vendôme

Guy
Concordia

McGill

St Laurent

Place
d'Armes

Canal de Lachine

Rue Jolicoeur

Place St Henri

Lionel
Groulx

Georges
Vanier

Bonaventure

Lucien-
L'Allier

Rue Guy

Square
Victoria

Rue Peel

Champ
de Mar

Angrignon

Rue St Patrick

Charlevoix

112

Rue Bridge

Parc
Agrignon

Monk

Jolicoeur

LaSalle

10

Canal de L'Aquaduc

Verdun

De l'Église

P
des K
(Île Notre Dar

VERDUN

MONTRÉAL NORD

Blvd Couture

Blvd Henri Bourassa

25

ST LÉONARD

125

Blvd Ray Lawson

40 Autoroute Métropolitaine

Saint Michel
Rue Jean Talon E

Anjou

Fabre   Iberville

Ave St Donat

Blvd Pie IX

Blvd Viau

Rue Beaubien

Ave Papineau

Ave de Lorimier

Rue d'Iberville

Blvd Rosemont

**Parc
Maisonneuve**

Honoré
Beaugrand

Radisson

Langelier

Jardin
Botanique

Cadillac

Blvd St Joseph E

du Mont Royal E

Rue Rachel E

**Parc
Olympique**

L'Assomption

Rue Hochelaga

Rue Norte Dame

Rue Sherbrooke

Pie IX   Viau

25

138

Joliette

Préfontaine

Rue Ontario E

Pont Tunnel Louis
Hippolyte Lafontaine

aine

Frontenac

Rue Ste Catherine E

Rue Notre Dame E

Parc
des Îles de
Boucherville

Papineau

St Lawrence River

Parc
des Îles
(Île St Hélène)

St Hélène   Longueuil

Rue St Charles

20   132

Ave Papineau

Rue St Laurent

Ch de Chambly

LONGUEUIL

132

15   134

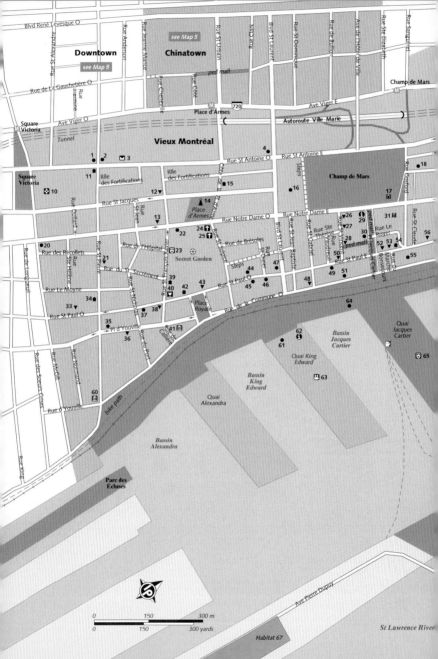

MAP 4 VIEUX MONTRÉAL

Blvd René Lévesque O

Rue de la Gauchetière O

Downtown
see Map 5

Chinatown
see Map 5

ped mall

Champ de Mars

Ave Viger E

Autoroute Ville Marie

Place d'Armes

720

Ave Viger O

Square Victoria

Tunnel

Vieux Montréal

Rue St Antoine O

Rue St Antoine E

4

Steps

Champ de Mars

18

1 2 3

Rlle des Fortifications

Rlle des Fortifications

15

16

17

Square Victoria

11

10

12

Rue St Jacques

14

Place d'Armes

Rue Notre Dame O

Rue Notre Dame E

26
29
27
30
31

13

22

Rue de Brésoles

28
52 53 54
50
55

56

24
25

Rue de l'Hôpital

23

Secret Garden

Steps

44
47
48
49 51

20

21

Rue des Récollets

Rue du Sacrement

39
40
42
43
45 46

64

34

33

38 37

Place Royale

Rue St Paul O

Rue de la Commune

35

41

62
61

Quai Jacques Cartier

36

Pl d'Youville

Bassin Jacques Cartier

65

Quai King Edward

63

60

bike path

Bassin King Edward

Rue d'Youville

Quai Alexandra

Bassin Alexandra

Parc des Écluses

0   150   300 m
0   150   300 yards

St Lawrence River

Habitat 67

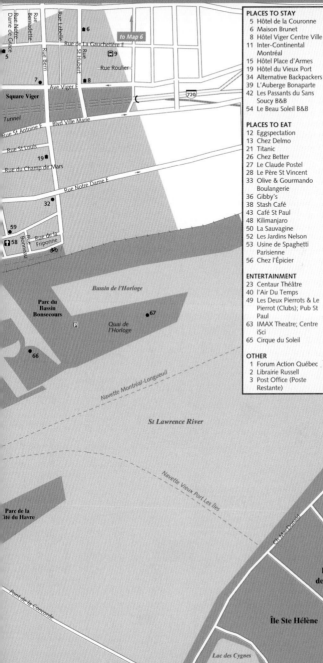

PLACES TO STAY
5 Hôtel de la Couronne
6 Maison Brunet
8 Hôtel Viger Centre Ville
11 Inter-Continental Montréal
15 Hôtel Place d'Armes
19 Hôtel du Vieux Port
34 Alternative Backpackers
39 L'Auberge Bonaparte
42 Les Passants du Sans Soucy B&B
54 Le Beau Soleil B&B

PLACES TO EAT
12 Eggspectation
13 Chez Delmo
21 Titanic
26 Chez Better
27 Le Claude Postel
28 Le Père St Vincent
33 Olive & Gourmando Boulangerie
36 Gibby's
43 Stash Café
43 Café St Paul
48 Kilimanjaro
50 La Sauvagine
52 Les Jardins Nelson
53 Usine de Spaghetti Parisienne
56 Chez l'Épicier

ENTERTAINMENT
23 Centaur Théâtre
40 l'Air Du Temps
42 Les Deux Pierrots & Le Pierrot (Clubs); Pub St Paul
63 IMAX Theatre; Centre iSci
65 Cirque du Soleil

OTHER
1 Forum Action Québec
2 Librairie Russell
3 Post Office (Poste Restante)
4 Simon's Camera
7 Union Français
9 Station Aérobus
10 Centre du Commerce Mondial
14 Monument Maisonneuve
16 Three Courthouses
17 Hôtel de Ville
18 Académies Culinaires du Québec
20 Cohoe's
22 Vieux Séminaire de St Sulpice
24 Basilique Notre Dame
25 Chapelle du Sacré Coeur
29 Tourist Information
30 Galerie Le Chariot
31 Château de Ramezay
32 Lieu Historique de Sir George Étienne Cartier
35 Centre d'Histoire de Montréal
37 Atelier Boutique de Cerfs Volants
41 Musée Pointe à Callière
44 Gallery 2000
45 Galerie Parchemine
46 Galerie St Dizier
47 La Guilde Graphique
51 Vélo-Tour
55 Bonsecours Market
57 Artisanat Canadien
58 Chapelle Notre Dame de Bonsecours; Musée Marguerite Bourgeoys
59 Maison Pierre du Calvet
60 Musée Marc-Aurèle Fortin
61 Flea Market
62 Tourist Information
64 Vélo Aventure (Bike Rental)
66 Pavillon du Bassin-Bonsecours
67 Sailors' Memorial Clock Tower

MAP 5 DOWNTOWN & CHINATOWN

PLACES TO STAY

1 Montréal Oasis
4 Manoir Ambrose
7 Royal Victoria College
8 Castel Durocher
11 Le Gîte Touristique du Centre Ville
14 Tour Trylon
19 Hôtel Pierre
20 Armor Manoir Sherbrooke
21 Le Riche-Bourg
22 Château & Hôtel Versailles
29 Ritz-Carlton
33 Hôtel Le Germain
39 Hôtel Casa Bella
40 B&B Revolution
42 Le Gîte du Plateau Mont-Royal
50 Hôtel Le St Malo
86 Hebergement l'Abri du Voyageur
88 La Villa de France
92 Chambres à Louer
107 Comfort Suites
113 Novotel
114 YWCA
122 YMCA
151 Aux Berges
152 HI Auberge de Montréal
153 Montréal Crescent
154 Hôtel du Nouveau Forum
157 Marriot Château Champlain
160 Hilton Montréal Bonaventure
161 La Tour Centre Ville
170 UQAM Residences
171 L'Américain

PLACES TO EAT

5 McGill University Student Union
12 Amalio's
13 Place Milton
16 Bueno Notte
18 Restaurant Globe
27 Katsura
35 Le Caveau
46 Razou; CÉGEP du Vieux Montréal (Swimming Pool)
49 Pique-Assiette
51 Provigo Supermarket
54 La Maison du Bedouin
57 Maison de Cari
60 Boustan
65 Joe's
69 Ferreira Café Trattoria
70 Bistro Rock Détente
71 Peel Pub
73 Ben's
74 Guy & Dodo Morali
96 Le Faubourg
99 Phaya Tai
100 Chez La Mère Michel
101 Bar-B-Barn
112 Arahova Souvlaki
117 Queue de Cheval
118 Mr Steer
120 Chez Parée
121 Café Presto
125 McLean's Pub
129 Reuben's
137 Il Facolaio; Dunn's
145 Frites Dorée's
173 Green Spot
174 Atwater Market
177 Le Relais des Sultans
179 École de Technologie Superieur

ENTERTAINMENT

9 Yellow Door Coffee House
10 Cinéma du Parc
16 Excentris Cinema
17 Le Swimming
45 Biddles; Jazz & Blues
45 Jello Bar
56 McKibbon's
58 Winnies; Winston Churchill Pub; Electric Avenue (Club)
59 Thursday's
61 Mad Hatter
63 Gerts; Laser Quest; Nautilus Plus (Fitness Center)
66 Sphinx (Club)
75 Paramount & IMAX Cinemas
87 Loft (Club)
89 Metropolis (Club)
90 Foufounes Electriques (Club)
91 Pub Ste Elisabeth
95 Sharx
102 Upstairs
103 Comedyworks
104 O'Donnell's
108 Club Zone
110 Hurley's Irish Pub
111 Brutopia
131 Metaforia Centre
133 737 Altitude (Club)
134 Le Vieux Dublin Pub & Restaurant
136 Isotori (Club)
140 Cubano's (Club); Academy Porta da Barra
143 Théâtre du Nouveau Monde
146 Monument National Theater
147 Club Soda
150 Comedy Nest
181 Tour de Ville Bar

OTHER
2 Côte des Neiges Dental Clinic
3 Grand Seminaire de Montréal
6 Musée Redpath
23 La Casa del Habano (Tobacco)
24 Concordia University
25 Musée des Beaux Arts; Musée des Arts Décoratifs
26 Holt Renfrew
30 American Express Travel Agency & Financial Services
31 Guilde Canadienne des Métier d'Art Québec
32 Cheap Thrills
34 Musée McCord
36 Pollack Concert Hall
38 Fourrures Dubarry
41 Musée Juste Pour Rire
43 Boutique Eva B
44 National Friendship Centre
47 Double Hook Bookshop
48 Montréal Forum
52 Lingerie Romance
53 1.000.000 Comix
55 Cybermac
62 Mt Stephen Club

64 Banque de Montréal
67 Chapters (Bookstore & Internet Access)
68 Odyssey Books
72 Les Cours Mont-Royal
76 La Maison Simons (Shopping)
77 Indigo (Books & Music)
78 Centre Eaton
79 Alouettes Billeterie
80 Cathédrale Christ Church
81 La Baie Department Store (Hudson Bay Co)
82 St James United Church
83 HSG Fur Group
84 Sam the Record Man
85 Musée d'Art Contemporain
93 Centre Canadien d'Architecture
94 Librairie Astro
97 Musée des Soeurs Grises

98 Pharmaprix
105 Le Café Electronique
106 H Poupart (Tobacco)
109 York Photo; Ogilvy
115 Urban Outfitters
116 CAA (Canadian Automobile Club)
119 Maison de la Presse Internationale
123 Currencies International
124 Metropolitan News Agency
126 HMV (Record Store)
127 Centre Infotouriste; Tip Tours; Salsathèque (Club)
128 Jean Coutu Pharmacy
130 Marks & Spencer
132 Main Post Office
135 Square Phillips
138 Future Shop
139 US Consulate
141 Spectrum de Montréal
142 Complexe Desjardins

144 Lingerie Romance
148 Zulu
149 Dance Gallery
155 Centre Molson
156 Gare Windsor (Train Station)
158 1000 Rue de la Gauchetière; Atrium (Ice Rink); British Council; UK Consulate
159 Gare Centrale (Main Train Station)
162 Basilique St Patrick
163 AFC Camera
172 Lussier Antique
175 Les Antiquités Grand Central
176 Lucie Favreau Antiques
178 Dow Planetarium
180 Le Baron
182 Bourse de Montréal
183 Bureau en Gros

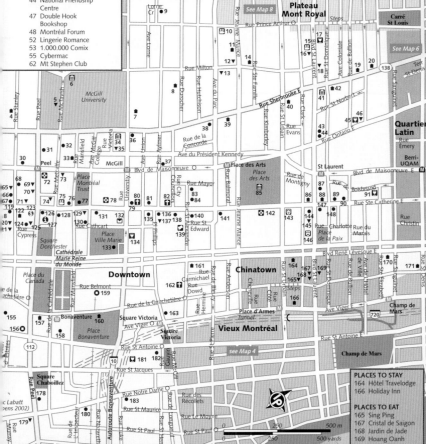

PLACES TO STAY
164 Hôtel Travelodge
166 Holiday Inn

PLACES TO EAT
165 Sing Ping
167 Cristal de Saigon
168 Jardin de Jade
169 Hoang Oanh

MAP 6 QUARTIER LATIN & THE VILLAGE

PLACES TO STAY
1 Castel St Denis
3 Hôtel de Paris; Auberge de Paris
8 Hôtel Villard
10 Hôtel Le Jardin d'Antoine
12 La Maison Jaune B&B
47 Hôtel St Denis
50 Hôtel Le Roberval

PLACES TO EAT
9 La Paryse; Jazzons
17 Le Commensal; Zyng
18 Café Croissant de Lune
49 Da Giovanni

ENTERTAINMENT
2 Tour de Ville
11 Bar Les Conneries
15 Quartier Latin Pub
16 Le Magellan Bar
20 Le St Sulpice
21 Bistro à Jojo
27 Théâtre St Denis

OTHER
19 Bibliothèque Nationale du Québec
26 Cinémathèque Québécoise
28 National Film Board
29 Voyages Campus
30 Main Bus Station
34 Centre de Design
35 Underworld
36 La Galerie de L'UQAM
48 Archambault Book Store

PLACES TO STAY
5 Le Gîte du Parc Lafontaine
22 Hotel Apartments A-1
23 Hôtel Louisbourg
31 Hôtel Le Breton
33 Turquoise B&B
40 Chez Roger Bontemps B&B
51 Studios du Quartier Latin
56 Bed & Breakfast du Village
58 Ruta Bagage B&B
61 Bourbon Entertainment Complex (Hôtel Le Bourbon; Le Track; The Mississippi Club)

PLACES TO EAT
14 Au Petit Extra
32 Pho Viet
38 Miyako
42 Bazou
43 Resto Bisous
45 Kilo

46 Metro (Supermarket)
53 Resto du Village
54 Girly's
55 Bijú
57 Bato Thai

ENTERTAINMENT
13 Lion d'Or (Club)
39 Cabaret l'Entre-Peau
41 Unity (Club)
44 Sisters
59 Le Drugstore
60 Sky Pub
63 Stud Bar

OTHER
4 Info-Sida (HIV/AIDS Information Center)
6 Central Public Library
7 Hôpital Notre Dame
24 A L'Antiquite Curiosite
25 Cité Deco
37 Buanderie du Village (Laundry)
52 Park
62 Banque de Montréal

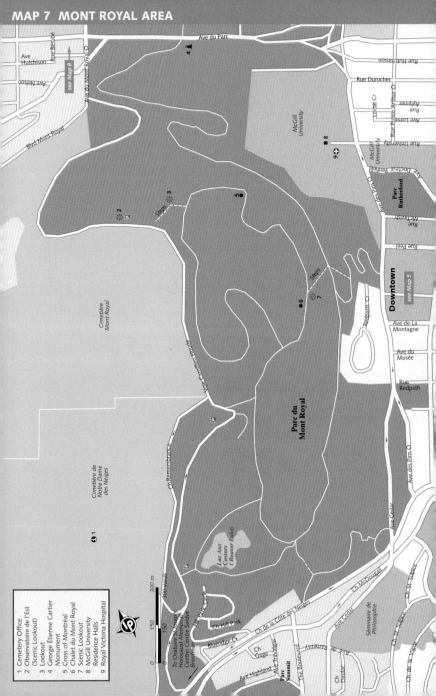

MAP 7 MONT ROYAL AREA

1 Cemetery Office
2 Observatoire de l'Est
   (Scenic Lookout)
3 Lookout
4 George Étienne Cartier
   Monument
5 Cross of Montréal
6 Chalet du Mont Royal
7 Scenic Lookout
8 McGill University
   Residence Halls
9 Royal Victoria Hospital

To Oratoire St-Joseph
Holocaust Memorial
Centre Centre Saidye
Bronfman

Cimetière de
Notre Dame
des Neiges

Cimetière
Mont Royal

Parc du
Mont Royal

Lac Aux
Castors
(Beaver Lake)

McGill
University

Parc
Rutherford

Downtown

see Map 5

see Map 8

Ave du Parc

Ave Hutchison

Ave Nelson

Rue Bérubé

Ave du Mont-Royal O

Blvd Mont Royal

Rue Durocher

Rue Hutchinson

Rue Aylmer

Rue Lorne Cr

Ave Lorne

Rue Prince Arthur O

Rue University

Ave Docteur Penfield

Rue Peel

Rue McTavish

Redpath Cr

Ave de La
Montagne

Ave du
Musée

Rue
Redpath

Ave des Pins O

Ave Cedar

Ch McDougall

Ch de la Côte des Neiges

Séminaire de
Philosophie

Ch St-Sulpice

Ave Cedar

Ave de la Vigie

Ch St-Sulpice

Parc
Summit

The Boulevard

Ave Trafalgar

Ave Highland

Ch
Gage

Ch
Dunlop

Ch Hill Park

Blueridge Ct

Fort
Peel
Circle

Ch Remembrance

Voie Camillien-Houde

Steps

Steps

0   150   300 m

0   150   300 yards

MAP 8 PLATEAU MONT ROYAL

see Map 9

Mile End

Parc Lahaie

Blvd St Joseph E

Blvd St Joseph O

Rue Bérubé

Ave du Parc
Rue Jeanne Mance
Ave de l'Esplanade
Rue St Urbain
Rue Clark
Blvd St Laurent
Rue St Dominique
Ave Coloniale
Rue Elmire
Rue de Bullion
Ave L'Hôtel de Ville
Ave Henri-Julien
Rue Drolet
Rue St Denis
Rue Rivard
Rue Gilford
Rue Prontiac
Rue Resther

Laurier

To La
Maison
du Bagel

Rue Villeneuve O   Rue Villeneuve E

335

1 ▼   Rue de Bienville

2 ▣

Rue Berri

8
9
11 ▼

3 ▼   Ave du Mont Royal O   Ave du Mont Royal E

4
7
10
12 ▼
Mont Royal

6
Ave Laval
13 ▣

5

Rue de Bullion
Ave L'Hôtel de Ville

Rue Marie-Anne O   Rue Marie-Anne E

Parc
Jeanne Mance

Plateau
Mont Royal

25 ■

24 ▣

Parc du
Mont Royal

Rue Rachel O   Rue Rachel E
▼20

22 ●   23 ●

21 ■

27 ▣

28 ●

30 ▼   31 ▼   32 ▼   Ave Duluth E   33 ●   34 ▣   35 ▼

Ave Duluth O   36

37 ▼

29 ●

41 ●

40 ▼   Rue Bagg

▼49

48 ●

46 ■

Rue St Denis

47 ▼

355

42 ▼
43 ▼

Rue St Cuthbert

Rue Napoléon

Rue Rivard
Rue Berri
Rue St Hubert

45
44 ▼

Rue Roy E

50 ◇   Ave des Pins O   Ave des Pins E

51 ▼   52 ▼

54 ▣

53 ▼
58 ▼

57 ▣

59 ▼

60 ●

61 ●

62 ●

63 ▼   ped mall   64 ▼

65 66 ●

Carré
St Louis

67 ▼
Rue Chenier
Sherbrooke

Rue
des Malines
68 ▼   69 ●

Rue de Rigaud

Ave du Parc
Rue Jeanne Mance
Rue Ste-Famille
Rue St Urbain
Rue Clark
Blvd St Laurent
Rue St Dominique
Ave Coloniale
Ave Bullion
Ave de l'Hôtel de Ville
Ave Laval
Ave Henri-Julien
Rue Drolet

Rue Guilbault
Rue Prince Arthur O

see Map 5   Downtown

see Map 6   Quartier Latin

Blvd St Joseph E

Rue Gilford

Ave du Mont Royal E

▼19

Rue Marie Anne E

Ave Bureau

▼26

Rue Rachel E

38 ⊞

Parc
La Fontaine

Rue
Napoléon

Napoléon

Université
du Québec
à Montréal

Rue Roy E
▼56

Rue Sherbrooke E

Rue Cherrier

The Village

see Map 6

Parc Persillier
Lachapelle

Marché
St Jaques

138

PLACES TO STAY
14 À la Dormance B&B
21 Auberge Chez Jean
25 Shézelles B&B
46 Bienvenue B&B
55 La Maison du Jardin
65 À La Belle Victorienne
    B&B
66 Pierre & Dominique B&B
68 Hotel de l'Institut

PLACES TO EAT
1   Ouzeri
3   Beauty's
11 La Binerie Mont Royal
12 Restaurant Rapido du
    Plateau
15 Porté Disparu
16 St Viateur Bagel & Cie
18 Bio Délices Inc
19 Ma-am-m Bolduc
20 Rotisserie Portugalia
26 Kamela Couscous
30 Nantha's Kitchen
31 L'Harmonie d'Asie
32 Chez José Boulangerie
35 Bistro Duluth
37 La Maison Grécque
40 Café Santropol
42 Coco Rico
43 Schwartz's
45 Waldman Plus (Fish
    Market & Restaurant)
47 Toqué!
49 Brûlerie St Denis
51 Caffé Elektra
53 Sushi et Boulettes
56 Le Toasteur
58 Il Sole
63 Mazurka
64 La Casa Grécque
67 Café Cherrier

ENTERTAINMENT
2   Théâtre du Rideau Vert
4   Jailhouse (Club)
5   Le Ballatou (Club)
6   Belmont (Club)
13 Quai Des Brumes
22 Passeport (Club)
23 Jingxi (Club)
24 Sofa
27 Barfly
28 Laïka (Club)
34 Bières et Compagnie
38 Théâtre de Verdure
41 Blizzarts
44 Tokyo Bar (Club)
48 Jazzi'z
54 Théâtre de Quat' Sous
59 Go-Go Lounge
60 Angel's; Jaï Bar (Clubs)
62 Café Campus (Club)
69 Blizzarts

OTHER
7   Rose Nanane
8   Rebella
9   Diabolik
10 Scarlett O'Hara
    Boutique
17 Centre de Surplus
29 Friperie St Laurent;
    Twist Encore; Mojo
33 Boutique Tourisme
    Jeunesse
36 Le Souk du Tassili;
    Kenzo Hair Stylists
39 La Maison des
    Cyclistes; Vélo Québec
50 Banque Laurentienne
52 Musique Noize
57 Cyberground Netcafé
61 Rotation

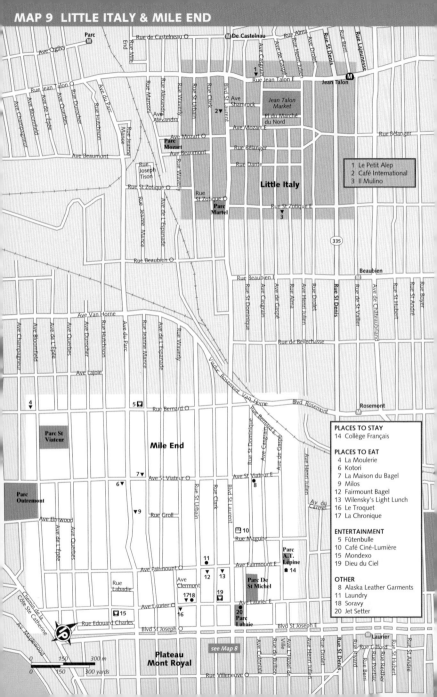

MAP 9 LITTLE ITALY & MILE END

Parc

Rue de Castelnau O   De Castelnau
Rue Alma   Rue St Denis   Rue Berri   Rue Lajeunesse
Ave Ogilvy

Rue Jean Talon O   Ave Casgrain   Rue de Castel   Rue Henri Julien   Rue Droiet

Rue de Castelnau
Rue Mile End
Rue Jean Talon E   **1**   Jean Talon

Rue Jean Talon O   Ave Shamrock   Jean Talon Market   Pl du Marché du Nord
Ave Alexandra   **2**▼   Ave Mozart   Rue Bélanger

Ave Mozart O   Ave Mozart

Parc Mozart   Ave Beaumont   Rue Bélanger   **Little Italy**
Ave Beaumont   Rue Dante

Rue Joseph Tison   Rue St Zotique O   Rue St Zotique E   **3**▼

Parc Murtel   335

Rue Beaubien O   Beaubien

Rue Beaubien E   Beaubien

1	Le Petit Alep
2	Café International
3	Il Mulino

Ave Van Horne   Rue St Dominique   Ave Casgrain   Rue de Gaspé   Rue Alma   Rue Henri Julien   Rue Droiet   Rue St Denis   Rue St Vallier   Ave de Chateaubriand   Rue St Hubert   Rue André   Rue Boyer

Ave Cajole   Rue de Bellechasse

Viaduc Rosemont Van Horne

4   Rue Bernard O   **5**   Blvd Rosemont   Rosemont

Parc St Viateur   **Mile End**

Rue Bernard E   Rue Casgrain   Rue de Gaspé   Ave Henri Julien

7▼   Ave St Viateur O   Ave St Viateur E   **8**

6▼   **Parc Outremont**

▼**9**   Rue Groll

Ave Elmwood

10

Rue Maguire

11   Parc A.T. Lépine

Ave Fairmount O   Ave Fairmount E   **14**

12   **13**

Rue Labadie   Parc De St Michel

17 18   **19**

15   Ave Clermont

Ave Laurier O   **16**   Ave Laurier E   **20** Parc Lahaie

Rue Edouard Charles   Blvd St Joseph   Blvd St Joseph E   Laurier

Plateau Mont Royal   see Map 8   Rue St Denis   Rue Berri

0   150   300 m
0   150   300 yards

Rue Villeneuve

MAP 10 PARC DES ÎLES

720

Rue St Antoine

see Map 5

Rue Panet

Rue Notre Dame

see Map 4

Downtown

Vieux Montréal

Rue de la Commune

Parc du Bassin Bonsecours

Quai de l'Horloge

Quai Jacques Cartier

St Lawrence River

Navette Montréal-Longueuil

Pont Jacques Cartier

Ch. MacDonald

Lac aux Dauphins

● 1

Port Ste Hélène

Chemin la Ronde

m 2

Île St Hélène

Tour de Lévis

Navette Vieux Port-Les Îles

Parc de la Cité du Havre

● 3

Pont de la Concorde

Île St Hélène

M

4 ☻ ● 5 m 6

134

Longueuil

Chemin du Chevron Le Moyne

Île Notre Dame

●

Rue St Charles Ouest

Chemin MacDonald

Passerelle du Cosmos

Lac des Cygnes

Place des Nations

Chenal Le Moyne

Pont des Îles

Parc des Îles

Ave Pierre Dupuy

Ave du Casino

Circ. Gilles Villeneuve

132

Longueuil

Blvd Lafayette

Rue Verchères

Rue Bouvier

Chemin Tiffin

Rue Rouville

Blvd Tascherau

Rue St Charles Ouest

7 ☆ ● 8

Rowing Basin

132

Parc de la Voie Maritime

Ave Vitré

Ave Morrissette

Ave Berkley

Ave Purtney

Blvd Desaulniers

Blvd Tascherau

Blvd Desaulniers

Lac des Régates

Canal de la Rive Sud

20

Ave Melton

Ave Dulwich

Ave Braxton

Ave Sanford

Ave Melton

Rue Riverside

Rue River

Ave Wood

Ave Oak

Ave Maple

Ave Curzon

Ave Sanford

Ave Braxton

Rue Logan

Rue Green

134

Ave Notre Dame

Ave Argyle

Ave Pine

Ave Victoria

Ave Home

Ave Aberdeen

Plage des Îles

Ave Fort

Ave Elm

Rue Webster

Rue L'Espérance

Rue Mercier

Blvd St Wilfrid Laurier

Ave St Wilfrid Laurier

Ave Provincial

Ave Bowdoin

Ave St Laurent

Ave Adam

Ave Edison

Ave Hudson

Blvd Bellard

112

N

0   250   500 m
0   250   500/yards

1 Tour de la Ronde Amusement Park
2 Musée David Stewart
3 l'Homme (Sculpture)
4 Information Kiosk
5 Plaisirs et Santé (Bike Rental)
6 Biosphère
7 Jardin des Floralies
8 Casino de Montréal

MAP LEGEND

ROUTES

City   Regional

Freeway
Toll Freeway
Primary Road
Secondary Road
Tertiary Road
Dirt Road

Pedestrian Mall
Steps
Tunnel
Trail
Walking Tour
Path

TRANSPORTATION

Train
Metro

Bus Route
Ferry

HYDROGRAPHY

River; Creek
Canal
Lake

Spring; Rapids
Waterfalls
Dry; Salt Lake

ROUTE SHIELDS

Trans-Canada Highway
(132) Provincial Highway

BOUNDARIES

International
Province

County
Disputed

AREAS

Beach
Building
Campus

Cemetery
Forest
Garden; Zoo

Golf Course
Park
Plaza

Reservation
Sports Field
Swamp; Mangrove

POPULATION SYMBOLS

◎ CAPITAL .... National Capital
◉ CAPITAL .... Provincial Capital

● **Large City** .... Large City
● **Medium City** .... Medium City

● Small City .... Small City
○ Town; Village .... Town; Village

MAP SYMBOLS

■ .... Place to Stay
▼ .... Place to Eat
● .... Point of Interest

Airfield	Church	Museum	Skiing - Downhill
Airport	Cinema	Observatory	Stately Home
Archeological Site; Ruin	Dive Site	Park	Surfing
Bank	Embassy; Consulate	Parking Area	Synagogue
Baseball Diamond	Footbridge	Pass	Tao Temple
Battlefield	Gas Station	Picnic Area	Taxi
Bike Trail	Hospital	Police Station	Telephone
Border Crossing	Information	Pool	Theater
Buddhist Temple	Internet Café	Post Office	Toilet - Public
Bus Station; Terminal	Lighthouse	Pub; Bar	Tomb
Cable Car; Chairlift	Lookout	RV Park	Trailhead
Campground	Mine	Shelter	Tram Stop
Castle	Mission	Shipwreck	Transportation
Cathedral	Monument	Shopping Mall	Volcano
Cave	Mountain	Skiing - Cross Country	Winery

Note: not all symbols displayed above appear in this book

LONELY PLANET OFFICES

Australia

Locked Bag 1, Footscray, Victoria 3011
☎ 03 8379 8000 fax 03 8379 8111
email: talk2us@lonelyplanet.com.au

UK

10a Spring Place, London NW5 3BH
☎ 020 7428 4800 fax 020 7428 4828
email: go@lonelyplanet.co.uk

USA

150 Linden St, Oakland, CA 94607
☎ 510 893 8555: TOLL FREE: 800 275 8555
fax 510 893 8572
email: info@lonelyplanet.com

France

1 rue du Dahomey, 75011 Paris
☎ 01 55 25 33 00 fax 01 55 25 33 01
email: bip@lonelyplanet.fr
www.lonelyplanet.fr

World Wide Web: www.lonelyplanet.com *or* AOL keyword: lp
Lonely Planet Images: lpi@lonelyplanet.com.au